Full Duty
Vermonters in the Civil War

State of Vermont.

EXECUTIVE DEPARTMENT, }
ST. JOHNSBURY, July 30, 1861. }

By an act of the Legislature passed April 26th, 1861, the Governor was "authorized and required to raise, organize and muster into service of the State without delay, two regiments of soldiers; and at such time as in his discretion it may appear necessary, four other regiments," &c.

Under this provision, two regiments,—being the 2d and 3d Vt. Vols.,—have been raised, uniformed, armed, equipped and mustered into the service of the United States for the term of three years or during the war.

The 1st Vermont Regiment having been detailed from the companies composing the uniform militia of the State, were mustered into the service of the United States, for three months' service, on the 2d day of May last. This Regiment, under the command of Col. J. W. Phelps, rendered important service at Newport News, Va., and during their term of enlistment have nobly sustained the honor of the State and the country. Their term of service will expire early in August.

The 2d Regiment having been ordered to Washington, participated in the disastrous battle of the 21st. The 3d Regiment has been ordered to Washington, where it still remains.

The events of the 21st instant, and the retreat of the United States army from the field near Manassas Junction, demonstrate the necessity of a greatly increased national force; and, although no formal requisition has been made upon me by the secretary of war, nor any apportionment of troops as the quota for this state communicated, yet the events referred to indicate clearly the necessity of exercising the discretionary power conferred on me by the aforesaid act, for raising and organizing additional regiments. Orders will therefore be issued immediately to the Adjutant and Inspector General for enlisting the 4th and 5th regiments of volunteers for three years, or during the war, to be tendered to the general government, so soon as it may be practicable to arm, equip and discipline the troops for service.

ERASTUS FAIRBANKS.

By His Excellency the Governor.
GEO. A. MERRILL, Private Sec'y.

UVM

Fairbanks proclamation calling up
the Fourth and Fifth Vermont regiments.

FULL DUTY

Vermonters in the Civil War

HOWARD COFFIN

Foreword by Edwin Bearss

THE COUNTRYMAN PRESS, INC.

Woodstock, Vermont

Library of Congress Cataloging-in-Publication Data
Coffin, Howard, 1942—
Full duty : Vermonters in the Civil War / Howard Coffin
foreword by Edwin Bearss.
p. cm.
Includes bibliographical references (p.) and index.
ISBN 0-88150-349-5
1. Vermont—History—Civil War, 1861—1865.   I. Title.
E533.9.C64   1993
973.7'443—dc20
93-32417   CIP

Designed by Glenn Suokko

Illustration research and selection by Jeffrey Marshall

Front cover photograph of detail from
Julian Scott's *The Battle of Cedar Creek*,
courtesy of Joseph Whitehorne

Map on inside of cover reprinted with kind permission of
Abbeville Press and Walton Rawls, editor
of *Great Civil War Heroes and Their Battles,* 1985.

Interior photographs courtesy of
University of Vermont (UVM)
Rokeby Museum
Library of Congress
Vermont Historical Society (VHS)
Howard Coffin Collection
Antietam National Battlefield, National Park Service
Waterbury Historical Society at the Waterbury Village Library
U.S. Army Military Institute, Carlisle Barracks, Carlisle, PA
St. Albans Historical Society
Peg Barry

Published by
The Countryman Press, Inc.
PO Box 175
Woodstock, Vermont 05091

Printed in the United States of America by
Capital City Printing Book Press
10 9 8 7 6 5 4 3 2

This book is dedicated to:
US Senator James Merrill Jeffords of Vermont,
who gave me the time to write and with whom it has been a great pleasure
to work for the preservation of Civil War battlefields.

My parents, Wallace Burbank Coffin and Arlene Jillson Coffin,
and my grandmother, Bertha Metcalf Coffin, all of whom
helped give me a sense of history.

My daughter, Anya Ingrid Coffin, and my twin brother, Bruce Metcalf Coffin,
fellow writers and explorers of Civil War places.

All those who work to save Civil War sites.

Contents

Foreword

Howard Coffin, because of his heritage, background, and interest, was predestined to write *Full Duty: Vermonters in the Civil War.* He is a fifth-generation Vermonter, with two great-grandfathers who fought in Green Mountain units during that terrible fratricidal struggle that etched itself in the American ethos more than any other in our common experience as a nation.

Born in Woodstock, Howard attended Lyndon State Teachers' College, left Vermont in the mid-1960s to serve a hitch in the US Army, and then went to work for the *Rutland Daily Herald* as a reporter covering state government, politics, and environmental issues. This was followed by seven years at Dartmouth College across the Connecticut River in New Hampshire, work in public relations, and five years as news director of the University of Vermont. Since 1990 he has been press secretary for Vermont's junior senator, Jim Jeffords.

More than a quarter century in journalism and public relations—beginning when my friend Howard was stationed at Fort Hood, Texas, as a member of the Second Armored Division ("Hell on Wheels")—enabled him to hone his writing and investigative skills. As a freelance author, he wrote dozens of articles, and his byline appeared frequently in the *Christian Science Monitor* and other respected newspapers and journals. In 1991 his first book, *UVM: A Special Place,* commemorating the bicentennial of the University of Vermont, was published.

As a child, long before he decided on a career, Howard was introduced to the Civil War by his mother. Entranced by her stories about Grandfather Elba Jillson's service in the Civil War as a private in the Ninth Vermont Infantry, he had her read out loud to him innumerable books about "The War."

It was in 1966, while an army reservist at summer camp at Fort A. P. Hill, Virginia, that Howard visited his first Civil War battlefield: Salem Church. There, on May 3–4, 1863, the Vermont Brigade battled Confederates. At that time the area was still rural. But since then this once peaceful countryside has been engulfed by shopping malls; Highway 3, the historic "Orange Plank Road" of the 1860s, has become "fast-food alley"; and Old Salem Church is now an atoll in the midst of burgeoning suburbia.

In the years between 1966 and 1989, Howard Coffin walked most of the eastern battlefields, paying particular attention to those where Vermonters marched, camped, fought, suffered, and died. To gain an appreciation for what we as Americans owe these soldiers in blue and gray, Coffin read their letters, journals, and reminiscences. As the years passed and other battlefields were either lost or threatened by development, Howard enlisted in the ranks of those fighting to preserve Civil War battlefields as a tangible link to those soldiers of the 1860s who dared to sacrifice their all—that future generations might live in freedom—and then he quickly became a leader in this struggle.

In 1989 Howard Coffin drafted a resolution calling on the US Congress to save battlefields, particularly in the Shenandoah Valley, where Vermonters had fought. The Vermont Legislature enacted the resolution, and Howard, some 18 months before he joined the senator's staff, carried the resolution to Jim Jeffords. The senator, an activist and environmentalist, on October 19, 1989, introduced a bill calling attention to the Civil War in the Shenandoah Valley. This date was the 125th anniversary of the Battle of Cedar Creek, a decisive struggle where the fate of the Army of the Shenandoah hung in the balance and a Union victory ensured Abraham Lincoln's reelection when the voters went to the polls 20 days later. Senator Jeffords proposed legislation directing the secretary of the interior to undertake a study to determine the feasibility of establishing a national battlefield park in the Shenandoah Valley to commemorate "Stonewall" Jackson's 1862 campaign and the 1864 campaign centering on the struggles between armies led by Generals Early and Sheridan. Too late to secure action in the First Session of the 101st Congress, it was acted upon by the Second Session and signed into law by President George Bush on November 28, 1990. As enacted, the legislation provided for a study by the secretary of the interior of Shenandoah Valley Civil War sites and the establishment of a Civil War Sites Advisory Commission.

The nation, and I, are the better because of Howard Coffin's initiative and the efforts of Senators Jeffords and Dale Bumpers of Arkansas to secure passage of the Civil War Sites Study Act of 1990. Howard and I serve as members of the Civil War Sites Advisory Commission, and because of this, I have gotten to know and appreciate Howard's dedication, wit, and perseverance. It has also given me the opportunity to write the foreword to *Full Duty*.

Howard Coffin, because of his background and interest, writes with keen appreciation for the subject—he writes from the heart. On the latter point, I speak with some authority. In World War II it was my privilege to serve with the marines in the Southwest Pacific, and, while hospitalized recovering from wounds received in the fight for Cape Gloucester, I began reading Civil War books. I started with Douglas Southall Freeman's three-volume *Lee's Lieutenants* and have continued this practice until today.

In writing *Full Duty* Coffin has honed a subject that will appeal to a broad spectrum—those interested in the trials and tribulations of their forebears, the legions of Civil War buffs, and those who find that readable history of the kind championed in my college days by Samuel E. Morrison and Robert Ferrell is more interesting than any novel. *Full Duty* falls into this class; it is not a book that, after reading a chapter or two, you will return to the bookcase and forget.

Vermont of the 1860s was one of those states—some in the North, others in the South—that went the extra mile for a cause that its citizens embraced. These states seemingly fit a mold. Populations were small; there were no metropolitan centers; most of the people were farmers; and, adjoining an international boundary or Indian frontier, the people were ruggedly independent and determined to fight for their beliefs. North of the Mason-Dixon line, states answering this description that come to mind are Vermont, New Hampshire, Maine, Iowa, Michigan, and Minnesota.

In the Civil War armies there were certain units that developed an *esprit* and that in combat seemed to stand a little taller and give a little more of themselves than others. Among the elite units that marched with the Army of the Potomac were the Old Vermont Brigade, the Iron Brigade, the Irish Brigade, and the Philadelphia Brigade. These were the rangers, paratroopers, navy seals, and marines of 130 years ago.

From first to last, Vermont, headed successively by three energetic and effective governors, did itself proud in its support of the Union. Thousands of men and boys, the state's most treasured resource, poured into the military, principally the army, to fight for preservation of the Union and, after January 1, 1863, the eradication of slavery, a cancer on the body politic that the founding fathers had first in 1776 and then in 1787 failed to address.

Vermont sent into the Federal armies more than 34,000 soldiers, organized into one heavy artillery regiment, one heavy artillery company, three companies of light artillery, three companies of sharpshooters, and one regiment of cavalry. In the Civil War, as in all wars since the 18th century, the infantry has been the backbone of the army, has suffered far greater casualties than the other combat arms, and has been the arbiter of defeat or victory.

In answer to "Father Abraham's" call, the Green Mountain State organized 17 infantry regiments. Mustered into federal service at Rutland, Burlington, St. Johnsbury, St. Albans, Montpelier, and Brattleboro, these regiments—beginning with the First Vermont Volunteer Infantry, a 90-day unit—entrained and headed south to defend the Union and crush the rebellion. Except for the five nine-month regiments, the other infantry units were in for three years. Most of the Vermonters, of whom one-sixth gave their lives in the war for the Union, were associated with the Army of the Potomac; the Seventh and Eighth infantry regiments and the First and Second companies of light artillery fought the war as far off as Louisiana, Florida, and Texas.

Howard Coffin tells the Vermonters' story with empathy and pride, which is understandable. To do so, wherever warranted, he employs the words of the participants found in diaries, journals, letters, and reminiscences. These actors from our American Iliad speak for themselves. We meet the men in blue as individuals and learn their agonies and triumphs in their own words.

While much of the narrative, as desired and expected, focuses on campaigns and battles, Coffin does not ignore the homefront. We get to know the wartime governors and the problems they confronted and mastered; we learn about life in the camps of instruction; we hear of the challenges faced by families in maintaining farms or family businesses with the father or sons in the army; and we experience the grief suffered by parents, widows, and orphans upon news of the death or wounding of loved ones on the distant battlefields and in hospitals and camps. The dramatic Confederate raid on St. Albans, as expected, commands attention.

Knowing of Howard Coffin's long interest in battlefield preservation, his willingness to get out and walk where the soldiers trod, and his inquiring mind, I was not surprised to find at the end of each campaign or battle chapter several paragraphs describing sites as they appear today. The purpose is twofold: to provide a preservation message by demonstrating that many hallowed fields yet unsullied are imminently threatened by urban sprawl and high-speed highways; and, second, to underscore that he is not an armchair historian, that before writing his history he familiarized himself with the lay of the land.

Full Duty has enhanced my appreciation of the important role that Vermonters and the Green Mountain State played in the Civil War. While I knew about Generals W. F. "Baldy" Smith, George J. Stannard, John Phelps, Stephen Thomas, and the other Grant, Howard Coffin introduced me to new friends. More importantly, he provided a context to better measure and appreciate what manner of men fought with Stannard at Gettysburg, in the Old Brigade at Spotsylvania's Bloody Angle, and with Thomas and the Eighth Vermont at Cedar Creek.

Edwin Bearss

As they marched, men fainted and fell, some with ghastly upturned faces, as if dead. Others struggled convulsively in the dust. They had no helpers. We were ordered to leave them in the dust where they fell.

I looked on the suffering men as martyrs of liberty, each bearing his cross from Gethsemane to his Golgotha, there to offer himself up to the good of others.

Lt. Stephen Brown, Second Vermont Brigade, on the long march to Gettysburg

Preface

Descending the high hills in a soft mist of autumn, maples red and gold and fields still green in the gentle morning light, I round a corner; in the valley are white-clapboard and red-brick houses, weathered barns, and a church steeple. Save for my car, the blacktopped road, and the telephone wires, this might be a long time ago, even before the Civil War.

But as I near the village, sunlight touches the marble figure of a soldier atop a monument, on which I find the names of 143 men who went from this place, Tunbridge, Vermont, to fight in the War between the States.

Henry James wrote, upon walking in his college's hall of honor for its Civil War dead, that it seemed impossible that the Civil War could touch even the campus of fair Harvard. I wonder how he would feel to read all those names in this village far up in the hills of New England.

From this quiet place young men went forth to fight at Chancellorsville, Gettysburg, Antietam, the Wilderness. Farm boys who had never been to Burlington were suddenly at the center of history, answering Abraham Lincoln's call to defend what he said was the last best hope of mankind.

To visit the battlefields one must travel to Virginia, Maryland, Pennsylvania, and Louisiana. But to understand the America of the Civil War period, in the North at least, there's no better place than Vermont. The Civil War erupted in a predominantly rural American nation, a country of small villages and farms. The look, the feel, of that America nowhere better abides than in Vermont.

The Civil War hit Vermont hard. Everywhere in the valleys and hills, the town and city streets, that truth becomes evident. The morning I drove into Tunbridge I'd just found the cellar hole of the home from which Pvt. Wilbur Fisk went to war. He served four years in the Vermont Brigade and sent home some of the finest of all soldier letters. The Fisk house had stood up a winding track, at the head of a steep-walled valley, today reachable only by foot or jeep.

The view extends south four ridges, with no other home in sight. The Civil War reached even there.

On a summer morning in 1861 the sad Fisks took their son to South Royalton and sent him off to war. The railroad station still stands by the South Royalton green with its Civil War memorial.

Drive up Route 110 from South Royalton, past the Tunbridge monument and into old Chelsea, and turn at the green up to Highland Cemetery, "consecrated in 1864." A monument states that "ladies of the Veterans Auxiliary aided by the sons of veterans of the Grand Army of the Republic" planted the maples that line the quiet drive. The November day I visited, though few colored leaves remained, flags flapping by Civil War graves made a blizzard of color on the hillside. I recalled a bit of poetry my brother once showed me:

> *On a thousand small town New England greens*
> *the old white churches hold their air*
> *of sparse, sincere rebellion; frayed flags*
> *quilt the graveyards of the Grand Army of the Republic.*

Nearby was the gravestone of Capt. Orville Bixby, killed in the Wilderness. John Bliss's stone tells that he was 51 years old when shot at Petersburg: "For his country he fought, for his country he died." Just down the hill is Stephen Kimball, 21 when he died at Fairfax Station: "Rest soldier, thy work is done."

Drive north through the narrow valleys and steep ridges on winding roads into West Topsham, where the gravestone of Charles Divoll, 28 when he fell in the Wilderness, stands in the front row by the road. A year and a half before, his brother Morris, 22, lying beside, had died just after Fredericksburg.

Continue north to Groton, with its 84 names on the town monument, then west on Route 302, where near the height of land stands the monument to William Scott, the sentinel found asleep but spared by Lincoln. Go on past old hill farms from which Vermont boys went forth to fight the wrong of slavery. Terribly many such homes received the dread news of another Vermont sacrifice, once again the chores falling harder still on wives and daughters, mothers and sisters. Drive to high Danville and its monument to 170 sons who donned Union blue. The name of Addison Preston is there, over whose body George Custer said, "There lies the best fighting colonel in the Cavalry Corps."

In the hills and valleys of old Vermont there is much to be learned of the Civil War and the America from which it emerged. The Green Mountain State wrote a record absolutely unsurpassed in the Union armies. Its story seems worth telling as this century after the Civil War ends and inscriptions on many Civil War gravestones fade, even in late afternoon light on south-facing hillsides.

The storied soldiers of Vermont came from Tunbridge, Chelsea, Danville, Groton, and Topsham; from Guilford, Arlington, Peru, Mount Holly, Derby Line, South Hero, Addison, Westford, and Fairfax; from Rutland, Burlington, Newport, Bennington, St. Albans, and Middlebury. They went to war from all 14 counties, every town, probably a gore or two. They went well prepared, sons of large, close families on self-sufficient farms where each person had tasks, was accountable, yet where cooperation was essential. Educated in one-room schools under close supervision, they learned the essentials, including history. Fun was self-made, and most learned early to shoot, to tramp the hills looking for deer and squirrels. On Sundays, most everyone worshiped in their faith, be it in church or around the kitchen table, where mother or father got out the Bible. Beliefs were firm; death was part of life and could come on the wings of angels. The Vermont that took its part in the Civil War produced young people who understood duty and hard work, who could walk forever and shoot straight. And they lacked street smarts, clever ways of getting out of things that should be done.

There were in this state, as the 1860s approached, firmly held convictions that the Union should be preserved and that slavery was wrong. But George Aiken allowed to me once that he wondered whether ideals or "the chance to get out from behind the back end of a pair of horses" sent more lads off to war.

I once asked the distinguished historian Frank VanDiver, a Texan and biographer of "Stonewall" Jackson, to assess the Vermont troops. He wrote:

> I am afraid I must bypass your question as to whether the Vermont Brigade was the best combat outfit in the war. As a practicing military historian, I cannot thus expose my flanks; but as a historian, southern or northern, I can pay tribute where it is due. Those good, tough Vermont men who stood firm on every field should be the envy of every soldier of every war. Were I a southern commander planning an assault, I would choose another unit as the point of attack if I could. If I were a northern leader planning a defense, I would anchor it on the Vermont Brigade. Although there may be units better known, few outfits have such an unblemished record as the Vermont Brigade. Vermont breeds good men who made and make good soldiers.

Out of the Vermont hills came some of the finest troops and fighting units of the American Civil War. The story of Vermont in the Civil War is one I thought Vermonters should know more of, as this century when so many of the Civil War soldiers died ebbs away. It is time to tell it when Civil War interest is high and while some Vermonters remember old men in fading blue uniforms.

It is told from their diaries, letters, and books, most especially with the guidance of the great Vermont Civil War account, G. G. Benedict's *Vermont in the Civil War*. This book couldn't have been written without it, nor could any book on the subject. But it has been six score and seven years since Benedict wrote, and it seems time for another look. Another more thorough book is planned. But years pass and the future is never certain. Let this stand for what it is for now. I heartily welcome, indeed seek, suggestions and corrections with an aim toward a better product next time.

Not all the Vermonters wrote of their experiences; much has been lost. Then there are the diaries that go blank on the days of great battles. But a substantial body of firsthand accounts exists, particularly in the archives of the University of Vermont and the Vermont Historical Society.

The Vermonters who went forth did their full duty. I have not yet done mine. But I hope that what has been produced is enjoyable, readable, and informative. I have enjoyed, for a quarter century, walking the fields of the Civil War. To those who hallowed that ground I owe, at least, this book.

Acknowledgments

With very special thanks to:
Barney Bloom, Vermont Historical Society
Edwin Cole Bearss, National Park Service chief historian
Edward Hoyt, historian, Montpelier
J. Kevin Graffagnino and Jeffrey Marshall,
University of Vermont Special Collections
T. D. Seymour Bassett, Vermont historian
Robert Krick, chief historian of the Fredericksburg and Spotsylvania
National Military Park
Peter Jennison, editor
Gregory Sanford, Vermont state archivist

With special thanks to:
Peg Barry
Cathy Beeler, Monocacy Battlefield
Bellows Falls Library
Bixby Library, Vergennes
Jerry Bochek, Newport News
Mary Bort
Brooks Memorial Library staff
Anthony Buono
Ken Burns
Chris Calkins, Petersburg
John Carnahan

Paul Carnahan, Vermont Historical Society
Earl Capron
Ralph Coffin
Marion Page and the Groton Library
Philip Cronenwett, Dartmouth College
Rep. George Crosby
Jack and Roselle Daley, Montpelier
Peggy Daniels, Fairbanks Museum
Patricia Delphia and friends
Doc Doubleday
Frank Dougherty
Grafton Historical Society
Dennis Frye, Harper's Ferry
John Hennessey, Manassas
Noel Harrison, Fredericksburg
Scott Hartwig, Gettysburg
Madeline Harwood, Manchester
Albert Jerman, Hildene
Mary Stewart Lee
Eugene Kosche, Bennington Museum
Robert E. L. Krick, historian, Richmond National Battlefield
Graham S. Newell
Gary Lord, Norwich University
John Lord, Johnson State College
John McAuslan
Linda McCarthy, Cedar Creek Foundation
Ruth McCarty, Lyndonville
Cathy, Kristin, and Erik Pearse
Marjorie Pierce
Rokeby
St. Johnsbury Atheneum
Mark Skinner Library
Richard Smyers
Ed Steele and Warren Hamm, St. Albans
Jack Tubbesing and Ben Ritter, Winchester
Whitney Walker
Steve Wakefield, Danville
Waterbury Public Library
Joseph Whitehorn, Middletown, Virginia
Susan Webb and Harriet Howard (Oliver Otis Howard's grandaughters)
John Williams, historian, Essex Junction

Erastus Fairbanks, Vermont governor as the war began.

VERMONT RESPONDS
TO LINCOLN'S CALL TO ARMS

"Vermont will do its full duty."

With those words (it is believed) the governor of the state of Vermont, Erastus Fairbanks, replied to a telegram sent him by the president of the United States of America, Abraham Lincoln, as the American Civil War began in the spring of 1861.

Lincoln had wired the following message to Fairbanks as Confederate States of America cannon compelled the surrender of Fort Sumter, defended by a federal garrison in the harbor of Charleston, South Carolina:

> *Strictly private and confidential*
> Gov. Erastus Fairbanks
> Montpelier, Vt.
>   Washington is in grave danger. What may we expect of Vermont?
>
> A. LINCOLN

More than a century later, in the process of editing and indexing the papers of Governor Fairbanks, a Vermont state archivist in Montpelier, Mary Greene Nye, found the forgotten telegram. She noted that in pencil, on its back, were written in Fairbanks's hand the words: "Vermont will do its full duty."

Sadly, the responding telegram has been lost. But it seems safe to assume that the penciled message was the governor's reply to the president.

Today those words seem to be a perfect statement of the will of Vermont's people as the Civil War began. As the subsequent bloody and demanding years would prove, the little state of Vermont, up in the northern hills of New England, stood full well ready to do its duty in the conflict. It would be the bloodiest war in America's history and require by far the greatest sacrifice, in blood and treasure, that Vermont has ever made for its nation. Vermont would indeed do its full duty. Lincoln's few words, "Washington is in grave danger," were accurate. Confederate camp fires could be seen just across the suddenly not so broad Potomac, and the capital city of the United States of America was almost deserted. Most of those who didn't need to be there, and many who did, had fled. The Confederate States of America had been formed, and Lincoln was in a city that many believed would be attacked at any moment.

Feelings in the Northern states were well summed up by Governor Fairbanks in a letter to one of Vermont's US senators, the Woodstock resident Jacob Collamer: "We have been upon the summit of a volcano for the past few months, which at any moment might have broken forth into an eruption, but for a restraining Providence."

The eruption came as shells arched through the night toward Fort Sumter, and on April 15 Lincoln issued a nationwide call for troops. Vermont was asked to send one regiment. Without waiting for any public sanction, Fairbanks responded to that call by issuing a proclamation ordering such a regiment to be formed. "Whereas an armed rebellion against the Government of the United States exists, the object of which is to subvert and revolutionize the Government; and whereas, the President of the United States through the Secretary of War, has made a requisition upon me for a regiment of men for immediate service, to which requisition I have responded by issuing the proper orders to the Adjutant General...."

From the very beginning, Vermont stood ready to fight for the salvation of the American Union and to defeat those who had shattered it. The attack on Sumter had evoked a most heated and patriotic response in Vermont. Flags suddenly seemed to be flying from every pole and window. Patriotic meetings were held in practically every community, including Burlington, where 1,000 people packed the city hall while hundreds more stood outside. The speaker was former Congressman George Perkins Marsh, about to leave Vermont to become Lincoln's minister to Italy.

"Our people, slow to move, are now roused," said Marsh, "and are swayed by a spirit mightier than any that has stirred them since Bunker Hill.... They will before long meet the Southrons face to face, and I venture to predict will make good General Washington's description, when he gave it as the result of his observations, that the Northern soldiers, if not in as great a hurry as some others to get into battle, were also not in so great a hurry to get out of it."

Marsh advised that the Vermont General Assembly should appropriate half a million dollars to support a war effort. As Marsh spoke, a large American flag was unfurled from the balcony, bringing the audience to its feet cheering until many were weeping like infants, one observer reported.

Fairbanks called the General Assembly into special session at Montpelier on April 23. The members of the House and Senate converged on the capital city, some on horseback, some by buckboard, no doubt a few on foot, but most by train. The *Burlington Free Press* reported: "The two brass field pieces, the

The State House in 1861.

trophies of the Battle of Bennington, which have so long had a post of honor in front of the Capitol, were speaking loudly for the Union here this morning. A beautiful National Flag, made by the ladies of Montpelier, had been put flying to the breeze from the staff of the Capitol, and was receiving a salute of 34 guns. They rang out well and woke an echo from many a heart as well as from many a hill."

The senators and representatives came to an almost brand-new State House, the old building having been destroyed by fire in 1857. That new State House is the one Vermont knows today, although additions have been made and the great dome, then painted red, was yet to receive its majestic gold leafing.

As the legislature began its official business, a legislator, Stephen Thomas (soon to be a colonel) of West Fairlee rose to say, "Until this rebellion shall have been put down, I have no friends to reward and no enemies to punish, and I trust that the whole strength and power of Vermont, both of men and of money, will be put into the field to sustain the government."

The House and Senate then met in joint session to hear an address by the governor. The man whom fate and the Vermont electorate had placed in the governorship at the darkest hour in American history was 68 years old and in the midst of a second one-year term as Vermont's chief executive. He was first and foremost a businessman, founder with his father and three brothers of E & T Fairbanks & Company. That pioneering scale enterprise had made St. Johnsbury a manufacturing center known throughout the nation. The family fortune had been assured in 1832 when brother Thaddeus patented the platform scale. The Fairbanks presence remains today in St. Johnsbury, especially in the august stone Fairbanks Museum and the high-windowed brick Athenaeum, both noble, enduring Fairbanks family gifts. Erastus Fairbanks was a strong and determined man, without much humor, but with business acumen. He was apparently a man of few words; yet the president had called, the state was suddenly and willingly ready to do its part to save the Union, and the legislature waited that spring day to hear what he would say.

The office of the governor in the Vermont State House looks much today as it did that long-ago April when Vermont's legislators gathered to hear their governor speak of war. Fairbanks is still a presence there, a marble bust in the southwest corner of the office portraying him with full beard, heavy eyebrows, a somewhat prominent nose, and a most serious expression. That determined, no-nonsense look certainly was upon his face that historic day as he sat at his desk contemplating, perhaps finally editing, the words he was about to say to the Vermont General Assembly. He sat in a chair carved by a Vermonter from the oak timbers of "Old Ironsides," on which he had served during the War of 1812. The chair is still in that office.

When Fairbanks's time came to speak, he stood at the rostrum in the House of Representatives, a room that appears now about as it did to him then. The rostrum remains, as does the great chandelier suspended above the center of Vermont's most historic room. Fairbanks stood before a portrait of George Washington, the only thing rescued when the old statehouse burned in 1857. (The painting now hangs in the State House's Cedar Creek room.) Fairbanks faced the members of the House at their desks in a semicircle. The members of the Senate sat on either side of the rostrum in the same high-backed formal chairs the senators still use for joint legislative sessions. The galleries were packed. Fairbanks donned his wire-rimmed spectacles and began to speak. He summoned all the literary talents his businessman's brain commanded, and perhaps more.

"Gentlemen of the Senate and House of Representatives," he began, "we are convened today in view of events of an extraordinary and very alarming character. The element of disunion which, in a portion of the United States, for many years, vented itself in threats and menaces, has culminated in open rebellion; and an unnatural causeless civil war has been precipitated against the general government."

Fairbanks declared that Vermont had been called on to raise a regiment of 780 officers and privates, and that he had ordered such a regiment formed. "The federal capitol is menaced by an imposing and well-armed military force, and the government itself, and the national archives, are in imminent peril," said the governor. Then came his appeal to the pocketbook, always a sensitive topic in Vermont: "The legislatures of other states have made liberal appropriations and extensive military arrangements for aiding the government, and their citizens are hastening to the rescue of our country's flag. We shall discredit our past history should we, in this crisis, suffer Vermont to be behind her sister states in her patriotic sacrifices for the preservation of the Union and the Constitution."

He concluded his remarks as follows:

The United States government must be sustained and the rebellion suppressed, at whatever cost of men and treasure; and it remains to be seen whether the vigorous preparations that are being made and the immense military force called into service by the president, are not the most probable and certain measures for a speedy and successful solution of the question. May that Divine Being who rules among the nations and directs the affairs of men, interpose by His merciful providence, and restore to us again the blessing of peace, under the aegis of our national Constitution.

Hours after the last words had sounded through the great hall, the legislature voted to appropriate not the half-million dollars the influential Marsh had advocated in his Burlington speech but a full one million dollars. And it authorized the raising and equipping of not one but seven military regiments. Further, it voted to give each private $7 a month in state pay, in addition to the $13 offered by the federal government. And the legislature voted provisions for a major state war tax.

At the close of one of the subsequent legislative meetings an attempt was made by the members to sing, en masse, "The Star-Spangled Banner." But in the atmosphere of excitement, nobody could get the tune properly started. That evening, however, a 25-person choir, each singer holding a small flag, gathered in the House gallery and led, with flags waving throughout the chamber, a successful rendering of the anthem. The special session was adjourned.

When news of Vermont's action reached New York City, the *New York World* proclaimed: "Vermont has a population of but 300,000, mostly farmers, and yet has made an appropriation of $1,000,000 to aid in maintaining the stars and stripes. Many have done nobly, but none, resources considered, have equalled this."

And word spread farther and wider, even reaching Henry Stevens at his home at 4 Trafalgar Square, London. Stevens was an antiquarian book dealer who, though born in Barnet, chose to live his life in London. He wrote to Fairbanks: "Vermont forever! I am prouder than ever to write G.M.B. [Green Mountain Boy] after my name seeing the noble stands that Vermont has taken in the great struggle. Let me congratulate the state on the impression it has made on this side of the Atlantic by its promptitude and self-sacrificing liberality."

In Washington, however, the American president was telling a group of volunteers as April ended: "I have desired as sincerely as any man—I sometimes think more than any other man—that our present difficulties might be settled without the shedding of blood. I will not say that all hope is yet gone."

But in Vermont, a full two weeks before Fairbanks had spoken, many were holding no such fond hopes. Up in northwest Vermont, in St. Albans, the commander of the Fourth Militia Regiment, George Jerrison Stannard, had notified Vermont's adjutant general that his regiment, all 200 men, was ready to march at two hours' notice. Stannard, who had a rendezvous with history in a Pennsylvania town called Gettysburg, had become the first Vermonter to officially volunteer his services.

UVM

Windsor's Old Constitution House.

THE ABOLITIONIST TRADITION

How had the war begun?

In the larger sense, did it begin when the first slave ship touched Africa or touched land in America? Or did it start when the first American master's lash cracked across the black back of a human being he considered his property? Or did it begin when old John Ruffin touched fire to fuse and the first shell hurtled from Morris Island toward dark Fort Sumter?

And when for Vermont? When did this little state's commitment to preserving the American Union and destroying slavery become so fervent as to ensure that more than one in ten Vermonters—nine in ten of them voluntarily—would go off to fight in a war from which they knew their chances of returning were decidedly limited? Certainly it happened long before Gov. Erastus Fairbanks issued the first call for troops. The argument over whether union or slavery was the great cause of the Civil War will never cease. But clearly, in Vermont at least, the slavery issue had long been important, for its residents quite simply considered the so-called peculiar institution to be a great wrong. Vermonters never had much use for slavery.

Perhaps it all began in that wood-frame house known today as the Old Constitution House, which still stands beside Windsor's wide main street. There, in the revolutionary war summer of 1777, representatives from throughout the land between Lake Champlain and the Connecticut River gathered to organize a political entity—a republic called Vermont.

In a warm July, muggy high-summer weather, they gathered in the local tavern, which then stood about a quarter mile south of its present location. They gathered anxiously at Windsor while a big British army under Maj. Gen. John Burgoyne was moving south along Lake Champlain toward the American defenses at Fort Ticonderoga and its companion fortifications at Mount Independence. Nevertheless, the nervous delegates set to work on July 2 to draft a constitution. The work went well but was not quite completed, when on July 8 a breathless rider brought news that the Americans had been forced to evacuate Ticonderoga and Mount Independence. What he did not know was that a battle had also occurred 20 miles closer, at Hubbardton, in the hills west of Rutland. As thoughts now turned from statesmanship to the welfare of homes and families, delegates prepared to leave, despite the unfinished work at hand. But suddenly out of the July heat came a rumbling, then a crashing, as a mighty storm was unleashed upon the Connecticut Valley. In the best Yankee tradition of not wasting time, the delegates went back to work while the storm raged. Before it ended, a constitution was adopted article by article. The first article stated:

> That all men are born equally free and independent and have certain natural, inherent, and inalienable rights, amongst which are the enjoying and defending of life and liberty, acquiring, possessing, and protecting property, and pursuing and obtaining happiness and safety: therefore no male person born in this country, or brought from over sea, ought to be holden by law, to serve any person as a servant, slave, or apprentice, after he arrives to the age of twenty-one years, unless they are bound by their own consent, after they arrive to such age, or bound by law for the payment of debts, damages, fines, costs or the like.

Vermont had adopted the first American constitution to outlaw slavery, or at least the enslaving of any male over 21 years of age. If it does not seem earthshaking today, it was a considerable step forward for the times, and it set a course from which Vermont would not falter. Later that historic year Capt. Ebenezer Allen and some fellow Vermonters returned from a raid into New York, near Ticonderoga, with a slave woman named Dinah Mattis and her child. Allen believed it to be "not right in the sight of God to keep slaves." He saw to it that Mattis was given a certificate of freedom from the Bennington town clerk. It stated that, according to an act of the Continental Congress, all prizes belonged to their captors and that therefore Dinah and her child had become the property of Allen and his men. The certificate gave mother and child the right "to pass and repass anywhere through the United States of America," and Mattis was "to trade and traffic for herself and child as though she was born free without being molested by any person or persons."

In 1786 the Vermont Legislature stated that anyone trying to take blacks out of the state would be violating state law. It added, "The idea of slavery is totally exploded from our free government."

Had the war against slavery begun for Vermont in Windsor that day of summer thunder, or on a fall day many years later, in 1828, in historic Old Bennington? Along its broad-shaded street where British prisoners were once paraded and where Vermonters ratified the US Constitution, stands a large stone with an impressive brass plaque. It states that at a spot 50 feet to the west William Lloyd Garrison edited *The Journal of the Times* from October 3, 1828 to March 27, 1829. Garrison, a slender, bespectacled, ascetic man, though only 28, had already made a name for himself as an abolitionist when he heeded the urging of some local antislavery people and came to Vermont from Boston to publish a newspaper.

"He dressed in black dress coat, black trousers, white vest and walked as erect as an Indian," one local remembered. John S. Robinson, later a governor of Vermont, recalled, "A pair of silver-mounted spectacles ride elegantly across his nose and his figure and appearance are not unlike that of a dandy."

Garrison arrived with the leaves at peak color in 1828, set up shop on what was already Vermont's most historic street, and began printing a newspaper. No less a personage than Horace Greeley later called it "about the ablest and most interesting newspaper ever issued in Vermont." In the first issue Garrison got things straight about editorial independence in stating the paper's motto: "Reason shall prevail more with us than the popular opinion." He wrote: "We have three objects in view, which we shall pursue through life, whether in this place or elsewhere—namely, the suppression of intemperance and its associated vices, the gradual emancipation of every slave in the Republic, and the perpetuity of national peace." He also advocated the forming of antislavery societies.

Notice.

The second annual Meeting of the Washington county Anti-Slavery Society, will be holden at the Free Church *this day*, commencing at 10 o'clock A. M.

Afternoon meeting at 1 o'clock.

A LIBERATED SLAVE, from one of the Southern States, will be present, and give some account of his perilous adventures in escaping from the "peculiar institutions" of the South. *Wednesday, Feb. 7.*

Broadside advertising a Washington County Anti-Slavery Society meeting.

Not many weeks had passed before Vermonters, at Garrison's urging, were flooding Congress with antislavery petitions. Writing in 1948 in his estimable book *Social Ferment in Vermont*, Richard Ludlum summed it up: "He supplied the impetus in Vermont and throughout the north that turned the antislavery movement into a crusade."

The abolitionists had come to Vermont, and they had found fertile ground to sow. Antislavery sentiment piled up in Vermont like snow in the Green Mountains. Garrison left the state the following spring to continue his crusading in Baltimore. En route he stopped in Boston to address a crowd in the Park Street Church. "I stand up here to obtain," he said, "the liberation of two millions of wretched, degraded beings, who are pining in hopeless bondage."

Many years later Garrison expressed fond memories of Vermont and its people, who he said "are possessed of large, somewhat roundabout sense." He also said, "A more hardy, individual, frank, generous race does not exist." And he recalled, "Oh there's nothing comparable to our clear blue sky, arching the high and eternal ramparts of nature which tower up on every side." He would return to Vermont in future years to speak against slavery, and when he did, his editorial aim of freeing the slaves while maintaining the peace had changed dramatically.

Garrison had been gone from Bennington eight years when, in 1836, a Vermont judge was asked to return a slave to its owner. From his high bench Theophilus Harrington decreed that he would honor "nothing less than a bill of sale from God almighty."

An antislavery society had been founded in Jamaica in 1833, the town thus gaining the label "birthplace of Vermont abolition." A year later 20 such societies were active. Meeting in state convention at Middlebury, the members stated that "no scheme has ever been proposed which offers any prospect of success but that of immediate emancipation."

In examining the antislavery movement in Vermont from 1832 to 1836, the historian John Myers has written, "A good case can be made for the thesis that Vermont became the first state to readily accept abolitionist doctrines."

Judge Jacob Collamer (later a US senator) declared that no attacks on free speech could be countenanced "even if the dissolution of the Union was being discussed." And in a church next door to his home, Woodstock Congregationalists proclaimed, "We consider slavery as it exists in the U.S. a violation of the law of God, altogether at variance with the Declaration of Independence and repugnant to the Gospel." Many Vermont churches were getting deeply involved in the antislavery movement.

Such home-grown antislavery preachers as Brookfield's Orange Scott and Orson S. Murray of Brandon took to horseback and spread the message of freedom throughout the state and beyond. Speakers came from across the Vermont borders: Garrison returned and later came Frederick Douglass and Wendell Phillips. Not all received warm welcomes. During an excursion around the state in 1834, Murray was threatened by a crowd in Burlington, snowballed in Randolph, and harassed in Windsor. Many years later an elderly Brattleboro woman, remembering her childhood, recalled the abolitionists with what even seemed a touch of ennui: "In the lecture courses which were given every winter in our village, such men as Charles Sumner, Wendell Phillips, Frederick Douglas and Cassius M. Clay (who had freed his own slaves) and others of the anti-slavery part, delivered burning addresses upon the state of our country, and predicted ruin if slavery continued."

By 1846 the *Rutland Herald* estimated that four of every five Vermonters were opposed to slavery. Vermonters began to petition the Congress to ban slavery in the expanding territories, much to the agitation of the Southern states. Legend holds that the Georgia Senate called on the president to "employ a sufficient number of ablebodied Irishmen to proceed to the State of Vermont and to dig a ditch around the limits of same and to float the thing into the Atlantic."

A committee of the Vermont Senate summed up attitudes in 1855 when it reported: "Born of a resistance to arbitrary power, her first breath that of freedom...how could her people be otherwise than haters of slavery...how can they do less than sympathize with every human being and every community which asserts the rights of all men to the blessings of their own something?"

In the Southern states there were rumblings of secession. Similar talk was also heard in Vermont. Thirty years after he had first come to the state, speaking where another abolitionist had once been snowballed, Garrison told a Randolph audience in 1858: "If the government is corrupt, put it away, and make a new government. When government has become subversive of its just ends, it is the right and duty of the people to alter and abolish it; this is what I was taught by George Washington and Benjamin Franklin and I thank them for it."

At the same time, 75 miles away on his Adirondack mountain farm, a man seen lately to have a strange new glint in his eyes was making plans for a foray into Virginia to start a slave uprising.

JOHN BROWN'S BODY

John Brown was past 50 when he became obsessed with the idea of setting free the slaves, and thereafter a touch of madness was seen in his gray-blue eyes. If many talked about freeing slaves, Brown did something about it, and in the end he swung from a Virginia gallows on a soft blue-sky day in the late autumn of 1859. Just before they hanged him, Brown handed a note to his jailer: "I John Brown am now quite certain that the crimes of this guilty land; will never be purged away; but with blood."

Not long thereafter the mighty Union armies marched south, and the bloody war that Brown foresaw was a reality. Those armies had a marching song, which ended "John Brown's body lies a-moldering in the grave. / But his soul goes marching on."

In his speech at New York City's Cooper Union in 1860, Abraham Lincoln assessed Brown's raid on Harpers Ferry, West Virginia: "That affair, in its philosophy, corresponds with the many attempts, related in history, at the assassination of kings and emperors. An enthusiast broods over the oppression of a people until he fancies himself commissioned by Heaven to liberate them. He ventures the attempt, which ends in little else than his own execution."

Lincoln was wrong about John Brown. Speaking 130 years later, the estimable Civil War historian Edwin Bearss was right. John Brown, he said, was "the single most important factor in bringing on the war."

John Brown was no stranger to Vermont. In 1849 he and his second wife Mary Ann Day, a native of Granville, New York, a little town that touches the Vermont border, moved to North Elba, New York, high in the Adirondacks, to help freed blacks who had settled on a large tract of land donated by the abolitionist Gerrit Smith. The Browns rented a farm on the road to Elizabethtown and for two years eked out an existence. Then they left, to return in 1855 and buy, just up the road from their old place, a small farm with a modest story-and-a-half house.

In that same year, 1855, Brown and five sons left for Kansas to support antislavery settlers, and they soon became involved in guerrilla warfare. Along Pottawatamie Creek, Brown led a group that included his boys and that, deep in the night, took five proslavery settlers from their homes and hacked them to death with swords. A son, Frederick, died in the Kansas fighting. His body was taken back to North Elba and buried by a large boulder in the front yard of the farm. Brown had already erected a memorial stone there to his father, a veteran of the revolutionary war. On the back of that stone he carved an inscription for his son:

> *Murdered at Oasawatamie*
> *August 30, 1856*

It had not been lost on Brown that Vermont had become a hotbed of antislavery sentiment. In 1856, when the Vermont Legislature appropriated $20,000 for the support of Vermonters settling in Kansas, Brown apparently tried to take advantage of the opportunity. In the papers of Sen. Jacob Collamer there is a letter from Clark Chapman sent to Collamer from Proctorsville, Vermont, on January 24, 1860. By then Brown was in his grave and Collamer had been named to a special Senate committee appointed to investigate Brown's Harpers Ferry raid. Chapman tells Collamer that Brown came to Proctorsville in 1856 to meet with Gov. Ryland Fletcher at Fletcher's home. An enclosed newspaper article from the *Vermont Journal*, printed at Windsor, was apparently written by Chapman. It reads, in part, that Brown had asked Fletcher if some old flintlock muskets belonging to the state of Vermont could possibly be "bought up cheap" and used "in Kansas to fight the Democratic Missourians should they invade the territory again this year."

Nothing much came of the investigating committee, and Fletcher was not called to testify on Brown's Vermont visit, as Chapman thought he perhaps should be. But Chapman's letter says that Brown, five years before the Civil War began, had gone to a little village in Windsor County to see the governor about some guns and possibly about at least part of 20,000 state dollars. It was certainly not the only time John Brown came to Vermont.

He was seldom in North Elba after 1855, though his much younger wife and children remained there struggling to make a living. But when at the farm he went down from the mountains and across Lake Champlain to Vergennes on shopping trips. Vergennes was on a railroad line, and its stores were better stocked than any establishments on the trackless New York side of the lake. Brown took the ferry at Westport, New York, operated by a family named Adams, that ran over to Arnold's Bay in Panton, five miles from Vergennes.

According to local reminiscences preserved in the Bixby Library, villagers who had dealings with Brown on his shopping trips found him kindly and likable, especially fond of children. (That's not surprising, for he had 20 of his own by two wives.) One man's handwritten reminiscence recalled selling goods to Brown at the Parker, Booth & Company store, located in the gray stone block that runs along the south side of Vergennes's main street just before it drops down to the Otter Creek bridge. The writer remembered that on what was apparently Brown's last shopping venture in Vergennes, "the winter before the Harpers Ferry affair, Brown came into town late in the day and bought a large bill of goods for his family. He asked Mr. Hawkins to show him some rope and after looking over the sizes, he bought 75 feet of the quarter inch. Mr. Hawkins always said that this was the rope which Brown used at Harpers Ferry to string across the road." (A legend persists in Vergennes that the rope was also employed in Brown's hanging.) It also appears that when Brown left North Elba for the final time, en route to Virginia and Harpers Ferry, he again took the Adams ferry from Westport to Panton. Brown went south possessed by the idea of starting a slave insurrection. If in later years Northern troops sang his name, in the South his name became anathema. Nothing was so feared in the slave states as a slave uprising, and what Brown was bent upon was a Nat Turner episode on the grand scale.

Brown chose for the start of his uprising a place that Thomas Jefferson once suggested might be the loveliest place on earth, where the Shenandoah and Potomac rivers meet amid high hills and steep cliffs. With 18 men and a batch of carbines and pikes to arm slaves, Brown moved into Harpers Ferry in the darkness of October 16, 1859. He seized the federal arsenal but was soon attacked by local militia and then by US Marines led by Lt. Col. Robert E. Lee. In the confusion the first man Brown's men killed was a free black.

Surrounded and under increasingly heavy small-arms fire, Brown's group holed up in a small engine house. With two of his sons dead and most of the rest of his men killed, wounded, or having fled, Brown was overwhelmed, severely wounded, and captured. Yet he recovered to stand trial in the courthouse at Charles Town, Virginia, over the ridge from Harpers Ferry. Back in North Elba, the abolitionist Thomas Wentworth Higginson visited Mary Ann Brown to tell her there was no hope for her husband. "Does it seem as if freedom were to gain or lose by this?" she asked. The trial was swift, the verdict "guilty," the sentence death.

On the eve of the December 2 hanging, the following editorial comment appeared in the *Rutland Herald*: "John Brown will die on the gallows; but there are sentiments of human nature that are universal, spontaneous and unconquerable....He has shown unflinching pluck for what he deems the right; he has perilled and sacrificed himself in a generous deed for others; and not they alone who approve the object of his ill-fated exploit, but they equally who disapprove that, feel in their innermost souls a response of admiration for the brave and generous old man."

Six weeks after Brown and his little band rode into Harpers Ferry, the old man had been hanged. His body came north by train from New York City to Rutland on December 5, accompanied by a small group that included Mrs. Brown and the Boston abolitionist Wendell Phillips. The *Rutland Herald* reported that the body remained at the depot in Rutland while Mrs. Brown and the gentlemen accompanying her spent the night across the street at the

Bardwell Hotel in Rutland where Mary Ann Brown stayed.

Bardwell Hotel. They took the very early train north the next morning.

On a light coating of snow, two sleighs met the train at the little railroad station in Vergennes. The casket, in a wooden box already damaged by souvenir hunters knifing out chunks, rode on one sleigh, Mrs. Brown and Phillips on the other. One contemporary account holds that a group of turkeys perked and clucked along behind the hearse sleigh. A crowd had gathered as the procession stopped outside the Stevens House at the town's main intersection, and there were demands, to no avail, that the casket be opened. Then the mournful little group proceeded down the hill, across the Otter Creek bridge, and out the Panton Road to Adam's ferry at Arnold's Bay. By nightfall the body had reached Elizabethtown in the shadow of the High Peaks and lay there overnight in the courthouse. Next morning, as a heavier coating of snow made the sledding easier, and with the horses straining as the Adirondacks steepened, the body was borne back to North Elba.

Presiding at the funeral, held in the front yard of the farmhouse, was the Reverend Joshua Young of the Unitarian church in Burlington. No local clergyman could be found to officiate. (Returning to Burlington, Young found that his service in North Elba was anything but appreciated. Not all Vermonters were rabidly abolitionist, and he soon lost his pulpit.)

The service began with the singing of Brown's favorite hymn, "Blow Ye Trumpet Blow." Wendell Phillips let loose with what was likely a lengthy eulogy. Young closed the service with the words, "I have fought a good fight, I have finished my course, I have kept the faith." Then John Brown's body was lowered into a grave marked by his father's memorial stone at the base of the boulder in the front yard. On the morning of his execution Brown had asked that his name, and the names of his sons Oliver and Watson, killed at Harpers Ferry, be added to the stone. It was done.

Harpers Ferry today looks much as it did when John Brown made his attack. Where the Shenandoah's waters mix with those of the Potomac stands the engine house, called Brown's fort, looking forlorn. Seven miles away, up through steep hills, the Kennedy house where Brown planned his attack is preserved, a log structure on a high stone foundation. (Stay on the road past the old house and one comes in another seven miles to the Antietam Battlefield, where Lincoln got the victory he needed to issue the preliminary Emancipation Proclamation.) Six miles away from Harpers Ferry, in Charles Town, the courthouse where Brown was tried stands in the center of town. The Jefferson County Museum, a block from the courthouse, displays the wagon that carried Brown and his coffin to the scaffold. Three blocks away, bounding a quiet, shaded, fenced-in lawn, a small marker denotes the gallows site.

The Rutland depot where Brown's body lay overnight is gone, leveled for a shopping center development. But the Bardwell Hotel is still there, now a retirement home. In Vergennes, the little red-frame railway depot where the body arrived remains, a storehouse now, on the north side of the little city. The Stevens House in the middle of Vergennes is a restaurant. It's also worth noting that Benjamin Franklin once spent the night overlooking Arnold's bay, in a house owned by a man named Ferris.

The Brown farm at North Elba is a state historic site. The farmhouse and barn are preserved. A high iron fence surrounds the great boulder and the graves in the front yard. In the middle of the circular driveway leading to the farm stands a statue of Brown, walking with a black youth, evidently explaining something. He has his hand on the lad's shoulder. I went to the grave one winter night, toward midnight and below zero. The boulder and the farmhouse were dim shapes against the stars that almost blazed in the moonless sky. As I looked back toward Lake Placid, the Big Dipper dominated the heavens. The profiles of Brown and the lad could be distinguished against a faint curtain of shifting, greenish light that crossed the northern sky. The northern lights were out that night, up by the constellation once called the Drinking Gourd.

VERMONT'S
UNDERGROUND RAILROAD

The Vermont author Rowland E. Robinson wrote in 1892:

> A line of the Underground Railroad holds its hidden way through Vermont, along which many a dark-skinned passenger secretly traveled, concealed during the day in the quiet stations, at night passing from one to another, helped onward by friendly hands until he reached Canada.... The star-guided fugitive might well feel an assurance of liberty when his foot touched the soil that in the old days had given freedom to Dinah Mattis and her child, and draw a freer breath in the state whose judge in the later years demanded of a master, before his runaway slave would be given up to him, that he should produce a bill of sale from the Almighty.

Escaped slaves seeking freedom were indeed star-guided. "Follow the Drinking Gourd" were words of an old song that set to music the directions given fugitives escaping the slaveholding South. The Drinking Gourd was the Big Dipper, with its two pointer stars locked always on the North Star. If they kept on walking toward the Drinking Gourd, sooner or later, and with good fortune, the slaves would reach free territory. As they moved north on certain cold, clear nights, other guiding celestial lights would emerge across the northern heavens. On some nights the aurora borealis would spread mysterious veils of light across the heavens to beckon north. As the fugitives journeyed, most became passengers on a secretive, intricate system of lodging and transport operated by abolitionists. It was called the Underground Railroad, and a branch of it came through Vermont, though just what routes it followed and just which buildings were its stations is unclear.

But in the town of Ferrisburg, along Lake Champlain in Chittenden

Rokeby, an important stop on the Underground Railroad.

County, off the main north-south road now called Route 7, a house that was most assuredly an Underground Railroad stop remains. Rokeby, now a museum, for nearly two centuries was home to the Robinsons, one of Vermont's remarkable families. The Robinsons traced their lineage to a manor house in England, a baronial place also called Rokeby. The English Rokeby is believed to have been named after the starlings, black birds also known as rokes, that called the house's grounds home. To this day, starlings often gather in great numbers in the trees around Vermont's Rokeby.

Best known of all the Robinsons was Rowland Evans Robinson, a distinguished writer who continued to produce books about Vermont after he became blind in his later years. His father was Rowland Thomas Robinson and his mother was Rachel Gilpin Robinson, both Quakers who dedicated themselves to helping slaves find freedom. But what of the rest of the Underground Railroad in Vermont? Stories of it persist in many towns. Far more houses are said to have been stops on the railroad than could possibly have been. Nobody will ever come close to knowing the truth, for the railroad was a secret, intricate system of transport that operated through whispered words and subtle signals. Not much was written down, for obvious reasons: the operators were breaking the law, conveying stolen property. Rather early in this century a writer named William H. Siebert made an effort to get at the facts. He may have come as close as anyone, yet his published results give us surprisingly few exact locations. Siebert had the benefit of talking with people who remembered pre–Civil War times, and he listed the general routes to Canada.

One route entered the state at its southeast corner and went up along the Connecticut River, moving inland at Windsor and Hartland to Woodstock. Along another route, the fugitives went up the Connecticut to Norwich, over to

Royalton, and on north to Montpelier. Another trail paralleled the Connecticut River only a short way before going inland through Townshend, Grafton, Cavendish, and on to South Woodstock and Woodstock. From Woodstock the way was north to Royalton and then on to Montpelier, which, like Woodstock, was an active depot. From Montpelier the path led to Hardwick, Albany, Barton, and Troy to Canada. Or the slaves were guided through Morrisville, Johnson, and Waterville, over to St. Albans, and on to Swanton and the border.

Another route entered the state at Bennington from Albany via Hoosick, New York, then went on to Manchester, up to Rutland, and through Middlebury, Weybridge, Vergennes, and the Robinsons' home of Rokeby to Burlington. From there it continued by boat on Lake Champlain to Canada or by road either up the lakeshore or through the Champlain islands. The refugees often were moved by water up the Lake Champlain canal from Albany to Whitehall and then on the lake to Canada, the steamers picking up and dropping off passengers as safety dictated. Another route along the New Hampshire side of the Connecticut River entered Vermont at the Northeast Kingdom town of Lunenburg from Franconia, New Hampshire.

Drive north today along Route 5 from Brattleboro to Norwich, up Route 7 from Bennington all the way to Swanton, or up winding Route 106 from Springfield to Woodstock, and one goes the way of the slaves, tired and worried, moving on foot, sometimes by wagon, through the cold, looking for the next safe house, the next station on the secret railroad. The slaves were secreted in train baggage cars, in the holds of lake steamers, and in the sometimes concealed rooms of private homes. In Woodstock, when I was growing up, I always heard tales that a cleverly disguised room had once been found in the big old White Cupboard Inn that stood at the town's main intersection. There were also tales of a tunnel that ran under the business district from the inn to Kedron Brook. An elderly lady once told me she saw what looked like a tunnel entrance when the foundation for the Woodstock Post Office was being dug in the 1930s. The owner of the big white house on the square was Titus Hutchinson, once a Vermont Supreme Court justice who put into practice the lofty antislavery principles long extolled by Vermont's judiciary.

The Hutchinson house endures as one of the great Vermont monuments, along with Rokeby, to the Underground Railroad. In both instances fugitive slaves were welcomed, sheltered, and sent on north. Some who stayed at the Hutchinson house surely passed through Rokeby.

As the war approached, the pacifist Robinsons believed that the nation should divide rather than go to war over the great issue. The Robinsons were friends of the major abolitionists, of Garrison, Phillips, and Frederick Douglass. The Robinson home is preserved today much as it was in those times; on the wall of the front parlor, a wonderfully cluttered Victorian reception room with piano and easels, is a framed handbill from 1843 advertising an antislavery convention in Ferrisburg. The speaker was Frederick Douglass, and after the convention, Douglass was invited to Rokeby for a reception. The carpet he trod, now frayed, still covers the parlor floor.

The Robinsons were prolific correspondents. Rokeby's collection of Robinson family letters includes a note from the abolitionist Oliver Johnson. On January 27, 1837, from Somerset County, Pennsylvania, Johnson wrote to Rowland T. Robinson:

I am now perhaps 30 miles from the state line. There are in this region at all times no small number of runaway slaves, but they are generally caught unless they proceed farther north. I saw yesterday, in this township, a stout man who ran away from Maryland. He is 28 years old, appeared to me to be an honest, likely man. He says he was sold with several others to a soul-driver for $1,000.... A reward of $200.00 has been offered for his apprehension, and it is not considered safe for him to remain here after winter has gone by as a search will no doubt find him.

He is very good to teaming, and knows how to manage horses. He says he could beat any man in the neighborhood where he lived, in Maryland, at mowing, cradling, or pitching.

He has intended going to Canada in the spring, but says he would prefer to stay in the U.S., if he could be safe. I have not doubt he would be perfectly safe with you.... It will be a great way for him to walk, but not worse than going to Canada. He can be furnished with the names of abolitionists on whom to call upon the way, and I think may reach Vermont in safety.

In April 1837 Johnson again wrote to Robinson about the same man:

I hope he will arrive in safety and prove to be an honest, faithful laborer—such a one as you need. If such should be the result, I shall have occasion to rejoice that I was instrumental in finding him a place where I am sure everything will be done to promote his happiness, and where the "laborer" will be considered "worthy of his hire," instead of being regarded as mere chattel and compelled to toil without any hope of reward.

Also in the Rokeby collection is a letter written in May 1851 to the Robinsons from Montreal by James Temple, an escaped slave. Temple began with a magnanimous thank-you to the Robinsons for sheltering him. Then he wrote: "I am at work at my trade getting a living looking through the glasses you gave me for which I never shall forget to be thankful I working for Mr. harding No 111 main street I think I shall soon be able to send for my family if I conclude to stay here. Please remember me to your colored people.... I shall never forget you and all your kindness to me may the peace of god keep you until the day of your deliverance."

From those letters it is clear that escaped slaves found not only refuge at Rokeby but employment on the Robinson farm as well. More than a decade before the Civil War, blacks were working in the fields of Rokeby, for wages, rather openly along the busy north-south road between Vergennes and Burlington. The letters challenge the presumption of dark-of-night secrecy throughout the entire Underground Railroad operation in Vermont. The two small rooms over Rokeby's great open-hearth kitchen, rooms that were quarters for hired help and virtually unchanged since the time of slavery, endure as a freedom shrine.

A letter in the Rokeby collection is a reply from Rowland T. Robinson to a slaveholder, dated May 1837:

> I regret … that the sum thou requires for the freedom of Jessee places this desirable object—the most anxious of his heart beyond his reach. Since leaving thy service he has by his industry and economy laid up 150$ & he is willing to give the whole of this sum for his freedom: and the whole of his savings is all that he can offer—for much as I and his other friends here may desire his liberty I am bound to inform thee without the least wish to offend that we cannot consciously contribute anything towards the purchase of a slave for his liberation; because we believe it would be recognizing a principle which God forbids.

In 1878 an aging William Lloyd Garrison wrote Rowland T. Robinson. The letter, from Boston on July 11, deals with what Garrison recalled as "the fiery old days":

> My dear and venerated friend … I always placed you high on my list of friends and co-laborers the most esteemed and the truest; and it affords me the greatest satisfaction to know that you have been preserved to hear the ringing of the jubilee bell, and to witness all those marvelous changes that have taken place in our land within less than a score of years. You have at last attained to the dignity of an octogenarian, while I have transcended the allotted "threescore years and ten." But many of the true-hearted men and women, who, from an early period, gave of themselves unreservedly to the cause of negro emancipation, have seen "the last of earth," leaving a comparatively small number to follow them in due time!
>
> I hope for a blessed reunion, under better conditions and on a higher plane; and the nearer I get to that "inevitable hour," which comes to all, and cannot be far distant, and may be very near, I see more and more clearly the divine beneficence of such a transition. It only remains for us to stand in our lot, and be "dressed for the flight, and ready to be gone." If we should not meet again in the flesh, I have an unshaken faith that we shall be permitted to do so when "clothed upon."
>
> Yours to uplift the fallen,
>
> WM. LLOYD GARRISON

Both Garrison and Robinson reached the inevitable hour the following year, 1879.

Back in the fiery old days, as the 1850s matured and more and more escaped slaves were following the northern stars, a new American political star was on the rise. On the western frontier a country lawyer named Abraham Lincoln was gaining a national reputation as a pugnacious and eloquent critic of slavery. But his rise to prominence was meeting a formidable challenge in a powerhouse of a little man born and raised in a Vermont Underground Railroad town.

Brandon, Vermont, native Stephen Douglas.

THE LITTLE GIANT

"Cedar Rail Farm" reads a sign in a farmyard in Brandon's Arnold District. There are plenty of cedar rail fences in the southern Champlain Valley, and since an old fence of that type runs along by the house, it seems a fair name; but one would be hard-pressed to find a worse name for a house where Stephen Douglas once lived. Douglas, "The Little Giant," twice in his political career ran up against a self-taught farm boy and self-made lawyer who used fence rails as a political symbol. Douglas and Abraham Lincoln squared off in two elections, Douglas winning the first, for the Senate, and Lincoln the second, for the presidency. But Douglas is best remembered for the first campaign and a series of debates in which he and Lincoln most clearly defined the issues pulling America into war with itself. Almost a century and a half later the Lincoln–Douglas debates stand as the most important elocutionary contests ever entered into by two Americans.

It is with good reason that Brandon honors Stephen Douglas, for he was one of the important Americans of his age. Though the case can be made that Douglas did not like slavery any better than Lincoln, from our perspective he looms as the more tolerant of human bondage. In the end, the people of Douglas's native state rejected him at the polls.

Today two historic markers on the north side of Brandon village proclaim a low, white-frame house beside the Baptist church to be the birthplace of Stephen Douglas. It's one of those old Vermont homes that goes on and on, added to again and again to accommodate growing families and prosperity. There, for a time, lived Dr. Stephen Arnold Douglas, whose wife Sarah Fisk gave birth on April 23, 1813 to a son they named Stephen. One summer evening two months later Dr. Douglas was sitting by the fire talking with his good friend James A. Conant and holding the infant Stephen. The doctor was suddenly stricken with a heart attack and died almost instantly, the baby falling from his grip into the open fire. Conant seized the boy, preventing any serious injury.

Soon after Dr. Douglas's death, Mrs. Douglas moved her little family out to the Arnold District to live on a farm owned by her brother. (To reach the farm today go north out of Brandon and turn left just past the Brandon Training School. One mile along is an abandoned brick schoolhouse, the Arnold District School, where Douglas got his early education. Turn left at the school; on the right side of the road is the farm to which the Douglas family moved, now called Cedar Rail Farm.) Young Stephen's years at the farm were difficult. The lad, often in poor health and small in stature, was pushed by a demanding uncle to do a heavy burden of work on the rocky and sometimes swampy acreage. Those demands certainly got in the way of school attendance but apparently did little to hamper Douglas's learning or his emerging brilliance. Neighbors began to compare him to his grandfather, Benajah Douglas, who represented Brandon in the state legislature and was known for his gift of gab.

Douglas was relieved when he was apprenticed to a cabinetmaker in Middlebury, Nahum Parker, to learn a trade he came to love. Douglas recalled years later: "I put on my apron and went to work, sawing table legs from two inch planks, making wash stands, bedsteads, etc. etc. I was delighted with the change of home and employment. There was a novelty about it that rendered it peculiarly interesting. My labor furnished exercise for the mind as well as the body. I have never been placed in a situation or been engaged in any business which I enjoyed to so great an extent as the cabinet shop."

In the front room of the Douglas birthplace in Brandon, long owned and maintained by the local Daughters of the American Revolution (DAR) chapter, stands a very substantial bureau. The drawers are dovetailed, and the signature of Stephen Douglas is proudly penciled on the back of the piece. At age 16 Douglas left Vermont, moving with his mother and her new husband to Canandaigua, New York. Stephen had already acquired an interest in politics, most specifically in the Democrat Andrew Jackson. Douglas remembered: "Whilst I lived with Mr. Parker, I formed a taste for reading, particularly political works.... At this time politics ran high in the presidential election between General Jackson and J. Q. Adams. My associate apprentices and myself were warm advocates of Gen. Jackson's claims, whilst our employer was an ardent supporter of Mr. Adams and Mr. Clay. From this moment my politics became fixed, and subsequent reading, reflection and observation have but confirmed my early attachment to the cause of Democracy."

Many years later, in 1851, 38 years old and representing Illinois in the US Senate, Douglas accepted an invitation to speak at Middlebury College's commencement exercises. Surely recalling his sometimes difficult childhood he said, "Vermont is a good state to be born in, a good state to be brought up in provided you emigrate early." Not surprisingly, the speech caused a stir. Lest anyone attribute his remarks to carelessness, note that Douglas once said in Illinois, "I came here when I was a boy, and found my mind liberalized and my opinions enlarged when I got on these broad prairies, with only the heavens to bound my vision, instead of having them circumscribed by the little narrow ridges that surround the valley where I was born."

After his controversial Middlebury speech, Douglas returned to Brandon just once more, during his presidential campaign of 1860, and was honored with a parade from the railroad station to his birthplace.

Douglas's rise after leaving Vermont was astonishing. Before he was 32 Douglas had served as Illinois secretary of state and as a state supreme court justice, and he had won a seat in Congress. In 1846 Illinois sent him to the Senate, where he became a power almost upon arrival.

At the same time another politician with fast-developing skills was on the rise in Illinois. Abraham Lincoln, one of the state's best lawyers, was elected to Congress in 1847. Though the two often disagreed, there is some evidence that Lincoln and Douglas were friendly. In their first electoral contest, when Douglas was convinced Lincoln had told a falsehood about him and "The Little Giant" suggested that the two should fight, Lincoln responded that it would prove nothing, "for he and I are the best friends in the world."

As the years passed, the men grew more apart philosophically, particularly on the slavery issue. Douglas, the Democrat, was of a mind that slavery was a matter best decided within each state and territory. Lincoln, meanwhile, was carving out strong support for his view that slavery ought not to expand with the nation. In 1856 Lincoln aligned himself with a new political party, the antislavery Republican party.

Illinois is a sizable state but not big enough for two thunderous and differing personalities such as Lincoln and Douglas. In 1856 Lincoln challenged Douglas's reelection to the US Senate, and a series of seven campaign debates was arranged. The topic of each was slavery and the future of the American union. Reporters from newspapers throughout the nation converged on the scenes in Illinois country towns, and crowds sometimes reached or surpassed 15,000 onlookers. The debaters did not disappoint. The contrast they made was far more than philosophical: Lincoln was six feet four, lanky and bony, with a high-pitched voice that reached even the most distant listener; Douglas was stocky, somewhat paunchy, and barely five feet tall, with a deeper voice that lacked Lincoln's carrying power. It was a fight to the finish, few verbal punches pulled, and the crowds cheered and jeered, laughed and hooted, shouted questions and comments. As one debate ended, some Republican supporters carried an embarrassed Lincoln from the stage in triumph. Douglas said his opponent was so weak from debating he was unable to walk.

Lincoln contended that a house divided could not stand, that America would fail as a nation if divided half slave and half free. Slavery, quite simply, was wrong and must not be allowed to expand westward. He charged that Douglas wanted no end to slavery, would as soon see it spread from sea to sea. Douglas said he saw no reason why America could not be half slave and half free. To abolish the peculiar institution would mean warfare between North and South, brother against brother. He called Lincoln a "black Republican" and charged that his opponent considered blacks to be the equal of whites. So it went, hot and often mean. At times the rhetoric soared. During the final debate, at Alton, Douglas presented the following defense of the doctrine of popular sovereignty:

> I will never violate or abandon that doctrine, if I have to stand alone. I have resisted the blandishments and threats of power on the one side, and seduction on the other, and have stood immovably for that principle, fighting for it when assailed by Northern mobs, or threatened by Southern hostility. I have defended it against the North and the South, and I will defend it against whoever assails it, and I will follow it wherever its logical conclusion leads me.

Lincoln was more than a match, at Alton, for instance:

> That is the issue which will continue in this country when these poor tongues of Judge Douglas and myself shall be silent. It is the eternal struggle between these two principles—right and wrong—throughout the world.... The one is the common right of humanity, and the other the divine right of kings. It is the same spirit that says, "You toil and work and earn bread, and I'll eat it."

When the seven contests had ended, though most observers thought Lincoln had won the debates, Douglas was narrowly reelected to the Senate. But Lincoln, in losing, had won a national reputation about the equal of Douglas's. Lucius Chittenden, a Vermonter who served in the Treasury Department in Washington for many years before, during, and after the Civil War, assessed the importance of the debates:

> Mr. Lincoln was defeated as a candidate for the Senate and Judge Douglas was elected. But this now famous debate had consequences of infinitely greater moment than the election of a Senator. It not only drew to Mr. Lincoln the support of a majority of the voters of Illinois; it marked out the lines upon which the future battle of slavery against freedom was to be fought. It established his title to the leadership of the army of freedom, as the most powerful and acceptable public speaker of his time. The people came to respect him as a statesman; to love him as one of themselves. Henceforth, wherever he was to be announced as a speaker, multitudes were to listen to him as the champion of freedom, the great orator of his time.

In 1860 Lincoln was the presidential nominee of the Republican party, having won his party's nomination with a significant amount of help from Vermont. After the first ballot of the Republican presidential convention, William Seward had more votes than Lincoln. But on the second ballot things began to change. The *Cincinnati Commercial* reported:

> The convention proceeded to a second ballot. Every man was fiercely enlisted in the struggle. The partisans of the various candidates were strung up to such a pitch of excitement as to render them incapable of patience, and cries of "Call the Roll" were fairly hissed through the teeth. The first gain for Lincoln was in New Hampshire. The Salmon P. Chase and the Frémont vote from that State were given

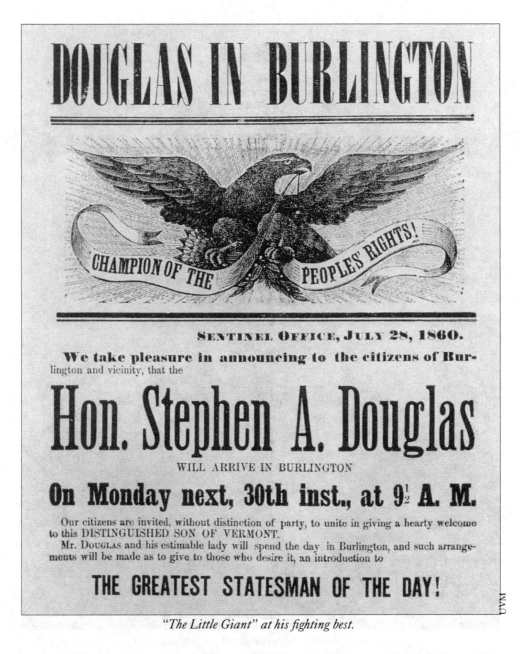

"The Little Giant" at his fighting best.

him. His next gain was the whole vote of Vermont. This was a blighting blow upon the Seward interest. The New Yorkers started as if an Orsini bomb had exploded.

Soon the nomination belonged to the Rail Splitter candidate, and in the presidential election he was again squared off against the Democrat Douglas. "The Little Giant," standard-bearer of a split party, campaigned long and passionately, saying he held the hope for keeping the country out of war. By election day he was exhausted. Lincoln, though receiving less than half the popular vote, won handily and claimed 80 percent of Vermont's votes, a state where he had never been seen.

Over 34,200 Vermonters fought for Abraham Lincoln.

Later, as the centennial of Douglas's birth approached, the people of Brandon made plans for a celebration precisely on Douglas's 100th birthday: April 23, 1913. More pressing events got in the way, and the thing finally took place on June 27. Some 2,500 people gathered in front of the Baptist church to hear a cornet band play and a former governor speak. Then came the highlight, the unveiling of a monument in a new little park in front of the birthplace. The unveiler was the grandson of Stephen A. Douglas, Martin Francis Douglas.

In truth, Douglas had done much to endear him to all the antislavery North

The Little Giant

just after his election loss to Lincoln. On inauguration day, Lincoln called on the rhetorical skills he had once trained on Douglas to voice his lingering hopes for peace. In an unmistakable gesture of unity, the frail-looking Douglas held Lincoln's hat while the new president spoke.

Lincoln said of his shattered nation: "We are not enemies, but friends. We must not be enemies. Though passion may have strained, it must not break our bonds of affection. The mystic chords of memory stretching from every battle-field, and patriot grave, to every living heart and hearthstone, all over this broad land, will yet swell the chorus of Union, when again touched, as surely they will be, by the better angels of our nature."

Thirty-nine days later Fort Sumter was under fire, and on Sunday, April 14, Lincoln prepared to make a national call for 75,000 troopers. That evening the White House was besieged by callers. One was Douglas, now looking pale and exhausted, there to offer his support and urge Lincoln to raise not 75,000 troopers but 200,000. They had a cordial meeting; Douglas pledged his support and went off into the night with Lincoln's thanks. They never met again. Douglas went west toward Illinois, speaking in several cities to call for unity behind the president. In Chicago a huge crowd applauded his words: "There are only two sides to the question. Every man must be for the United States or against it. There can be no neutrals in this war, only patriots—or traitors."

His strength fast ebbing, Douglas was soon back in his Chicago home, the Tremont House hotel, confined to bed. His family gathered round him as his last hours dwindled to minutes. Before he lost consciousness, Douglas managed to say that he wanted his children to respect and obey the Constitution. One week later a regiment from Douglas's native state, come to answer the call of Lincoln (and Douglas), was under fire in the first battle of the Civil War, at a Virginia crossroads hamlet called Big Bethel.

THE FIRST VERMONT REGIMENT

As war drew near, the armed forces of the United States were under the command of a War of 1812 relic, an old and tired man so bloated and weakened by ailments that he was unable to mount a horse. Yet there was nothing wrong with Lt. Gen. Winfield Scott's mind, and at the outset of hostilities he devised a plan for defeating the South by controlling the Mississippi River and blockading Southern ports. It became known as the Anaconda Plan, and after Scott's retirement in late 1861 others seized on it as the strategy that eventually brought Union victory. And Scott made pure sense in the spring of 1861 when he responded to the news that men were training in Vermont. "I want your Vermont regiments, all of them," he said. "I have not forgotten the Vermont men on the Niagara frontier. No, I remember the Vermont men in the War of 1812."

Scott not only wanted but desperately needed Vermont soldiers. At the outbreak of the Civil War just 16,000 men served in the army of the United States of America, and most were scattered throughout the vast West at various forts and outposts. Certainly military preparedness was at a low ebb in Vermont, for the state and the nation had enjoyed many years of peace. A tradition of "June trainings" had once existed in Vermont, whereby young men would turn out on the town green or fairgrounds for military drill under the direction of old soldiers. But over the years they had deteriorated. The Burlington historian T. D. Seymour Bassett once wrote of "the degradation of June trainings into a mere picnic whose sometimes alcoholic aroma offended temperance men." Bassett also noted that, according to a saying at the time, the troops were given just three commands: "Mount! Drink! Fall off!"

In 1858 Gov. Ryland Fletcher, who had met with John Brown, invited what remained of various militia companies throughout Vermont to assemble at

UVM

First Vermont's camp at Brattleboro, by George Houghton.

Brandon for an inspection and review. To his amazement companies showed up from Woodstock, Granville, Burlington, Middlebury, Swanton, St. Albans, Bellows Falls, and Cavendish, along with the local Brandon Grays. A torchlight parade got it started, and next day Governor Fletcher took command and ordered his little army to attack a rocky hill at the far end of the drill field. The big crowd cheered mightily as the Vermont lads stormed to almost bloodless victory, save for the injury of three men by the premature discharge of an old cannon. The Brandon muster, in addition to providing a good time for all, served an important purpose. It was widely written and talked about and rekindled interest in the local militia.

In the summer of 1860, when Gov. Hiland Hall ordered a muster at Montpelier, 900 men appeared, one company led by the redoubtable George Stannard. Some men were willing to volunteer when called, but at the close of 1860 the state of Vermont listed as its military property just 957 aged muskets, 6 fieldpieces, and 503 practically useless Colt pistols.

Events moved quickly in 1861. In April, with the firing on Sumter, Governor Fairbanks ordered a special legislative session and the call-up of a regiment of troops, Vermont's share of Lincoln's requested 75,000 men. Suddenly companies were drilling everywhere. The Vermont adjutant general, Horace H. Baxter of Rutland, dispatched the Vermont quartermaster general to the federal armory at Springfield, Massachusetts, for rifle-muskets. Being turned away, he went to Boston, where Gov. John A. Andrew saw to it he got 300. The women of Vermont set about making gray uniforms for a Vermont regiment. By May 7 no less than 56 full companies had organized throughout the state.

The outbreak of hostilities in the South was nowhere greeted with more excitement than on the plain at Norwich, above the Connecticut River. Among the instructors at Norwich University was Alonzo Jackman, a brigadier general of the Vermont militia. Jackman was one of the first Vermonters to volunteer his services for the war, but Governor Fairbanks responded: "There is a duty, a very patriotic duty for you to perform; that is, to remain at the military college and qualify young men for duty as officers, and thus you will do your state the best service." Jackman stayed at the school, and it made a powerful contribution to the Civil War, both for the North and the South. Two-thirds of the 1,013 cadets who attended Norwich between 1835 and 1865 went to war, most as officers. A total of 23 graduates became generals in the Union army. Four graduates became general officers in the Confederate armies. No military school, save for Annapolis and West Point, produced more Union army officers than Norwich. One graduate, Gideon Welles, became Abraham Lincoln's secretary of the navy.

The First Vermont Regiment was designated by order of Governor Fairbanks on April 27, 1861. It included companies from Brandon, Woodstock, Cavendish, Middlebury, Swanton, Burlington, St. Albans, Northfield, Rutland, and Bradford, six of which had already conquered that hill in Brandon. Col. John W. Phelps of Brattleboro, a West Pointer who had served with Winfield Scott in the Mexican War and been wounded, was appointed commander. Peter T. Washburn of Woodstock, a lawyer and commander of the Woodstock Light Infantry, which was generally conceded to be the state's best infantry company, was named second in command. The men were ordered to gather May 2 on the fairgrounds at Rutland. The Burlington Light Guard left home that morning, and the *Burlington Free Press* reported, "Amid cheering and the waving of handkerchiefs, and good byes and God bless you's from thousands of lips, the long train moved away." The first night in camp at Rutland, a frigid wind swept down off Pico and Killington and blew down tents.

On May 8 the First Vermont Regiment was officially mustered into the US Army by Lt. Col. Gabriel J. Rains, a career army officer and veteran of the Seminole and Mexican wars sent up from Washington for the purpose. Rains was a South Carolinian who made little secret of his sympathies with the cause of secession, and his reputation preceded him. Still, Rains was an official designated by the federal government, and he swore the Vermont troops into the US Army for a period of three months. Governor Fairbanks presented Colonel Phelps with Vermont and American flags, saying:

> In your hands, supported by these troops, I feel that this flag will never be dishonored, nor the State of Vermont disgraced. I charge you to remember that this flag represents but one star in that other flag, which I now present, bearing the national emblem, the stars and stripes. Vermont claims no separate nationality. Her citizens, ever loyal to the Union and the Constitution, will rally in their strength for the preservation of the national government and the honor of our country's flag.

As the ceremony ended, orders arrived directing the First Vermont to

UVM

Woodstock's Peter Washburn led Vermonters
at Big Bethel.

proceed south. General Scott wanted the regiment added to the garrison at Fort Monroe, at the entrance to Hampton Roads in Virginia—Confederate territory. On May 9, 1861 a 20-car train took the regiment to Troy, New York, where a large crowd gathered. The *Troy Times* reported: "The strong, sturdy looks of the men, their ability to withstand hardships, and the entire absence of small men from the ranks, were observed by all. By general acclaim the regiment was pronounced to be the finest ever seen in this section of the country. Every man bore himself like a true soldier and gentleman. We understand there are 100 graduates of colleges in the ranks, besides many men of large business interests and wealth in the State."

From Troy the train chugged into New York City, a place most of the farm boys turned soldiers had only heard about. Arriving in the morning, they marched down Fifth Avenue and Broadway to encamp in City Park. The Vermonters wore new gray uniforms and, in the tradition of the Green Mountain Boys, a sprig of evergreen in their caps. Indeed, one parade onlooker, seeing Colonel Phelps and asking the identity of "that big Vermont colonel," got the response, "That? Oh that is old Ethan Allen resurrected."

Another onlooker exclaimed, "Father Abraham, ain't them boomers!"

The *New York Sun* said, "It is an interesting study to move about among those troops of stalwart, kingly, yet modest men—every mother's son every inch a man. More formidable troops fought not with Allen, or Stark, or Cromwell."

One tall farm boy who doubtless had never been to Burlington and who had walked 15 miles from the family farm to enlist, now found himself a Gotham celebrity. His physique and good looks attracted a crowd as he stood by the sidewalk during a break in the march. Suddenly a carriage drew up and a young man sprang from it to grasp the Vermonter's hand and exclaim, "You are the most splendid specimen of humanity I ever met."

Early the next afternoon the First Vermont formed up on Broadway and marched for the docks, where the steamer *Alabama* waited. Most of the Vermonters had never been aboard an ocean-going vessel, and this one was so crowded that four companies had to pass the journey in the hold. Virtually all the hill-country troops were seasick through most of the day-and-a-half voyage, but on May 13 the impressive, moated citadel of Fort Monroe came into view on the Virginia shore. Located at Point Comfort fronting on the Chesapeake Bay, at the tip of the Virginia peninsula that separates the York and James rivers, Monroe's big guns commanded the waters of Hampton Roads. Four years later Confederate president Jefferson Davis was imprisoned there in a small, cold cell, for a time in irons.

But now the war was just beginning, and a regiment of Vermont farm boys was encamped near a Federal fortification on land the Confederate States of America considered its own. On May 19 they witnessed their first fighting. In the evening the booming of cannon was heard, and the men rushed to waterside. Across Hampton Roads a Union gunboat was lobbing shells into a rebel battery, and the battery was firing back. Next day, war's reality hit home: Pvt. Benjamin Underwood of Bradford became the first Vermont soldier to give his life for the Union, dying not of an enemy bullet but of measles. The death brought sadness to the entire regiment, and Underwood was buried with great ceremony in a little cemetery overlooking Chesapeake Bay. His death was an omen, for disease would claim more Vermonters in the Civil War than enemy fire.

Two days later Maj. Gen. Benjamin F. Butler, a Massachusetts politician turned general, arrived at Fort Monroe to take command. Butler promptly ordered Colonel Phelps and his regiment to make a reconnaissance to nearby Hampton. On May 23 Colonel Phelps set his troops in motion down the road toward the town, thus making the first reconnaissance of the war by US soldiers on Virginia soil. As the Vermonters approached Hampton, a Virginia colonel on a white horse rode up to Colonel Phelps and demanded to know where he was going and what he was doing. In those early days of the Civil War, the Confederate colonel was not shot or captured but politely told that if the Union troops were not harmed, no damage would be done to Hampton. The colonel wheeled his horse and rode back to a bridge leading into town. Phelps's men immediately saw smoke and, dashing ahead, found several planks afire. At the far end of the span a gun carriage was found; the cannon it bore had been dumped in the river by some nervous local militia to prevent capture.

After looking around the largely deserted village of Hampton, the Vermonters marched back to the fort, accompanied by several freedom-seeking blacks. Two days later a local resident came to reclaim his property. General Butler promptly refused, declaring the blacks to be "contrabands of war," and kept them within the fort's protection. A Vermont soldier wrote home to Burlington: "There are lots of negroes coming in every day for protection. I have no means of knowledge, but have heard there are between 300 and 400 at the fort … more coming in almost every hour."

On May 26 the First Vermont was transported to Newport News, where a long earthwork was constructed to protect Camp Phelps. Colonel Phelps was put in charge of his namesake camp, and Lieutenant Colonel Washburn was given command of the regiment. Night after night, still more slaves came to the camp and were promptly put under military protection. Lt. Roswell Farnham of Bradford wrote home: "We are all enjoying ourselves first rate, and probably have not half the anxiety that our friends at home have. The weather here is delightful and it never is as warm as further inland. We have a good sea breeze and are entirely out of the range of the swamps.… I think we are as safe as we can possibly be and we have no apprehension of an attack."

While it has long been popularly believed that Bull Run was the first conflict of the Civil War, I always knew better. I played much baseball during the long, slow summer days of my youth, about anywhere in Woodstock there was enough space to throw a ball. We lads often played in Tribou Park, at the intersection of Central and Pleasant streets, a place dedicated to the memory of Woodstock's Civil War veterans. It's a small, triangular piece of land with a Civil War monument topped by a marble Union soldier. Some very special rules had to be made up to accommodate a ball game, and one of them was that a corner of the monument's base was first base. I had long noted that on the monument were carved the words "From Big Bethel to Appomattox. Ever fearless, ever faithful." Everyone knew the Civil War ended with Appomattox, so I figured it must have started with a battle called Big Bethel.

Big Bethel was not really a battle. But it earned a significant mention in history because it was one of the war's first fights, the winners made much of it, and the losers took it hard. It happened because General Butler got word that the Confederates had thrown up entrenchments behind a creek near a hamlet called Big Bethel, eight miles out on the Yorktown Road. Butler decided to send a force to seize them, some 2,500 men to march in two columns by night, within attacking distance of the Confederate position. The columns were given the distinctively Yankee word *Boston* to shout back and forth to identify themselves as friends.

Only a portion of the First Vermont was sent—the Woodstock, Bradford, Northfield, Burlington, and Rutland companies, under Colonel Washburn, about 500 men altogether. They got started about midnight, well back in one column, stumbling along most excitedly through the blessedly cool Virginia summer night off toward what was likely to be their first real fight. Well short of Big Bethel they heard firing. Up ahead the expedition had begun to unravel. Before meeting any Confederates, some New York outfits on parallel roads caught sight of each other in the first light of June 10 and began shooting, friend at friend. Shouts of "Boston" were to no avail. The shooting had a comic aspect until the growing light revealed the cost. Twenty-one men had been shot, at least two mortally. Moving to the area, Washburn deployed his troops and cautiously advanced. Seeing men in the distance that he suspected were friendly, Washburn ordered his Vermonters to holler "Boston." Artillery shells came in response, again friendly fire, passing harmlessly overhead.

In this state of disarray Washburn, among other commanders, thought a return to camp was in order. But higher command said no. Spirits were further dampened when scouts came in to report Confederate strength along the Big Bethel earthworks at 20,000 men, probably 20 times their actual strength.

Washburn was ordered toward the left flank of the enemy's earthworks, and he marched off through the woods in the growing heat of the day. Meanwhile, the main Federal attack was being launched toward the center of the Confederate line, with little spirit or effect. A marsh was crossed and the deep creek forded, and Washburn deployed his men along the crest of a low wooded ridge. They were the only organized Federal soldiers to reach the Confederate side of the creek. Less than 100 yards to the front were the rebel earthworks, bristling with muskets. Washburn's men opened fire and several minutes passed before shots came back, sailing high over the Vermonters' heads. Lieutenant Farnham recalled:

> The fire was returned to some extent and several men were killed and wounded at this point, but soon the fire of the rebels nearly ceased, and suggestions were made of an advance, but just then a bugle in the rear, across the creek, sounded the retreat and Lieutenant Colonel Washburn withdrew his men by the same route that they went in, across the creek and marsh. The enemy brought their artillery to bear upon the retreating forces and for a time made it lively for them.

The Battle of Big Bethel was over. As the retreat began, Pvt. Reuben Parker of Woodstock stopped to help a fallen soldier, was quickly surrounded by angry Southerners, and was subsequently sent off to prison in Richmond. Ten days later he was back with the First Vermont, always claiming to be the first prisoner exchanged during the war. On the way back to camp, a local man named Whiting stepped from his house and took a shot at the Vermonters. In later, grimmer days the man might have been summarily executed, but this day he was reprimanded with several swift Vermont kicks.

When it was over, Washburn praised his men for having behaved like veterans. Lieutenant Farnham summed up Big Bethel in a letter several days later, taking issue with some newspaper accounts:

> The fact is there was no bayonet fighting, and none of our men came near enough to the enemy to be bayoneted, unless the enemy had guns four to six rods long. Our boys engaged them nearer than anybody else, for we were no more than four or five rods off. The fact is while we were fighting the other regiments were withdrawing from the field, and we were so far to the right (our right) that we were lost sight of. We could not see one of the regiments nor were we in the least sustained. When the order to retreat came, the wonder is that we were not all cut off, for the enemy had outflanked us on our right, instead of our outflanking them, and gave us a peppering of…canister as we withdrew. It is well they did not follow us at once, for if they had,

we should have been in danger of being entirely cut off. The only reason they did not, is because we had poured such a storm of lead upon them for the few moments we were engaged.

Farnham and his troops settled back into camp. Packages arrived from mothers and wives containing home-cooked food, underwear, socks, sometimes a quilt. Measles spread. Pvt. Dana Whitney of Woodstock and a New York soldier took some mules and strayed beyond camp. Confederates shot Whitney dead. Three Vermonters were slightly wounded a few days later, trying to steal some Confederate cattle.

The three-month enlistment of the First Vermont expired on August 2. The regiment embarked two days later from Fort Monroe and sailed to New Haven, where it boarded trains for home. Years later a Brattleboro woman, Mrs. Levi K. Estey Fuller, remembered the First Vermont's return:

When it was learned the regiment was on its way back to Vermont, the citizens of our village planned a grand reception, with music and torch lights, but it was so late at night when they arrived that Lieutenant Colonel Washburn, who was in command, had them stay in the train and march to the fairgrounds the next morning, where they pitched camp…and stayed eight days. They were visited early and late by the citizens. There were 17 sick men who were placed in a temporary hospital, arranged for them in the upper story of the old Brattleboro House, and one died there. These soldiers were for most of us the first real soldiers we had ever seen.

After their long week in Brattleboro the men headed home to smaller but no less enthusiastic hometown receptions. The history of the First Vermont Regiment in the Civil War was complete. All but five of its men had returned safely. But of the 753 mustered out, more than 600 would sign on with other regiments. By the time the First got home, the Second Vermont Regiment had formed, gone south, and been bloodied along a winding Virginia stream called Bull Run.

THE SECOND VERMONT
AT BULL RUN

Under the eaves of the Eagle Tavern in East Poultney, built in 1790 and still operated as a hotel, is a little one-bed space known as the Horace Greeley Room. Nobody knows for sure if Greeley slept there, but it's known he roomed at the tavern, and since he was young and had little money, it's a good bet the smallest guest room was his. Greeley came to East Poultney in 1826 at the age of 14 to learn printing. Before he took a room at the tavern, he walked 11 miles to work each day from his home in West Haven. Greeley learned his lessons well during his four-year apprenticeship in the office of the *Northern Spectator*, owned by George Jones, future founder of the *New York Times*. Greeley recalled years later that he had been among those who turned out on the village green to prevent a fugitive slave from being recaptured.

Greeley went on to major achievements, founding the *New York Tribune* in 1841 and using it to espouse his antislavery views. (He certainly was influenced by his Vermont newspaper contemporary William Lloyd Garrison.) Though he initially opposed Lincoln for president, when war neared he supported him, and in the summer of 1861 Greeley was pushing the administration and the military to be more aggressive.

"Forward to Richmond. Forward to Richmond," Greeley printed time and again. Since caution was being counseled by Lincoln and old General Scott, and by the new man brought in to lead the army, Irvin McDowell, Greeley and the firebrands caused considerable discomfort. Everyone knew a sizable rebel army was building just 25 miles from Washington, protecting an important railroad junction near Manassas along a stream called Bull Run. Greeley and others wanted action, and McDowell had in and around Washington some 30,000 armed men. The Confederates at Manassas numbered about 20,000, though

*Horace Greeley learned newspapering
in Poultney.*

other regiments were only a few hours away by rail in the Shenandoah Valley.

Within McDowell's army was the Second Vermont Regiment, newly organized and sent south by Erastus Fairbanks. The Second was a picked regiment, chosen by Adjutant General Baxter from some 60 Vermont militia companies. He selected the Brattleboro, Burlington, Castleton, Fletcher, Ludlow, Montpelier, Tunbridge, Waterbury, and Vergennes outfits. Israel Richardson, a Fairfax native living in Michigan, refused command of the regiment, so Fairbanks turned, at Richardson's recommendation, to another Michigan resident, Henry Whiting. The men didn't like Whiting because he wasn't a Vermonter, and the Vermont soldiers were always suspicious of old-line military men. Whiting was class of 1841 at West Point. (They did accept the West Pointer named second in command, George Stannard.)

The Second Vermont, destined to fight in most of the major battles of the Civil War in the East, assembled at Burlington on June 6. It immediately became the greatest attention-getter in Vermont, with people visiting by the hundreds each day to see the regiment drill. In late June orders came to report to Washington, and early on the morning of the 24th the 868 men marched through Burlington to board a 20-car train. Crowds greeted them in Troy and then in New York City, where the papers gave this Vermont contingent, too, a stirring review: "The First regiment of Vermont have already figured with honor to themselves on the battlefield, and it is evident from the physique and general cut of the Second, that they will not be second to the first on the field of action…. The men are nearly all six footers."

The Second Vermont marched through Baltimore to change trains, where it discovered that it was getting into hostile territory. A soldier recalled, "The line was half a mile long, the perspiration ran off the men like rain. Occasionally some old lady would wave her handkerchief, but aside from that we were received in silence and allowed to depart the same way."

The regiment reached Washington on June 26 and set up camp three-fourths of a mile east of the Capitol. It still had much to learn. A soldier writing to the *Burlington Free Press* said of the local company: "We also practice some target shooting. Several of the boys make rather bungling work of this; for instance, one boy in loading...put in his first cartridge wrong side up, and afterward put three loads on top of that. The target wasn't hit by nary a one of those shots. We have hardly become reconciled to our guns yet."

After two weeks of drill, the regiment crossed the Potomac and marched five miles into the Virginia countryside, where McDowell was forming his army. One Vermonter observed on the way, "The slaves at work in the fields through which we pass if in sight of the massa or massa's residence, looked on in silence and saw us pass, but when they were assured that no one was watching, such demonstrations as they gave vent to I never have seen before."

One night, in camp at a place called Brush Hill, a private from Roxbury, Victor Goodrich, until a few weeks before a blacksmith, hopped up on a wooden box and began to dance a jig—a little clogging, maybe. "Boys, I am going to have one more good dance and it may be my last," he said. The men liked Goodrich and no doubt they laughed, but what he said stayed with them.

The Second joined two Maine regiments to form a brigade in a division commanded by an old Pennsylvania regular, Samuel Heintzleman. The brigade commander was Oliver Otis Howard, a Maine man. O. O. Howard, as he was known, was to become something of an important figure in the war, with a knack for being on battlefields at important times. He was a career soldier and a most pious man, too pious for the taste of many soldiers.

This July of 1861, Lincoln, Scott, and McDowell were abandoning a policy of slow preparedness and deciding it was time to move. Greeley was heeded. On July 16, led by a regiment of New York Zouaves dressed like Arabian knights, McDowell's 35,000-man army began to march toward Bull Run, where 22,000 Confederates under Pierre Gustave Toutant Beauregard waited.

McDowell got his inexperienced Yankees out to Bull Run in rather good time, then he delayed. It was July 20 before he was ready to attack. The Confederates had a strong defensive position behind meandering and high-banked Bull Run. The direct route of attack would have been along the Warrenton Pike, across the creek on an arched stone bridge and into the center of the Confederate line. McDowell first proposed an attack around the right flank of the Confederate army. Had that happened, the Second Vermont might have been in the front ranks. Instead, McDowell chose to make a show of attacking the Confederate center, then tried to turn the left flank of the enemy line. It was not a bad battle plan, but while McDowell developed it, the advantage was building for the Confederates.

As the day of battle dawned, additional rebel troops were arriving from the Shenandoah Valley. Among them were some men under an eccentric college professor who had once spent a few days in Vermont. In the midsummer of 1860 a quiet Southern man with his wife had come to Brattleboro to seek relief from his ailments at the local mineral spring, a place once visited by a strongly abolitionist Boston lady, Julia Ward Howe. The man's complaints were dyspepsia (stomachaches) and bad eyes. He had already sought relief at several springs in the North, and the Brattleboro waters didn't offer much help, either. So he went on to Northampton, Massachusetts, a community to which his wife, Anna, took an instant liking, choosing to remain for a few days after her husband departed for Lexington, Virginia, and his teaching duties at Virginia Military Institute. In fact, she wrote home of "the Connecticut River winding through the loveliest of emerald valleys, with fine mountain scenery." Her husband's name was Thomas Jonathan Jackson, and one year later he was to acquire the nickname "Stonewall" on a fiery hilltop above Bull Run.

On Saturday, July 20, the Vermonters heard skirmishing, and there was a feeling that the following day would be a big day. That night Colonel Howard addressed his troops and said that it was likely to be the last time they would all meet on earth. He talked about the dangers that lay ahead. It was, perhaps, just what the soldiers did not want to hear.

The Vermonters were roused at about 2:30 A.M., and with the rest of Heintzleman's division, prepared to move. Like most of McDowell's army, the Second was directed to swing upstream to Sudley Ford to wade Bull Run, then down the far side to attack the Confederate left. Most of the army got that done by midday; then the fighting along the heights beyond Bull Run became intense. The Vermonters heard the boom of cannon and the racket of small arms, and it seemed likely they'd be fighting very soon. But as the division swung north, Howard's brigade was halted by McDowell and ordered to stay where it was, in reserve.

The principal battle developed on and around Henry House Hill, a long field-topped ridge rising from the south side of Youngs Branch. The battle surged across that hilltop with one side seeming to have the advantage, then the other. The Union forces were apparently going to carry the day. But as they prepared for what was to be the victorious charge, more and more Shenandoah Valley soldiers, some 24 hours off trains, were forming a line of battle behind the military crest of the hill. Positioned by the Virginia Military Institute's Thomas Jackson, they were sternly told not to move, no matter how many Yankees came up behind the Henry House.

One Confederate officer looked to Jackson and his men and told his rattled men and boys to emulate the Virginians. "There stands Jackson like a stone wall," said the officer, who fell dead several hours later. The Yankees ran up against that stone wall, and the whole attack came to a bloody halt. Meanwhile, after several hours of waiting, the Vermonters and the rest of Howard's brigade began moving toward the sound of firing on Henry House Hill.

The route the Vermonters took to the battlefield led upstream east of Bull Run for three miles, then near Sudley Church the brigade crossed the 50-foot-wide stream and headed back toward the action. "We were two hours coming in

Second Vermont at Bull Run, by James Hope.

to the battle field," a Vermont soldier recalled, "and as we neared it the incessant roar of cannon, mingled with the rattle of musketry, and the many wounded we met being conveyed to the houses used as hospitals, told us that it was a frightful struggle."

Another member of the Second Vermont recalled the cries of the wounded: "Oh, for God's sake, a drop of water," and, "Don't step on me, boys."

Colonel Howard remembered: "I formed my brigade lines, the Second Vermont and Fourth Maine in the front, and the Third and Fifth Maine in the second line. When forming, I so stationed myself, mounted, that the men, marching by twos, should pass me. I closely observed them. Most were pale and thoughtful. Many looked up into my face and smiled."

Capt. James Hope of Castleton remembered, "We were not allowed a moment to rest, or even time to take a drink of mud, called water, in the ditch, but were hurried to the field." As the Vermonters and the rest of Howard's brigade crossed the Warrenton Pike and moved uphill, a shell burst in the ranks and instantly killed Cpl. Russell H. Benjamin. The Brattleboro railroad worker, recently married, had won a spot with the regimental color guard because he was a good soldier. Now he had become the first Vermonter to die in a Civil War battle. The same shell also carried away the right arm of First Sgt. Urban A. Woodbury of Elmore and left him helpless. He was captured late in the day and spent the next three months in Confederate prisons. Still another shell wounded 10 Vermonters.

According to Captain Hope: "In the face of the murderous shower ... brought finally behind a wooded hill, we were formed in line, marched up through the woods over the top of the hill, which was a rough pasture ground, where we halted in front of the foe, and dressed our line, a fairer mark than we made never was placed before a marksman."

One Vermont soldier recalled: "Our brigade marched in line of battle, with charged bayonets, the smoke and dust so thick that we could not see a rod ahead of us, and the cannon balls and shells from the enemy's battery falling thick around us."

The Second had come atop Chinn Ridge to face the left end of the main enemy line, extended over from Henry House Hill. As the regiment took position, the men could see rebel troops advancing to their right, beyond their flank. Straight ahead were South Carolina troops, not 300 yards distant. The Vermonters halted, took aim, and sent several volleys toward the foe, who promptly took cover in the woods. "The enemy was so sheltered and at such a distance ... our fire seemed utterly useless," one Vermonter recalled.

By this time the Battle of Bull Run had been decided. On Henry House Hill, Beauregard, who had arrived at the point of danger, sent his men forward to yell "like furies"—the impressive debut of the Southern battle cry, the rebel yell. The Union line wavered and gave way. Howard's brigade was now alone out on the right.

Some Maine soldiers moved in behind the Vermont regiment, firing uncomfortably close over their heads. All the while, more Confederate artillery was coming to bear on Howard's brigade. Howard recalled: "It was a hot place. Every hostile battery shot produced confusion, and as a rule our enemy could not be seen."

The order to retreat came, and the brigade began an orderly withdrawal back down Chinn Ridge. Somebody forgot to tell Company A, out by itself to the right. George Stannard went out to order it back with the rest of the regiment. The order was at first refused. Then Company A came back to the fold, as some Confederates loosed a tremendous long-range volley in its direction: miraculously the torrent of bullets hit only one Vermonter.

Within a few minutes the retreat reached the Warrenton Turnpike, jammed with troops and wagons. Confederate shells screamed in, units were mingled and broken, and men ran for their lives. Rumors were shouted that the Confederate Black Horse Cavalry was about to sweep down on the road. The Vermonters, who could run with the best of them, went in the direction they had come, toward Sudley Ford and across Bull Run. "Troops were now flying in all directions, and our men began to run," said a Burlington soldier. The Second Vermont eventually regained its original campsite but rested for only an hour before moving on 10 miles to Fairfax Court House, where many fell exhausted, asleep as they hit the ground.

Bull Run was a bad day for the Union. Vermont troops had now been in two Virginia fights, both losses. But Bull Run was far bigger than Big Bethel. Some 450 Union men were killed, 1,100 wounded, and perhaps 1,800 captured. About 400 Confederates were killed and 1,500 wounded, but only 13 were captured. The Second's casualties were 2 men killed, 34 wounded, and 30 captured.

One man who didn't come back was Private Goodrich, who had danced on the box a few long days before. As the regiment had moved onto Chinn Ridge, a musket ball slammed through his head. His body was left where it fell and buried by Confederates.

Another Green Mountain boy who fought at Bull Run, Edson Emery of Tunbridge, kept a diary; its entries provide a succinct summation of a failed campaign.

Sunday, July 7, 1861
115 degrees in the shade. A good many drunk and some fighting.

July 9
132 degrees in the shade. 200 degrees in the sun.

July 10
Philo [brother Philo Emery] was sick, probably measles.

July 15
Philo is not any better. Into the woods on picket guard.

July 17
Had an awful long march.

July 18
Heard the cannon. Marched near Manassas, awful hard march. Philo is better.

July 20
Orders to march at 2 a.m.

July 21
Left camp at Centerville at 6 a.m. Double quick most of the way about six miles. Went into the field and fought for about 30 minutes. It was awful. The bullets come like hail.
Then we retreated in confusion.
Loss is heavy.
Old Jeff and Beauregard it is said had 85,000 while we had only about 25,000.

EDSON EMERY

Melvin Dwinell, who had gone south to live and had enlisted in the Eighth Georgia Infantry, wrote home to his parents in East Calais:

Sunday last I was in the midst of one of the hardest battles that ever occurred in America—I am without a scratch or even a bullet hole in my clothes—five of our men fell dead at my side.
If I should meet any of my relatives on the battlefield in Lincoln's army they will there be considered as my enemies and treated as such. My heart is with the south.

Long after the Civil War, Joshua Lawrence Chamberlain of Maine spoke on the battlefield at Gettysburg, where he had fought. "In great deeds something abides," he said. "On great fields something stays. Forms change and pass; bodies disappear; but spirits linger, to consecrate ground for the vision-place of souls."

Bull Run, compared to Gettysburg and others, was not a large battle. Three times as many men were shot on the same ground a year later during the second battle of Bull Run. But it was the first major fight, and it changed the entire nation, North and South, confronting it with the bloody reality of a big and long war.

At Bull Run today, almost a century and a third later, as Chamberlain said, something abides. The spirit or feel of the Civil War does not, it seems to me, abide in places where many men fought and died that have since been desecrated, paved over, and built upon. But in places where even a small part of the field remains as it was, spirits seem to linger. Such a place is the battlefield at Bull Run. (Follow Route 66 west of Washington and, if traffic is light, one reaches it in little more than a half hour.) There's a battlefield park of some 4,000 acres of fields and woods. Though surrounded by unchecked development, Manassas National Battlefield Park is a quiet, lovely, seemingly rural place.

Most tourists go to the visitor's center to see the slide show and pick up their brochures, then perhaps walk out toward the reconstructed Henry house and the grave of Judith Henry. They look a long time at the statue of "Stonewall" Jackson sitting atop his horse and defiantly facing the direction of the Union advance. Down in the valley toward the creek are other famous Bull Run landmarks—the Stone House, which served as a hospital, and the Stone Bridge, over which one brigade of the Union army retreated. Ask directions of the park rangers to reach Chinn Ridge, where the Second Vermont fought. It's south of the visitor's center, a quiet open rise where deer graze in the evening and where Vermonters were in their first major battle of the Civil War. At the end of Chinn Ridge Drive is a traffic circle, about where the Vermont troops stood and fired.

THE VERMONT REGIMENTS
ASSEMBLE

Until it fell in the late 1980s, a beech tree with a scythe blade embedded in it stood in a field gone to brush off Sharpshooter Road in North Fayston. Legend holds that a young man named Wheeler had been mowing one day in 1861, all the while pondering the fact that a military company was drilling in Montpelier. He lodged the scythe in the tree and went down to the house to tell his folks he was going to enlist. He went off the next morning, never to return, killed on a Southern battlefield and buried in an unmarked grave. His folks never let the scythe be disturbed, and over the years the tree grew around the blade and held it fast.

There are other scythe tree legends in Vermont, tales that symbolize the mood of the summer of 1861, when Vermont got ready for war and began sending boys south. Companies were organizing in most towns of any size and were given jaunty names, such as the Equinox Rifles of Manchester, the Ransom Guards of St. Albans, the Allen Grays of Brandon. Calais had its Lafayette Artillery, Benson its Valley Guards, Castleton its Green Mountain Guards, and Rutland the Green Mountain Lancers. By the time the leaves turned in 1861, Vermont had organized, equipped, and sent to war six full regiments. One, the First Vermont, had already ended its three-month term, though most of its soldiers promptly signed up with other outfits. By fall some 5,000 Vermonters were under arms.

Most Vermonters seemed caught up in the military spirit. Years later, Judge F. M. Butler, who had grown up in Jamaica, that hotbed of abolition, remembered a day in his childhood:

The Jamaica company of enlisted men were training backwards and forwards, up and down the Main Street, past the hotel, commanded by their officers, and led by the stirring music of a snare-drum and two fifes. A United States flag was strung from a rope from the Muzzy Store to the Holton house and swung over the center of Main Street.

I had come to the village with my father to see the training and hear the music. I stood in front of the Muzzy Store with a large crowd of other boys, a little ahead, of course, of the old men, watching the proceedings. A neighbor had also come to the village for the same purpose. He was then a man of middle age, strong, vigorous, with full long beard, broad shouldered, well built and would weigh probably 200 pounds.

He had been talking quite loud and was the center of a small knot of men.... He declared that the soldiers were going south to commit murder for a few damned niggers, and Jamaica would pay for it.... The company marched rapidly past the hotel and under the flag to the tune of "Yankee Doodle." They swung out into line and halted under the flag. The music stopped, they broke ranks, then rushed up to the Muzzy Store.... They seized our neighbor, some by the whiskers, some by the shoulders, some by the arms, and forcibly led him down under the flag.

I was frightened almost to death. They pulled his whiskers and lifted him from behind for I saw their boots come away from him ... and repeatedly commanded him to cheer. The leader started him off with "Hip-Hip" and he cheered for the flag and he cheered and he cheered again. Between every cheer they commanded him to cheer louder.... In less time than it takes to tell it, the bugle called, the soldiers rushed for the line, the command was given, three cheers went up for the flag ... and the vigorous marching and countermarching went on.

In the mountain village of Wilmington still another company was drilling before it was ordered to Brattleboro for muster. On a warm Sunday afternoon the townspeople held a send-off in a pleasant grove near the center of the village. A feast was devoured; the ceremonies began with a prayer and the reading of several poems composed for the occasion. The highlight was the presentation of a sword by the patriotic ladies of the town to the company commander, Capt. Henry F. Dix. Miss Sarah Morgan, a local schoolteacher, was selected to make the presentation. In an age of overblown rhetoric, much was expected of speakers. Miss Morgan did not disappoint.

The ponderous doors of war that have so long been closed in our country are again thrown open. Our boasted land trembles beneath the tread of armed men. The war cry has sounded through sunny valleys, over wide prairies, and even on these green hills where quiet had reigned since the brave Green Mountain Boys helped to make our land a nation among nations. And now to the glory of their sons be it spoken, that when again the command "to arms" has rung out, so many brave ones from these peaceful homes stand ready to do what their strong arms can do to plant our grand old stars and stripes where they shall wave alike o'er these green-clad hills, and the orange groves of the sunny south.

Captain Dix accepted the sword with this response:

We believe our cause is just; we go to battle for the right, and we have the strongest assurance that you feel a deep interest in our welfare. We know your best wishes will accompany us, and we believe that in a few months when grim-visaged war shall have smoothed his wrinkled brow, when the angel of peace shall revisit our shores, when the clash of war and the din of battle shall be exchanged for the pleasing pursuits of domestic life and we return to our peaceful homes among the green hills of Vermont, the plaudits of a rescued people will welcome us.

The band played, and next day the Wilmington company went to Brattleboro, then off to war. Except for those sent home sick or with wounds, it would be three years before most would return. Of course, some never came home at all.

A rifle company had organized in the town of West Windsor—the West Windsor Guards. One day two local black men came down to the drill field and asked to join. But Abel Prince, 35, and Thomas Little, 26, were quickly turned away. Eighteen months later they would go down to Boston, where a young Brahmin, Robert Gould Shaw, was putting together a regiment of blacks. It was designated the 54th Massachusetts and, when it finally received permission to fight, ended up on a beach beside Charleston Harbor facing a formidable fortification called Fort Wagner. The 54th tried mightily to capture the fort but failed, at a terrible cost. For its zeal, the regiment won lasting fame and glory. Prince and Little were but two of 68 Vermonters who served in the 54th Massachusetts.

A monument at the entrance to the Brattleboro Union High School athletic fields records that 10,200 volunteers mustered into the service there, and 4,666 veterans mustered out. On the monument is a bas relief depiction of two soldiers. One, neat in full uniform, holds a rifle-musket and bears a serious expression. He is, of course, mustering in. The other, mustering out, has a bandaged head but is waving his hat, letting out a cheer, glad to be home.

That Brattleboro field was the most important of all Vermont's mustering centers, though soldiers also came to fields in Rutland, St. Johnsbury, St. Albans, Montpelier, and Burlington to sign up. The men who encamped at Brattleboro wrote of the tall pine trees, and, indeed, tall pines still stand at the far side of the field. The original site encompassed much more than today's athletic and school complex and extended into what now are surrounding neighborhoods.

Charles Ross, who grew up in Brattleboro, camped there as the Fourth Vermont trained in the summer of 1861 and kept a diary.

Sat. Aug. 16
Arrived at Brattleboro about 3 o'clock.... I find the camp on a pleasant plane about a mile from town.

Sunday 17
A very pleasant day but a very unpleasant one for me being the first in camp. I fear I shall find many such days but I hope I shall not have any disposition to let fail my

religious feeling.... Wanted to go to church but could not get out of camp as we were called out to supper 4 of our men fell out as they were faint. I am tough as a horse.

Monday 18
Our Com. has been inspected today. Some have been thrown out. What my lot is I do not know. I have recd a Greatcoat, Blanket, Kanteen & Blowse from the Gov. also some shivering for my coat. I wish I could get in some place as I am not where I wish I could be.

Wednesday 20
I do not like the way I am tented. I would like to be in a tent with my own chosen comrades. I am feeling pretty mean and have the Wild-axe-handles, but I hope to get over it soon. I am pretty tired. Have drilled pretty well all day.

Thursday 21
Felt pretty mean this morning. Did not drill before breakfast but have done all my duty rest of the day.... Think I shall like camp life as soon as I get used to it. I do not like so much swearing.

Saturday 23
Bought six pears & apples all cost .09 and also got one blanket marked for .05.... Did not drill this morning before breakfast as I felt mean.

Monday 25
Did not get off duty till near 9 o'clock this morning.... Did not sleep very warm last night. It was cold and foggy.

Tuesday 26
I should like to have it rain and settle the dust a little.... We have one or two that are quite sick.

Thursday 28
We met with quite a loss in our company today. Our Capt. was promoted and we are left without a Capt. I am sorry for our com. and glad for the capt. Harland & I got our pictures taken today for .75. We have had rain tonight all the camp is a float.

Friday 29
Did not sleep this last night very comfortable as I was wet at the legs. Have not done a great deal at company drill but have been on Battallion drill twice. Have spent for apples .03. I wished I had not eat them for I feel I shall have the wild-ax-handles.

Sunday 31
It has been quite pleasant all day.... Went down to the river and had a good wash

this forenoon. Attended the meeting this afternoon and heard a very good sermon from a good man.

September, Monday 1

It is raining quite hard and is quite disagreeable.... Have been mustered into the U.S. service but did not receive any pay.

Tuesday 2

Have just received my first pay.... I fear I shall sleep cold. Do not think much of this way of living.

Wednesday 3

Went down town this morning on dead dutys. one of our company had died and the company went down to escort his body to the depot.... I am 24 years old to day another birthday I fear I never shall see.

Ross, though in many battles and confined for a time in the Confederate prison at Andersonville, survived the war.

Ross's Fourth Vermont Regiment formed on July 30 in response to the sorry news from Bull Run. Governor Fairbanks, skeptical of talk about a short war, ordered two more regiments of three-year enlistees. The men of the Fourth named their Brattleboro encampment Camp Holbrook in honor of Frederick Holbrook, of Brattleboro, who had just succeeded Fairbanks as governor. As Ross noted, it rained the first week and 300 of the 1,042 men of the regiment quickly got sick.

Frederick Holbrook, Vermont's second Civil War governor.

Command of the Fourth was offered to Col. Peter Washburn, leader of the Vermont troops at Big Bethel. He declined because of ill health but later succeeded Horace Baxter as Vermont adjutant general. Edwin H. Stoughton of Bellows Falls, 23, just two years out of West Point, was assigned. His 19-year-old brother Charles was appointed major. The Fourth left Brattleboro by train on September 21, 1861.

The Third Vermont Regiment organized about the same time as the Second, but the Third had been slower to gather and thus missed Bull Run. It assembled at Camp Baxter on the old Caledonia County fairgrounds just south of St. Johnsbury, where in later years the Cardiff Giant would lie in state and Buffalo Bill Cody would perform in his Wild West show. The main fair building was expanded to a length of 340 feet, and three-tier bunks for 1,000 men were

VHS

The Third Vermont at the St. Johnsbury fairgrounds.

installed. By early July all 882 men had arrived, and about a third of them promptly came down with measles. Still, they were impressive physical specimens, as a tailor from Boston, John Earle, noted: "I've made uniforms for many officers and men in most of the New England states, but I never put the tape on such a set of men as these."

Discipline at Camp Baxter proved wanting. A man named Pike operated a refreshment saloon in the camp, and one night some soldiers decided to steal what they wanted. A guard fired at the would-be thieves trying to batter down the door; Sgt. John Terrill of Canaan was killed and another man wounded. Years later historian T. D. Seymour Bassett wrote of the Vermont camps, "Insubordination, intoxication and AWOL's were…epidemic, the results of camp conditions, delays, disappointments over equipment and arms, dislike of officers, and civilian habits."

While in camp, the Vermont regiments were the objects of intense public interest. Crowds came every day to watch the drills or spend time with friends and loved ones. Railroads offered special excursions to the camp towns. On July 4 a ceremony was held at Camp Baxter with Governor Fairbanks present. More than 10,000 people stood several rows deep around the large drill field and on the surrounding hillsides. The thing got going with the firing of a 34-shot salute from a cannon posted on a high bluff. After a good deal of drilling, Fairbanks presented an ornate regimental flag made by the ladies of the community. Lt. Col. Breed N. Hyde accepted, saying, "It shall with God's blessing be returned, tried in battle, its folds bearing records of deeds that you, sir, and the citizens of Vermont shall be proud to say were done by the Green Mountain Boys."

Governor Fairbanks hoped to appoint as commander of the Third Regiment Col. John Phelps, who had led the First Vermont to Virginia, but since Phelps had already been assigned elsewhere by the War Department, command was given to Lieutenant Colonel Hyde, of Hyde Park. Hyde came from a long military lineage, his grandfather having fought at Bunker Hill and his father in the War of 1812, and Hyde himself had graduated from the US Military Academy. A Waterbury physician, Dr. Henry Janes, was named regimental surgeon. On July 24 the Third Vermont marched down to the St. Johnsbury railroad station, where a train waited to take the men to the nation's capital.

The Fifth Vermont Regiment, summoned in late July, rendezvoused on Henry Seymour's farm north of St. Albans. The Fifth, too, named its encampment Camp Holbrook. Another West Point graduate, Henry A. Smalley of Burlington, commanded. Lewis A. Grant of Rockingham was named second in command, and Redfield Proctor of Cavendish was major. The 1,006 men of the regiment, in new blue uniforms, left for the war zone on September 23, still needing a good deal of training.

To the Montpelier fairgrounds in late September came the men who would make up the Sixth Vermont Regiment. The commander was Nathan Lord, Jr., son of the president of Dartmouth College and already a veteran, having served under Maj. Gen. George Brinton McClellan in the mountains of western Virginia. On Saturday morning, October 19, most of the city of Montpelier turned out in a steady rain to say farewell.

An artillery unit, the First Vermont Artillery, commanded by George Duncan of Shaftsbury, also assembled at Montpelier, then moved to Brattleboro for drill. Two more Vermont artillery units would be organized.

At the beginning of October Erastus Fairbanks's term of office expired. As the General Assembly convened in Montpelier for its annual session, Fairbanks gave his final address. He stood at the rostrum in the House of Representatives, where, not half a year before, he had made the first call for men and money to support the war effort. Now his work was done.

He reported in a businesslike manner that six Vermont regiments had been raised and equipped, that a company of sharpshooters had gone to Washington, and that a second company was being organized. He also noted that a cavalry regiment was being put together, and that artillery units were organizing. He ended his governorship with an invocation, "May our heavenly Father interpose to deliver our beloved country from its present calamity and from those perils which threaten it, and restore to it again the blessings of peace, union and prosperity."

Fairbanks's successor, Frederick Holbrook, soon called for more Vermont troops. A steady stream of men was flowing from the hills and valleys of old Vermont to the fields of old Virginia.

THE VIRGINIA ENCAMPMENTS

On childhood Sunday afternoons, in the days before television reached the deep valleys of Vermont, my mother and father, brother and sister, aunts, uncles, and cousins would gather at the old farmhouse north of South Pomfret that was the home of my maternal grandparents, Hal and Anna Jillson. After supper everyone assembled in the parlor, where grandmother seated herself at the piano, Uncle Alan took his guitar from its case, and grandfather tuned up his harmonica. Everyone joined in old songs until well into the evening; the words of many are still engraved in my mind. Years later I learned that some were camp songs, brought home from the Civil War by my great-grandfather Elba Jillson, who had gone off to war from that very house. We sang "Tramp, Tramp, Tramp," "The Vacant Chair," "Just before the Battle, Mother," "Tenting Tonight."

Those songs of war, lovely and haunting, are part of a mystique about Civil War camp life. The days and weeks between the battles seem, popularly at least, to have been a quiet, song-filled time of comradeship and thoughts of home. But in fact camp life was sometimes more deadly than battle, and it was at its worst in the damp fall and winter of 1861–62. The Vermont troops would come to be regarded as among the finest in the war, but at this early stage the camps almost did them in before they got a chance to fight.

After Bull Run the Second Vermont Regiment was exhausted and discouraged, with too few tents and blankets. Still, Gen. Irvin McDowell reviewed the regiment in early August and found it in "good condition."

One incident affected morale. The Second Vermont's commander, Col. Henry Whiting, had never been popular, and after the battle it was alleged that he had been less than eager to expose himself to bullets and shells. Maj. Charles H. Joyce, the second in command, apparently in accordance with the wishes of the men, charged Whiting with what amounted to cowardice, in a letter he wrote to a Burlington newspaper. Joyce, a Northfield lawyer who later would represent Vermont in Congress, was most popular with the troops. Yet he was arrested by Whiting and confined to camp. After several weeks of inquiries, higher authorities deemed that Joyce had been punished enough and could resume his duties. His return to camp was greeted with cheers.

After the Bull Run campaign, the Second was moved from the Virginia countryside back to the defenses of Washington. Spirits rose when the men were greeted by the Third Vermont Regiment, less than two weeks from home. The two Vermont regiments were assigned to guard the Chain Bridge, west of the capital, that spanned the Potomac and connected Tennellytown with Fairfax County. This relatively safe position boosted morale, and spirits were definitely raised by the news that the army had a new commander.

Gen. George McClellan was summoned by President Lincoln after McClellan had won some small but famous victories in the mountains of western Virginia. Vermonters got a firsthand look at McClellan, dashing in a brand-new uniform and riding a splendid horse. From the Georgetown Heights the Vermonters had been moved a mile into Virginia to help a New York regiment build two huge earthwork forts. One afternoon General McClellan showed up in the company of a very tall, lanky, and rather homely gentleman wearing a stovepipe hat. President Lincoln and McClellan moved among the Vermonters shaking hundreds of eager hands.

Building forts was backbreaking and exhausting work, and as the nights cooled, despite their welcome relief, more and more men were waking up feeling poorly. The Vermonters, together in their growing discomfort, were now commanded by a St. Albans native, the West Pointer William Farrar Smith, better known as "Baldy." Smith intended to merge all the Vermont regiments into a brigade that he would lead. But first he had to direct construction of the forts, named Ethan Allen and Marcy. Fort Marcy still stands beside the George Washington Parkway west of Washington, preserved and open to the public.

Being in enemy territory, though only a mile deep, was nervous duty. Time and again the men were turned out in the middle of the night, sometimes for hours, for mostly imaginary emergencies. In late September they were pulled out of camp, made part of a 5,000-man force, and moved several miles toward a Confederate hilltop position. Near Lewinsville, in an engagement reminiscent of Big Bethel, some Northern units fired at each other, and the scrap ended in confusion and retreat. About 100 members of the Second Vermont got so disgusted that they refused to fall in for picket duty next day.

The Third Vermont joined a 2,000-man expedition also sent toward Lewinsville. On the way back an artillery unit commanded by the Confederate cavalryman James Ewell Brown (Jeb) Stuart got the Vermonters in range. Two men were killed and several wounded.

War gave many of the Vermont troops their first look at a wider world. Frederick M. Gale of Barre wrote home to his uncle about the things he had seen.

I am in Washington, the seat of the best government that ever existed.
I started from Brattleboro Saturday at 12 o'clock and got here Monday afternoon

UVM

The Fifth Vermont at Camp Griffin in Virginia.

about 4. I never saw such a variety of land as I have since I left Barre. I thought it was poor enough between Bellows Falls and Brattleboro. But down here in Delaware and Maryland it looks hard. There was some of the nicest farms in Massachusetts that I ever saw.

I don't remember of seeing a farm in New Jersey or Delaware or Maryland that I would take the gift of.

Gale went on to report that he had seen, from the train, "one man breaking up with one mule and [I] thought the land must be pretty soft, but when we got here I found it different. We pitched our tents and we couldn't drive a hard wood stake into it. I thought I had seen dust blow before, but never 'till now."

The Fourth and Fifth Vermont regiments arrived in late September as the weather began to sour and joined the other Vermont units at an encampment they named Camp Griffin. At first it had a rather welcome look: broad fields broken by little hills and tall forests, with here and there a plantation house. Troops arrived daily until about 20,000 men camped among those hills and vales. But with the rains came bone-chilling night fogs. Camp Griffin got bad.

By mid-October all five Vermont infantry regiments were in Virginia. A soldier in the Fifth wrote home to Manchester in mid-November describing the routine of camp life.

At 5 o'clock in the morning comes the roll call, when each man tumbles unceremoniously out of bed to answer his name.

Then comes our breakfast.... At 7 o'clock is the knapsack drill ... it tends to

75

develop our muscles and learns us to endure hardships. At 10 o'clock is skirmish drill.

At 12 o'clock we have dinner. In the interval, between drills, we are occupied in cleaning oiling and repairing our guns.

In the afternoon, at half past one o'clock is the brigade drill, which lasts all afternoon, and at sundown is the dress parade, then supper.

We receive our letters in the evening…. At 8 o'clock is the evening roll call. Then we prepare to sleep. At 8:30 comes taps, then the lights are blown out and the camp is still.

Another Vermonter, Julius Clark, wrote his mother, "It is awful hard work down here."

By late fall "Baldy" Smith had been elevated to the command of a division, and the Vermont regiments were led by William H. T. Brooks. Nights grew colder, tents leaked, and the men still lacked an adequate number of blankets and warm clothes. One soldier in the Fifth, George P. Bixby, wrote to his brother in Shrewsbury.

The Sixth regiment has lost more men…. The measles was the trouble with the men the biggest part.

We are getting hard drills now and we drill all the afternoon and two hours in the forenoon.

I wrote to you about sending a bed quilt. I hope you have sent it before now for I need it very much…the weather is cold and damp here now but not any snow nor the ground is not frozen hardly any it is frosty nights here now something like October in Vermont.

We have a stove in our tent now. We bought one the other day for 40 cents apiece pipe and all.

As fall deepened, mumps, whooping cough, chicken pox, diarrhea, dysentery, typhoid fever, and even malaria ran rampant. In late October General Smith telegraphed Governor Holbrook requesting 850 coats, 1,500 pairs of pants, and 100 tents. Colonel Whiting followed with a message to the legislature asking for clothing and tents. The War Department found out and declared that it would handle supplies. Not until mid-November did additional clothing begin to arrive. Attendance at religious services soared.

Capt. Charles P. Dudley of Manchester wrote a letter home from Camp Griffin that was published in the local *Manchester Journal*.

The weather is cold here. We have had a strong wind all the past day and night, and the men are now suffering for want of better sleeping blankets. It is not for myself that I care; I can stand everything …cold, heat, sickness if it comes, death if it must, and not complain or fear, but to look on and see others needing comforts, necessaries that cannot be had, makes me sick at heart….

Poor soldiers! Unused to privations, having had all the comforts of life, it is hard to come down to its simplest needs. Many of my company have been sick, some 10 of them have been very sick, but are now getting better.

I am sick at heart at times when I go into the hospital and see the suffering ones. I shall be glad to receive blankets from Manchester people. We shall have to get them transported to us, but the men MUST HAVE THEM.

Watching this all from afar was Vermont's new governor, Frederick C. Holbrook of Brattleboro. Holbrook, as the coming months would prove, was a man of action, and in November he dispatched Dr. Edward E. Phelps of Brattleboro, one of Vermont's most respected physicians, to Camp Griffin for an investigation. Phelps came back with disheartening findings. Of the 4,939 Vermonters in camp, Phelps determined that 1,086 were excused from duty because of illness. He noted that the Vermont regiments had been too long stationary in their camps, on soil that had become saturated with "noxious elements." But he was at a loss to explain why those conditions so affected the Vermonters and not units from other states that were in similar circumstances.

The surgeon general of the Army of the Potomac, Dr. Charles S. Tripler, also had a look at the Vermont camps. He reported:

In November, 1861, with a mean ratio of 6.5 percent sick in the whole army, twelve Massachusetts regiments gave an average of 50 sick each; five Vermont, an average of 144 each; and 35 Pennsylvania, an average of 61 each. In January, 1862, the 12th Massachusetts, 1,005 strong, had but four sick; the 13th, 1,003 strong, but 11; while the 15th, 809 strong, had 68. In the same month the Fifth Vermont, 1,000 strong, had 271 sick; the Fourth, 1,047 strong, had 244 sick; while the Second, 1,021 strong, had but 87, and the Third, 900 strong, had but 84. All these regiments were in the same brigade and encamped side by side.

Tripler suggested that severe fatigue duty on entrenchments, exposure on picket duty, and frequent alarms could be among the causes.

Surgeon General Tripler issued another report on January 28, 1862: "The Vermont regiments in Brooks's brigade give us the largest ratio of sick of all the troops in this army, and that ratio had not essentially varied for the last three months." Tripler went on: "While writing I have received another weekly report from the Vermont brigade, which shows a large increase of sick over that of the preceding week.... The food of our men is now good and they are gradually improving in their cooking. The clothing of the men is generally good. I do not think any deficiency in this respect has anything to do with the fevers that scourge our Vermont troops."

Susceptibility to disease would haunt Vermont soldiers throughout the Civil War; the reason remains a mystery. Surgeon General Tripler concluded his report with a guess, "I believe there is a nostalgic element in those regiments affecting them unfavorably."

Did he mean that homesickness was playing a part? He never said. But looking back almost a century and a third later, it seems likely that those farm boys were paying a severe price for having grown up in the hills of pristine Vermont. Having failed to develop immunities that city boys got early from close contact with many fellow humans, the Vermont lads were prey to all kinds of strange microbes when they reached the crowded Virginia camps. And in those camps more and more Vermont soldiers were being detached on burial details to lay comrades to rest in the Virginia soil more than 500 miles from the snow-clad hills of home.

Slowly conditions improved. The onset of deep winter, even with some snow, seemed to have a beneficial, perhaps even a nostalgic effect of a positive nature. Better clothing and tents arrived. Tripler made room for the more seriously ill and contagious Vermonters in military hospitals by sending conva-lescents to Philadelphia. Log houses were built to replace tents, and more attention was paid to sanitation. And in January a thaw came upon the land that caused the suspension of drills for several weeks. Everybody got a good rest. As March approached, cheering news came from the West. A general named Grant had captured two forts—Henry and Donelson—along the Tennessee and Cumberland rivers. His terms, "Unconditional Surrender," won U. S. Grant a new nom-de-guerre.

On November 20 thousands of spectators converged on Bailey's Crossroads in Virginia for a grand review of the Army of the Potomac. William H. Herrick of St. Johnsbury, a member of the Third Vermont's band, wrote in his diary:

About noon the thunder of artillery announced the arrival of the commander-in-chief, the troops are called to attention and soon after the party came into sight, Gen. McClellan riding a horse length ahead of the rest of the party, his cap off in acknowledgment of the enthusiastic greeting of the soldiers—plainly dressed but riding a magnificent horse. It may have been the excitement and enthusiasm of the time and place, but he seemed the fit leader of this splendid army and I felt that it would be a pleasure to follow him TO THE DEATH if need be such, I have no doubt were the feelings of every soldier in the field and they found vent in such tremendous cheers as I never heard before—each regiment taking it up as he passed their lines.

In the reviewing party were the president who was very conspicuous, not only from being a full head taller, but his plain citizen's dress contrasted with the uniforms with which he was surrounded.... They made rapidly down the line of each division, the soldiers cheering with much enthusiasm and the bands playing. Afterward they took up a position on a hill at one end of the field and the troops began marching in review. The bands of each brigade were combined. That of the first brigade got through first rate but ours blundered terribly, pretty uneasy in our nervousness and excitement....

After this we marched directly off the field and for home, the fields, the hillsides, the housetops and everything within seeing distance of the field was full of spectators and the sides of the road, for miles away were lined with carriages of every kind.

Houghton photo of a Vermont burial at Camp Griffin.

Herrick also remembered the march to the grand review field: "Other regiments joined us till the road was filled as far as the eye could reach with a line of glittering bayonets and as our long line wound, over hill, through forests and wide valleys, it was the most picturesque view of soldiering I had ever seen."

On the hillside with the official reviewing party was an invited guest, the suffragette and abolitionist Julia Ward Howe of Boston, who returned to her room at Willard's Hotel in Washington that night and wrote a poem inspired by a marching song she likely heard that day, "John Brown's Body." Certainly, she recalled the long lines of glittering bayonets Herrick had remembered when she wrote:

> *I have read the fiery gospel*
> *Writ in burnished rows of steel.*
> *As ye deal with my contemnors,*
> *So with you my grace shall deal*
> *Let the hero born of woman*
> *Crush the serpent with his heel,*
> *His truth goes marching on.*

She called her poem "Battle Hymn of the Republic."

As winter wore on, with more and more days showing hints of spring, thoughts turned to the coming battles. Lt. Samuel Sumner of Troy wrote to his parents on March 6: "I have a great curiosity to know how I shall stand fire. It is the heighth of my ambition that I may meet it as becomes a man fighting in the right and if it should be my fortune to survive the war I can proudly say that I was one to help preserve the country in its hour of peril." Sumner had less than four months to live, destined to be killed in action on June 29.

Today at Langley, Virginia, within the massive headquarters complex of the Central Intelligence Agency known to the thousands who work there as "the campus," a permanent exhibit honors the Vermont soldiers. The CIA stands on land that was Camp Griffin, and photographs show the troops there, one depicting the Fifth Vermont lined up before its tents, with two large rocks in the foreground. Take Dolley Madison Parkway from the CIA complex; turn into Kurtz Road and stop before the one-story brick house at Number 1331. In the front yard, most clearly visible and unchanged, are those two rocks. A few hundred yards away, along a private drive lined with great trees, is an old brick house, "Salona." Called Smoot's Hill during the war, it was headquarters for Camp Griffin.

GEN. WILLIAM SMITH'S
"OLD BRIGADE"

In truth, Vermont's William Farrar "Baldy" Smith wasn't too bad a general. Smith had one bright and shining moment midway through the war, getting an army under U. S. Grant out of a very tight spot. Then he had a terrible moment in mid-June 1864 when he blew a chance to cut the war short by several months. He rose fast early because he was an experienced officer and had a friend in a very high place. He had known George McClellan for a long time, and Smith used that relationship to his benefit, and to Vermont's. In the fall of 1861 Smith went to McClellan and asked that he be allowed to form a brigade made up exclusively of Vermont regiments. That was against a Union army policy, based on the concern that if a one-state brigade got badly shot up, then a whole state might lose its taste for war. But McClellan was at the height of his power, and he gave quick approval to Smith's request.

Smith later wrote in a book of wartime reminiscences, "I asked General McClellan to give me the Vermont troops in one brigade, which he did, and I have always been proud of the record it made in the war." The Vermont Brigade was born, composed of the Second, Third, Fourth, Fifth, and Sixth Vermont regiments. They promptly went into camp together and got sick. But as spring approached, most of the men were recovering, ready to fight and write one of the proudest records of the war. Bruce Catton called the brigade "one of the two or three best in the army." It was also the only brigade in the Union Army of the Potomac that served throughout the war permanently composed of one state's units and named after that state. (There was a brief period in 1862 when a nine-month New Jersey regiment was made part of the brigade.)

Smith was a native Vermonter, born in St. Albans into a prominent family. A cousin was John Gregory Smith, a lawyer and railroad owner who would be the

William Farrar "Baldy" Smith.

last of Vermont's three Civil War governors. The cousin went to West Point, where he got the name "Baldy" for a thin spot on the top of his head. Everybody said he was brilliant; he was fourth in his class of 1845. In a peacetime army he chose the engineers, and in 1859 he was in Chicago, overseeing construction of a lighthouse. There he met McClellan, out of the army and a vice president of the Illinois Central Railroad. They became friends.

Later in the Civil War, months after he got his Vermont brigade approved, Smith would have all kinds of trouble with superior officers, turning several high-ranking generals very much against him and badly damaging his military career. But McClellan liked him, and Smith's men liked him because he looked after their needs. He also was known by fellow officers for keeping a very well stocked headquarters, visitors sometimes wakened with a glass of champagne.

In the summer of 1861 Smith had been appointed commander of the Third Vermont. He was then put in command of the forces protecting Chain Bridge at Washington, and soon thereafter was given command of a division. His Vermont Brigade was the first unit made a part of that division.

In late October a member of McClellan's staff, William H. T. Brooks, 42, succeeded Smith as commander of the Vermont Brigade. Though born in Ohio, Brooks was the son of a Montpelier native. The troops forgave his flatlander status, and they also ignored his well-known lack of sympathy for antislavery causes. He was tall and powerful, a West Pointer and a battle-tested veteran of the Mexican War and the western frontier who, the soldiers would soon discover, showed no outward fear of minié balls.

Brooks saw his sick regiments through the bad fall and winter of 1861–62, and in the spring began to whip them into fighting shape. As March

Mexican War vet W. H. T. Brooks led the Vermont Brigade.

arrived, McClellan at long last got his army into motion and began the move toward Richmond. The Vermonters were ready to fight, to write the first chapter in what would be their brigade's remarkable combat record.

Nearly a quarter century after the war, in 1889, Frank Moore published a book called *The Civil War in Song and Story*. Someone, whose name has been lost, contributed a chapter on the Vermont Brigade that remains perhaps its finest tribute. The book describes the author as "one who did not belong to [the Vermont Brigade], and who never was in Vermont." It reads, in part:

THE VERMONT BRIGADE—They were honest farmers turned vagabonds. They were simple countrymen changed into heroes. They were quiet townsmen that had become rovers. They stole ancient horses and bony cows on the march. They pillaged moderately in other things. They swept the dairies, and they stripped the orchards for miles where they travelled. They chased rabbits when they went into camp, after long marches, and they yelled like wild Indians when neighboring camps were silent through fatigue. They were ill disciplined and familiar with their officers. They swaggered in a cool, impudent way, and looked down with a patronizing Yankee coolness upon all regiments that were better drilled, and upon that part of the army generally that did not belong to the Vermont brigade. They were strangely proud, not of themselves individually, but of the brigade collectively; for they knew perfectly well they were the best fighters in the known world. They were long of limb, and could outmarch the army. They were individually self-reliant and skillful in the use of arms; and they honestly believed that the Vermont brigade could not be beaten by all the combined armies of the rebellion.

They were veterans in fighting qualities almost from their first skirmish. This was at Lee's Mills. They crossed a narrow dam under fire, made the attack they were instructed to make, and came back, wading deep in the water, with a steadiness that surprised the army. They were an incorrigible, irregular, noisy set of rascals. They were much sworn at during their four years of service; yet they were at all times a pet brigade. There were but two things they would do—march and fight; and these they did in a manner peculiarly their own. They had a long, slow, swinging stride on the march, which distanced everything that followed them. They had a quiet, attentive, earnest, individual way of fighting that made them terrific in battle. Each man knew that his neighbor in the ranks was not going to run away; and he knew, also, that he himself intended to remain where he was. Accordingly, none of the attention of the line was directed from the important duty of loading and firing, rapidly and carefully. When moving into action, and while hotly engaged, they made queer, quaint jokes, and enjoyed them greatly. They crowed like cocks, they ba-a-ed like sheep, they neighed like horses, they bellowed like bulls, they barked like dogs, and they counterfeited, with excellent effect, the indescribable music of the mule. When, perchance, they held a picket line in a forest, it seemed as if Noah's ark had gone to pieces there....

There were many regiments equal to the Vermont regiments in actual battle, and some that, like the Fifth New York volunteers, not only equalled them in fighting qualities, but greatly surpassed them in drill, discipline, and appearance on parade. As a brigade, however, they were undoubtedly the best brigade in the army of the Potomac, for they not only fought as well as it was possible to fight, but they could outmarch, with the utmost ease, any other organization in the army.

It was the intention of the writer only to refer to this brigade as furnishing the best type of the American soldier; but this article has grown beyond its intended limit, and we have, therefore, not the space to examine into the causes of this superiority. Two, however, may be briefly stated. First, that the regiments from Vermont were brigaded together. This rule, strange to say, seemed to work well only in regard to the smaller states, like Vermont and New Jersey. Second, the fact that Vermont, during the first year of the war, recruited for her regiments, and kept them full. Regimental and company officers, knowing that their ranks would be filled up, discharged men freely, and thus managed to get rid of their weak and worthless soldiers. For these reasons the Vermonters were good men. They were fortunate, moreover, in having such commanders as General W. F. Smith and W. T. H. Brooks. It naturally resulted from this combination of circumstances that they became a great power in battle, and earned a reputation of which every man and woman in Vermont may well be proud.

The Vermont Brigade broke camp with the rest of the Army of the Potomac in the spring of 1862 and headed toward an engagement where its fighting qualities would for the first time be severely tested, at a boggy place on the Virginia peninsula called Lee's Mills—a destination Civil War historians seldom mention but one that Vermonters can never forget.

WILLIAM SCOTT'S PARDON

Route 302, William Scott Memorial Highway, between Barre and Wells River, winding through white-clapboard villages, vintage farms amid high pastures, and steep wooded hills, is named for Vermont's most famous Civil War private. William Scott of Groton may in fact have been the best known of all the hundreds of thousands of privates who served in the Union armies.

East from Barre, beyond the heights of Orange, the road eventually begins a long descent toward the village of Groton, with the great mass of New Hampshire's Moosilauke Mountain in the distance. The high Presidential Range of the White Mountains is suddenly visible beyond a granite monument on the south side of the road. The monument stands where Thomas Scott, who migrated from Scotland in 1825, and his wife Mary (Wormwood) Scott made their home when the Civil War began. They farmed what looks like poor land, now boulder-strewn pastures gone to brush and back to woods. The monument honors the Scotts' son William, the "Sleeping Sentinel."

The Scotts settled there with eight children—seven boys and a daughter. Thomas and Mary Scott certainly needed all the help they could get on the farm. An army friend of William Scott's remembered: "William always worked at home.... His father always had his wages. His father was in very reduced circumstances."

But the Scotts saw to it that the children were schooled and received strong religious training, as William's letters attest. When the war broke out in 1861, five of the boys were old enough to serve: William, Daniel, George, John, and Joseph joined up and went south.

William Scott enlisted at Montpelier and went on to St. Johnsbury to join the encampment of the Third Vermont Regiment. A regimental bandmember recalled that Scott just couldn't learn to march. He was always getting kicked by the feet of those behind and stepping on the heels of those ahead. He was

William Scott, the Sleeping Sentinel.

described as "a big, awkward country lad who had a heart as big as he was." He was popular with his fellow soldiers, despite the kicks and stumbles, and on the night of August 30, 1861 he took the place of a friend assigned to picket duty, though he had had that duty the night before.

By then the Third had encamped on the Georgetown heights overlooking Chain Bridge. The regiment's job was to guard that strategic bridge, night and day; nearby was the Georgetown reservoir, which provided much of the capital city's drinking water. On the night of August 31 William Scott and two other Vermont soldiers were stationed near the north end of the Chain Bridge, looking toward the Virginia bluffs a half mile away.

Between 2 and 3 A.M. the officer of the guard, Capt. Thomas House from St. Albans, found Scott and his fellow pickets sleeping. "When I found them all asleep I tried to find out whose duty it was to have been awake at the time. They all said it was Scott's and Scott admitted that it was his duty," Captain House stated. Scott was arrested and charged with violation of the 46th Article of War—having been a regularly posted sentinel who went to sleep at his post. The penalty for that offense was death.

A 12-man court-martial, all Vermonters, was appointed by the regimental commander, Col. Breed Hyde. The 12 men, including Maj. Wheelock G. Veazey and Col. George Stannard, met on September 5 and summoned Captain House to recount his discovery of the sleeping sentinels. Though Scott pleaded not guilty, Captain House's testimony was conclusive. Scott was sentenced to be shot four days later, September 9. (The execution order, signed not by but for General McClellan, is preserved at the Fairbanks Museum in St. Johnsbury.) William Scott, just six weeks off a Vermont farm, was about to become the first soldier in the Army of the Potomac to be executed.

Scott's comrades were shocked, and they set to work to right, if they could, what they considered an injustice. The help of the Reverend Moses Parmlee of Underhill, the regimental chaplain, was quickly enlisted. Parmlee later said of Scott, "His exterior was plain, but he had a warm and honest heart. He slept at his post because of sheer exhaustion and not because he lacked vigilance." Parmlee and the men wrote a petition asking that Scott be pardoned and got the signatures of 191 officers and men of the Third Vermont. "Baldy" Smith signed.

Word of Scott's plight quickly spread beyond the ranks of the army. In fact, the case became something of a cause célèbre. Newspapers in Vermont and throughout the North ran stories. Many editorialized, most in favor of mercy. But the *New York Times* was of no such mind, backing the death sentence "to prevent the recurrence of a similar dereliction among our troops."

The *National Republican* of Washington stated, "We are opposed to capital punishment, but if there is an offense for which a man should be put to death, we think young Scott committed it."

More than a century later, one of Vermont's finest journalists, Bernard Crosier of North Springfield, an army veteran, produced a finely written accounting of the Scott affair. It included this appraisal of the case against the Groton lad: "If the death penalty sounds harsh for merely falling asleep, it has to be remembered that the Union forces had been badly-routed at Manassas only four days before the Vermont regiment started guarding the bridge. Gen. P. G. T. Beauregard's combined army was only 10 miles south of the river, and a sleeping sentinel could mean the loss of Washington."

Reverend Parmlee wrote that he got on a horse and, two days before the scheduled execution, went to "the president's house," where "we were unable to gain a personal interview, but were assured the case was receiving careful consideration." That night the commander of the Army of the Potomac, General McClellan, wrote to his wife, "Mr. Lincoln came this morning to ask me to pardon a man that I ordered to be shot." According to Carl Sandburg, the biographer of Lincoln, the president said: "I could not think of going into eternity with the blood of that poor young man on my skirts. It is not to be wondered at that a boy, raised on the farm, probably in the habit of going to bed at dark, should, when required to watch, fall asleep; and I cannot consent to shooting him for such an act."

Later, Lincoln added, "Well, I have made one family happy, but I don't know about the discipline of the army." Lincoln ordered the execution stopped.

But nobody told Scott.

On the morning of September 9 the Third Vermont was assembled in a three-sided formation. Six men were chosen as a firing squad. One was a private from Brattleboro, Luke I. Ferriter. He recalled many years later that each squad member was given one bullet each, five of which were blanks, so that no man could be sure he had fired the fatal shot. (More likely, it was one blank and five live rounds.) "We were all shaking in nervousness," Ferriter recalled. Ferriter saw Scott led, trembling, out of a tent with a white cap pulled over his head. Another soldier said Scott was white and shaking, barely able to support himself. Another witness said the condemned was "deadly pale, and an occasional shudder shook his exhausted frame." Scott did not ask for mercy.

An officer stepped forward to pronounce what was expected to be the order of execution. He read:

Headquarters of the Army of the Potomac
Washington, Sept. 8
Private William Scott, of Company K. of the Third regiment of Vermont volunteers, having been found guilty by court-martial of sleeping on his post while a sentinel on picket guard, has been sentenced to be shot, and the sentence has been approved and ordered to be executed. The commanding officers of the brigade, the regiment and the company, of the command, together with many other privates and officers of his regiment, have earnestly appealed to the Major General commanding, to spare the life of the offender, and the president of the United States has expressed a wish that as this is the first condemnation to death in this army for this crime, mercy may be extended to the criminal. This fact, viewed in connection with the inexperience of the condemned soldier, his previous good conduct and general good character, and the urgent entreaties made in his behalf, have determined the major general commanding to grant the pardon so earnestly prayed for. This act of clemency must not be understood as affording a precedent for any future case. The duty of a sentinel is of such a nature, that its neglect by sleeping upon or deserting his post may endanger the safety of a command, or even of the whole army, and all nations affix to the offence the penalty of death. Private William Scott of Co. K of the Third regiment of Vermont volunteers, will be released from confinement and returned to duty.

By command of Maj. General McClellan

S. WILLIAMS, ASST. ADJT. GENERAL

Writing 30 years later, a Vermonter who was there, Pvt. David Morgan of Vergennes, a member of the Third Regiment's band, recalled, "I still see poor broken down and dejected Scott who, much to my surprise, evinced no particular emotion when the pardon was read."

But the ranks erupted in cheers, both for Scott and for President Lincoln. Firing squad member Ferriter later claimed that Lincoln stepped from the ranks to acknowledge the cheers, but that seems to have been a figment of Ferriter's imagination. Despite a persistent legend that Lincoln visited the execution site to be sure his commutation was heeded, no other evidence places him there. Scott, shaken, went back to duty. Chaplain Parmlee wrote some months later: "I returned to camp to meet Scott, released and perfectly happy. He went about his duties as if determined to prove himself worthy of the pardon he was granted. He was always a faithful soldier, but after his pardon he was doubly so."

A month later, Scott wrote home:

Dear absent friend,
I received your letter, and was glad to hear that you and the rest what are left are well....

I think it high time that we are looking for our souls' welfare. Time is but short at the longest. We are certain death is like a thief which cometh in the night when we think not.

I heard that Edwin Darling was dead and Burnham, too. Charles Emery got a letter which told us the news, but may God be with the widows and the fatherless. By the hand of God helping me, I shall some day outride the storms of affliction and land my soul on the other side of Jordan and head our weary souls home to rest where there shall be no death. There we shall have it all peace and harmony. It stands us in hand to be ready for death any time, for in such an hour as you think not the son of man cometh to destroy the earth.

From your friend,

WILLIAM SCOTT

Somehow Thomas Scott found enough money and went down to Wells River and boarded a train, bent on personally thanking the president. When he got to Washington, Scott went straight to the White House and was admitted to the president's office. There a Vermont farmer in his only passable suit of clothes faced the tall, lanky, homespun man who was his son's commander in chief, a product of the dirt-floor shacks of frontier farms. There's only one source that confirms this meeting, but one can imagine the Vermont hill farmer face to face with the president of the United States of America. Tom Scott had a hard time getting out the words, gratitude for sparing the life of his son. Lincoln knew what to say. We are told that he asked Mr. Scott how he could manage the farm with five of his seven sons gone. Then the conversation turned to farming, the prospects for the coming year. Lincoln knew the season ahead would be hard on the Scott farm without the older boys; according to the source, when Scott departed, Lincoln slipped him a $10 bill. He also gave him a pass to visit his sons in the camps. Tom Scott apparently went out to the camps in northern Virginia, saw his boys, and returned to Washington and got on the train north to Wells River, to his depleted family and his farm high in the Groton hills. It was sugaring time and there was much work to be done.

Many years after the war, in 1892, there was an exchange of correspondence concerning the Scott matter prompted, apparently, by a newspaper article. It all raised the possibility that the charges and death sentence had, to a point, been staged.

In the papers of "Baldy" Smith, at the Vermont Historical Society, is a letter written by Smith in 1892 to Redfield Proctor:

> We found great trouble with the new troops was to get them to understand the responsibilities of a sentinel, and the disasters which might arise from a soldier in the picket line going to sleep. That trouble was getting to be serious and no amount of preaching about duty and danger seemed to produce any effect. It was finally arranged with headquarters that I was to take one good case and prefer the proper charges in due form. A court was then to be ordered and as the case was to be one in which there should be no doubt about the evidence.... The programme was carried out to the letter upon William Scott, Third Vermont Regiment, who was the first indubitable case secured.... So far as Mr. Lincoln was concerned it must have been purely a matter of form from the time the papers were placed before him. There was no idea but that he would issue the pardon.

Those who have studied "Baldy" Smith's writings caution that he often strayed from the truth when referring to his troubled war years. But his observations on the Scott matter are supported by a letter in the Smith papers from Wheelock Veazey. "I got the impression," Veazey wrote, "that there was an understanding that reached through army headquarters to the president that the whole business was to be a matter of form rather than real substance, for the sake of its moral effect on the army."

Smith also wrote that he visited Scott to tell him that, in the end, he would be spared. Scott, he said, was not so sure.

WASTED LIVES AT LEE'S MILLS

In Virginia in 1862 the long, unhealthy winter ended with the call of bugles floating on the moist and flower-scented breeze. General McClellan had finally decided to move his Army of the Potomac into action. As the army broke camp, its most famous private, William Scott, sent a letter home.

> Dear absent but not forgotten friend,
> I seat myself to write that I am well and hope that when these few scribbled lines reach you, they will find you the same. The Groton boys are all well now. We haven't had much snow here this winter, but I'd rather see all the snow that ever fell in Vermont than endure here. It is very cold and wet. The mud is awfully deep. We moved from Camp Griffin and moved to Flint Hill and stopped there five days, and then moved to within five miles of Alexandria. We expect to go down to the coast soon. We are in the woods now. The night we came from Flint Hill it rained all night. It rained like everything and we never slept a wink all night. A soldier's life is nothing more or less than a dog's life.

Toward the end of his letter he added, "I should like to get some new sugar to eat." He knew the sap would soon be running in Vermont.

But the weather improved. Another Vermont private, Julius Clark, wrote home: "We are all in good spirits.... The weather is like April in Vermont.... I can read...by moonlight."

On Sunday, March 23, with bands playing and flags flying, the Vermonters were put aboard ships and steamed down the Potomac. In the morning a sight familiar to veterans of the First Vermont Regiment loomed on the shore—the ramparts of Fort Monroe. The Vermont Brigade, all five regiments together, landed with the rest of "Baldy" Smith's 13,000-man division at the tip of the Virginia Peninsula, between the York and James rivers. The division went some

Larkin Mead sketch of Vermonters at Lee's Mills.

eight miles inland, not far from the scene of the Big Bethel fight, and encountered enemy riflemen. A few shots were exchanged; the division was promptly withdrawn to encamp near Newport News. By April 4 the entire Army of the Potomac was on the Peninsula. A pleasant week of swimming and feasting on oysters followed while McClellan decided what to do. On April 5 the division was again marched up the Peninsula some 10 miles until it came to a river, on the other side of which were some very impressive Confederate earthworks.

The Confederates had suspected that McClellan might try a move up the Peninsula toward Richmond, and for two months slaves and soldiers had been building fortifications on the west bank of the Warwick River, a sluggish stream that flows almost entirely across the Peninsula. Not only were the earthworks formidable, but dams had been constructed as well, turning a wide creek into a series of shallow ponds, a daunting military obstacle. Where Smith's division was posted, a dam built near a mill owned by a man named Lee had created a pond 50 yards wide. As the Vermonters cautiously approached its banks, artillery began firing from earthworks on the other side. Upstream, around the historic village of Yorktown, another Federal column was at a standstill, facing similar obstacles.

McClellan's 65,000-man army was now on the scene confronting 13,000 Confederates commanded by Maj. Gen. John Magruder. Fond of acting in amateur theatricals, Magruder began shooting at Federals everywhere and marching parts of his small army around and around to make it look like a force many times its size. He had a most appreciative audience in McClellan, always convinced he was outnumbered and now appealing to Lincoln for more troops. The Federal advance was stalled.

The Vermonters camped in a clearing where the Garrow family farmhouse had recently stood. They were put to work helping improve roads and building earthworks to protect the artillery. Some of the men were posted by the river on picket duty, occasionally exchanging shots with Confederates. At this point, news reached the Army of the Potomac that lifted everyone's spirits. Out on the Tennessee River, U. S. Grant had won another victory, at Shiloh.

Meanwhile, on the opposite shore of the Warwick where the open riverbank flats met the woods, the Confederates were busy strengthening fortifications. McClellan ordered "Baldy" Smith and the Vermont Brigade to attack them; in the early morning of April 16 the Vermonters prepared to fight. Units of the Third and Fourth Vermont regiments were advanced to the riverbank above the Lee's Mills dam, where the creek was impressively wide. On the far side, out in the open, were Confederate rifle pits, backed by high earthworks at the edge of the woods. Smith's men opened fire, which was promptly returned, and artillery on both sides fired intermittently, putting a stop to work on the Confederate defenses. McClellan himself appeared on the scene, well back from the river, surrounded by staff and orderlies, and told Smith to send men across the water and occupy the enemy's works. But he also cautioned against a general engagement and told him to withdraw if serious resistance developed. Those were strange orders, since Magruder or any Confederate commander would surely offer serious resistance if his main defensive line were in danger. But Smith did as he was told.

Skirmishers were placed in the swampy woods by the water to distract the Confederate riflemen. Three cannon were wheeled out into the Garrow field to fire directly at the enemy works. Colonel Hyde's Third Vermont made the attack. Two companies, one commanded by Capt. Fernando C. Harrington of Charleston, the other by Capt. Samuel Pingree of Hartford, were to wade the stream holding cartridge boxes and rifle-muskets well above their heads. They faced a discouraging prospect: a swamp, a pond 150 feet across, then open ground on the far shore protected by rifle pits. Beyond those pits lay the high earthworks, giving the riflemen and cannon in them clear fields of fire.

About 3 P.M. the Union artillery opened in earnest, at once getting a spirited

Houghton photo of Vermont troops crossing the dam at Lee's Mills after the battle.

reply from the Southern gunners. Just before the order to advance was given, Captain Harrington came up to Captain Pingree and announced that he was unwell and unable to go forward. (Later Harrington insisted he had crossed the stream, indeed had rescued a battle flag.) Pingree gave the order to advance and out of the woods went two companies of Vermonters, 192 men. In the front rank was William Scott.

A soldier in the Third Vermont remembered: "We marched steadily at the quick to the edge of the stream, and plunged in, on the run, the water deepened unexpectedly.... The killed and wounded began to fall the instant of entering the stream."

George French, a corporal in the Third Vermont, until a few months earlier a teamster in his hometown of Cambridge beneath Mount Mansfield, recalled:

On we pushed, climbing over logs, roots and every kind of impediment which floated in the water or rested on the ground, firing as we had opportunity, until the channel of the creek was past, and the depth of water began to diminish. Then the gleam of our steadily advancing bayonets began to strike a terror to the rebel hearts and one by one they leaped from behind their breastworks and took cover in the thickets behind. Now commenced a scene which beggars all description. Firmly grasping our trusty rifles we rushed on, shouting, firing, yelling—and ere we set foot on dry land every rebel had left the pits in front of us. I cannot tell you what followed. It makes my heart sick to think of it. Let it suffice to say we held them there at bay for a long hour, waiting, oh how anxiously for reinforcements. The ground was dotted with our comrades dead and the creek was crimson with the blood of our wounded.

After a brief fight the North Carolina and Georgia soldiers holding the rifle pits retreated to the earthworks. The Vermonters gave a loud cheer and started for them, only to be stopped by a deadly volley and by Captain Pingree, who saw the futility of such a frontal assault.

William Scott was hit just as the first row of Vermonters came onto dry land. Some said five, some said six bullets tore into the body of the Sleeping Sentinel, and he went down at water's edge.

The Vermonters held to the captured rifle pits for protection, but more and more Confederates came up, and more and more Vermonters were getting shot. Pingree, wounded in the leg, asked Colonel Hyde for permission to withdraw. No reply came. For a half hour the Vermonters hung on grimly, taking more fire, with Confederates working their way around the flanks. Captain Pingree sent another messenger back to Hyde and was hit again, a bullet taking away a thumb. At last an exhausted soldier emerged from the deadly water with word from Hyde. Yes, Pingree could now bring his men back.

Corporal French wrote, "As we waded back, weary and sick of heart, the water fairly boiled around us with bullets."

A young soldier from Lamoille County said, "It was just like sap boiling in that stream, the bullets fell so thick."

Of the 192 men who had crossed the stream, just 100 came back unharmed. Division commander "Baldy" Smith later said, "Among the four companies of the Third Vermont who crossed the creek, there were more individual acts of heroism performed than I ever read of in a great battle."

The wounded and dying were carried to the shelter of trenches and woods. The firing on both sides died. Then, incredibly, orders came to resume the attack. Col. Edwin Stoughton was ordered to send four companies of his Fourth Vermont across the Lee's Mills dam to storm a one-gun battery on the opposite shore. Stoughton ordered his men forward, with bayonets fixed, but they were met by a furious fire and driven back to the cover of the woods. Two men were killed and twelve wounded. Stoughton and another soldier came back together, dragging a wounded man. Meanwhile, downstream, the Sixth Vermont Regiment also had orders to cross the river. The Sixth Vermont's Capt. David B. Davenport of Roxbury was wounded while wading the stream and was helped from the water to safety by an 11-year-old drummer boy—his son Henry. As the boy returned to the stream to get water for his father, a bullet knocked the cup from his hands. (The elder Davenport would recover from his wound, only to die of sickness in camp.)

Most of the men of the Sixth reached the enemy shore hardly scathed as the result of their swift attack and some inaccurate enemy fire, but the Confederates began to sight in with accuracy. Three of the five company commanders who went across were quickly hit, one fatally. Some Vermonters rushed the enemy rifle pits but were quickly repulsed. Sgt. Edward Holton of Williston, seeing a color bearer shot, bolted forward, grabbed the fallen flag, and eventually carried it back across the water. He was unhurt. Col. Nathan Lord, commanding the regiment, saw that the whole enterprise was hopeless and, acting with a dispatch that Colonel Hyde had lacked, took it upon himself to order a retreat.

The fight at Lee's Mills was over. It had been a waste. Two weeks later, the Confederates abandoned the Warwick River lines. Two days after the battle, under a flag of truce, a Confederate officer and a Union officer met in the middle of the Lee's Mills dam and reached an agreement for returning the Vermont dead. The meeting was cordial, and the Confederate acknowledged considerable losses on his side. As a result, 29 blackened bodies were carried by Confederates to the middle of the dam, where they were handed to Vermont soldiers, who buried them in the woods of the Garrow farm. When it was all over, Vermont's loss at Lee's Mills was put at 44 killed and 148 wounded. In subsequent days, 21 more Vermonters died of wounds.

"The Battle of Lee's Mills" is what Vermonters call that bloody fight along the Warwick River that 16th day of April 1862. Confederates called it the Battle of the Chimneys or the Battle of Dam No. 1. When it was over, "Baldy" Smith had some explaining to do, especially concerning why the attack had been renewed. Rumors spread that he had been drunk and had fallen from his horse. A military court of inquiry quickly exonerated Smith, who had the support of many Vermont Brigade officers. Smith later said, "The moment I found resistance serious and the numbers opposed great, I acted in obedience to the warning instructions of the general-in-chief, and withdrew the small numbers of troops exposed from under fire."

In the Third Vermont was a 16-year-old drummer boy from Johnson, Julian Scott, who twice crossed the deadly water of the Warwick River to bring back wounded. "He pulled out no less than nine of his fellow soldiers," said a comrade. "Ephram Brown, who was helping him, was himself shot through the thigh in the inside and disabled. Scott waded back like the boy hero he is, and brought him safely over." Scott was unhurt and later, for his actions, became the first Vermonter awarded the Medal of Honor. Well after the war Scott painted some of the finest of all Civil War paintings, including *The Battle of Cedar Creek*, which hangs in the State House.

It isn't clear whether Julian Scott knew William Scott. Someone had carried the terribly wounded William back across the river to the shelter of the woods. At least one of the bullets that tore through Scott's body hit the stomach, and such wounds were almost always fatal—the worst kind, according to the soldiers, who called them "gut shots." The tough farm boy lived on into the next morning, through what must have been a night of agony. Scott was under the care of surgeon Henry Janes of Waterbury, who later said there was nothing he could do for the lad.

A friend of Scott's, Charles Emery, wrote home on April 19 to "Friend Priscilla":

The bullets whistled around me most of the day, but none of them hit me. Willie Scott was killed on making the charge he had five bullets in his body.

I see where he was buried. He was buried in a peach grove the trees was blossomed out.

Others said cherry blossoms were in bloom when Scott's body was laid to rest with other Vermont soldiers on the Garrow farm. All agreed that when his grave was dug, the bones of an American soldier of the revolutionary war were unearthed.

Carl Sandburg wrote that William Scott, "among the fresh growths and blooms of Virginia springtime at Lee's Mills took the burning messages of six bullets into his body.... All he could give Lincoln or his country or his God was now given."

There was considerable disagreement about Scott's final words, though the popular account held that he thanked Abraham Lincoln for having given him the chance to die honorably for his country. One sergeant in the Third Vermont who knew Scott quoted him as saying, "Tell the boys to avenge my death."

The papers picked up the story, and Francis De Haes Janvier published a verse in Scott's honor. Janvier was invited to the White House to read his creation for the Lincolns. It concluded:

While yet his voice grew tremulous, and death bedimmed his eye—
He called his comrades to attest, he had not feared to die!

And, in his last expiring breath, a prayer to heaven was sent—
That God, with his unfailing grace, would bless our President.

A large and thriving city like Newport News in Virginia might be the last place one would expect to find a well-preserved Civil War battlefield. But the people of that city have had the good sense to set aside some 8,000 open acres as a municipal park, the largest city park east of the Mississippi. Within that park, where a slow river flows between wooded banks, is the battlefield of Lee's Mills, looking today much as it did in 1862. In the mid-1980s I saw mention in a guidebook that a Civil War battlefield was preserved in the great Newport News city park. Could it possibly be Lee's Mills? A call to the city parks office confirmed that it was. A week later I arrived in Newport News and found a superbly preserved little battlefield. The earthworks and artillery positions occupied by the Vermonters before and after the battle survive in woods and fields of what was the Garrow farm. Warwick Creek is wider and deeper now, and a pedestrian footbridge takes Civil War buffs, fishermen, and picnickers across. The bridge is built on what the locals call Dam No. 1, the dam that widened the Warwick River where the Vermonters fought and across which some of the Vermonters futilely charged. On the far shore are the rifle pits the Vermonters captured, and beyond them, in the woods, are the huge earthworks that General Magruder's men and slaves constructed—some of the best preserved of all Civil War earthworks.

Beside the still waters of the dammed Warwick River is a painting of the battle, depicting the Vermonters attacking through the water. An accompanying tablet reads: "Two hundred men of the Third Vermont Infantry waded across the Warwick River under close fire and gained the Confederate rifle pits on the north shore. Rallying from the surprise attack of the 'Green Mountain Boys,' the southerners drove them back with considerable loss to the invaders."

The day I visited, I inquired for the whereabouts of the Vermont burials. I was told that in 1866 the US government had established a military cemetery at nearby Yorktown. The Vermonters were disinterred from the battlefield and reburied in that cemetery. A park ranger took me to the cemetery, shaded by cedars and surrounded by a brick wall. It lies between a Confederate fortification and a reconstructed French artillery position from the Revolutionary War.

The cemetery contains 2,000 Union graves. I walked among them for some time before beginning to find Vermonters. There lay Seymour Wells, John Savory, Walter Vance, Charles Wells, Frank Thomas, Austin Boynton, William Godfrey. And a little farther on was another of those small, militarily uniform headstones set flush with the ground, with the name William Scott.

Five hundred miles away in Groton, up across the road from the Scott monument where the Scott house once stood, is an old stone-walled cemetery with a Scott family plot. Just one son who went to war lies there, Joseph, who came home wounded and did not live long. The other boys who went to fight—William, George, and Daniel—never came home.

Clearly, the Scott monument in Groton is far more than a remembrance of one famous Union private. It is a monument to an American family's monumental sacrifice for the causes of freedom and unity. Thomas and Mary Scott gave five sons to the Union and only one survived. It was a terrible gift, and not long after the war, perhaps too much haunted by sad memories, the Scotts left their upland farm. Or perhaps they gave up the farm because, as Lincoln had feared, Tom Scott simply couldn't do all the work without those boys.

One day I was doing research in the wondrous library of the Vermont Historical Society and asked for a folder of material on Scott. As I leafed through the pages on pages of information, I came upon a letter in Scott's hand, the one in which he expressed the fond hope that "I should like to get some new sugar to eat," his last letter. It seems to me one of Vermont's great treasures. Sleep well, Sleeping Sentinel.

THE FIRST VERMONT CAVALRY

In the Chittenden County town of Westford, the Congregational church sits on a rise at the head of the green. Below, at the near end of the green, is a statue, a monument to a former pastor who went to war in 1862 and became known as "the fighting chaplain" of Vermont's only cavalry unit. Though the legendary Vermont Brigade has commanded history's attention, the First Vermont Cavalry was one of the Union army's best.

The granite statue pictures a bearded man with a Bible in hand, dressed in a Civil War uniform with a cavalry hat, brim upturned on one side. He is the Reverend John H. Woodward. Born in Charlotte in 1809, he grew up principally in Franklin County, and in 1836 married "a most estimable lady," Emily Morehouse of Shelburne, the same year he entered the ministry. The next year he assumed the pulpit of the Westford Congregational Church.

Woodward was past his 50th birthday and serving as a state senator when, in the fall of 1861, he learned that a Vermont cavalry regiment was being formed at Burlington. Upon arriving at the drill field on the north side of the city, christened Camp Ethan Allen by the men, Woodward volunteered as chaplain of the regiment. The First Vermont Cavalry was a thoroughly democratic outfit, having been raised under federal, not state, authority and thus authorized to elect its own officers. The men chose Woodward as their spiritual leader. They got more than a minister.

At first the regiment was drilled on foot, but horses were quickly shipped in and branded with a "US" on forefoot and foreshoulder. The horses, mainly Vermont Morgans, were each between five and nine years old and 15 and 16 hands high, as required by federal regulations.

The First Vermont Cavalry, 966 men and mounts strong, boarded five trains totaling 153 cars at Burlington on December 14 and started south. Before reaching New York City, the regiment lost one man, James Horgan, who fell

CAVALRY HORSES

WANTED!

The Subscriber will pur-

chase Horses suitable for Cavalry uses, at   county

of   Vermont, on

the   days of   1862.

Joseph Lance.

UVM

The First Vermont Cavalry preferred Vermont Morgans.

from a car and died under the train's wheels. On arriving, the regiment saddled up for a long ride into New Jersey to board other trains. Passing through the slippery, slimy city streets in the rain, men and horses fell down. It might have seemed comical if some men and mounts hadn't been injured. The unit nevertheless got the standard rave reviews from the local press. The *Newark Advertiser* reported: "The Green Mountain Boys arrived about four o'clock and marched up Market Street amid the liveliest tokens of enthusiasm. The men are of a superior class, with the true Yankee grit blazing from their eyes. The horses are small, compact and sinewy, and evidently capable of great endurance. It was the general remark that so splendid a body of animals had never been seen together in this city."

Reaching Washington at night, the regiment was bivouacked in an abandoned Capitol Hill cemetery, where some men fell into freshly dug graves. On the day before Christmas the regiment started for Annapolis. A corporal who experienced the march wrote:

Our appearance must have been picturesque. In addition to our equipments of sabre, pistol, haversack, canteen, lariat, rope and pin, feed-bag and blankets, we had cups, plates, frying-pans, coffee-pots, shawls, mattresses, pillows, valises, satchels, brushes, and other things too numerous to mention—all in some unaccountable way attached to our horses and ourselves, so that we had, when mounted, breastworks in our front and bulwarks in our rear. With horses unused to marching, and riders unused to riding, and officers unused to everything in the service, we went most of the way at a pace little short of a charge.

At Annapolis the regiment continued its drill and said good-bye to its founder and first commander, Col. Lemuel Platt of Colchester, who had sought and received federal permission to raise the regiment, and from the first had said he didn't intend to stay long in the service. He was without military experience and past 50, and at Annapolis he tendered his resignation to chief of cavalry Brig. Gen. George Stoneman. His replacement was the 33-year-old West Pointer Jonas P. Holliday, to whom the men took an instant liking, even though he was a New Yorker. The Vermonters spent a rather quiet winter at Annapolis, generally free of the disease plaguing the Vermont infantry not so many miles away in Virginia. In early March 1862 orders came to move, first back to Washington, and then along the Potomac into western Maryland. After a two-week encampment at Edwards Ferry, on March 29 the regiment reached the scene of John Brown's capture, Harpers Ferry.

Harpers Ferry lies at the so-called lower end of the Shenandoah Valley, where the Shenandoah River joins the Potomac. Soon the Vermont horsemen were headed up the valley where help was badly needed, for "Stonewall" Jackson was on the loose, having begun his Valley Campaign. Jackson began his maneuvers by attacking at Kernstown on March 23. Though Jackson had run into an unexpectedly large Union force and been forced to withdraw, he had pinned down Gen. Nathaniel Banks and the main Federal force in the valley, to which the First Vermont Cavalry was now being attached.

The Vermont cavalry got its first look at the horror of war as it rode south on the Valley Pike past the Kernstown battlefield. Fresh graves, battered wagons, dead horses, and wounded men were everywhere. It was a depressing sight, and four days later, on April 5, as the regiment crossed Cedar Creek and Fisher's Hill, the unit was again profoundly shocked. Regimental commander Holliday turned off on a side road along Tumbling Run, unholstered his pistol, and blew his brains out. "He seemed to be in feeble health," one Vermonter recalled, "weighed down by his responsibility, able to sleep but little, laborious, anxious, troubled, nervous." Cavalryman William Wells of Waterbury wrote to his parents:

He rode down from the road to the run (the Shenandoah) about 50 or 60 rods from the road. There dismounted, hitched his horse, took out a revolver and shot himself and fell into the river. He shot himself in the middle of the forehead. The ball did not come out. The adjutant and orderly were within about 40 rods from him. When they got to the run he was just floating away.... I do not know the cause of the act. We shall miss him very much.

That night regimental surgeon George S. Gale comforted the men. "Gentlemen," he said, "our duty is with the living and not the dead. There is material enough in this regiment to save it."

Jackson had taken most of his army for a rest, off around the south end of Massanutten Mountain and up into a hollow in the Blue Ridge Mountains. But he had left a cavalry screen under the capable leadership of Turner Ashby. One April morning well before sunrise, some Vermonters approached the village of Mount Jackson and saw Confederates torching a covered bridge. The cavalry lined up, bugles sounded, and the Vermont horsemen made their first combat charge. The outnumbered Confederates quickly galloped to safety on high ground; the Vermonters put out the fire, using their horses' feedbags. Artillery shells suddenly began slamming in, one plunging through part of the bridge but miraculously hurting no one. The Vermont fire fighters were most pleased to see reinforcements arrive, Chaplain Woodward, with drawn sword, in front. The frontline of battle was the last place most soldiers expected to see their pastor. General Banks's men subsequently advanced through the charred but usable bridge.

Several days later, three cavalry companies rode off around the south end of Massanutten Mountain in search of Jackson's main force, and, spotting enemy horsemen, the Vermonters galloped ahead. Cpl. John Hatch of Danville took after a slow Confederate and seized him, just as Hatch was struck by a musket ball. The Vermont cavalryman managed to bring in his captive before he fainted. He died next day, the first member of the regiment killed by hostile fire.

Banks's army went into camp around the village of New Market, with cavalry patrols watching the surrounding hostile territory. Spotting enemy cavalry riding leisurely one afternoon, some Vermonters gave chase and the outnumbered Confederates accelerated. Chaplain Woodward remembered:

> The horses of the captain and the chaplain being the fleetest, they were some distance in advance, and drew so near to the retreating foe as to give them several shots. Coming to a road that turned to the left, two of the flying rebels leaped from their horses and fled into a house a little way from the corner. I followed them.
>
> On entering the house an elderly lady broke out in an unearthly screaming, "O dear, O dear, the Yankees have come!"
>
> I opened a door into a bedroom, and seeing two feet protruding from under the counterpane, raised it and said: "Jonathan, come out! I want you!"
>
> He came out, and proved to be the son of the woman, who was now entirely beside herself. I tried to calm her, telling her that the terrible Yankees would not harm her or her son if they behaved themselves. By this time our men had come up, and I delivered the prisoner to them, and going into another room found the other man. Two of our men took the prisoners on behind them, on their horses, and we started back.

In the next few days word reached the Federal camps around Harrisonburg and New Market that "Stonewall" Jackson had fought and won a brisk little battle at McDowell, in the Alleghenies. General Banks decided to distance himself and moved back north, down the valley to the village of Strasburg, where he felt at least temporarily safe.

Jackson rightfully called his infantrymen "foot cavalrymen" because they could do things like march 160 miles in two weeks. He brought his force back from the mountains, linked up with Richard S. Ewell, and drove his men up the Luray Valley, screened from Banks by long Massanutten Mountain. On May 23 Jackson overwhelmed a small Union force at Front Royal, and suddenly Banks was in deep trouble.

Banks retreated north along the Valley Pike en route to Winchester, wagon trains and cavalry coming last. As the wagons came up the pike, Jackson's lead elements attacked at the village of Middletown. As one group of Vermont cavalrymen rode out of that village, it found a tangle of wagons clogging the pike. The Vermonters drew sabers and charged. It was a mistake. Awaiting in the traffic jam were Confederate infantry and a cannon, which delivered two charges of canister. Jackson later reported that "this road was literally obstructed with the mingled and confused mass of struggling and dying horses and riders."

William Wells wrote: "The shells were coming all about us as we stood in the street. We supposed that our infantry and artillery were engaged, but come to find out Banks was at Winchester with all his force except cavalry …and Jackson was between us and Banks. The only way to get out was to charge toward Winchester about 12 miles on the Pike all the way under enemy fire which I can assure you was anything but pleasant."

Regiment commander Charles H. Tompkins arrived in Middleton as the fight was ending. He later reported:

> I proceeded as far as the suburbs of Middletown, where I found the enemy in force—their line of infantry was very extensive and was well supported by cavalry and artillery. My regiment was formed in column of squadrons in readiness to charge…. Perceiving the enemy were advancing in too large force for successful opposition to be made, I deemed it advisable to retire in order, abandon the wagons, and make an attempt to join General [John P.] Hatch by making a detour to the left…. The entire baggage train of the regiment was abandoned and fired, and rendered utterly useless to the enemy. My horses were foraged but the men were without food and were completely exhausted from the fatigues of the day.

That night the Vermonters, some in large groups, others in small knots, and some individually, began riding into Winchester to join the rest of the army taking its position on low hills. By morning more than half the Vermont regiment, about 500 men, had rejoined Banks. Jackson attacked with only a portion of his army. Banks's soldiers fought for their survival. The Vermonters were first posted south of Winchester, helping to hold off the Confederates as stragglers and a few more wagons came in. But as artillery began to find its mark, they were withdrawn through the streets of the city. One Vermont trooper was ambushed by a citizen of the town and shot dead. As Jackson moved to encircle Winchester, Banks withdrew north. In the end, Banks got his army away and kept moving, all the way across the Potomac River.

The Vermonters crossed on May 26 at Williamsport and promptly went into camp. As rolls were called, first counts set the number of missing men at 300. But two days later 200 of them appeared, all having made their way to safety by various moonlit and wooded ways. Among those coming in unharmed was Chaplain Woodward, who summed things up in a letter to Vermont: "Our retreat from Virginia was rapid, our disasters considerable, and our escape wonderful, considering all the circumstances."

Cavalryman George Everest wrote home: "All of our baggage wagons were taken, so that we have got no tents or cooking utensils, or anything but what we had on our backs. I lost a pair of shirts and three pair of footings and about a quire of writing paper, a bunch of envelopes and a few postage stamps."

William Wells wrote, "Everything that I had in my trunk and elsewhere except what I had on my back is gone to Dixie."

The Vermonters got some rest north of the Potomac. Then they came cautiously back into the lower end of the Shenandoah Valley, around battered Winchester. They found few Confederates to trouble them, for Jackson and his army had vanished. Having defeated Banks and then two more Union armies to complete his Valley Campaign, "Stonewall" put his men on trains bound east. They chugged through the Blue Ridge and across the Virginia piedmont toward Richmond to join the fight to defend the Confederate capital, to be the hardest fighting in the East thus far.

THE EQUINOX GUARDS
AT SAVAGE'S STATION

Within the Army of the Potomac trudging toward Richmond was a company of soldiers from Manchester, a unit organized in the spring of 1861. On summer evenings it paraded around town, often with a band playing. Some nights the men were fed free of charge at Vanderlip's. When they stayed to drill the next day, they slept in the courthouse across the road. A total of 93 men enlisted; each private was paid $18 a month, plus a $3.50 clothing allowance and a promise of $100 at discharge. Patriotic spirits bloomed in the summer air. Dr. Ezra Edson put an advertisement in the *Manchester Journal* seeking lumber workers. "No persons opposed to the General Government in putting down the present unhallowed rebellion need apply."

The militia men called themselves the Equinox Guards. Among them were five sons of Peter Cummings—Henry, Hiram, Silas, William, and Edward—and their first cousin, William H. Cummings. Also in the ranks was Horace Clayton, married to one of the brothers' sisters. One evening the Reverend and Mrs. James Anderson held a reception in their garden. Mrs. Anderson had taught many of the men in her Sunday school classes, and after the company marched in through a flower-decked arborway, she gave a moving and motherly speech that the townspeople, and the men, fondly recalled in the difficult months ahead.

Then the time came to join the Fifth Vermont Regiment assembling at St. Albans. On that fateful mid-September day the company formed in the street opposite the Equinox House. The order to march was given, and the men faced right and started up the street for the Manchester Depot railway station. The Manchester Cornet Band led the procession, followed by wagons and most of the town's citizens, many in tears as the men, with bayonets gleaming, boarded the train. In St. Albans they were designated Company E of the Fifth Vermont Regiment and soon were sent to the war zone.

The Fifth was spared the bloody fight at Lee's Mills, after which McClellan took a long look at the abandoned Yorktown works, then resumed his long-interrupted march up the Peninsula. On the first day out the army got a taste of the Vermonters' soon-to-be-legendary marching ability. Union Maj. Gen. Erasmus Keyes, on realizing that a long column of troops led by Vermonters had passed a point where they were to have halted, told an orderly, "If your horse has bottom enough to catch up with the Vermont Brigade, I want you to overtake them and order a halt. Tell them we are not going to Richmond today."

The Army of the Potomac, reaching the outskirts of Williamsburg, confronted another formidable line of fortifications. McClellan attacked on May 5, 1862. The fighting lasted most of the day, and the armies suffered more than 3,900 casualties. The Vermonters never got into action, but they saw the terrible effects of the fight. A soldier writing to the *Rutland Herald* described, "Arms and legs broken and shot off ... bowels torn and running out of the body, faces disfigured by all manner of wounds." At the scene of a hand-to-hand fight, "Men with hands clutched in each others' hair, or with one hand on the opponent's throat, the weapon of each at the same instant reaching some vital spot, fall clutched in the embrace of death."

The Confederates, as they had done at Yorktown, abandoned their fortifications and moved on up the Peninsula, closer to Richmond.

Spring in Virginia meant a good deal of rain. Soldiers were pulled out of line to lift and pull cannons and wagons out of the mire. One day a tall Vermont soldier somehow got separated from his regiment and was slopping along through the mud, doing his best to catch up. Reaching a crossroads, he spotted a local man and asked, "Where does this road lead?"

"To hell," came the answer.

"I calculate I'm most there," said the soldier.

Near the Union supply depot of White House, where George Washington had once courted his bride-to-be, McClellan ordered a major reorganization of his army, structuring his forces, he hoped, for the final battle that would capture Richmond and end the war. Henceforth the Vermont Brigade would be part of a new army unit, a corps composed of two divisions, those led by "Baldy" Smith and Brig. Gen. Henry Slocum. Commander of the corps would be Maj. Gen. William B. Franklin, an 1843 graduate of the US Military Academy and a classmate of U. S. Grant. Franklin had been number 1 in his class, Grant number 21. Franklin's outfit was named the Sixth Corps, and the Vermont Brigade would be part of the Sixth Corps as long as the war lasted.

By the end of May the Army of the Potomac had come within six miles of the Confederate capital. At night the long line of Union camp fires was visible from the outskirts of Richmond across the Chickahominy River, normally a quiet little stream but now swollen by spring floodwaters. The Vermont Brigade went into camp on the right wing of the Union army, well back from the river. Then it moved in closer to overlook the Chickahominy. On a still Sunday morning the

UVM

White House near Richmond, where Vermonters camped.

Union soldiers could hear the Richmond church bells. The Vermonters were set to work improving local roads, which had become mud troughs. A soldier in the Second Vermont wrote home:

> A marked evidence of the spirit of our volunteer free soldiery was offered yesterday. Part of our regiment was sent out to bridge over water courses and corduroy the road to prepare it for the passage of the artillery. Long pine sticks had to be carried by hand many of them over half a mile, and then floated to where needed. Many stripped off their clothes; others plunged in with them on; all working nobly, till three deep and swift channels were spanned and the low places corduroyed. Others labored still more severely and did not come in till midnight. Things now seem ready for our passage over the river, so that we may move on to Richmond.

By the end of May only the swollen Chickahominy separated McClellan and his 100,000-man Army of the Potomac from the 70,000 Confederates under Gen. Joseph E. Johnston. McClellan edged still further forward, having advanced two of his five corps, about 40,000 men, across the river. Johnston, who had retreated some 60 miles up the Peninsula from Yorktown, lashed out on May 31. The battle was vicious and confused, amid Chickahominy swamps and farm fields. Each side sent about 40,000 men into action. When it was over, Seven Pines, also called Fair Oaks, proved to be the bloodiest battle of the war in the East thus far. Among the casualties was General Johnston, seriously wounded and out of the war for a time. Confederate president Jefferson Davis promptly named his military advisor, Robert E. Lee, to replace Johnston. The war was about to change.

The Vermonters, in their positions north of the Chickahominy, missed the Battle of Seven Pines entirely. Throughout the two-day battle they heard artillery and then small-arms fire. When word came of the enemy's repulse, on the morning of June 5, the Sixth Corps crossed the Chickahominy, and the Vermont Brigade went into camp north of Fair Oaks at the Golding farm. They were scarcely five miles from Richmond, and during the next 19 days they occasionally came under fire from Confederate artillery. They were also in range of enemy sharpshooters, and several men were wounded while buying supplies at a sutler's store. On June 19 H. J. Peck, a sharpshooter, wrote home: "The weather here is every day like some of the hottest days of summer in Vermont.... The rebels fight desperately, yet they must know they are about played out." The rebels were anything but "played out."

On June 26 Confederates under that old actor General Magruder, charged with holding the Richmond lines, attacked at Mechanicsville. The fight was, in a way, one among newfound friends. In the preceding days some of the Vermont soldiers had been meeting with Confederates between the lines for conversation and an exchange of goods. "Yesterday the pickets swapped canteens with the rebels, our men giving a canteen of coffee for a canteen of whiskey," one Vermonter remembered. The trading was brisk and friendly. But when the fighting started, all pleasantries were forgotten. At dusk the Fourth and Sixth Vermont regiments confronted Georgians who came marching across a wide field. The Vermonters started shooting, and the Confederates went back into the woods whence they had come and returned the fire. When it ended well after dark, 15 Vermonters had been shot, one mortally.

The next day, with "Stonewall" Jackson on the field, Lee attacked north of the Chickahominy River, launching the second in a series of engagements that came to be known as the Seven Days. The Battle of Mechanicsville, June 26, 1862, produced 2,000 casualties. The Vermont Brigade was spared, having been well south of the river and out of the fight.

On the 27th the Confederates attacked at Gaines's Mills. By day's end 15,000 Northern and Southern troopers were shot or captured. The Vermonters stood at the ready but were not called into action. Next day the entire army moved south and east toward the James. Smith's division, including the Vermont Brigade, found itself in the rear of the Union army, where action was quite likely to develop. On the 28th some units of the brigade came under heavy artillery fire; two men were killed and six wounded. As the slow march south was resumed, the Vermonters passed piles of Federal supplies set afire to prevent capture.

The Vermont Brigade reached Savage's Station about noon on June 29. The Fifth Vermont Regiment, including the boys in Manchester's Company E, had marched past the station when it was suddenly ordered to halt. A soldier in Company E, writing home on July 6, said:

At five o'clock we were nearly three miles beyond Savage's Station when rapid fire was heard in that direction and our brigade had orders to "about face." When we reached the station, the engagement was already going on. The almost maddening excitement and the whistling of the bullets and the rush of ...canister is all that I can remember as our gallant boys charged bayonets nearly up to the enemy with a yell that still rings in my ears. We halted within a short musket range of the enemy and piled our northern lead into them for nearly an hour....

But at what a sacrifice to us! The field where we stood was black with dead and wounded. We had been exposed nearly all the time to a murderous fire from three directions.... Our company suffered more severely than any other as we were in exact range of a gun that was pouring ...canister through us, cutting our men down like grass.

The Fifth Vermont and the Manchester boys were in the worst of the action at Savage's Station. As the Fifth advanced along the Williamsburg Road, it came upon another Union regiment hunkered down in the woods, refusing to move. The Fifth's commander Col. Lewis A. Grant recalled, "I remember as if it was yesterday the way we tramped over that line of cringing men, cursing them soundly for their cowardice."

As the Fifth emerged from the woods, it faced a hollow filled with Confederate riflemen, supported by Confederate artillery placed on a rise; a perfect defensive position. Adding to the Fifth's peril was a monster Confederate cannon mounted on a railroad car firing huge shells. Colonel Grant, perhaps unwisely, ordered a charge. The Fifth Vermont was torn apart. The men of Company E, the Manchester boys, were slaughtered.

As Sgt. Lucius Bigelow of Burlington said: "We could not, allowing for shirks and feeble men, blown by double-quicking, have carried more than 400 muskets into battle. We lost in 20 minutes 206 men, killed and wounded. In spite of this awful loss the regiment held its ground and quelled the fire of the enemy; and it was difficult to make the men understand why they should retreat after dark; for they felt that they had held their ground and won the day."

While the Fifth was being riddled, the Sixth Vermont was advancing on its left through woods and suddenly came under severe fire from Confederates on its flank. In the deepening twilight 60 men were hit by foes they could barely see.

The Third Vermont was groping ahead when challenged from the woods ahead by a stern voice: "Who are you?"

"The Third Vermont," someone said, and bullets cut into the Vermonters' ranks. The Third held its position until after dark, under fire all the while.

At 9:30 a thunderstorm erupted over the smoky battlefield, and at about 10:00 the Vermonters were finally ordered to withdraw. Men who were not hurt carried or supported wounded and dazed men along the rough road past Savage's Station, revealed in flashes from the thundering skies. Many wounded Vermonters had to be left behind, and some died on the field or in hospitals that were soon captured by the Confederates, always lacking adequate medical supplies for their own wounded.

Among those who stayed behind was a surgeon in the Vermont Brigade with the appropriate name of Sawin, William J., from Chicopee, Massachusetts. Sawin walked the battlefield the next day and recalled, "Thirty men of the Fifth Vermont were found lying side-by-side, dressed in as perfect a line as for a dress parade, who were all stricken down by one discharge of …canister from the enemy's batteries."

Writing many years after the battle, the veteran Confederate general D. H. Hill recalled, "About half a mile from the Station (Savage's) we saw what seemed to be an entire regiment of Federals cold in death, and learned that a Vermont regiment had made a desperate charge upon the division of McLaws, and had been almost annihilated."

Company E, the Equinox Guards, went into the fight with 57 men. Only seven came out unharmed. Twenty-seven had been killed or mortally wounded. The Cummings brothers fought side by side with brother-in-law Clayton. Henry, the oldest brother, got shot in the thigh and was discharged three months later. He went home to his wife, Mary Jane, and a son, but he never fully recovered, dying of the effects of his wounds at age 67, in 1885. Silas, Edmund, and Hiram were captured and died of their wounds as prisoners. William was shot and helped from the battlefield. His leg was amputated, but he died nonetheless in a Union hospital. Cousin W. H. H. Cummings died in prison of a shattered leg. And brother-in-law Horace Clayton was shot dead on the field, leaving a wife, Laura, and three sons. The loss of the five boys (six if Clayton is counted) is believed to have been the greatest suffered by any Union family in one battle in the entire war.

The sad news from Savage's Station reached Manchester on the Fourth of July, when the local paper published a letter just received from Lee Orvis, written from the front to his sister: "I have got dreadful news to communicate. In the last fight before Richmond all of Co. E 5th Vermont Volunteers were killed wounded or taken prisoners, with the exception of seven."

Manchester was in a state of mourning. The *Manchester Journal* editorialized: "If ever there was a sad and gloomy hour in this valley, it was that which brought us the first terrible tidings of those most near and dear to us who were engaged in the recent battles before Richmond. In more than one of our homes there was a grief and agony no words can depict."

When the final count was made, the Vermont Brigade had lost 358 men at Savage's Station: 71 were killed, 270 were wounded, and 17 were missing; 36 men later died of wounds, The Fifth Vermont had suffered more casualties than would any Vermont regiment in a single battle in the entire war.

Sometime after daylight next morning, the battered Vermont Brigade crossed White Oak Bridge and moved to a temporary rest on the heights beyond. Most of the Vermonters slept on the fields as the Virginia day grew hotter and as the last of the Army of the Potomac passed by. About two in the afternoon, the troops were rudely awakened. "Stonewall" Jackson had got 30 cannon into position on a nearby hillside and opened fire on the fields where the Vermonters rested. Sixth Corps commander William Franklin later said, "It commenced with a severity I never heard equalled in the field."

A surgeon in a New York regiment recalled:

Unutterable confusion prevailed for a time; riderless horses galloped madly to the rear; officers wandered without commands, and men were left without directions how to act. Generals Smith and Davidson occupied an old fashioned wooden house, which stood upon the brow of the elevation above and facing the bridge. About it were many orderlies, holding their horses. The first volley riddled the house with shells. The gray-haired owner of the house (Mr. Britton) was cut in two as he stood in the door, and several other persons were injured.

General Smith, at the moment the cannonade opened, was engaged at his rude toilet; his departure from the house was so hasty that he left his watch, which he did not recover. He coolly walked to a less exposed position and devoted himself to restoring order.

Like their general, the Vermonters scurried off to find shelter, mainly in the woods. Col. Wheelock G. Veazey of the Third Vermont got men from behind trees and into battle line. A regiment from another state posted nearby lined up, then ran away. The artillery fire finally slackened, and an attack by Jackson against the Vermont position, expected all day, never materialized. Meanwhile, two miles away at Glendale, other Confederates were making a desperate attempt to disrupt the Union retreat. They failed.

The Army of the Potomac went on south and east, headed for Harrison's Landing, where deep-draft supply boats could dock. The Confederates followed; several miles short of the landing, McClellan drew his forces up on the crest of a long, gradual, open slope called Malvern Hill. Line on line of Union infantry waited for the Confederates, backed by dozens of cannons and gunboats in the nearby James River. Lee ordered an attack. It was hopeless. After an afternoon of slaughter in which more than 5,000 Confederates fell, the attack was called off. The weary Vermont Brigade, posted well out of the way of the fighting, was spared the battle of Malvern Hill. Some Vermont sharpshooters, however, were in the thick of it.

The Vermont troops were among the last to leave Malvern Hill, having stood again as a rear guard as the army resumed its march to Harrison's Landing. It moved out in a torrential rain. Colonel Veazey described the scene:

No person can give any conception of the wake of a retreating army after such a campaign in such a country. It simply beggared description. Stragglers sick and dying, arms of every description, stores of all kinds, abandoned wagons, broken down horses and mules, mud so deep that no bottom could be reached. All these at every step; and then add the sickening feeling of defeat and retreat, and the momentary expectation of a rear attack, and no help within reach. Weary, hungry, exhausted, sick, what torment could be added, except the loss of honor? Such was our dreary march as a rear guard to Harrison's Landing.

A soldier in the Third Vermont summed up his experiences in a letter written home on July 12: "In the last two weeks we have seen some hard times. Men who are not killed are worn out and sick. There was five days I was without eating and sleeping. I have never been so bad off and darn dirty before."

The Vermont Brigade stayed at Harrison's Landing for six rainy weeks. Within the ranks there was deep respect for a little drummer boy who had marched up the Peninsula, then endured the fury of the Seven Days. Willie Johnson of the Third Vermont was just 12 years old when he enlisted at St. Johnsbury; now he was a battle veteran. Willie was the only drummer boy in "Baldy" Smith's entire division to reach Harrison's Landing still in possession of his drum. Secretary of War Edwin M. Stanton found out, and the lad from Vermont was brought to Washington and given the Medal of Honor.

On July 8 a grand review of the Army of the Potomac was held. A member of the Fifth Vermont wrote home: "President Lincoln arrived in camp and reviewed our whole army.... As our brigade was on the extreme right, he did not reach us until long after sundown when he passed along our lines by moonlight on horseback, followed by a staff of about 200 mounted officers. When he got to the end he bowed, put his hat on and gently rode away. I shall make no remarks on the old gentleman as I only saw him by moonlight."

Finally marching orders came, and the Army of the Potomac left its base at Harrison's Landing. Lee didn't interfere. The march back down the Peninsula, under a blistering midsummer Virginia sun, led through familiar places. They tramped across the Chickahominy, through Williamsburg and Yorktown, across the Warwick River near Lee's Mills, and on by Big Bethel, coming to rest at Fort Monroe, where the campaign had started. The Peninsula Campaign had ended in failure. The Vermonters with many units of the army went by steamer to Alexandria, near Washington, disembarking on August 24. As they got there, deep trouble was brewing not far west. Robert E. Lee and "Stonewall" Jackson were on the move from Richmond, coming north to Union territory.

Word of the great failure of the Peninsula Campaign hit Washington hard, and a post Bull Run–like sadness settled on the city. Yet on July 2 President Lincoln signed legislation that spoke to a continuing vast hope for the future of the American nation. The president thus made law of Vermont Senator Justin Smith Morrill's Land Grant College Act, which gave western public lands to the states for the purpose of funding agricultural colleges. It proved to be the basis on which many fine colleges of higher learning would rise, including the University of Vermont.

In Manchester the courthouse still stands along the main street where the Equinox Guards were quartered when they drilled in the summer of 1861. The north end of the Equinox House across the street housed Vanderlip's, where the men were sometimes fed. On the street between the Equinox House and the courthouse, a monument to Manchester's soldiers has been erected. The red railroad station at Manchester Depot, where Company E departed, is now a storehouse. Up on the nearest hill is the Factory Point Cemetery, which contains a monument to Manchester's Civil War dead and the grave of one of the Cummings boys.

In Richmond is a broad grassy park on a hilltop called Chimborazo, overlooking the James River, where the largest of all Civil War hospitals once stood. A two-story brick building houses the headquarters of the Richmond National Battlefield Park. There one can obtain maps and directions for a 90-mile tour of what remains of the local battlefields, including those of the Seven Days. Driving out of the old Confederate capital, one passes remnants of the city's earthen defenses. The road leads down across the Chickahominy River and out to the great battlefields of the Seven Days. One steaming July day I tried to find the Savage's Station battlefield and got to the general area only to encounter a snarl of highways. Savage's Station is mostly lost to progress, to concrete and the internal combustion engine's demands. But I did find a bit of the old Williamsburg Road that dead-ends against a four-lane road. By a patch of woods I found a marker noting that a battle had been fought. I gathered from some reckoning and an old map that I was about on the spot where the Fifth Vermont made its bloody charge. I stood awhile, then walked in the green woods where the leaves muffled the noise of passing cars. I moved on through White Oak Swamp and up Malvern Hill, where there's a small exhibit shelter and, when it works, a tape recording that describes the battle. I sat a long while on the hilltop, looking down the long slope where 5,000 Confederates fell trying to get to the place where I now passed a quiet late afternoon. At Malvern Hill, even in that little patch of woods amid the highways at what once was Savage's Station, the aura abides. Darkness hovered over Richmond when I reached my hotel.

———————————————————

GOVERNOR HOLBROOK
INTERVENES

As the Army of the Potomac was preparing for its spring offensive, about to materialize as the disastrous Peninsula Campaign of 1862, two young Vermont artists went south. Larkin Mead, already a well-known sculptor, and George Houghton, a photographer, left their Brattleboro homes to follow the Vermont Brigade. Mead had become instantly famous one winter morning in Brattleboro in 1857. Townspeople going to work found, at the intersection of Linden and Main streets, a gleaming white angel carved of ice and snow. (Brattleboro's Brooks Memorial Library today displays a marble replica.) Mead and some friends had labored through the previous night on the work of art. In the days before it melted, people came from near and far to see the wonder. It was not only an artistic triumph but a fine public relations ploy as well. Newspapers along the East Coast praised it.

Houghton operated a photography studio in the third floor of the gray stone block of buildings that still stands along the east side of Brattleboro's Main Street. Soldiers sent to the Brattleboro encampment made it a point to stop there, to obtain carte de visite images of themselves in uniform. Then Houghton went south to take pictures of the Vermont Brigade in Virginia, for sale to the people back home.

Mead went to war at the invitation of Gen. William Farrar "Baldy" Smith, who apparently hired Mead to make sketches of enemy fortifications. Mead was soon selling drawings to *Harper's Weekly* in New York City. He went with the Vermont Brigade to the Virginia Peninsula but came home after a bullet whizzed by his ear, either from a Confederate sharpshooter or a nervous Yankee picket. Houghton stayed a while longer before returning to his photography studio in Brattleboro. By that time he had produced the finest photographic record of the

Vermont soldiers at war, and one of the best of the entire war, rivaling the work of Mathew Brady and Alexander Gardner.

Both men had wanderlusts, and Houghton soon went west, dying in Minnesota in 1870. Mead sailed for Europe not long after his war experience, setting up a studio in Florence and becoming a well-known sculptor.

The fact that Mead and Houghton could move freely with the armies, recording scenes of anything they wanted, speaks to the Civil War's remarkable lack of military censorship. Throughout the war a torrent of information steadily came back to Vermont from the armies, untouched by military information specialists. Of course, the major newspapers had their correspondents recording the battles and campaigns. Those accounts were eagerly read throughout Vermont, in small towns, often by some loud-voiced citizen from the steps of the general store. Vermont newspapers regularly printed letters sent home from soldiers, not only giving vivid accounts of events at the front but also expressing strong opinions.

One Vermont paper, Montpelier's *Green Mountain Freeman*, had a correspondent in the ranks of the Vermont Brigade, Pvt. Wilbur Fisk of the Second Vermont. Fisk was a schoolteacher in Tunbridge before the war. As a war correspondent he signed his letters home "anti-rebel." He expressed opinions freely and gave vivid accounts of battles, marches, encampments, and various soldier attitudes. As the Vermont Brigade moved toward Antietam, Fisk wrote, "I certainly hope that after this campaign, we can write of something besides disaster, slaughter, defeat, and skedaddle."

A member of the Second Vermont wrote home to the *Rutland Courier* early in the war: "The papers do not mention this movement, therefore I judge it is a forbidden subject to them. Their reporters have but little opportunity to do so. No one is allowed to pass the bridge."

With such information coming daily from the armies, the fact that the war was going badly for the Union forces was most clear to the people of Vermont during the summer of 1862. Certainly the gloomy state of things was not lost on Vermont's new governor, Frederick Holbrook, who set out to do what he could to turn things around. Vermont had three Civil War chief executives, and the least known may well have been the best of all. Erastus Fairbanks, governor when the war began, and John Gregory Smith, governor when it ended, were best known. In between, the little ship of state was ably captained by Holbrook. His was the only governorship that took place entirely within the war.

Frederick Holbrook was not a native Vermonter, having been born on February 15, 1813 in East Windsor, Connecticut. But his parents moved to Brattleboro when he was a boy, and he got most of his schooling there, though he graduated from a private school in Massachusetts. He worked for several years in a bookshop in Boston and while in that city pursued his lifelong love of music. Gifted with a considerable singing voice, Holbrook became an active member of the city's Handel and Haydn Society.

Back in Vermont, he bought a farm in Brattleboro and then, in 1831, made a long trip through Europe to study European agricultural practices. Holbrook returned convinced that European farming methods were far superior. He began writing his considered opinions on agriculture; soon his articles were being published in scientific journals. A newspaper in Albany, New York, agreed to print a monthly farming column. Holbrook not only wrote about improving agriculture but actually did something about it, beginning experiments with a new type of plow.

As the war approached, Holbrook had become well known throughout Vermont, was elected president of the Vermont Agricultural Society, and was chosen to represent Windham County in the Vermont Senate. When the war began and fellow Republican Erastus Fairbanks stepped down, Holbrook was easily elected governor. His friend James J. Tyler recalled:

> Mr. Holbrook was, in the years of mature manhood, a man of striking and impressive presence. He was a little more than six feet in height, broad-shouldered, weighed about 190 pounds, well-proportioned, erect, dignified, yet unassuming, his head large and perfectly-formed, his handsome face always wearing a pleasant smile, his manner courteous and deferential; but under his affability he carried an unbending will. His was the simple life. He disliked ostentation, lived plainly but well, loved his garden and believed that his work in it, continued till he was past 90, prolonged his life.... He was not a learned man in the scholastic meaning of the term, but he was exceedingly well read and well informed.

Holbrook took office in the fall of 1861, delivering his inaugural address to the General Assembly on October 22. He began by saying he would have preferred to talk "on the favorite pursuit of my life," the promotion of agriculture. But the principal business of state was war. Holbrook then tried to summarize the feeling of Vermonters toward the conflict. "They are willing," he judged, "to expend their blood and treasure, if need be, to the fullest extent of their means to aid the national government in crushing this causeless rebellion."

If he was right, there remained untapped within Vermont a great reserve of personal sacrifice. Holbrook lost no time in putting that theory to the test, promptly creating the Seventh and Eighth infantry regiments. He also ordered formation of two more artillery batteries. Then Holbrook formed the Ninth Vermont Regiment and, a bit later, the 10th and 11th. As the war news continued to be grim, Holbrook sent a letter to President Lincoln, and later recalled the circumstances:

> The call in 1862 for 300,000 three-year volunteers, followed very soon after in that year for 300,000 nine-months men, resulted from a letter I wrote to the president earnestly and frankly setting forth the fact, well known to us, from my point of outlook, that a very large additional force was immediately needed to crush the rebellion, and urging him at once to call for 500,000 three-years volunteers, assuring him that the people of the loyal states would respond to such a call; and that if the government hesitated from lack of funds to arm and equip so large a force, then, so far as Vermont was concerned, the state would arm and equip its quota of

such call to the acceptance of such military inspector as the government might appoint, and would wait on the government for reimbursement at such times as it should be in funds....

On receiving the letter, the President, Secretary of War (Edwin M. Stanton) and Provost Marshall General Simon Draper, had a session over it at the secretary's office, the president taking out my letter and saying, "I have a letter from Governor Holbrook of Vermont which solves all my doubts and difficulties about calling for more men."

General Draper was immediately dispatched to Vermont to call on and confer with me, and have such a paper formulated as I thought the loyal governors would be willing to sign, recommending and endorsing such a call for men, and General Draper appearing at my office two days later, such a paper was agreed upon.

A letter calling on Lincoln to make a major call-up of troops was circulated to the Northern states' governors for their signatures. Holbrook remembered:

While preparations for issuing the call were in progress at Washington, Governor Richard Yates of Illinois, not yet knowing what steps were being taken to reinforce the Union army, wrote a desponding letter to President Lincoln about the discouraging aspects of the war. He was a brother lawyer and intimate friend of Mr. Lincoln's and so the president, in his characteristic way, at once telegraphed this reply to Governor Yates' letter—"Wait a little, Dick, and see the salvation of the Lord." Within a day or two after, Governor Yates received the call for more volunteers.

Upon receiving the call I at once wrote to the president again, thanking him for the call, but expressed the opinion that it should have been for a larger number of men, and hoping it would be succeeded very soon by another call, for I felt certain they would be needed to bring the War to a close. Very soon after the call for 300,000 nine months' men did come. Those two calls brought the war to a close.

In Vermont, the 10th and 11th infantry regiments were headed south by early September. While they formed, Holbrook issued on August 13 a proclamation ordering the organizing of five more regiments, to be made up of troops enlisting for just nine months. That proclamation read in part: "Let no young man capable of bearing arms in defense of his country linger at this important period. Let the president feel the strengthened influence of our prompt and hearty response to his call. Let Vermont be one of the first states to respond with her quota."

As a result, the 12th, 13th, 14th, 15th, and 16th Vermont regiments reported to Brattleboro in early October. Late that month the regiments were formally organized into the Second Vermont Brigade. Later in the war, soon before his second gubernatorial term expired, Holbrook would order up the 17th Vermont Regiment, the last from Vermont.

The majority of Vermonters who served in the Civil War did so in regiments organized by Governor Holbrook, but he did far more than send thousands of

Vermont boys to fight and die. After Lee's Mills, the battle that produced the state's first heavy losses, Holbrook intervened in the care of the sick and wounded. On April 16, 1862 most of the 148 Vermont wounded were moved from the banks of the Warwick River to the safety of Fort Monroe. Reports of poor conditions at the old masonry fort began to reach Vermont, chiefly in letters from the wounded. Governor Holbrook sent a telegram to Secretary of War Stanton asking whether the Vermont wounded could be sent home if suitable accommodations were provided. At the same time, Adj. Gen. Peter Washburn was dispatched by Holbrook to Washington to ask that the old US Marine hospital in Burlington, which had never been used, be turned over to the state of Vermont for a hospital.

The War Department agreed to give the state the building, then, with reluctance, agreed to send the wounded Vermonters home. Washburn went from Washington to Fort Monroe, starting home with 115 wounded men. Most made it to Burlington to be cared for in the state's first army hospital. It was to be the first of three.

In October 1863 Holbrook again badgered the War Department, this time concerning the fate of the Ninth Vermont Regiment. That outfit had been captured at Harper's Ferry and sent to cold Camp Douglas in Chicago to await exchange. Hearing reports of poor conditions at Camp Douglas, Holbrook wrote Secretary of War Stanton on October 13:

Sir,

I have the honor to call your attention to the condition of the 9th Regiment of Vermont Volunteers, who were captured at Harper's Ferry and paroled. They are now encamped near Chicago, Ill. and are without sufficient shelter, many without blankets and necessary clothing. They are encamped upon a level tract of land and whenever it rains (as it has most of the time since they arrived there) the ground is converted into the worst kind of mud. Being encamped near a large city they are subject to many temptations, and it is almost impossible for the officers to preserve strict discipline. In consequence of their situation the men are becoming sick and discouraged.

Holbrook went on to ask that the regiment be moved to a healthier location. Yet it was well into the following spring before the Ninth Vermont was moved out of Chicago and headed back toward the war.

Undaunted, as the winter of 1862–63 deepened, Holbrook again confronted Washington about the condition of Vermont's soldiers. In fact, in December he went to Washington on what he called "a special mission." Many years later, Holbrook put the story in his own words. He had observed, he said,

with pain the anxiety of many families in Vermont, occasioned by the numbers of our troops who were disabled and confined to the hospitals in and around Washington and in the camps, wasting away from their sufferings, from homesickness and from the influence of a malarial climate. The casualties of army life by sickness were perhaps proportionately larger among our Vermonters than among those from other sections.... Under these circumstances numbers of our citizens made long and trying journeys, at an expense which many could ill afford, to look after their disabled boys.

To allay the anxieties of friends and save lives of the soldiers, the writer felt that effective measures must be taken. He therefore at this time appealed to the United States authorities to establish a military hospital in Vermont for the treatment and care of the sick and wounded Vermont soldiers. When the plans were first submitted to the president and the secretary of war they were regarded as inexpedient and impractical of execution. It was thought that many of the disabled men would die under the fatigue and exposure of such long transportation back to their state; and it was suggested that possibly some might be lost by desertion. It was said also that the plan would be an unmilitary innovation....

After repeated meetings and discussions, the writer made an official and formal proposition to take the barrack buildings, of which there were many, owned by the government on the camp grounds at Brattleboro, remove them to a sheltered situation at one end of the grounds, placing them in a hollow square, and to fit them up with plastered walls, good floors, chimneys, provisions for ventilation, an abundance of pure spring water and all needed appliances and facilities for hospital purposes. This was to be done under the care and supervision of Surgeon [Edward E.] Phelps, of established Army experience and reputation, and at the expense of the state of Vermont.

Holbrook also asked that Vermont agents be allowed to search US Army hospitals to find Vermont soldiers in need of treatment back home. It was a radical proposal, so much state intervention in the matters of the national military. The secretary of war finally consented, with the caution that it was all an experiment and might be ended in six months. Holbrook said that was fine and went back to Brattleboro with permission for his hospital.

He recalled:

Directly on returning to Brattleboro the work of moving buildings and fitting them for hospital use according to agreement was begun, and by the middle of February was completed. The whole was accepted by the government medical inspector and the disabled men began at once to arrive. Before the end of the following summer, the hospital was full, some men having been sent from neighboring states to occupy rooms not needed by Vermonters. During the summer and autumn, hospital tents were erected to enlarge accommodations, and these were occupied by men from several other states, so that from 1,500 to 2,000 patients were treated at a time, those who had recovered being sent to the front again and new cases taking their place. The hospital was soon credited by the United States medical inspector with perfecting a larger percentage of cures than any United States military hospital elsewhere could show.

The six-month experiment continued until the war ended. The Brattleboro hospital was built at one end of the soldiers' encampment; one wonders what effect the sight of the wounded and dismembered had on new recruits.

Holbrook wrote that the success of the hospital caused the federal government to sanction other hospitals in many states. The result, he said, was that thousands of men who otherwise would have died were saved—many, of course, to be returned to the front. Holbrook claimed that of the 4,500 soldiers who were treated at the Brattleboro hospital, only 95 died.

Long after the war, Holbrook was asked to name the chief accomplishments of his governorship. He said he was proud of raising all those units and of starting the military hospitals. But he said the thing he liked best was convincing some Boston banker friends to give the state of Vermont highly favorable interest rates on loans to finance its part in the war.

On September 12, 1906 a memorial stone was dedicated on the site of the Brattleboro hospital and encampment. Many Vermont veterans of the Civil War were present. The *Vermont Phoenix* began its story:

> A monument of enduring granite now stands a silent sentinel to mark the field in Brattleboro which was the rendezvous of the Vermont troops during the Civil War and which was the site of a government hospital during a part of that great struggle. It was dedicated Wednesday afternoon and the dedicatory exercises form an important chapter in the history of Brattleboro.... In connection with the event the annual reunion of the Windham County Veterans Association was held, which gave to the occasion a two-fold interest. About 1,200 people attended the exercises.

The monument stands at the entrance to the Brattleboro Union High School playing fields, its inscription stating that 10,200 volunteers were mustered into the service on that field and 4,666 veterans mustered out there. Governor Holbrook took exception with one of those figures. The old chief executive was still alert in 1906 when the memorial was dedicated, though unable to attend. He sent a message, read for him, in which he proudly recounted his role in urging Abraham Lincoln to summon more troops. Later Holbrook wrote that the correct number of troops mustered in at Brattleboro should have read 13,856, not 10,200.

One has to look closely when entering the Brattleboro Union High School grounds to spot the old Civil War memorial. It's at the gateway, though there's talk of finding it a less-cluttered location. Along the edge of the bluff, in Brattleboro's Prospect Hill Cemetery, is a grouping of small stones set around a flagstaff, the final resting place for 20 soldiers who died in the Civil War hospital at Brattleboro. The plot commands a view down the Connecticut River Valley. There lie boys who never went home, from Pennsylvania, New Hamphire, Maine, Ohio, New York, Michigan, and Massachusetts. Two stones say "unknown." Frederick Holbrook's grave is nearby.

RUTLAND'S
RIPLEY BROTHERS

In Rutland were two brothers who, given their family position, might well have chosen to spend the Civil War far from conflict. Edward Hastings Ripley and William Y. Y. Ripley came from a family of wealth and power, of summers at Saratoga Springs and intellectual evenings at home attended by servants. A sister, Julia Ripley Dorr, was a well-known poet of her time and entertained many of the great literary figures of the era in her Rutland home. The father, William Young Ripley, had amassed a fortune by organizing the first marble company in Rutland County. Three sons, Edward, William, and Charles, wore the Union blue and two became war heroes. Despite their backgrounds of privilege, the lads were tough as the rock in their father's quarries, and when war came, they couldn't wait to go off and fight.

William commanded a distinctive unit. In the summer of 1861 the nation's best-known marksman, Hiram Berdan of New York, convinced the War Department that the Union army needed sharpshooters. Since the ranks of the Confederate army were known to contain many well-known marksmen, Berdan was quickly given the go-ahead to organize the US Sharpshooters. They would eventually comprise 18 companies, three from Vermont, a total by war's end of 620 Vermont marksmen, by far the largest number per capita from any state. From the start there was an element of elitism to the sharpshooters. The uniform, instead of the regular army blue, was of green cloth, a distinctive kepi, and the marksmen wore leather leggings and carried knapsacks of tanned leather with the hair still on.

To qualify, a man showed up with his rifle at a tryout, one of several throughout the state. Many of the farm boys, who had hunted squirrels about as long as they could remember, often met the test. One tryout was held at the fairgrounds in Rutland, and the Ira town history includes the following account:

William Y. Y. Ripley led
Vermont sharpshooters.

Edward Hastings Ripley became
a brigadier general.

Colonel Berdan issued circulars and advertised for enlistments, but made it necessary for the right to enlist that the applicant should be able to shoot 10 consecutive
bullets from a rifle, offhand, without a rest, into a 10 inch ring at a distance of 40
yards.... Early in September it was announced that a meeting would be held at the
fair grounds in Rutland for the purpose of giving those who desired to enlist in the
Vermont company in this regiment, an opportunity to make the required target
and enroll their names for the war....

On the morning of the day set for the test, two boys, brothers, go down from the
hills with a horse and buggy and, after hitching their horse under the meeting house
shed in the village, with their rifles saunter down to the fair grounds, where they find
a large crowd of people who had assembled to witness the shooting, which was under
the control of Wm. Y. Y. Ripley, who afterwards became lieutenant colonel of the
regiment. The rifles were heavy muzzle-loading target rifles, for at the time breech-
loaders were comparatively unknown, and entirely unknown in the mountains of
Vermont.

When the targets were in place and the distance measured, the elder of the boys
stepped to the line and, carefully loading his rifle, commenced firing. The first shot
was a wild shot, but inside the ring; so were all the 10 consecutive shots, many of
them being almost in the center of the target. The younger of the boys then walked
to the line and, although somewhat nervous at first, he succeeded in placing 10
bullets within the ring. As each shot was fired and the target master placed a black
patch over the bullet hole in the white target, a cheer went up from the crowd, which
encouraged the boys in their efforts. A great many who desired to get into this
regiment attempted to make the necessary target, but few succeeded. A few days

afterward the order of Colonel Berdan was modified as to allow good riflemen to enlist in this company, and it was soon filled, the test having been found too severe for procuring enlistments.

Company F assembled at West Randolph in mid-September 1861, shipped south almost immediately, and started training at the Camp of Instruction in Washington. The 113 Vermonters were made part of the First US Sharpshooters Regiment, trained by Colonel Berdan himself, known as the best marksman in America. When President Lincoln and General McClellan stopped by, Berdan pointed out a man-sized and man-shaped target 600 yards distant and boasted that he would put a bullet in the right eye. He did. Then the president took a rifle from a Vermonter named Peck and tried some shots.

In November William Ripley of Rutland, who had served in the First Vermont Regiment at Big Bethel, was appointed commander of the First US Sharpshooters, to the delight of his fellow Vermonters. His brother Edward wrote of him, "William enjoyed his reputation as a marksman and liked to demonstrate his ability by throwing two potatoes in the air and sending a bullet through both."

Back home, a second sharpshooter company was organized at West Randolph. In late November it, too, came to Washington and was incorporated as Company E of the Second Regiment of US Sharpshooters. In early January a third Vermont company, organized at Brattleboro, arrived at Camp of Instruction and was designated Company H of the Second US Sharpshooters Regiment. All three Vermont companies served throughout the war.

In spring Ripley's First Sharpshooters were ordered to join the Army of the Potomac on the Virginia Peninsula. Near Lee's Mills, Cpl. Charles Peck of St. Johnsbury, the man who had handed his rifle to Abraham Lincoln in Washington, was hit by a sniper's bullet, getting what he called "an ounce of lead" in the leg. Peck always claimed to have been the first Yankee to shed blood in the Peninsula Campaign. In the days along the Warwick River, the sharpshooters kept careful watch on the enemy works. One day Ripley took a rifle and silenced a Confederate marksman firing long-range at his men from the far side of the river. The Vermont sharpshooters moved with the army to the outskirts of Richmond and then through the long and bloody Seven Days of fighting and retreating.

When the army turned to face Lee's Confederates on Malvern Hill, the sharpshooters, unlike the Vermont Brigade, were hotly involved. On the long slope they held an advanced position against the Confederate lines that came on and on, almost suicidally, against the all but impregnable Union position. Ripley's men were particularly effective in wreaking havoc on a Confederate battery that tried to get in position on the Union flank. The sharpshooters shot down the cannoneers as they attempted to unlimber and fire from a distant hillock. After the war William Ripley met a member of the Confederate battery who told him, "We went in a battery and came out a wreck. We stayed 10 minutes by the watch and came out with one gun, 10 men and two horses, and without firing a shot."

The bloody Seven Days ended at Malvern Hill.

The Vermonters fought until late afternoon when they were withdrawn, with four men wounded and ammunition running short. A sergeant among the sharpshooters, long after the war, described Colonel Ripley in battle to Ripley's son: "Git behind them trees sed the Colonel…but they was young an' playful an' kep' on bein careless. Jes then a shell come a-smashin over us, rippin off branches, an' yer Pa, he sung out, 'Now God damn ye, will ye git behind trees.' His voice was like it come from a mile off an it sounded jes like a minnie ball, a-whistlin and a-stingin through the woods. We skedaddled and took cover."

Colonel Ripley was one of the last to leave the field, staying to direct some infantrymen forming to confront still another desperate advance. He was on horseback and suddenly felt a numbness in his right leg. Ripley looked down, and saw his boot filled with blood; a musket ball had shattered the bone. An orderly tied a handkerchief around the leg, but Ripley's horse was hit by three shots and fell dead atop his rider. Ripley was dragged from beneath the animal, placed in an ambulance, and removed from the field, then left behind as the army retreated. But some of Ripley's men, learning that he'd been deserted, went back, found him, and carried him away by stretcher just before the Confederates arrived. That surely saved his life, for even under the care of doctors in a Union hospital he nearly died.

After returning to Washington the Vermont sharpshooters moved west to join the newly formed Army of Virginia under Maj. Gen. John Pope. "Stonewall" Jackson was loose in northern Virginia, and Pope finally found him near the old Bull Run battlefield. There was a reunion of Vermont sharpshooters at the battle called Second Bull Run, also called Second Manassas. Ripley's First US Sharpshooters Regiment found themselves in a tight position, in a sunken road just 40 yards in front of Jackson's line. They were finally withdrawn, and during a lull in the fighting they came upon Companies E and H of the Second US

Sharpshooters. Those companies had had a rough trip toward Bull Run, getting in a train wreck. Greetings were briefly exchanged as the war roared in the background. Then the companies went their own ways, with E and H moving along the Warrenton Pike to engage Jackson's riflemen from behind a rail fence. Next day Pope's entire army was in retreat after a smashing flank attack engineered by General Lee and Lt. Gen. James Longstreet. The sharpshooters were the only Vermont units engaged at Second Bull Run. William Ripley had been forced to follow events from afar. Narrowly escaping amputation, he went home to Rutland to recover, with a promise that he would command the 10th Vermont Regiment, then forming. But he was never well enough to return to war and was instead active in organizing and training the Vermont Home Guards. Later he was awarded the Medal of Honor for his heroism at Malvern Hill.

William Ripley's brother, Edward Hastings Ripley, was a medical student at Schenectady's Union College when the war began, fretting that it would all be over before he got a chance to fight. He wrote:

> Father seemed particularly anxious, as it was his desire that one of his sons adopt a profession. I had therefore mapped out a career of study to follow on graduation. These peaceful days abruptly ended as, during one warm and beautiful May day forenoon, I drove into Rutland and found the streets alive with stirring news. President Lincoln had that morning issued a call for 300,000 more men. Instantly I felt the hour had come. I drove quickly to find Father and Mother and break my news to them. I rushed into the garden and through it, down towards the old elm. My eager eyes caught sight of them sitting together on the double seat under the swinging branches of that beautiful tree. Love, peace, plenty, contentment were all idealized in that one ineffaceable picture, father with his silken white hair, and mother with her light dress and garden shade-hat.
>
> I felt I had to make short work of it or I was lost. So I said, "Well, Father, Mr. Lincoln has had to call for 300,000 more men and I must go now. I have waited as long as I can. I hope I shall go with my parents' approval and consent." Father hesitated for an instant and then said, "Edward! you must do what seems your duty."

In response to Lincoln's call, Governor Holbrook had ordered up the Ninth Vermont Regiment. Edward Ripley recruited a Rutland company, and when the regiment gathered at Brattleboro, he was named its captain. George Stannard was appointed commander of the Ninth Vermont. The regiment was in Brattleboro about long enough to draw weapons. "On Friday we went down and got our muskets and strange to say, no one was hurt," a Rutland soldier recalled, adding, "guns are very dangerous things in the hands of new recruits, even if they have neither stock, lock, or barrel."

The Ninth left Brattleboro on July 15, 1862 and went straight to Washington and across the Potomac, camping for a few days near Alexandria. Then its 1,000 men were put on trains and moved west to Winchester, Virginia, at the northern end of the Shenandoah Valley. The regiment had a rather pleasant, though hard-working, stay at Winchester, constructing a hilltop fort.

Ripley wrote home:

> A few nights since, wishing to get a bath in a brook—one of my men said he had been to an elegant place to bathe, so we took him along to show us. We went out through the town down past Senator [James M.] Mason's ruined mansion, and stopped at a break in the garden wall. We went through and found ourselves in most beautifully laid out grounds, with a regular swift, dashing, clear cold Vermont trout brook rushing round in among the beautiful trees.
>
> "This is the place," said the man.

The easy days at Winchester ended with news that "Stonewall" Jackson, taking little time to savor victory at Second Bull Run, was on the move in the Ninth Vermont's direction. The regiment was ordered to historic Harpers Ferry, where 12,000 Federal troops were being assembled in hopes of keeping the strategic location out of Confederate hands. Driven by Stannard, the Vermonters made a forced march of 30 miles. On arrival, they were placed under the command of a man with a shaky military record and a reputed weakness for booze—Col. Dixon S. Miles. Miles soon had his hands full, as scouts reported "Stonewall" Jackson and many Confederates drawing near.

From the first, the Vermonters knew they might be in a tight spot. Ripley later likened being at Harpers Ferry to being "in the bottom of a bowl." Harpers Ferry, as previously noted, is a triangle of land bordered on one side by the Shenandoah and on another by the Potomac. On the far sides of each river, sheer cliffs rise to summits known as Maryland Heights and Loudoun Heights. On the third side, away from the river, is the high ground of Bolivar Heights, from which

Harpers Ferry from Loudoun Heights.

126

the Shenandoah Valley rolls away south. The Vermonters went into camp on Bolivar Heights. Colonel Stannard, from the first, did not like the look of things, particularly Miles's refusal to strongly fortify the high ground, and he volunteered his Ninth Vermont for isolated duty on Maryland Heights and Loudoun Heights. The offer was refused as three columns of Confederates under "Stonewall" himself approached.

One night, looking along the Shenandoah Valley, the Vermonters saw a long line of Confederate camp fires. Miles at last posted some men on the heights, but they were far too few. The Ninth Vermont watched—on September 13—as fighting broke out on Maryland Heights, and Federal troops were slowly forced to withdraw from the summit. Confederates were then seen on Loudoun Heights. And rebels under Ambrose Powell Hill were pressing in toward the camps on Bolivar Heights.

On the afternoon of September 14, as Ripley recalled,

Major [Edwin] Stowell and I were lying on our backs in the grass behind our tents watching our shell lift themselves up so wearisomely in their long flight toward the hostile working parties, when suddenly I saw two, three, four, half a dozen puffs of smoke burst out in the very centre of them, and we jumped to our feet, clapped our hands, and hurrahed in delight: "Our guns have the range, and the rebels have got to go." Suddenly, in the very centre of [Julius] White's brigade, there was a crash, then another and another, and columns of dirt and smoke leaped into the air, as though a dozen young volcanoes had burst forth. Stowell caught the situation quicker than I, and exclaimed: "it's their guns!" In an instant the bivouac turned into the appearance of a disturbed ant-hill.

Harpers Ferry was surrounded. As the shells zeroed in, Stannard hurriedly marched his men from place to place. He kept it up until dusk, when the shelling slackened. That night the Federal position was ringed by thousands of Confederate camp fires. The morning brought more intense shelling as the Confederates moved artillery to closer range.

The long butternut battle lines forming out in the fields to the south were too much for Miles. Despite the strong protests of Stannard that a stubborn fight should be made, Miles surrendered the Harpers Ferry garrison. Not so Stannard. He formed up the Ninth Vermont and marched them down the road into Harpers Ferry, bound for a pontoon bridge and escape. But as he reached the river, an orderly arrived from headquarters and ordered the Vermonters back up the hill to surrender with the rest. Stannard took a long look at the far side of the river and, like a good soldier, obeyed orders.

One Union outfit did escape from Harpers Ferry. In the spring of 1862 students at Norwich University and Dartmouth College, just across the Connecticut River, had organized a cavalry troop. The College Cavaliers joined a Rhode Island cavalry unit, which ended up at surrounded Harpers Ferry. The collegians galloped out before the surrender, racing up through the Maryland mountains. They broke through Confederate lines and were free men, able to depart for home when their enlistments expired a few days later.

Reluctantly the Ninth Vermont went back to its shot-torn campground and stacked arms. The Confederates immediately swarmed in. Ripley recalled:

> A group of mounted officers sat on their horses in the road in front of the street of company E. It began to be whispered about that the one with full and sandy beard was the redoubtable Stonewall Jackson. We stood on the side, watching him and not knowing whether to resent the intrusion of his men or not. Suddenly, I saw Lieutenant Quimby of company E, a hot-headed, bold fellow, stride out of his street down to the side of Jackson's horse and say, "Are you Stonewall Jackson?"
> Jackson replied, "Yes."
> Then said Quimby, "Did you not agree to protect us under the terms of the surrender?"
> "Yes," said Jackson.
> "Then, by God, sir," said Quimby, "I want you to drive these lousy thieves of yours out of my camp and stop them robbing my men."
> We were terror stricken at Quimby's rage and audacity, and looked for a scene; but Jackson said quietly, "This is all wrong and I will see it stopped," and turning to one of his staff he sent him to order the men out of our camp; but this was not done until much damage and loss was inflicted upon us.

Another story about Jackson emerged from Harpers Ferry. As the Vermonters reluctantly surrendered and marched back into camp, "Stonewall" sat on his horse watching them pass and noticed that some were in tears. "Don't feel bad, men, don't feel bad," Jackson said. "God's will must be done."

One of the last artillery rounds fired at Harpers Ferry took the life of the hapless Colonel Miles. Ripley summed things up: "Few disasters of the war exceeded that of Harpers Ferry in the folly which caused it. Miles was a man of indolent habits and loose principles, with a mind enervated by past and possibly continued self-indulgence—on this there is conflicting evidence…he was too proud as an old West Point officer to seek and follow the advice of his volunteer officers, several of whom could have carried the defense of the place to a brilliant issue."

The surrender of Harpers Ferry knocked the Ninth Vermont out of action for eight months. The captured Vermonters were paroled by General Jackson to stay out of the war until exchanged for Confederate prisoners. The Vermonters were shipped to Camp Douglas, a former encampment for Southern prisoners near Chicago that was, coincidentally, named for Stephen Douglas. They spent a long winter, generally living like prisoners themselves. Ripley, in letters home, worried that his regiment was becoming the subject of shame, having been in only one engagement, in which it had surrendered. During the winter Stannard moved on to command the Second Vermont Brigade and Ripley became the Ninth's colonel. It would be spring before the Ninth was back in action, at a backwater of the war in Virginia. But there were stars in the regiment's future, and a general's star in Edward Ripley's.

Bird's-eye view of Camp Douglas, Chicago.

After Jackson had paroled the Vermonters, he immediately set his forces in motion. When the long line of Confederates passed the Vermonters' camp, Ripley recorded the scene:

That night I lay beside the Charles Town Pike and watched until morning the grimy columns come pouring up from the pontoons. It was a weird, uncanny sight, and drove sleep from my eyes. It was something demon-like; a scene from an Inferno. They were silent as ghosts; ruthless and rushing in their speed; ragged, earth colored, dishevelled and devilish, as tho' they were keen on the scent of the hot blood that was already steaming up from the opening struggle at Antietam, and thirsting for it. Their sliding dog-trot was as tho' on snow-shoes. The shuffle of their badly shod feet on the hard surface of the Pike was so rapid as to be continuous like the hiss of a great serpent, broken only by the roar of the batteries as they came rushing by on the trot, or the jingling of the sabres of the Cavalry. The spectral, ghostly picture will never be erased from my memory. The next day we took up our unhappy march for an unknown destination.

The Confederates Ripley watched, Jackson's legendary foot cavalry, were bound for the village of Sharpsburg, Maryland, a dozen miles away, where a battle had already begun along winding Antietam Creek. It was to produce the bloodiest single day of the war, and the Vermont Brigade would be there.

COSTLY VICTORY AT ANTIETAM

After the Peninsula Campaign, the Old Brigade remained at Harrison's Landing for several long weeks. Then it marched back down the Peninsula, boarded transports for shipment to the Washington area, and moved west as action developed around Manassas. General Pope had been dealt a crushing defeat at Second Bull Run by Robert E. Lee. Abraham Lincoln summoned the general he knew could pull the beaten Union armies together into an effective fighting machine: he asked General McClellan to again assume full command, and McClellan promptly accepted. The Vermonters cheered the news.

There was little time to spare. Flushed by his victories at Cedar Mountain and Second Bull Run, Lee was intent on bringing the war to Union territory. He drove his army into Maryland, and McClellan, having combined Pope's Army of Virginia with the Army of the Potomac, set off in pursuit. At the beginning of the second week of September, McClellan, with five army corps, some 80,000 men, marched west through Maryland, and on September 13, 1862 the Vermont Brigade was five miles southeast of Frederick. On that day McClellan was granted an extraordinary piece of good fortune. In a grove of trees where a Confederate unit had recently camped, a copy of Lee's campaign plan was found and promptly delivered to the Union commander. It told McClellan that Lee's army was off beyond South Mountain and divided into four columns, all miles apart. Prompt action could mean the piecemeal destruction of the Army of Northern Virginia. McClellan started off in the right direction with a good strategy in mind. His orders to the Sixth Corps, including the Vermonters, were to clear the way over South Mountain.

Dispatches came in the evening ordering a march at first light. To get the job done, the orders should have read "move immediately," but it was morning before the troops were on the road. The Vermont Brigade arrived in Burkittsville a little past noon; their view of the task ahead must have been discouraging. The

130

road up and over South Mountain, through rocky Crampton's Gap, led steeply up a hill that loomed over the village. Confederates were there, some in a lane lined with stone walls that paralleled the hillside. Fortunately for the Vermonters that day, there just weren't enough Confederates to man it properly. The ones that were there, dismounted Virginian horse soldiers under Col. Tom Munford, put up a brisk if brief fight.

The attack on Crampton's Gap was begun by other units of the Sixth Corps, which ran up Burkittsville's only street, with sharpshooters' bullets coming from some houses alongside, and cheers of Maryland women from others. Burkittsville was considerably Union in sentiment. The early attackers veered to the right of the Crampton's Gap Road, firing as they moved uphill and taking fire from above. Then came the Vermonters, with commander William H. T. Brooks ordering Col. Edwin Stoughton's Fourth Vermont and Bennington's Maj. J. H. Walbridge's Second Vermont to lead the attack. One Vermont soldier reported to his local newspaper, the *Bennington Banner*: "As we passed through Burkittsville we were cheered by the ladies of the town....We passed through the entire length of the village, the shot and shell of the enemy flying like Satan's angels over our heads."

At the foot of the hill the Vermonters took shelter behind a barn until ordered to attack. The soldier wrote:

> We filed from behind the barn, halted and came to a front as coolly as if on drill. Next came the order to charge and forward we went at double quick, our lieutenant colonel leading the way a yard or two in front of the colors, which were flying out to the breeze....We halted a moment as we came to the stone wall, bounding the field, across which we had charged, but it was not long before the order came to move on and onward we moved over the wall, through the woods, up the mountain sides, sweeping with irresistible force everything before us.

In a half hour the Vermonters were at the crest with other Sixth Corps units. Crampton's Gap had been taken. At the summit 115 Confederates surrendered to Colonel Stoughton. The Battle of Crampton's Gap had cost the Vermont Brigade just 1 man killed and 22 wounded.

To the north other Union units were seizing Fox's and Turner's gaps, and by dark three passes over South Mountain were in Union control. The way to Lee's army had been substantially opened and, had McClellan ordered haste, the Union garrison at Harpers Ferry, including the Ninth Vermont, just a few short miles beyond, might have been saved.

The summer after the fight on South Mountain, Joseph Case Rutherford, an army surgeon, visited the battlefield. He wrote to his wife, Hannah Chase Rutherford, in Newport:

> We are now laying on the old battlefield of South Mountain fought last September. It was a terrible battle. The rebs lost 800 men killed, we 250. They were all buried on top of the mountain....Our men drove the rebs up the side of the moun-

tain, through the woods and when they got to the top to what is called by the natives "the 10 acre lot," there the rebs made a stand behind a series of stone walls, 3 in number, but our men bravely drove them from cover.

You can judge the fierceness of the fight by our men by this.…The walls are capped by 2 and 3 rails. One of our officers who visited the spot counted 84 bullet holes in one length of these rails and 120 in another.

Lee and his divided 45,000-man army were in trouble, with a Union force twice its size coming in over the mountains and looking for a fight. The Southern commander issued orders for his divisions to converge on a low ridge that ran north-southeast of the Potomac, east of the village of Sharpsburg. Nearby, lazy Antietam Creek ran through a lush green farm valley, and on the hills beyond, McClellan began assembling his Union host of 80,000 men. The shooting started on September 16. Lee's back was to the river, and he had little choice but to fight. The Vermont Brigade spent the night five miles from the battlefield, in farm country west of South Mountain known as Pleasant Valley. In the morning, with gunfire already cracking on the September air, the brigade was marched up near Antietam Creek. They were held for a time near a stone bridge, with Confederates on the hillside beyond, a bridge later to gain the name "Burnside's Bridge." Then they marched north toward the center of the Union line, where some bloody fighting had already taken place. As the morning wore on and the firing increased to a terrible din, with smoke filling the fields and woods, the Vermonters prepared to go in.

Unbeknownst to the men of the Old Brigade, some Vermont troops had already been engaged on the Antietam battlefield. The men of the Second Vermont Sharpshooters had been fighting on the right of the Union line, advancing in the vicinity of the Miller Cornfield. Joseph Hooker, who saw many bloody Civil War battlefields, said that cornfield was the worst, filled with mangled bodies and dying men.

Had the Union army been better used, the Civil War might have been decided at Antietam. But McClellan fought a piecemeal battle. First, he attacked the Confederate left and got repulsed and repulsed again. Then he struck at the center and was driven back with frightful losses. Finally, as the day grew late, McClellan ordered Ambrose E. Burnside to hit the weakened Confederate right. He did, after frittering away precious time taking the bridge destined to bear his name. When Burnside finally got across and came booming in toward Sharpsburg, he met Confederate forces just arrived from Harpers Ferry. The battle ended in a bloody stalemate.

The story of the Vermont Brigade at Antietam is one of what might have been. By the time the Vermonters were ordered onto the battlefield, with the rest of the Sixth Corps, Union attacks on the rebel left had failed. Not long before the Vermonters went in, a tough native of the Green Mountain State had fallen in battle. Israel Richardson, born in Fairfax and a West Point graduate, was old army. A descendant of Israel Putnam, Richardson had fought Seminoles in Florida and participated in most of the major Mexican War battles alongside

Antietam National Battlefield, National Park Service

Vermont skirmishers at Antietam (detail of panoramic painting by James Hope).

Winfield Scott, winning the nickname "Fighting Dick." Early in the war he refused command of the Second Vermont Regiment; on September 17, 1862, he was leading a division in the Second Corps in the thickest of the late-morning fighting. Richardson had a well-deserved reputation for fearlessness, and on that morning, amid the shot and shell, he was moving his massive frame along his line of troops, booming encouragement. Then he was wounded as he went to the rear to bring up artillery, and he had to be carried from the field. He lingered six weeks and died in early November.

The Vermont Brigade was finally summoned to action about noon, advancing through a gruesome field where battle had already raged in failed attempts to crack the Confederate line around a Dunkard church. A newspaper correspondent described the Vermonters' advance as follows: "(Baldy) Smith was ordered to retake the cornfields and woods which had been so hotly contested. It was done in the handsomest style. His Maine and Vermont regiments and the rest went forward on the run and, cheering as they went, swept like an avalanche through the cornfield, fell upon the woods, cleared them in 10 minutes, and held them.... The field and its ghastly harvest which the grim reaper had gathered remained with us."

Samuel Pingree of the Third Vermont later wrote: "As we came near a large cornfield we of the Vermont Brigade were faced to the right and swept through the cornfield towards the enemy. At the further edge of the cornfield we were halted, and alignment made and we lay down in front of the dead lane and orchard and we lay there as near as I can recollect all night."

The Vermonters were ordered to halt as they came up toward the Dunkard church and in sight of the battered rebel line beyond. Then the brigade was withdrawn about 200 yards to the cover of a low ridge. There it held through the day, amid considerable shot and shell, with a man occasionally getting hit, returning fire when a target presented itself. Though a few Vermonters were occasionally seriously wounded, one soldier reported that men on both sides of him were hit by spent bullets that did not break the skin. All the while the battle raged off to the south, but the Vermonters never got the order to go forward again. Indeed, the entire Sixth Corps, despite Gen. William B. Franklin's entreaties to McClellan, remained at a standstill. Confederate sharpshooters were the main problem. General Brooks, cut from the same cloth as Israel Richardson, ignored them, pacing along his line. Finally a rebel bullet found its mark, striking him in the mouth and knocking out two teeth.

A man standing nearby ran to the brigade commander and asked Brooks if he were hurt.

"No," said the tough old soldier, "had a tooth pulled." He remained along the battle line until dark.

The battle died with the light of day, and when it was over, the Vermont Brigade had lost just 25 men killed and wounded. They paid a mild price, considering that almost 23,000 soldiers North and South had been killed, wounded, or captured.

While McClellan had failed to win the decisive victory that seemed at hand, Lee's invasion of the North was stopped. The two armies stared at each other for another day, then Lee moved off on the night of September 18 on the long retreat to Virginia. McClellan, true to form, did not pursue.

The battlefield was a place of horror as the numbers of dead and wounded overwhelmed burial parties and medical capabilities. Pvt. Horace Tower, of Clarendon, in the Second Vermont, recalled: "We went up to where the dead and wounded lay between their line and ours, and such a sight never was seen; there were killed and wounded rebels lying three deep…the worst of all was to hear the wounded men cry for water and for help to get them off."

More of Antietam's aftermath comes through in a letter written by a New Hampshire soldier, Joseph Everest, who had a son in the Vermont cavalry. The elder Everest had enlisted at the age of 54 after his son George, 17, went to White River Junction and took the train to Burlington, where he joined the Vermont cavalry. At Antietam, Joseph Everest, with his New Hampshire regiment, was wounded near the Miller Cornfield, and he wrote the following letter while lying gravely wounded on the battlefield:

> My dear wife,
> I write this on my knees being unable to stand in consequence of wound from bullet through my thigh, which has been very painful, rendering me very weak from loss of blood. It is now 48 hours since I fell. I am yet on the ground but hope to be taken to hospital soon. You may possibly see it reported that I am dead. I write this to relieve you and hope it may reach you in time, I fell in the battle near Sharpsburg, Md. From your husband, with praise to God for my life.
>   My love to all,
>   J. W. Everest

Everest was eventually moved to a field hospital, where he wrote:

On the ground about 4 rods from where they brot me one week ago tomorrow. September 24 near the battlefield where I have remained ever since under a shed on some straw with about 20 others: 4 with their legs taken off, the rest wounded in various ways....I am very weak and suffer extremely from pain in my shoulders & back in consequence of lying in the rain & cold since I was wounded.... Where our regiment are I don't know. They never sent anybody to look after the dead or wounded. Mr. Cole kindly procured me a clean shirt and drawers, my shirt was black with blood, and stiff. I have not seen George nor heard from him for weeks....There are so many here to care for, and I consider myself very fortunate in being brot from the field. Portions of both armies passed over me during the day. 3 times one rebel cocked his gun and levelled at my head. I begged him to spare my life, and he did so.

Everest's son George eventually learned in a letter from his mother of his father's plight and got time away from his Vermont regiment to visit his father, by then moved to a hospital in Washington. The son wrote to his mother:

When I went in he was asleep, and I passed by him and looked at every one in the tent before I made up my mind that it was him, he had grown poor and altered so much. He was very glad to see me, and I stayed with him three or four hours. Got him some lemons, sugar, crackers....The doctor says he is doing just as well as can be expected. Says he won't be well so quick as it would be on a younger man, but thinks it will get well in time, so that he will not be lame. While I was there he got a letter from you with ten dollars in it.

Joseph Everest died a few days later. His son went on through the war almost another year, then was shot in a cavalry fight soon after the Battle of Gettysburg. He also died after lying unattended on the field for a long time.

Abraham Lincoln went to Sharpsburg and visited the wounded in field hospitals such as housed Joseph Everest. He also had a visit with General McClellan. Not long afterward, as McClellan ignored the president's entreaties to pursue Lee's battered army, the president's patience with his commander again expired. McClellan was relieved of command. George Brinton McClellan was out of the war for good. Still, the soldiers of the Army of the Potomac had a special place in their hearts for their old commander. As late as January 5, 1863 Pvt. John Morse wrote home to his wife Jane in Bethel, "I think McClellan is the man yet."

Back home, as the summer of 1862 waned, the featured speaker at the Rutland Fair was the newspaper publisher Horace Greeley. Speaking a week before Antietam, Greeley said: "War is not the natural state of man. His true destiny, his true glory, are found in the quiet walks of peace. God grants that the manifold sufferings, the sacrifices, the bereavements of this strife be not endured in vain...that the Bow of Providence may soon irradiate our sky...and that from our afflictions, the agonies, of this crisis may arrive the stately fabric of impartial and universal freedom."

Abraham Lincoln had been looking for a victory, and if Antietam wasn't a decisive victory, he nevertheless seized on it and made a prophet of Horace Greeley. On September 22, five days after Antietam, the president issued his controversial preliminary Emancipation Proclamation, to take effect January 1, 1863. The abolitionist Rufus Kinsley, who lived in Fletcher before enlisting, was soldiering with the Eighth Vermont in the Louisiana bayous when word reached him of the proclamation. He wrote in his diary: "Thank God, the word has at last been spoken. Light begins to break through. Let the sons of earth rejoice. Sing paeans to liberty. Let tyranny die."

The countryside west of Frederick, Maryland, is broken by a series of ridges, and it is easy to see why it reminded the Vermont soldiers of home. One summer afternoon I found Burkittsville along the base of South Mountain, its single street still lined with houses predating the war. That village is one of the remarkable places where it's still possible to know you're in about the same setting as the Vermont soldiers.

Antietam is one of the loveliest and best preserved of all Civil War battlefields, marble monuments set in fertile farmland where cows graze and corn grows. Along Antietam Creek graceful old stone bridges survive from the day war came their way. The visitor's center stands on a hilltop near the center of Robert E. Lee's long line. There are battle relics, an excellent audiovisual presentation that tells Antietam's story, and, in the observation room, four paintings by a Vermonter. James Hope, who wrote about his experiences at the first battle at Bull Run, was 43 when he reached Antietam as a captain in the Second Vermont but was kept out of combat because of poor health. During the fighting he was thus free to make a series of sketches that became the basis for his paintings. The image they accurately convey is one of two vast armies meeting in a bloody struggle. Everywhere there are dead and wounded, dark spots on the autumn fields, numerous as crows at harvest.

Two monuments to Vermont soldiers stand at Antietam. One, beside the Miller Cornfield, honors the Vermont sharpshooters. The Vermont Brigade monument, behind the little crest that gave some cover, stands near the national battlefield visitor's center. A national cemetery is located on high ground just outside Sharpsburg where the last Union attacks were stopped. Thousands of graves are arrayed in a great circle around a massive granite statue of a soldier of the Union. The Vermonters are buried on the south side. There are 60 graves, Vermont dead having been brought in from other battlefields, including South Mountain and the fight nearly a year later at Funkstown, to join the few Vermonters killed at Antietam. It is a place where birds sing, and I once disturbed a huge black snake sunning itself among the Vermont stones.

BURNSIDE'S FAILURE
AT FREDERICKSBURG

North of South Royalton, where a sign along the Tunbridge road marks the Washington County line, a dirt road bears off sharply to climb steeply into the hills from whence flow the White River's branches. Follow it a half mile; on the right is the old Button Cemetery. Each year, a new American flag is placed by a certain gravestone in the first row. On the stone is carved in weathered letters:

Charles
Son of Oel and Anna
Cleveland
was killed in battle
at Fredericksburg, Va.
Dec. 13, 1862
Age 19 yrs., 6 mos.

Charles Cleveland lies alongside his mother and father, who near Christmas day in 1862 had gone down to the South Royalton railroad station to fetch his plain board coffin. Probably they took the buckboard up the hill to the high graveyard among the open fields and pine forests for the burial in the family plot. They stood proud and cold and sad on a Vermont winter day to lay their Charlie to rest.

The sight of that hillside grave reminds one of the useless waste of life at the great battle of Fredericksburg, Virginia, in December 1862. There, Federal troops, led by another incompetent commander, were shot down in waves as they bravely advanced across frozen and open fields. The Vermont troops were fortunate; they missed the worst of the fighting. But every Union soldier who fell at Fredericksburg fell for no good military purpose.

In the aftermath of the Battle of Antietam in September 1862, the Vermont Brigade welcomed 250 fresh troops from Vermont to its ranks. Then it got a huge addition, 1,000 soldiers of a new regiment, the 26th New Jersey. Like the troops of the Second Vermont Brigade, the Jerseymen were nine-month enlistees. It would not always be a happy partnership.

"The 26th New Jersey regiment belongs to this brigade—a regiment of nine months men who came out here with big bounties, and, of course, has seen more hardships, endured more privations, and suffered more generally than any of the old soldiers ever dreamed of," recalled Pvt. Wilbur Fisk of the Second Vermont. "The boys call them 'two hundred dollar men,' and they take wicked delight in playing their pranks on them whenever they have the chance."

One officer of the New Jersey outfit saw it this way: "We were emphatically a green regiment when we entered on active service. But we had one great advantage. We were brigaded with veterans, and with veterans, too, who had won a high reputation in the Peninsula and Maryland campaigns. Their example was our real teacher in the art of war."

So the Vermont Brigade had grown, but then it lost a popular commander, William Brooks. The gruff old veteran, promoted to command of a division, issued a farewell to his troops:

> The brigadier general commanding this brigade hereby relinquishes its command. In thus terminating an official connection which has existed for precisely a year, the general commanding experiences much regret. He is not unmindful that his own reputation has been identified with and dependent upon that of those who have served under him; and it is with great gratification that he thanks them for the noble manner in which they have sustained him, in the performance of his arduous duties in camp and field. He will watch their future career with deep interest, and trusts he will ever have occasion to feel proud that his name has been associated with the Vermont Brigade.

The brigade's officers met to discuss what might be a fitting farewell gift. At first they decided on a horse and saddle, but nobody could be found bold enough to make the presentation. Finally, a collection was taken and a silver service was (probably anonymously) set before the general's tent. Gruff old Brooks received it with tears in his eyes and found himself unable to speak.

In Brooks's place the Vermonters got just what they did not want. Col. Henry Whiting of the Second Regiment, that Michigander who the soldiers always suspected lacked the heart for combat, was named to head the Old Brigade. There were more changes in the wind: General McClellan was on his way back to civilian life for his failure to pursue Lee after Antietam, and Lincoln, on November 7, appointed Ambrose E. Burnside to command the Army of the Potomac. Burnside took the job with some reluctance, the old soldier (for whom sideburns were named) lacked confidence in his ability to command a huge army. Subsequent events would bear him out. Burnside promptly reorganized his army, dividing it into three "grand divisions." Gen. William Franklin was elevated from command of the Sixth Corps to lead the Left Grand Division. The Sixth Corps was now commanded by "Baldy" Smith, and the division of that corps in which the Vermont Brigade now served was given to Brig. Gen. Albion P. Howe, a Maine man and a West Pointer.

All this was happening after the army had moved south and east from western Maryland and the valley of Antietam Creek. As the Vermonters came back across South Mountain and through Burkittsville, they grumbled that McClellan had been unjustly dealt with. Most seemed to hope "Little Mac" would get another chance to command the 120,000-man army, now moving into the Confederacy and toward the banks of the Rappahannock River, a wide stream that flows from the Blue Ridge foothills through the Virginia piedmont to the sea. President Lincoln had reluctantly approved Burnside's strategy of moving on Richmond via Fredericksburg. That Virginia port city, located at the fall line above which the Rappahannock is no longer navigable, was precisely halfway, and in a direct line, between the two national capitals—Washington and Richmond. Clearly, it was destined for bloodshed.

After many marches, then delays, Burnside concentrated his army on the heights at Falmouth, across the Rappahannock from Fredericksburg. Burnside had been waiting for pontoons on which his army could cross the bridgeless river. By the time they arrived, his intentions were no longer a mystery, and Robert E. Lee was gathering 80,000 soldiers along the low hills beyond the Rappahannock. Lt. Gen. James Longstreet was there, and just as Burnside prepared to attack, "Stonewall" Jackson and his men tramped in, filing into carefully selected defensive positions.

Beyond the once-peaceful town of Fredericksburg the river plain extended almost a mile to a low ridge. At the base of it was a road, in places sunken below ground level, and where it was at ground level, a stone wall ran along it. Lee posted four ranks of infantry in the so-called Sunken Road, and on the low hills above, known locally as Marye's Heights and Willis Hill, he placed artillery. It proved to be one of the finest defensive positions ever taken by the Army of Northern Virginia. Southeast of Fredericksburg, Marye's Heights and Willis Hill became higher hills. The river plain widened to farm fields, broken here and there by a stream. A railroad line and a road slashed across the plain, coming up from Richmond. Lee aligned infantry at the edge of the woods, supported by cannon back on the hills. To attack Lee, the Yankees would have to cross an expanse of open plain, against massed and protected infantry and artillery. Burnside could have opted for another strategy, perhaps moving upriver to flank the Confederates off their low hills. He chose a frontal attack.

The Vermonters crossed the Rappahannock on pontoon bridges in the vanguard of Franklin's Left Grand Division and came onto the Confederate side of the river where the plain is widest, more than a mile of fields between the river and the low, Confederate-held hills. They advanced to the Richmond Stage Road, which cuts across the plain, and then were deployed as skirmishers to protect the gathering Yankee forces. On that Friday, December 12, there was considerable shooting, particularly along the line held by Col. Charles Joyce's Second Vermont. At one point, the Second advanced to push back a line of pesky Confederate skirmishers and then withstood an attempt by the Confederates to regain the lost ground.

Saturday morning, December 13, dawned foggy. As the mists lifted a little past midmorning, an awesome sight confronted the Confederates on their heights. On the plains below was the vast Army of the Potomac, more than 100,000 men, all in line with flags flying and bayonets gleaming. It was such a spectacle that even General Longstreet had misgivings about the strength of the Confederate position. An artillery commander quickly assured him that once his cannon went into action, a chicken couldn't live on that plain.

The story of the Vermont Brigade at Fredericksburg is a sidebar to a sidebar of the main action. The brigade was posted out beyond the highway, with the railroad in front and its right flank touching the steep bank of Deep Run. Saturday was a day of fierce, one-sided fighting, suffering, and dying, much of it in front of the Sunken Road and Marye's Heights. Where the Vermonters lay, action got heated up in the morning when elements of a rebel brigade under William Dorsey Pender advanced toward the Union lines and were repulsed with the help of the Second Vermont. In the afternoon a more serious probe was launched by Alabama troops, part of John Bell Hood's division. As they came on, the Third Vermont was moved along Deep Run ravine out to the railroad tracks. A Vermont Brigade surgeon described the attack:

It was interesting to see them crawling through the woods and dry grass, and forming a line of battle in the horizontal position, awaiting the foe....They waited in position an hour or more when it was evident the rebels were approaching. Three regiments of North Carolina troops advanced upon the position of the 3d. Our boys heads could be seen by the enemy, and they fired upon us, killing and wounding 5 of the 3d. This was a time of intense excitement for the boys were eager to spring upon the enemy, but they were not yet near enough. Soon the order was given for them to rise and fire. They did fire and that was the last seen of the advancing enemies.

Confederate general Pender later wrote an account of the attack:

After the heat of the action on the right, the enemy advanced a brigade up Deep Run, throwing one regiment somewhat in advance, which so sheltered itself behind the trees, as to get near enough to take an officer and 15 men of the Sixteenth North Carolina prisoners, who were protecting the left flank of the regiment. This left the regiment to be raked by a fire from down the railroad track. The colonel drew his regiment back to the ditch and held his ground until General [Evander] Law sent forward two regiments to its assistance.

The Confederates lost nearly 300 men in that action.

The principal Federal offensive in the area of the battlefield where the Vermonters were located was directed by Maj. Gen. George Gordon Meade to the south of the Vermonters. Meade made a strong infantry attack on "Stonewall" Jackson's lines; the Federals broke through in a swampy area where the Confederate line was weak (perhaps because some Confederates didn't like standing in icy swamp water). But Jackson hurried in reinforcements and the Federals were sent reeling back, the line restored. The Fourth Vermont advanced in support of the attack, though well out of the frontline, and received the heaviest loss of any Vermont regiment that day. Confederate cannon on the hills helped break Meade's attack and probably inflicted most of the Vermont casualties. All of this fighting, off on the left end of the Union line, however, was dwarfed by the slaughter in front of Marye's Heights and Willis Hill.

That morning, General Lee stood at his command post on the highest hill, roughly opposite from where the Vermonters fought, and saw the rising fog reveal the mighty Union army. He said something to the effect that it was a good thing war is so horrible, or men might come to love it too much. On the plains beside Fredericksburg, the Union infantry then marched up toward the Sunken Road, and the reality of war was suddenly most apparent. The Northern troops were mowed down as they came on and on. Some Yankee regiments were said to lean forward as if marching into a driving wind and rain. The rebels in the Sunken Road and the cannon on the hills pulverized the attackers. The plain between the road and the houses of Fredericksburg was littered with dead and dying men. Yet orders still came from Burnside, on the heights across the river, to keep on attacking. Not one Union soldier reached the Sunken Road all day long. The slaughter ended only when it became too dark to fight. Through the long night, trees cracked in the cold, and many of the wounded pinned down on the open fields froze to death.

The next day Burnside wanted to renew the assault. But his generals who had seen the reality of Saturday's brave attempts close up said no. The two armies faced each other through Sunday, the Vermonters on skirmish line at times giving and receiving fire. Sunday night was colder than the previous night, and as the stars came out, the northern sky began to take on color. The northern lights that sometimes served as beacons to fugitive slaves gave a strange luminescence to the horrible battlefield, where the dead and wounded still lay between the lines.

On Monday the Vermont Brigade was relieved and marched back across the pontoon bridges to the heights of Falmouth. The Vermonters, though spared the worst of Fredericksburg, had paid a considerable price. The brigade suffered 24 killed and 127 wounded. General Howe, in his official report on the battle, said the Vermonters "gallantly maintained at all points" their line. "They stood unmoved for three days and nights under the direct and enfilading fire of the enemy's batteries, and at all times exhibited a discipline and soldiership worthy of veterans of the first class."

Under cover of the darkness of Monday night the rest of the Army of the Potomac moved back across the Rappahannock, and the Battle of Fredericksburg was over.

On Sunday, as the Vermonters and the Confederates warily watched each other across the open fields, Charles Cleveland was killed. He was out on picket in advance of the main Union line with other members of the Fourth Vermont. Some of the boys were standing too close around a flag when a Confederate gun crew took aim and let loose an exploding shell. It was a direct hit; four men died instantly, among them Cleveland, and 14 more were wounded. Young Cleveland's body was sent back across the river to Falmouth and to the undertakers who followed the army. His body was put in a box and sent north to his family, to rest in Button Cemetery high in the Tunbridge hills. The other men killed by that dreadful shot were Privates Tyler Joy of Westminster, Oliver Pease of Townshend, and Herman Kent of Montpelier.

After this senseless battle the Union army went into camp on the heights of Falmouth. The troops built shanties with fireplaces, but the old camp sicknesses quickly spread, and by January 1, 1863 the Vermont Brigade had just 2,760 of its 3,933 men present for duty.

On January 20 Burnside turned everyone out of camp and sent the army up along the Rappahannock on frozen roads. His aim was to reach the upstream fords behind Lee and flank him off those deadly Fredericksburg heights. The Vermonters were out in the lead of one column, but before they'd gotten far, the sky clouded over and heavy rains came. Soon the entire army was bogged down in roads that became long, bottomless mud holes. The Vermonters had marched toward a shallow spot in the river called Banks's Ford, where Burnside planned to put part of his forces across. The pontoon boats and their wagons got mired in the slop, and the Vermonters were put to work hauling them. It took 100 men to budge a single wagon.

Burnside presently came up to encourage the men. One Vermonter set down his impressions: "As he rode through our division in the afternoon, with only two staff officers, himself and horse covered with mud, his hat rim turned down to shed the rain, his face careworn with the sudden disarrangement of his plans, we could but think that the soldier on foot, oppressed with the weight of knapsack, haversack and gun, bore an easy load compared with that of the commander of the army."

A soldier in the Fifth Vermont, Julius Lewis of Poultney, had quite a different view:

So we got all ready and started up the river to get across. They called it 16 miles that we marched that day it was a hard march. This was Tuesday and that night it began to rain and the next day about noon we was ordered to pack up and so we did and started for the river. When we had got about a mile the Col said he wanted us to hold low. So says I to old Lewis I guess that we are in for drawing blood. But I did not care where they did put me but came to go 1/2 a mile farther we found out whats the matter. We had come down there to help draw the pontoon wagons out of the mud. You better believe we had some fun if it did rain like the devil. They would put about three companies onto the ropes and let them rip. The mud was up to our asses and more too. Well we worked there until night and then came back to where we started Tuesday night. You can make up your own mind what kind of a night we had with our clothes wet as piss and still it was raining. The next day they give us a good portion of whiskey so that made it all right with us. Some of the boys got as drunk as the devil. We stayed there that day and night and Friday we came back to our old camp. You better believe we was glad to get here too. I think Old Burnside has shit his breeches this time.

After three days in the muck, Burnside called a halt; his exhausted army went back into camp, and the "Mud March" went down in history as another great failure. Soon thereafter Abraham Lincoln relieved Burnside of command and put Joseph Hooker in charge of the Army of the Potomac. Hooker had a nickname, "Fighting Joe"; in the spring he would set off to fight, and the Vermonters would find themselves back across the Rappahannock. That time they would be face to face with Marye's Heights.

A national military park and cemetery are located in Fredericksburg today. Some 14,000 Federal soldiers rest on Marye's Heights and Willis Hill, places many of them died trying to capture. Great trees shade the well-tended lawns and long lines of headstones, and one can survey the Fredericksburg battlefield, where the waste of the Federal attacks becomes quickly apparent. Below, in the Sunken Road, some of the original stone wall that sheltered Confederate riflemen remains. The plain across which the Union divisions attacked is filled with houses. Just two blocks toward town, and parallel to the Sunken Road, is Littlepage Street, as far as any Union soldier advanced.

South of town, along the base of the line of hills, are preserved miles of Confederate trenches. Though development increases, the fields before them are mostly open and a sign marks Deep Run, a brook that winds from the hills to the Rappahannock. The Vermont Brigade fought along its banks.

THE SEVENTH AND EIGHTH
IN LOUISIANA

"This is the hardest place I ever saw. There is nothing here but sand, not hardly a spear of grass to be seen, nor even a stone, as far as the eye can see." A Vermont soldier thus recorded his first view of Ship Island, off the south coast of Mississippi, not far from where the Mississippi River emerges from its long delta and flows into the Gulf of Mexico. Rather early in the war it came into Union hands when captured by a force under command of a Vermonter, John W. Phelps of Brattleboro, who had led the first regiment Vermont sent to war. Vermont troops were soon headed its way, two full regiments with artillery. Some troops likened their first view of Ship Island to something snow-covered floating in the sea. The image fast faded when they got ashore.

Although the story of Vermont in the Civil War is often associated with the great battlefields of the East, Vermont troops did much fighting elsewhere. When Gov. Frederick Holbrook called the Seventh and Eighth regiments, their destinies were to take them far south. The Seventh passed the war in very southern climes. The Eighth spent most of the war in Louisiana, before coming north to join in the finale. Also dispatched to Louisiana were the First and Second Vermont batteries, both to spend their terms of service along the Gulf Coast.

The Eighth Vermont Regiment was organized late in the fall of 1861 as a part of the New England Division put together by Maj. Gen. Benjamin Butler, under whom the First Vermont had served early in the war. Butler went to Montpelier to offer command of the Eighth, at Governor Holbrook's recommendation, to Stephen Thomas of Bethel, the Democratic state senator who so enthusiastically supported Governor Fairbanks's call for the first Vermont war appropriation. While in Montpelier, Butler, who never missed a chance at a public appearance, spoke to the legislature: "The North will win," he assured, "for it can build ships, manufacture armament, supply food, run railroads. What can the South expect when it even depends on Vermont schoolmarms to teach it?"

Thomas, 51 and totally without military experience, accepted Butler's offer with some reluctance. But the six-term Vermont House member and two-term senator, twice the Democratic nominee for lieutenant governor, finally agreed and became the only Vermonter to command a three-year regiment a full three years. The *Rutland Courier* said on his appointment: "Colonel Thomas has no aristocratic airs or pomposity about him, but should the enemies of the Union come into hailing distance of the Eighth Vermont Regiment, they may expect to hear a second Ethan Allen exclaim, 'By the great eternal, let the old Stars and Stripes alone.'"

The regiment gathered at Brattleboro in January 1862. On March 4, after a cold encampment fraught with sickness, the regiment boarded a train for New York City. There it marched down to the East River docks and boarded two ships, the *Wallace* and the *James Hovey*. On board, sealed orders were opened revealing the regiment's destination to be Ship Island. Pvt. Rufus Kinsley sailed on the *Wallace*; his diary entries describe a long and difficult voyage.

> March 13. Seasick myself. O dear, sick enough: sea sick, and sick of the sea. Wish I were home, sugaring off for Aunt Elvira, or some of the girls....The air hot as harvest.
>
> March 14. Dead calm, and all hands dead sick. Ship surrounded by school of porpoise, highly tickled at the sight of Yankees, who looked, in their blueish hats and greenish coats, as they were sprawling around the decks and hanging over the rails, quite like a cargo of overgrown bullfrogs.
>
> March 16. Awakened at 2 in the morning, by the howling of the tempest, and the pitching of the ship, setting me on one end, and then suddenly on the other. Moveables lashed to their places, and the sick to their berths....Many were frightened out of their wits. Before noon storm abated.
>
> March 18. Getting over sea-sickness a little: have had a hard time of it; and have seen a sad sight this evening:—a poor old father burying his son at sea. E. L. Davis, of Co. I died at 9:15 p.m., and at 9:30 was thrown to the sharks....The body was wrapped in a blanket with iron slugs tied to the feet, and slid over the side on a plank.
>
> March 27. Made the Bahama islands: First land seen for seventeen days.....Terribly hot: most of us badly blistered.
>
> April 5. Made Ship Island, after having sailed four weeks, with almost nothing to eat, and much of the time with only a half pint of water per day.
>
> April 6 (Sunday). Six of the Maine boys were drowned while bathing. Bed of white sand as loose as meal. No floors to our tents. Found 10,000 troops on the island, and an enormous fort, mounting guns with bores as large as a flour barrel. Island nine miles long, and one-half mile wide at the west end; at the east end, two miles. East end covered with pine, and various other trees; inhabited by alligators, and all the snakes in the catalogue; besides wild fowl in abundance. A great variety of flowers. West end, all sand.

The Eighth endured a month on Ship Island as part of Butler's steadily growing force, which soon numbered more than 14,000 men. The aim was to capture the Confederacy's largest city, New Orleans, 75 miles away. One day a tropical storm nearly swamped the entire island, and on another the heavy booming of cannon was heard in the distance. Flag-officer David Farragut and his fleet, bristling with cannon, had sailed up the Mississippi River and attacked the two forts protecting the Crescent City. After a blazing night battle early on April 24, Farragut arrived at the New Orleans docks. The city surrendered. Soon thereafter General Butler brought his army of occupation upriver and disembarked among a most hostile populace.

General Butler, named by President Lincoln as military governor of Louisiana, was the epitome of a Yankee political general. Totally without military experience as the war began, Butler got a commission and a generalship purely because of his clout. A Massachusetts man with a genius for the maneuverings of politics, Butler went down in history as one of the war's inept generals. But he did know something about government and, when told to govern Louisiana, quickly brought the rebellious city of New Orleans under control. Early on, the locals gave him the nickname "Spoons" for his alleged pilfering. Later, they attached the name "Beast," which stuck for the rest of the war. Butler clamped martial law on New Orleans, took the local police force out of power, and replaced it with soldiers. The Vermonters briefly played New Orleans cops.

At the end of May the Eighth Vermont was ordered across the river to the town of Algiers, no more hospitable than New Orleans. Almost from the moment the Vermonters set foot there, escaped slaves came to their camp seeking refuge. One day a black man arrived closely followed by his master, who proceeded to beat him in front of the troops. The master was promptly thrown out of camp. Among the abolitionists in the ranks of the Eighth was the diarist Kinsley, who gave religious teaching to the escaped slaves. Kinsley recorded in his diary on June 17:

> Visited during the day several plantations, and saw enough of the horrors of slavery to make me an Abolitionist forever. On each plantation in all this section of country is a large building called a hospital, with only two rooms. In one may be seen the stocks, gnout, thumbscrew, ball and chain, rings and chain, by which victims are fastened flat to the floor; and others, by which they are bound to perpendicular posts; iron yokes of different patterns, hand cuffs, whips, and other instruments of torture, for the benefit of those who had been guilty of loving liberty more than life, but had failed in their efforts to obtain the coveted boon.

The numbers of slaves began to overwhelm the Eighth, and many were sent a half dozen miles upriver to General Phelps's headquarters, at Carrollton, where the Seventh Vermont Regiment camped. Phelps, at 50, a longtime army veteran, had once fought the Seminole Indians. But he had refused to participate in the Mexican War, viewing it as a move to gain slave territory. His abolitionist fervor continued unabated into 1862, and, back in the deep South, he not only welcomed fugitive slaves at Carrollton but also began drilling them. Word of this development spread like a fire alarm. Phelps, the Louisianans said, was a war criminal. He escalated tensions by asking for enough muskets to arm three black regiments, reasoning, in a letter to Butler:

> The negroes increase rapidly. There are doubtless now 600 able-bodied men in camp. These, added to those who are suffering uselessly in the prisons and jails of New Orleans and vicinity, and feeding from the general stock of provisions, would make a good regiment of 1,000 men, who might contribute as much to the preservation of law and order as a regiment of caucasians and probably much more. Now a mere burden, they might become a beneficent element of governmental power.

Butler, already the first Union commander to give refuge to slaves, back at Fort Monroe, and already dealing with a rebellious populace, denied the request. Phelps promptly resigned his commission and left the war. When this was announced to the troops, a ceremony was quickly organized on the camp parade ground. The men stood in formation while the regimental band played "Hail to the Chief." Some speeches were made, and the regiment, en masse, sang "Auld Lang Syne."

Phelps proved to be a man barely ahead of his time. Before many weeks had passed, Butler had a change of heart and, urged in part by Colonel Thomas, approved the training of black troops.

Not only was the Eighth Vermont charged with keeping order in Algiers, but it also was to help patrol the surrounding territory, a waterlogged, bayou-laced countryside full of local militia. In late June, 30 Vermonters, under Capt. Alvin Franklin of Newfane, went west on a locomotive and passenger car along the Opelousas and Great Western Railroad toward a station called Bayou des Allemands, to investigate reports that Confederates were tearing up track. As the train was moving through cane fields near Raceland, a horseman was seen crossing the tracks. The train stopped and a scouting party was sent ahead. It was an ambush. Bullets slammed into the train, hitting several men and killing the engineer. Captain Franklin was hit five times but remained in command, directing his men's return fire. Then he leaped from the train, ran through a hail of bullets to

Stephen Thomas led the Eighth Vermont.

Howard Coffin Collection

147

the locomotive and, with the help of the fireman, got it in reverse—just in time, for Confederates were tearing up track in the rear. The scouting party jumped aboard as the train moved out. The track wreckers were scattered before they could complete their job, and the train returned to friendly lines, with five men killed and seven wounded. It was the first taste of combat for the Eighth Vermont. Kinsley noted in his diary, "The dead and wounded brought in look bad, very bad."

The regiment spent a miserable summer in and around Algiers, affected by heat and sickness. In late August Colonel Thomas led 200 men toward Saint Charles Court House after hearing reports that enemy soldiers were rounding up cattle. Shots were exchanged, and Thomas came marching back, followed by 500 blacks, about 1,000 cattle, and hundreds of sheep and mules.

In midsummer Confederate Maj. Gen. Richard Taylor arrived in his native state to formalize and strengthen resistance to the occupying Yankees. He quickly took aim at the Federal garrison now at Bayou des Allemands and called in Texas cavalrymen. Reaching Boutte Station, Taylor surprised and captured the few men on duty. Then he and his men lay in wait for an approaching train, carrying some 60 men of the Eighth Vermont. The train was caught in a crossfire; all the men could have been lost, had it not been for the bravery of Pvt. Louis J. Ingalls, a Belvidere man. Seeing that a switch on the track had been thrown, Ingalls leaped from the train and ran ahead to correct the situation. He did, but took three bullets and a blast of buckshot. Ingalls lived, and the train got away, but only after 14 men were killed and 22 wounded.

The Confederates advanced toward Bayou des Allemands. Outnumbered, the defending detachment commander ran up the white flag. Colonel Thomas, who had started out from Algiers in a rescue attempt, was forced to turn back when his train hit a cow and derailed. At Bayou des Allemands, 138 men of his regiment surrendered. The prisoners were eventually marched to Vicksburg and paroled, with the exception of two soldiers, Privates Charles Wills of Randolph and Edward Spear of Braintree. They were held to be executed in reprisal for the execution of some Confederate guerrillas in Missouri. But Confederate president Jefferson Davis intervened. Wills made it back to his unit, but Spear died before returning to Union lines. Far less lucky were seven captured soldiers of German descent who had joined the Eighth Vermont at New Orleans. The Confederates charged them with desertion, claiming they had previously enlisted in Southern units. On October 23 Bernard Hurst, Diedrich Bahne, John Leichleider, Michael Leichleider, Michael Mosman, Frank Paul, and Gustave Becker were executed. They were lined up and shot next to graves they were forced to dig, according to Thomas, who questioned some prisoners.

A well-regarded young Union general, Godfrey Weitzel, now entered the action. Out of West Point seven years, he was familiar with the region, having done engineering for the US government at New Orleans before the war. As fall came, Weitzel set in motion a western expedition aimed at bringing some of the unruly countryside under firm Union control. Colonel Thomas and the Eighth

Vermont were ordered to move back through Bayou des Allemands and beyond. To make certain the colonel had a force adequate for this venture into hostile territory, Weitzel gave him 1,000 additional men—members of the First Regiment Louisiana Native Guards, all blacks. On September 24 Thomas took his Eighth and the Native Guards out along the railroad line. It took three days to reach Bayou des Allemands. Thomas later wrote, "The command pulled the luxuriant grass from over 20 miles of track, built eighteen culverts from 10 to 20 feet in length; rebuilt what was estimated as four miles of track; rebuilt a bridge 470 feet long; drove the enemy from the road, and captured seven cannon, all in one week."

There were signs that Confederate soldiers were nearby. When the expedition reached Bayou des Allemands, the black regiment was assembled at the station, and Colonel Thomas mounted a railroad car and ordered quiet. Then he spoke, and though his exact words have been lost, he said that everyone should expect to face combat soon and that when the fighting began, those before him would at long last have the opportunity to begin avenging the vast history of wrongs long committed against their race. Then Thomas gave a stern warning: when the fighting started, any man who flinched would be shot on the spot. Out in that canebrake clearing deep in the snaky bayou country of old Louisiana, the black soldiers began to cheer. They were more than ready to fight.

Thomas ended the meeting and got his men in marching order, blacks and whites shouldering rifle-muskets and heading off side by side to war. He might have recalled some words once spoken by Frederick Douglass: "Once let the black man get upon his person the brass letters, 'U.S.,' let him get an eagle on his buttons and a musket on his shoulder and bullets in his pocket, and there is no power on earth which can deny that he has earned the right of citizenship in the United States."

The Vermonters and their new comrades at arms never found any Confederates to fight, so the testing of blacks in battle would have to wait.

After more hard labor repairing railroads, the expedition came to rest in early December at Brashear City, 50 miles west of Algiers. The Vermonters remained there more than a month. As the old year ended, they got news that General Butler had been relieved of his Louisiana command, to be replaced by Maj. Gen. Nathaniel Banks, under whom the Vermont cavalry had served in the Shenandoah Valley. The men of the Eighth seemed sad to see old "Beast" go. But back in the camp of the Seventh Vermont, the men cheered.

Bidding the black regiment farewell, the Eighth received orders to join an expedition commanded by General Weitzel. Some 4,000 men, with gunboats for cover, were to deal with a heavily armed Confederate gunboat, *Cotton*, which had been harassing Union troops and shipping along a bayou west of Brashear City. Weitzel found the ship in mid-January, and in action remembered as the Battle of the *Cotton*, the Vermonters, protected by sharpshooters, overran Confederate rifle pits protecting the warship. Rufus Kinsley described the battle's end in his diary:

After firing a few shots, we charged on the rifle pits, and took 37 prisoners and 45 guns with ammunition. We found 100 rifle pits, occupied by 150 of the enemy's sharpshooters; but our numbers were so few that most of them made their escape. Cotton by this time badly disabled and backing off up the bay, which, for some miles along here is only 400 to 1,000 feet wide. Our party deployed as skirmishers, and followed her, with Colonel Thomas and men in supporting distance in the rear. When near the Cotton, a rebel battery on the other side, before undiscovered, under cover of which the cotton lay, opened upon us with vigor, filling the air with bursting bombs and solid shot, which mowed the cane on every side.

The Vermonters were forced to withdraw. But that night, in Kinsley's words, "We were startled from our very pleasant dreams at three this morning, by an explosion, which proved to be the Cotton, which had burned her magazine and then blew up. The end of our expedition being then accomplished, we returned to Brashear City, the sharpshooters of the 8th being honored with a passage on one of the gunboats."

In his official report of the action, General Weitzel wrote: "The Eighth Vermont, Colonel Thomas,…reflected the highest credit upon itself by the splendid manner in which they cleared the enemy's rifle pits on the east bank and afterwards pursued them. This regiment took 41 prisoners, three wounded, and killed four of the enemy. This regiment lost none, because it flanked and surprised the enemy completely."

Not long after the battle, while the Eighth was resting, it was placed officially in General Weitzel's brigade. The regiment, for the rest of the war, would be a part of a new army corps, the 19th. As spring 1863 arrived, the Eighth Vermont was ordered by General Banks to march west through Louisiana, on a major expedition involving many thousands of men. In a fight at Bisland, one Vermonter was killed and seven wounded. The inconclusive engagement produced a report by a correspondent for the *Boston Traveller* who wrote:

But two or three officers remained on their horses. Among them, very conspicuously sat, perfectly upright and still, Colonel Thomas of the Eighth Vermont. His regiment was at the extreme right, and supported A battery where the shot fell the thickest. Not a single man ran, or showed any disposition to do so. Twice during the heavy cannonading, General Weitzel sent Lieutenant Smith of his staff to warn the colonel that he was exposing himself unduly, and begging him to dismount. The reply of the great-hearted officer was: 'Colonel Thomas sends his compliment to General Weitzel, and begs to inform him that he did not come down here to get off his horse for any damned rebels.'

As Thomas rode slowly along his line of battle, he repeated the words, "Steady, men. Stand firm. Old Vermont is looking at you."

General Grant's forces were fighting up along the Mississippi, maneuvering to capture the Confederate stronghold on the high bluffs at Vicksburg and to bring the river under Union control. Grant needed General Banks's men. Soon they were on their way, in the heat of another Louisiana summer, toward a fortified town called Port Hudson, and a long siege.

The other Vermont regiment in Louisiana, the Seventh, had already advanced on Vicksburg and come back sick and discouraged. The Seventh had arrived in the South after its organization by Governor Holbrook late in 1861. The unit gathered at the Rutland Fairgrounds the following February of 1862, where the manager of a local marble quarry, George T. Roberts, took command. The regiment's major was William C. Holbrook of Brattleboro, the governor's son. These Vermonters, too, were assigned as part of General Butler's New England division and ordered to New Orleans, an assignment the men vainly protested. In the ranks of the Seventh were a large number of men who had served in the First Vermont, under Butler around Fort Monroe, and they did not have fond memories of the man.

They, like the Eighth, endured an arduous sea voyage to Ship Island. On arrival, they immediately got in trouble with General Butler, who felt they took too long coming ashore. The Vermonters insisted, against orders, on bringing all their equipment, which proved a wise decision when a bad storm struck days later. Butler took great umbrage at what he considered a personal affront; and old "Beast" was not the forgiving kind. The Seventh Vermont would pay a price for crossing Ben Butler.

The Seventh was assigned to General Phelps's command and directed to Carrollton, six miles up the Mississippi from New Orleans. There it remained until early June, spending considerable time taking in the blacks who came to camp in search of freedom. In mid-June General Butler issued an ill-conceived order: "Proceed to Vicksburg...take the town or have it burned at all hazards." To seize the Gibraltar of the Mississippi, he assigned a fleet under Admiral Farragut and just 4,000 soldiers, including the Seventh Vermont, all under the command of Gen. Thomas Williams. The small army was put ashore across the river from the Confederate citadel, with orders to dig a canal through a narrow neck of land where the Mississippi made a great bend. They were, in effect, to divert the river from Vicksburg and the Confederate fortress's guns, leave the place high and dry and thus make its capture unnecessary. To help, some 1,200 blacks from nearby plantations were brought in to aid in the digging. It was a hopeless task.

As summer wore on, the Vermonters, encamped among stagnant pools in the growing heat, began to get sick. Malaria spread in the mosquito-filled lowlands; soon, nearly everybody was prostrate. The digging went on, and the men christened the canal "Butler's Ditch." The Mississippi would not cooperate; before a halt was called, only about 100 Vermonters of the 750 who had gone up to Vicksburg were fit for duty. Finally, the attempt at Vicksburg was abandoned and the Seventh Vermont moved its sick to an embarkation point. Surgeon Enoch Blanchard of Lyndon descibed the departure: "By some means, I scarcely know how, we got 300 sick and helpless men over to the levee opposite Vicksburg, without tents or blankets, and without food or medicines. Just at night it began to rain in a drizzling sort of way. I managed to get a limited supply of crackers and tea and spent the night wading through the mud distributing these articles of nourishment."

General Williams withdrew his depleted force down the river to Baton Rouge. They didn't rest long, because a Confederate force of 5,000, under Gen. John C. Breckinridge, was immediately dispatched toward Baton Rouge with orders to seize the town. Waiting were but 2,500 Union troops. General Williams, a Mexican War veteran, was not at his best and his defenses were poorly prepared. But when the Confederates arrived, their numbers had also been severely reduced by sickness. Nevertheless, on August 5, they attacked through a morning fog. The result was a confused battle, most especially for the Vermonters.

When it began, the Seventh Vermont, with less than 250 able to fight, was posted toward the right of the long Union battle line. But as the action developed, the Vermonters were shifted by General Williams to the left, where the Confederate pressure was developing most heavily. The Seventh was actually posted in a second battle line, somewhat behind an Indiana regiment. The Confederates stormed in, and the rifle fire got more and more intense. At some point, General Williams rode up and found that the Vermonters weren't firing. He asked why not and was told they feared hitting the Indianians. Williams gave the order to fire and the Vermonters obeyed. From the foggy woods to the front hurried an Indiana soldier, protesting that his men were getting hit. Major Holbrook described the action:

> At this time the fog and smoke was so thick that it was next to impossible. Colonel Fullam, who had gone forward to reconnoiter and to ascertain, if possible, the position of the 21st Indiana, was unable to locate it with certainty, and could only learn that it had moved further to the right. About the same time some of Manning's guns went into battery in rear of the regiment and opened an indiscriminate fire which greatly endangered our position. Finding the men were so exposed as to be subjected to a heavier fire from our own troops behind than from the enemy in front Colonel Roberts moved the regiment back to its original position in front of the camp.

A bullet hit Roberts in the neck and, as he was carried to the rear, another hit him in the stomach. The colonel died two agonizing days later. Meanwhile, off to the Vermonters' right, General Williams went down with a fatal wound. The Confederate attack was finally halted with the help of Union gunboats in the Mississippi River. The Battle of Baton Rouge ended with a Confederate repulse and a narrow Union victory. Less than a month later, Baton Rouge was abandoned to the Confederates.

But the battle was far from over for the Vermonters. Four days after the firing stopped, an order came from General Butler's headquarters, signed by the general himself. It read, in part:

The commanding general has carefully reviewed the official reports of the action of August 5th at Baton Rouge, to collect the evidence of the gallant deeds and meritorious services of those engaged in that brilliant victory. The name of the lamented and gallant General Williams has already passed into history. Colonel Roberts of the Seventh Vermont volunteers, fell mortally wounded rallying his men. He was worthy of a better disciplined regiment and a better fate. Glorious as it is to die for one's country, yet his regiment gave him the inexpressible pain of seeing it break in confusion when not pressed by the enemy and refuse to march to the aid of the outnumbered and almost overwhelmed Indianians. The Seventh Vermont regiment, by a fatal mistake, had already fired into the same regiment they had refused to support, killing and wounding several. The commanding general therefore excepts the Seventh Vermont from General Orders No. 57, and will not permit their colors to be inscribed with a name (Battle of Baton Rouge) which could bring to its officers and men no proud thought. It is further ordered that the colors of that regiment be not borne by them until such time as they shall have earned the right to them, and the earliest opportunity will be given this regiment to show whether they are worthy descendants of those who fought beside Allen and with Starke at Bennington.

Butler's censure was harsh. Colonel Holbrook, having been promoted to replace the dead Colonel Roberts as regimental commander, went immediately to Butler and protested, to no avail.

The news soon reached Governor Holbrook who declared, "these charges are believed to be grossly unjust and have stirred up the people of Vermont."

A court of inquiry was demanded and held; Colonel Holbrook charged it was comprised of Butler's people. It found that the Vermonters had not abandoned their colors, as had been alleged. As a result, permission was given for the regiment to carry its colors again. But the court held firm on disallowing the name of Baton Rouge to be added to those colors. The Seventh Vermont was disheartened. The regiment had, after all, suffered much on the long sea voyage, on Ship Island, at Vicksburg, and then in battle at Baton Rouge.

After Baton Rouge, the Seventh returned to Carrollton, where the encampment was christened Camp Williams, in honor of the deceased general. But the men quickly gave it another name, "Camp Death," as disease took a heavy toll in the swampy location. Finally, late in September, the regiment was ordered to sea again. The Seventh Vermont was bound for Pensacola, Florida, where it would spend most of the rest of the war, with mosquitos generally a greater threat than rebels.

MORE VERMONT TROOPS
IN VIRGINIA

As the second winter of the war deepened, more Vermonters than ever before were in the war zone: 15 infantry regiments, a cavalry regiment, 3 companies of sharpshooters, and 2 artillery companies.

The Army of the Potomac, including the Vermont Brigade, went into winter camp on the north bank of the Rappahannock River, still recovering from the disastrous encounter at Fredericksburg and the subsequent exertions of the Mud March. Wilbur Fisk of the Second Vermont wrote:

One can hardly suppress a feeling of regret, to see land so fair so ruthlessly destroyed by the demon of war. Miles on miles of as finely timbered country as was ever produced, are stripped, laid waste, bared to the earth wherever the army has been. Fences have been converted into fuel, and houses without number burned to the ground. Universal ruin is marked everywhere. It cannot be otherwise. Soldiers will not respect forest nor fences when they are benumbed with cold, nor will they be content to take any less than their needs require for the sake of economy or to spare the pockets or the homes of the secesh [i.e., secessionist] inhabitants. Virginia is a guilty state, and her day of retribution seems to be at hand.

Just south of the Rappahannock was Robert E. Lee's Army of Northern Virginia; the opposing armies lived rather peaceably through the winter, separated by the wide river. At times, Union and Confederate soldiers crossed over to exchange conversation, newspapers, and tobacco. The Vermonters in winter camp made small huts with fireplaces and kept as warm as possible. But once again, they were hit by disease, though less severely than during the previous winter. The army was better cared for, better supplied and organized, thanks to

A. A. Carter sketched the Fourth Vermont on the Mud March.

its new commander, Joseph Hooker. Fisk saw him during a grand review of the Army of the Potomac and wrote:

> He is not at all such a looking man as one would associate with the name of "fighting Joe." He has a smooth, pleasing countenance, light hair, a keen eye, though not so piercing, perhaps, as McClellan. He looks more like some venerated minister of the Gospel than a General. But I had not the opportunity to get a very distinct impression of him. I only saw him as he rode rapidly by the ranks, viewing each regiment in front and rear. If I was to give my own impression of the man, I should call him of a mild, good-natured disposition, not at all rash or reckless, as some seem to have an idea....I like the appearance of the old hero very much.

Hooker reorganized his army and the War Department shipped McClellan's friend, "Baldy" Smith, off to Pennsylvania. In his place, as commander of the Sixth Corps, Hooker chose a longtime army veteran who had distinguished himself at Antietam. John Sedgwick, a Connecticut Yankee, was named commander of the Vermont Brigade's corps; "Uncle John" quickly earned his men's admiration. Under Sedgwick, the Sixth Corps badge, its square-proportioned Greek cross insignia, became one of the most famous corps symbols in the Union armies.

In February 1863 the Vermont Brigade itself got a new commander when the unpopular Col. Henry Whiting resigned from the army. He was replaced by Col. Lewis A. Grant, a Brattleboro native risen to command of the Second Vermont Regiment despite having had no military experience prior to the war. But Grant was a born fighter, and one Vermont infantryman said of the new commander, "Grant is as proud of his men as his men are proud of him."

There had also been changes at the regimental level. The five regiments were now commanded as follows:

Second Regiment: James H. Walbridge of Bennington, who had taken that one company out all by itself at the first battle of Bull Run and even refused George Stannard's entreaties to return to the line.

Third Regiment: Col. Thomas O. Seaver of Pomfret, who also had gained a reputation for bravery under fire while serving as a company commander.

Fourth Regiment: Col. Charles B. Stoughton of Bellows Falls, a West Pointer, had replaced his brother Edwin. The brother had been appointed commander of the newly formed Second Vermont Brigade.

Fifth Regiment: Lt. Col. John R. Lewis of Burlington, who had been second in command to Grant and then had risen to succeed him when Grant was named Vermont Brigade commander.

Lewis A. Grant, last commander of the Old Brigade.

Sixth Regiment: Col. Elisha L. Barney of Swanton, who had gotten his baptism of fire along the Warwick River.

The Vermont Brigade spent a rather uneventful winter along the Rappahannock, keeping a watchful eye on the Confederates, shivering on the far bank of the river (about as wide as the Winooski west of Waterbury).

A memorable battle, in which nobody on either side was killed, took place in February when the new regiment in the Old Brigade, the 26th New Jersey, challenged the Third and Fourth Vermont Regiments to a snowball fight. The 26th was a big regiment, numbering as many men as both Vermont units, so the battle was about even, at least in numbers. Combat was set for February 25, and a huge crowd of soldiers lined the field. The men were put into line of battle by their officers, skirmishers were advanced, and the fighting began. The Vermonters, as was their custom, went in hard. These farm boys had grown up flinging snowballs on school playgrounds, and the fight was over rather quickly. The two Vermont regiments even captured the colonel, adjutant, and quartermaster of the New Jersey regiment and their horses.

The New Jersey men were also bested in another way during the winter encampment. The Second Vermont had been experiencing an annoying and continuous loss of fresh meat from its regimental store. Some of the men came to believe that the meat was being taken by members of the 26th New Jersey. One night Vermonters crept into the New Jersey camp and pilfered the commander's pet Newfoundland dog. When they returned to camp, the dog was slaughtered and dressed, then hung in the tent of the Second Vermont quartermaster's store. That night the carcass disappeared, and the thieves' tracks were followed to the New Jersey camp. The Vermont soldiers figured that dog meat was henceforth on the New Jersey menu, perhaps even the regimental commander's table. The story quickly spread through the ranks of the Army of the Potomac, and for a time the New Jersey men were greeted with woofs and bow-wows.

In early April President Lincoln joined his new commander, General Hooker, in a review of the Army of the Potomac, with a strength of 113,000 men. The Vermont brigade contained 3,343 of that number, though winter sickness left about half confined to tents or hospital. Wilbur Fisk wrote:

> We were reviewed by President Lincoln last Wednesday. The honorable gentle-man looked thin and careworn. No doubt it would be a great relief to him as well as to the country at large if the nation was free from the dire calamity of civil war. Perhaps my immagination added the unusual paleness to his cheek, and the expression of care that his countenance wore, but, certainly, as he passed by where we were standing, and I had a chance to see his face fully, I for the moment, doubted the statement, so often made in newspapers, lately, that our President is enjoying the finest health and the best of spirits.

The Old Brigade was no longer the only Vermont brigade in the war. In response to Lincoln's call, Governor Holbrook had called up the Second Vermont Brigade. It consisted, like the Old Brigade, of five regiments: the 12th, 13th, 14th, 15th, and 16th. The men were enlisted for just nine months, but their terms would cover, just barely, the three days of one of the two most important battles of the war. The Second Vermont Brigade numbered nearly 5,000 men when it was organized. Command was given to Edwin H. Stoughton, who had previously led the Third Vermont Regiment. Like his brother, Stoughton was a West Point graduate from Bellows Falls, also trained as a lawyer. Nobody ever questioned Stoughton's bravery, but within a very short time many questioned his common sense.

The commanders of the five regiments were as follows:

12th Regiment: Col. Asa P. Blunt of St. Johnsbury, a combat veteran having served with the Third Vermont and then with the Sixth Vermont as its second in command.
13th Regiment: Col. Francis V. Randall of Montpelier, a veteran of 15 months' service in the Old Brigade. Randall was a lawyer in Montpelier when the war began, had served two terms as Roxbury's representative to the legislature, and had been state's attorney of Washington County.
14th Regiment: Col. William T. Nichols of Rutland, the first man to respond when William Ripley organized his Rutland Light Guard when the war broke out. He had fought at Big Bethel and then been elected to the legislature.
15th Regiment: Col. Redfield Proctor of Cavendish. A Dartmouth College and Albany Law School graduate, Proctor was a law partner of his cousin Isaac Redfield in Boston when the war began. He served as an officer in the Third Vermont, then

was on Gen. William F. Smith's staff but fell sick and had to return home. Recovered, he was given command of a regiment.

16th Regiment: Col. Wheelock G. Veazey of Springfield, another Dartmouth graduate, had just opened a law office in Springfield when the war began. He too had served on "Baldy" Smith's staff and had for a time, during the Peninsula Campaign, commanded the Fifth Vermont.

The Second Vermont Brigade arrived in late October to set up camp at Springbank, a Virginia plantation the soldiers named Camp Vermont. On December 7 General Stoughton took command; a few days later, the brigade was moved to the vicinity of Burke Station, several miles south of a crossroads village known as Fairfax Court House.

In Virginia at this time were three other Vermont regiments. The Ninth, with George Stannard commanding and Edwin Hastings Ripley second in command, had at long last been released from confinement at Camp Douglas in Chicago. In late March the regiment had boarded trains to escort 2,500 Confederate prisoners to City Point, not far from Richmond, where they were exchanged for Union prisoners. In mid-April the Ninth took position near Suffolk, some 20 miles southwest of Norfolk, where the Confederate generals James Longstreet and D. H. Hill had suddenly appeared.

A Ripley commanded the Ninth Vermont, and another Ripley almost commanded the 10th. But the severe wound William Ripley had received at Malvern Hill was still making his life miserable when, in the late summer of 1862, he was offered command of the new 10th Vermont. Ripley was forced to refuse, so Alfred A. B. Jewett, a Swanton native, was given the colonelcy. Jewett had been a business partner of Elisha Barney, now commander of the Sixth Vermont. He was a veteran of the First Vermont and Big Bethel.

The 10th gathered at Brattleboro, then moved to Washington in the late summer of 1862. Sent west of the capital for guard duty along the Chesapeake and Ohio Canal, it heard the distant rumble of cannon from the Antietam campaign. The campground was muddy and sickly, and five men died of disease almost immediately. The 10th was made part of Washington's outer defenses, quartered west of the city where the Monocacy River enters the Potomac. The regiment spent a quiet winter on the banks of a river destined to give its name to a battle in which the 10th would play an important part.

Another new regiment, the 11th

Alfred Jewett organized the 10th Vermont.

VHS

Vermont soldier (probably Lyman Labbarree of Underhill) with Sixth Corps cross.

Vermont, was also in the field as the war's second winter came early for Virginia, with snow six inches deep by mid-November. Its commander was James M. Warner of Middlebury, West Point class of 1860. He had served as quartermaster at Fort Wise in Colorado under post commander John Sedgwick and had taken command when Sedgwick went East to fight. Warner was 26 when assigned to the 10th Vermont, which reached Washington in September to garrison the city's fortifications. There was a shortage of artillerymen, so as winter began, the 11th Vermont Infantry became the First Artillery, 11th Vermont Volunteers. Infantrymen became cannoneers. The troops out on the frontlines had a disdain for men who served around the capital. Because they manned heavy artillery, did little marching, and supposedly got plenty to eat, the fighting troops called them "the heavies." The 11th Vermont spent the winter of 1862–63 and much time thereafter in the defenses of Washington, well out of action.

The First Vermont Cavalry had been almost constantly active since it contested "Stonewall" Jackson's Valley Campaign. After retreating from the valley with Banks's beaten army, it regrouped north of the Potomac, then made a series of probes into northern Virginia, some into the Shenandoah Valley, where there were brushes with the enemy. For a while the Vermonters became part of a command led by the noted cavalryman John Buford, destined for fame at Gettysburg. During John Pope's failed campaign that ended at Bull Run, the Vermont cavalry rode down to Gordonsville and got in a fight with the Virginia cavalry. The Virginians got the early advantage until some Vermonters led by Capt. William Wells formed a line and held it. Then several Vermonters got shot in a skirmish at Orange Court House. The Vermont cavalry missed the big battles at Cedar Mountain and Bull Run but was almost constantly in the saddle; when things quieted down late in August, one company commander, Capt. Addison Preston of Danville, wrote: "I have but 24 men fit for duty. The rest are worn out. We have had scarcely a moment's rest night or day since the battle of Cedar Mountain. Sometimes we have been in front of the enemy, sometimes in his rear. Twice we have marched for miles with one divison of the rebel army in our front and another close in our rear, on the same road." By the end of August the regiment had just 400 men fit for duty, less than half its full compliment.

In late September the Vermont horsemen went on a reconnaissance to the Blue Ridge Mountains and found Ashby's Gap held by Confederates. The Vermonters charged and, though met by a sudden blast of rifle fire, broke the Confederate line. In the charge, company commander Preston had burst through the enemy's front and rear lines when two Confederates with pistols drawn wedged him between them and began to ride away. Preston hit one Confederate with the hilt of his sword. The other fired, hitting the Vermonter in the right arm as another shot grazed his side. But Preston got away and just managed to reach Union lines before he fainted from loss of blood.

Early in the winter the regiment was withdrawn closer to Washington, where patroling and skirmishing continued. Soon 500 fresh and badly needed Vermont horses arrived, mostly Morgans. In early January a new company arrived from Vermont, putting the regiment back near a full compliment of 1,034 men and horses. There would be little rest for the Vermont cavalry during the winter months.

In winter camp the men sang a song that looked to the time "when this cruel war is over." It wasn't over, not by half. And the worst was yet to come.

EDWIN STOUGHTON AND
JOHN MOSBY

Not long after the war, Herman Melville visited the scenes of battle in Virginia and, returning to New England, wrote a group of Civil War poems. One, "The Scout toward Aldie," describes a Union cavalry patrol riding into country known to be frequented by a Confederate partisan commander named Mosby. Melville likened the countryside to shark-infested water, an apt comparison, for much of northern Virginia, particularly south and west of Washington out to the Blue Ridge Mountains, was known during the Civil War as Mosby's Confederacy. Lt. Col. John Singleton Mosby, a lawyer turned soldier, led a band of some 800 partisan fighters, usually operating in small groups. His domain was gentle farmland dotted by small villages, and his men worked those farms and peopled those villages. They were part-time soldiers, quiet folk by day who took up pistol and sword by night when summoned to some secret rendezvous by quiet word of mouth sent forth by their leader. They would emerge as if out of the Virginia soil to attack some unsuspecting Union force. Mosby and his rangers became the bane of the existence of thousands of Union soldiers, and in the winter of 1862–63 a lot of Vermonters got to know Mosby, especially one young general of infantry.

As winter began the Vermont cavalry had returned to full strength after a hard-riding and -fighting summer and fall. John W. Woodward, son of the cavalry's fighting chaplain, John H. Woodward, arrived with reinforcements, a newly organized cavalry company. Young Woodward had enlisted in August 1862 upon graduating from the University of Vermont. He stayed in Vermont several months helping to organize a company of horsemen, which elected him its leader, then said good-bye to his Westford home and the young lady he planned to marry.

The Vermont cavalrymen were patrolling Mosby's Confederacy, many stationed in small groups at isolated picket posts, on lonely and risky duty. On March 2, 1863 two companies of cavalry, one under the newly arrived Captain Woodward, went looking for Mosby on a scout toward Aldie. Receiving a report that no enemy were in the village, they rode in and dismounted to feed their horses in the yard of a gristmill. Some of the troopers took their mounts to a nearby blacksmith for shoes. Suddenly Mosby himself and about 30 horsemen came pounding up to the mill and quickly made 16 Vermonters their prisoners. The rest jumped on their horses and scattered for the countryside—all except Captain Woodward.

Before Mosby's arrival Woodward, uneasy, had ridden alone outside the village for a look around. On hearing shots he started back, to be met at a bridge by two of Mosby's men. A bullet struck Woodward's horse, which fell on the young officer, pinning him to the ground. A Confederate rode up close, firing his pistol, until the Vermonter managed to draw his own pistol and shoot the man dead. As others closed in to finish off Woodward, John Mosby appeared and put a stop to it. Impressed by Woodward's bravery, the Confederate commander ordered the wounded cavalryman taken to a nearby house and put to bed. Mosby and his men then rode away with their prisoners, the Confederate later saying that Woodward had killed one of his best men. Young Woodward was soon out of bed and back with his company.

Other members of the First Vermont Cavalry had another firsthand encounter with Mosby a few days later. A detachment of 25 was just ending 48 hours of picket duty at an isolated post, near the hamlet of Herndon Station, when 50 horsemen were seen approaching. The tired Vermonters were lounging around a sawmill and took little notice, for the men in front wore blue coats. Then shots came from the bluecoats; the Vermonters took cover in an old sawmill. The Confederates began firing into the mill, badly wounding one Vermonter. Mosby shouted that unless the men in the tinder-dry mill quickly gave up, the place would be burned. The Vermonters surrendered.

At that moment, in a nearby house, five Vermont cavalry officers were having dinner. They had been in the area as part of a commission, investigating charges that some Yankee soldiers had been stealing from local civilians. Mosby's men saw the Vermonters' horses, surrounded the house, and captured all five men. Among them was William Wells, who had joined the Vermont cavalry as a private as the unit was forming in Burlington. He had reached the rank of major, but now his fast-rising military career was interrupted, for Mosby sent him to Libby Prison with the other four Vermont officers. They would spend two months in that filthy and overcrowded tobacco warehouse near the Richmond waterfront before being exchanged. Wells wrote a letter home while under guard: "Today about 1 p.m....Just as we got through eating we heard a yell and pistol shots. Upon looking out the window we saw about 50 men, Confederates, Mosby. We are on the road to Richmond."

In late March 130 Vermont horsemen under Capt. Henry Flint of Irasburg rode toward Leesburg on being told that Mosby was in the vicinity. Mosby was indeed nearby, bedded down with 80 of his men in the fence-enclosed barnyard of a farmer named Haskel. The Vermonters almost had Mosby. But one of his men had decided to spend the night at a farmhouse a couple of miles down the road. Seeing the Vermonters ride past, he cut cross-country to warn his commander. When the Vermonters charged, Mosby's rangers were ready, just barely. The Confederates fired from behind fences, and the Vermonters, who attacked before their full force arrived, had no chance. Six bullets hit Captain Flint and he fell dead. Those who were not shot turned their horses and tried to get away.

Mosby's men gave chase, and a running fight ensued for several miles down the road toward Dranesville. When it ended, 7 Vermonters were dead, 22 wounded, and 82 captured. Mosby also took 95 good Vermont horses. These Vermont prisoners were also taken to Richmond, then exchanged a month later. Through the winter the Vermont cavalrymen stood a wary watch on Mosby's Confederacy, patrolling deep into enemy territory toward Aldie, Leesburg, and Catlett's Station.

Mosby saved his greatest triumph of the winter for the nearly 5,000 nine-month enlistees of the Second Vermont Brigade and their commander, just-appointed Brig. Gen. Edwin H. Stoughton. Soon after arriving from Vermont the brigade was posted 15 miles southwest of Washington near the country cross-roads known as Burke Station or Fairfax Court House. In late December Mosby joined cavalry commander Jeb Stuart on a raid that took them near the courthouse. The venture amounted to little, for Stuart's approach was discovered; some Vermont soldiers contributed to its failure by firing on the approaching

Edwin Stoughton, left, brother Charles, center, and Col. Harry Worthen, pictured in Virginia by Houghton.

Confederates. Still, Mosby had a good look at the Vermont lines and found them porous enough for a small unit to slip through.

The Second Vermont Brigade was guarding a seven-mile front below Fairfax Court House when heavy snow fell. The troopers snuggled down in log huts abandoned by other Union soldiers. The Second's General Stoughton certainly kept warm; he set up headquarters in the village of Fairfax Court House in the comfortable brick house of a Dr. William Gunnell. Then he invited his mother and his sisters down from Bellows Falls. With a regimental band at his beck and call, Stoughton was fond of inviting friends and dignitaries to join him in reviewing the troops.

The goings-on at Stoughton's comfortable headquarters caused grumbling, according to the historian T. D. Seymour Bassett: "He galloped about on his fine horse, occupied a handsome house, and lived the life of Riley....He gave splendid dinner parties at his quarters in Fairfax Court House, and an invitation to be his guest was considered a great distinction....He had in his house ma, sisters, two New York ladies and a piano."

In retrospect it seems clear that Stoughton lacked sufficient maturity for the position he held. But a convivial life-style was not rare in Union headquarters: Joe Hooker, over on the Rappahannock, was having a fine old time as the winter wore on. Still, Stoughton should have known better. He was, after all, a graduate of the US Military Academy, class of 1859. At 23 he had commanded the Fourth Vermont through the Peninsula Campaign, said to be the youngest colonel in the entire army. His men didn't like him much, and long after the war a private in the Second Brigade, Alonzo Sherman of Underhill, recalled that Stoughton made himself unpopular by arresting soldiers for failure to salute properly. "The Vermont boys at the time were more accustomed to getting up a winter's woodpile than they were to giving the regular army salute," Sherman said.

The soldiers also noted that the general did not seem to be paying much attention to his own safety; if he weren't careful, he might just be "gobbled" some night. The brigade outposts some three miles out were supposed to serve as headquarters security, but as Mosby had observed, they were scattered. "The risk of such an operation has been apparent even to the privates," wrote George Benedict in the 12th Vermont, "and has been a matter of frequent remarks among officers and men, for weeks past. How could they protect him as long as he kept his headquarters at such a distance from them?"

The Confederate raider, with 30 handpicked men, left Aldie at nightfall on March 8, bound for Fairfax Court House. The night was very dark, and a misty rain fell on the snowy fields. John Mosby lived until 1916, and late in life wrote a reminiscence of that night for a popular magazine:

> On account of the muddy roads we kept on the pike until we got within two or three miles of the camps; then we turned off and passed through a gap in the line between them. We could see campfires to the left and to the right, but no one challenged us. The soldiers in their tents were peacefully dreaming; occasionally an owl hooted, and a rabbit on its nocturnal rounds went skipping before us....

The Gunnell House where Mosby siezed Stoughton.

It was about two o'clock in the morning when we entered the town. No sentinel halted us; all who saw us in the dark thought we were their own cavalry. We were dressed in gray; but one color could not be distinguished from another. There were a few guards in town; they made no resistance....

We halted at the court house, and I divided the command into squads and sent them out to gather prisoners and horses. We found the telegraph operator sleeping in a tent, and took him, as we did not want him to send off any messages about us. We cut the wires. With six men I rode to Stoughton's headquarters. There were several tents in the yard, but the tenants were asleep. I knocked on the front door, a window above opened, and someone asked, "Who are you?" There was an answer, "Fifth New York Cavalry, with dispatches for General Stoughton."

A staff officer, Lieutenant Prentiss, in his night-dress, opened the door. I whispered my name in his ear, and told him to go with me to Stoughton's room. He led the way upstairs. We found the man of war in bed dreaming like the Turk when Markos Bozzaris waked him up. I did not stand on ceremony, but after striking a light gave the General a spank. He rose and in an imperious tone asked, "What does this mean?" I told him who I was; that Stuart's cavalry was in possession of the town; that Jackson was at Centreville; and bade him dress quickly. He asked me to take him to Fitz Lee; they had been cadets together at West Point.

Mosby and his men spent about an hour in Fairfax Court House. When they left, they took General Stoughton, a handful of officers, 15 privates of whom several were Vermonters, and 55 horses. As the procession rode out of the village, Lt. Col. Robert Johnstone of the Fifth New York Cavalry, staying in a nearby house with his wife, came to the doorway in his birthday suit to inquire of the horsemen who they were. Realizing they were Confederates, he turned and ran back through the house and into the backyard, where he dove under the outhouse. Mosby sent men in pursuit, to no avail. The party moved on into the countryside as the sky began to lighten. Not long before dawn, Mosby's raiders and their prisoners passed through the Federal lines and on to safety.

Mosby delivered his prisoners to Culpeper and Brig. Gen. Fitzhugh Lee, nephew of Robert E. Lee, who had indeed known Stoughton at West Point. Lee

On Road to Richmond
March 17 1863 10 P.M.

Bro Charles

To day about
1 P.M. Capt Scoville Co F
Lt Cheny Co C & myself
started to visit picests at
Herndon, just as we got
ready to leave Mr Hanes
offered to give us some
Dinner, just as we
got through eating we
heard a yell & pistol shots
upon looking out the window
we saw about 50 men
Confederates. Mosby We are on
the road to Richmond
they let us ride our
horses thus far, guess
they will as far as
Culpeper when we late

Mosby had only 18 men at Fort ——

William Wells wrote home en route to Libby Prison.

UVM

166

treated his former fellow cadet rather well, but without hesitation sent him on to Richmond and the dread Libby Prison.

Back in the ranks of the Second Vermont Brigade, a private from Hartland, Benjamin Hatch, wrote to his wife: "Thare haint nothing hapend that suited everybody so well as it did to have the rebs take old Stoughton. I presume the newspapers wil try to make a great story of it but it suits everyone that had anything to do with him. We know the scamp here as well as the papers do. He has wanted to go to the front for some time and now he has gone."

Mosby continued his surprise attacks through the winter and into spring, though never again bagging as high-ranking a trophy as General Stoughton. As the weather warmed, the Union cavalry began to take some measure of revenge. One May night Capt. Addison Preston took a patrol out Mosby-style at midnight to scout along the Bull Run Mountains. In one of the gaps in the long ridge, Preston met some of Jeb Stuart's cavalry. After a hot fight amid the rocks and woods of Thoroughfare Gap, Preston set some 50 of Stuart's men in hasty retreat. A fortnight later, Preston encountered Mosby.

When Mosby attacked a Union supply train just up the tracks from Catlett's station, a Vermont cavalry detachment happened to be camped only five miles away, along Kettle Run. Mosby had used a howitzer to blast the train's locomotive, and the sound of its explosion sent the Vermonters to their horses. They covered the five miles in half an hour and found that Mosby had already made off with mailbags, plenty of fresh fish, and other treasured supplies. Preston paused for no more than a glance at the mess, then headed down the road, intent on overtaking the Confederate raiders. They were found soon enough, atop a rise where the road ran through a deep cut, with howitzer in the road and dismounted cavalry in a short line of battle behind it.

Some New York cavalrymen were with the Vermonters, and they immediately charged up the hill. Mosby's howitzer boomed, and 10 of the New Yorkers lay dead or wounded. Two companies of Vermonters then went galloping up, to be met by another blast of cannon. But the rebel cannoneer waited too long, for he hit only one target, a horse. The Vermonters burst into the Confederate ranks; the rebels got the worst of a brief and fierce hand-to-hand fight. Mosby's men scattered to the woods, most of them getting away. Mosby escaped, but only after a Vermonter whacked him on the shoulder with a sabre. The Vermonters came home with Mosby's precious howitzer, at a cost of just one man killed, Sgt. Job Corey of Tinmouth, and seven wounded. One Confederate who later died of his wounds was an English adventurer, Captain Haskins, a Crimean War veteran.

The Vermonters extracted some vengeance from John Singleton Mosby, but it was no help to Edwin Stoughton, who was confined in Libby Prison for two months. When he returned to Union territory, he found his military career at an end. His nomination as brigadier general, awaiting US Senate approval at the time of his capture, had been withdrawn by President Lincoln. Stoughton was left without military rank or military assignment, as the affair attracted national attention. Lincoln sealed Stoughton's doom when he said, on hearing that one of his generals had been seized from his own bed by a Confederate raider, that he didn't much mind the loss of a brigadier general, for he could make another in five minutes. "But those horses cost $125 apiece."

Mosby later said of Stoughton, "Great injustice has been done him. He was entirely blameless. If anyone was to blame it was [Sir Percy] Wyndham, who commanded the cavalry outposts and let me slip in."

Stoughton was finished, and he went back to Vermont to study law with his father, B. F. Stoughton, a prominent attorney. They practiced together in New York City and in Bellows Falls for a time. But Stoughton had become sick while in Libby Prison, and he never fully recovered. He died in 1868, having just turned 30.

Some of Mosby's Confederacy today retains the rural look and feel of Civil War days, but suburban Washington is expanding along ever-widening roads. Where development has not done its worst, the territory once ruled by the Confederate cavalryman is still lovely. One finds what remains of it out beyond Dulles Airport and the city of Manassas, some 30 miles to the east and southeast of Washington. Little towns like Aldie, Waterford, Marshall, and Catlett retain the look and feel of the Civil War. And there are still back roads to wander, past farms and woods, roads that rise and fall over the low hills and across streams locally called runs. All the places have their Civil War histories, and it is still possible to imagine how those Yankee troopers must have felt in that unfamiliar land, never knowing when John Singleton Mosby might appear over a rise, out of a forest, from behind some barn.

Suburbia has swallowed most of the open country around Fairfax Court House, where Stoughton had his headquarters that fateful winter of 1862–63. In the center of the bustling little metropolis, a red-brick church remains on the site of the church Stoughton attended. And just behind it is the two-story, red-brick rectory, added to a bit since Civil War times, but nonetheless the Dr. Gunnell house where Mosby found the Vermont general.

Half a thousand miles north in Bellows Falls, behind another Episcopal church, is the Immanuel Cemetery. A large blocky memorial stone stands off in the shaded northeast corner with the name Stoughton carved in it. Each Stoughton family member has a smaller stone, and the general's is there, though the carving has faded badly and it is now all but impossible to read his name.

DEATH AT CHANCELLORSVILLE

Through the winter of 1862–63 Confederate soldiers stood watch on the heights of Fredericksburg, from which they had brutally repulsed Ambrose Burnside's Army of the Potomac in December. As April was about to become May, Joseph Hooker roused his rested and refitted Army of the Potomac out of its camps north of the Rappahannock River to begin a military campaign known ever after as Chancellorsville.

Hooker had a good plan. He would leave a considerable force to threaten another attack at Fredericksburg. While Lee's attention was directed there, he would move the bulk of his army along the Rappahannock, cross many miles upstream, and come in behind the Confederates. On April 27 a mass of 50,000 Union soldiers, with 30,000 more soon to follow, marched up the north side of the river. Three days later, Thursday, April 30, Hooker's force reached a country crossroads known locally as Chancellorsville. Hooker had outflanked Lee, and he boasted that the Confederate commander must either come out and fight him or ingloriously flee. Lee came out and fought, though outnumbered about 110,000 to 60,000. Robert E. Lee always fought, and his defeat of Hooker at Chancellorsville may have demonstrated the greatest generalship of the entire war.

The Vermont Brigade, with the Sixth Corps, was left across the river from Fredericksburg while Hooker marched upstream. The Sixth Corps's job was to keep Lee's attention on the old river crossings where the whole army had moved to attack at Fredericksburg in December. While John Sedgwick put part of his 30,000 men across the river, the Vermont Brigade remained on the far side through Friday night, May 2. As the day wore on, the Vermonters could hear a growing rumble to the west as Hooker and Lee collided near Chancellorsville. The racket died only as the nearly full moon rose.

Lee, discovering that Hooker had stolen a march on him, left 10,000 troops under Jubal Early on the Fredericksburg heights and marched west with his other 50,000 men to confront Hooker. "Fighting Joe," for reasons never fully explained, stopped his advance as soon as Lee's lead elements began shooting, and he ordered his army to pull back and dig in. Outnumbered, Robert E. Lee suddenly had the upper hand. That night, around a camp fire by a woodland crossroads, Lee and "Stonewall" Jackson planned one of the war's most daring maneuvers. At dawn Jackson would take 25,000 men on a 12-mile march across Hooker's front, to strike its weak right flank.

About midnight on Saturday, with the day-long relentless sound of battle to the west finally easing, the Vermont Brigade crossed the Rappahannock on a pontoon bridge south of Fredericksburg—back to the ground where they'd done their part in the Battle of Fredericksburg in December, on the wide river plain confronting the Confederate-held hills. That night, corps commander Sedgwick received an order from General Hooker to fight his way out to join him. Hooker had good reason to summon help. Near dusk on Saturday, May 2, as Hooker's unsuspecting soldiers were cooking supper, Jackson's 25,000 yelling Confederates rushed out of the woods, destroying the weak west end of the Union line. The victims were the men of the 11th Corps, New Yorkers mostly, commanded by Maj. Gen. Oliver Otis Howard, that most religious man who had commanded Vermonters at First Bull Run.

If Howard's generalship has been questioned, nobody ever doubted his courage. Howard thrust an American flag under the stump of the right arm he'd lost on the Peninsula and rode into the fray to rally his troops. But when the situation finally stabilized in the smoky darkness near Chancellorsville, Howard's corps had been steamrolled two full miles. Hooker, still with a numerically superior army, was nearly paralyzed by uncertainty.

In the moonlight the triumphant Jackson rode out to reconnoiter in the smoldering woods and was accidentally shot by his own men. He died a week later.

Hooker's SOS to Sedgwick was a mean order because it meant that the Sixth Corps, reinforced by one division of the Second Corps, must do what the entire Army of the Potomac had failed to do less than five months earlier—carry the Fredericksburg heights. Sedgwick knew that, in December, not a Union soldier had reached the Confederate works along the infamous Sunken Road. But he would try.

In the dark of early Sunday morning, the Vermonters were marched north toward Fredericksburg. The first

Oliver Otis Howard at Chancellorsville.

Howard Coffin Collection

light of morning revealed the brigade facing the daunting Fredericksburg heights, with infantry along the base and cannon crowning the crests. Though the Sixth Corps had been south of this area in the earlier battle, the men were acutely aware of what had happened in the fields they now faced.

Through the morning Federal artillery lobbed shells over the Vermonters' heads, softening up the Confederate positions. Albion Howe, commanding the division to which the Vermonters belonged, received orders from Sedgwick a little before noon. He put his men into three storming columns, two under the command of Vermonters, massed along the Stage Road, three-quarters of a mile from the main Confederate line. They stood in readiness along the south bank of Hazel Run, a stream that flowed through a break in the Confederate-held heights. To the right of Hazel Run was Willis Hill, the southern end of Marye's Heights. Directly ahead, to the left of the stream, was the long line of hills extending south, generally known as Lee's Hill because Robert E. Lee had had his command post there in December.

Off to the north, or right, of the Vermonters were other Sixth Corps attackers poised to make a direct assault against the Sunken Road over the ground strewn with Union dead in December. The troops were ordered to remove knapsacks and to press ahead quickly without stopping to fire, a mistake Sedgwick believed had contributed to Union failure the previous winter.

A Wisconsin regiment off to the right was told: "You will not fire a gun and you will not stop until you get the order to halt. You will never get that order."

Sedgwick's reinforced Sixth Corps faced fields showing spring flowers and, beyond, thousands of veteran Confederate soldiers. The battle flags were out, bugles sounded, and the lines went ahead in a spectacular show of strength. The men attacking directly at the Sunken Road caught it worst, recoiled, went on, recoiled again, and then continued to advance in the face of artillery and rifle fire from road and heights.

The Vermont troops took their share of casualties as they moved along Hazel Run. Lewis Grant remembered: "The lines started over the plain at double quick in splendid style, the rebels opening at the same time all their batteries on the heights, pouring a terrible fire on the advancing lines; but on they went, driving the rebels before them."

Small-arms fire poured from Confederates behind the railroad track that crossed the Fredericksburg plain, and men were hit. The Sixth and Second Vermont regiments were in the front of the advance, moving toward the break in the heights where Hazel Run came through. As the attack crossed the tracks, the Sixth Vermont veered right, toward the south end of Marye's Heights. It paused where the steepness afforded some protection and a chance for the men to catch their breath. The 33rd New York moved just ahead. Lewis Grant said that the 33rd was the first regiment to reach the top, just before the Sixth Vermont. One member of the Sixth said: "Death-dealing shells plow our ranks, but still the advancing columns press onward and upward over one after another of the enemy's works and Fredericksburg is ours." Suddenly Vermont and New York troops were on the heights above the Sunken Road and the entire position began to give way.

The Second Vermont and the rest of the Vermont Brigade stayed to the south of Hazel Run, moving toward Lee's Hill. The Second, with the 26th New Jersey, went up the north end, the right end of the hill, with the Third, Fourth, and Fifth regiments to the left, and slightly behind, moving up the hill's face. The Fifth Vermont stayed back, protecting a battery. The attack was the New Jersey regiment's baptism of heavy fire. Wilbur Fisk in the Second Vermont certainly didn't like what he saw of their debut:

The 26th New Jersey was to take the lead, ours to follow and support them, and other regiments were to advance on our right and left. The boys started with confidence and alacrity, cheering as they went. The rebels opened on us from every piece they had, from a 24 pounder to a pocket pistol. Our batteries played over our heads and helped us all they could. The air seemed to be full of hissing shot and bursting shells. The roar was terrific and it required men of nerve to stand it. The Jerseys faltered; they did not run, but their regiment became so completely broken up that but little could be expected of them. There didn't seem to be any ranks anywhere. They were scattered all over the ground, so that a shell could hardly burst amiss....

Colonel Grant saw at once that to expect anything from that regiment would be hanging his hopes on a rope of sand, so he ordered the Second Vermont to the right of them, and we rushed up the hill ahead. Some from the Jersey regiment, more brave than the rest, joined with us and fought like heroes till the engagement was over.

The hill up which we charged, was covered with brush besides being very steep and every way difficult to climb. At the right there was a deep ravine also filled with brush and felled trees. The right of the regiment had to make their way up through this. The rebs had set fire to the brush on top of the hill, and the hot, suffocating smoke drifted into our faces, but we moved straight onward, regardless of everything. The air was intensely hot and sultry, the fire of the rebel musketry as we neared the top of the hill, was hot, too, but not a man flinched. While we were crossing the flat and till we got to the foot of the hill, our regiment kept in as good a line as if they were on a drill. Among this brush and smoke and bullets, this, of course, was impossible. We halted a moment in a rebel rifle pit to take breath, when at the word from Col. Grant, "Up now my brave boys and give it to them," we pushed forward as fast as possible....

At the top of the hill we were met with a more terrific shower of bullets than before. For a moment our regiment wavered. A little way beyond us through the smoke, the rebels could be seen hesitating the same way. Their officers were trying to rally them. It was a critical moment....Now was the precious moment to strike. Oh! if our boys only would rally—thank God they did. They rallied in stoutly, and drove the rebs to the eminence beyond.

An officer in a New Jersey regiment also described the fight:

As we approached the foot of the hills, we could see the rebel gunners limbering up their pieces. The Second Vermont, which had got a little ahead of us, were now moving up the steep slope on our right, in beautiful line; and presently we also commenced the ascent. A terrible volley thinned the ranks of the Vermonters; but they pressed on, and the enemy began to give away. As we reached the top of the hill we could see the flying foe, crossing through a gully and ascending the rise of ground opposite. The terrible Fredericksburg Heights had been captured.

Lewis Grant said after the battle: "The Second Vermont was the first regiment in the principal work on the highest range of hills, and the Sixth Vermont was the second regiment in the works on the lower range of hills commanding Fredericksburg. The heights were carried by storm at the point of the bayonet." As the Union attack rolled to the top of Lee's Hill, the Confederates retreated to a rise several hundred yards to the rear. The Second Vermont scarcely had time to catch its breath before ordered to join in an assault on that rise. They went ahead, and took heavy casualties. The men of the Third, Fourth, and Sixth regiments, reaching the top, pounded each other on the back and cheered. But the final grim tally showed that 132 men of the Vermont Brigade had been killed or wounded, 105 men in the Second Vermont alone.

The men were allowed time to return to the plain to pick up knapsacks. Sedgwick then ordered his corps to march west toward Chancellorsville, to link with Hooker as soon as possible. Well into the afternoon the lead elements of the Sixth, the division under former Vermont Brigade commander William Brooks, began to take fire from a low ridge ahead; around the little red-brick Salem Church were Confederate infantry and artillery, miles closer than they were thought to be. Brooks pressed ahead to the ridge and encountered a growing enemy force. What the corps soon faced, as it found out, was far more than a rear guard. By daybreak on May 4, the corps confronted a sizable share of the Army of Northern Virginia. Once Hooker had been dealt with, Lee was free to concentrate on the Sixth Corps. Lee would soon personally direct the action at Salem Church, intent on dealing the Sixth Corps a death blow.

Sedgwick quickly gave up hope of reaching Hooker and withdrew into a three-sided defensive position on high ground back toward Fredericksburg. Now he was threatened on three sides, for Jubal Early quickly retook the Fredericksburg heights lost the previous day. When day broke on Sunday, May 4, the Sixth Corps was dug in and braced for a morning assault. The Vermont Brigade, in Howe's Division, was posted on the east side of the three-sided Sixth Corps position, the most vulnerable part of the line, where it bent and headed west to join Brooks's division.

The morning dawned quietly and remained so as the sun rose high. The Vermonters had a good night's sleep and had finished breakfast when, as Private Fisk recalled: "Everything seemed to be as well as heart could wish, and our anticipations rose high of an early and glorious victory. But our hopes were quickly annihilated when a volley of rebel shells fired from the very hill we had taken Sunday, came hissing over our heads and bursting in our midst." Not long after, Confederate infantry probed the Union positions. Then all was quiet. Lee was, in fact, preparing an attack on Howe's division, one that would hit hardest where the Vermonters stood. Around five o'clock the Confederates struck, "with a violence I never before encountered," said General Howe.

The ground the Vermonters held faced an area broken by ravines and rises. Jubal Early's men, smarting from their temporary loss of the supposedly impregnable Fredericksburg heights, and bent on revenge, threw themselves directly against the Vermonters and the rest of Howe's division. The Fifth Vermont was to the front and took fire first, as a Vermont soldier recalled: "As the Confederate line neared the Fifth Vermont's veterans of Savage's Station, the terrain caused it to bear to the right. The Fifth's Colonel Lewis swung his men abreast of the attackers, and delivered a heavy fire into the flank of the gray infantry. When a longer battle line approached, Lewis retreated to higher ground."

The action shifted to the Second and Third Vermont and the 26th New Jersey. The long Confederate line came close, the New Jersey men fired, then moved back seeking cover. The Second Vermont rose and delivered a volley into the Confederate ranks. Then the Third Vermont fired, and the Confederate attack halted.

A rebel brigade swarmed up a steep slope, the crest of which was held by Col. Charles Stoughton's Fourth Vermont. The Vermonters waited, stood, and shot en masse; the attackers were mowed down.

The Vermont regiments had been shifting to meet the advancing Confederate waves, and as they did so, a gap appeared to open in the Vermont lines. The next rebel advance headed for it, battle flags flying. Just out of sight was Col. Elisha Barney's Sixth Vermont, keeping down. A member of the Sixth Vermont said: "It was the Green Mountain Boys against the chivalry of Louisiana." Another remembered: "They are close upon us and still our regiment is ordered to lie down and hold their fire...many are wounded by the shower of bullets which fall on us from the right and left....It is now time for us to act and, rising, we pour a murderous volley into their ranks."

Another Confederate attack was broken. Now the Vermonters rose, as did some of the 26th New Jersey, and with bayonets fixed, moved down the bloody slope toward their dazed enemy. More than 200 Confederates surrendered.

A member of the New Jersey regiment saw the action this way: "The Sixth Vermont lay behind a little rise of ground, awaiting the onset of the rebel hosts. Although the enemy was at least three times their number, for there was a whole brigade of them, the gallant Vermonters let them come until they were actually within a few feet, and then, rising, poured in a volley which literally decimated the foe."

It was evening and the Vermonters withdrew, awaiting another attack. Wilbur Fisk recalled:

Daylight had faded, but a full moon shone brightly and an enemy could be seen almost as well as in the day time. A few pieces of artillery was posted just to the left of us and as soon as the enemy advanced from the woods they opened on them with grape and cannister. The effect was grand. I never saw more splendid artillery firing. At every discharge the ...[cannister] could be heard rattling against the trees like throwing a handfull of pebbles against the side of a building. No enemy could stand such a fire, and they were soon driven back.

General Howe said:

The enemy, apparently thinking our left was giving way, rallied and confidently advanced until they brought their flank opposite the woods in which was placed those sterling soldiers of the Vermont Brigade. At the favorable moment this brigade opened its fire on the flank of the enemy's columns, and immediately the batteries in front opened a direct fire. The effect of this flank and direct fire on the enemy was most marked. In a short time not a hostile shot came into our lines. Darkness now came on. Soon the moon rose and lighted up the field; but not a rebel could be seen between our lines and the Heights of Fredericksburg.

In his book *Ordeal by Fire* the historian Fletcher Pratt put it another way: "Toward evening Early put a brigade into column for one last effort, with the war-cry 'Remember Jackson,' but a Vermont regiment as hard as the hills that gave them birth stood up to receive it hand to hand and the retreat of the Union army was secure."

In the darkness General Sedgwick withdrew toward the Rappahannock and Banks's Ford, while Howe's division protected the rear. The men of the Vermont Brigade were the last to go, beginning their two-mile tramp to the river about midnight. Sometime thereafter the Confederates discovered the Sixth Corps's retreat and took up pursuit. Lee had, after all, hoped to smash the reinforced corps before it got away. In desperation he mounted a night attack, hitting at the last remnants of the Vermonters protecting the pontoon bridge at Banks's Ford. It amounted to little as the Sixth Corps moved to the safety of the Rappahannock's far bank. Upstream the next night Hooker's big army did the same thing.

"It was daylight, though fortunately foggy, when the last of us crossed the bridge at Banks's Ford," a soldier in the Sixth Vermont remembered. Another said the last Vermonters crossed in boats, the bridge having been dismantled. George Benedict wrote: "As daylight [on the 5th] crept over the eastern hills the last of the brigade marched wearily up the heights on the northern shore. They dropped as soon as they were halted and slept till noon, their rest hardly broken by the shells from the enemy's batteries across the river which fell along the lines of sleeping soldiers."

Chancellorsville had been a resounding Union defeat. Lincoln spent endless hours at the War Department's telegraph office in Washington, reading dispatches from the front. In that office were two young Vermonters, Albert Chandler of Randolph and Charles Tinker of Chelsea. The War Department employed only four cryptographers, and two came from Orange County in Vermont. One or both may have been present when the disastrous news came in from Chancellorsville and Lincoln exclaimed, "What will the country say?"

The Sixth Corps's taking of the Fredericksburg heights became known as Second Fredericksburg. The ensuing action as Lee blocked Sedgwick's march to join Hooker was called Salem Church. The national military park at Fredericksburg, as previously noted, contains much of the Sunken Road, including a section of original stone wall. Along the road there's an enlarged picture taken just after the battle, showing Confederate dead lying in that bloody lane. Lee's Hill is part of the military park at Fredericksburg and can be climbed in gentle switchbacks on a walking trail. Out toward Chancellorsville, beside four-lane Route 3, the old wartime Orange Plank Road, stands little Salem Church.

Salem Church is the first Civil War site I ever visited. One summer Saturday afternoon in 1966, on weekend army pass, I found it amid rolling fields just off Interstate 95 near Fredericksburg. A sign beside the two-story, red-brick structure described the battle and how Confederate sharpshooters had occupied its upper story. I walked to the east side of the building and found, to my utter amazement, that the wall was pock-marked by bullets. I was hooked on the Civil War for life, "Civil warped" as a Mississippi historian once put it.

A quarter century has passed since my first visit, and I have returned to Salem Church at least once every year since. Gradually, I watched the little building, in which the severed limbs of wounded men were once stacked like cordwood, become enveloped by unregulated development. Today Salem Church is a little red church amid a sea of shopping malls, housing developments, gas stations, and fast-food emporiums. The battlefield is lost and gone forever. I have likened its fate to watching an old friend die. Salem Church's demise is fair warning that if the battlefields of the Civil War are not permanently protected, they will eventually be destroyed.

At the Chancellorsville Battlefield visitor's center 10 miles west, a slide show describes the Chancellorsville campaign, including the fighting around Salem Church. The narration concludes with the words: "Walk this hallowed ground. Listen for the distant voices on the ageless wind. These quiet woods and fields are always here to remind us how much we owe to the sacrifice of others. Here they came, here they fought, and here they died. What they lost, we lost. What they gained, we gained."

In early May of 1863 the armies, North and South, suffered nearly 30,000 battle casualties in the woods and fields around Chancellorsville, Salem Church, and Fredericksburg. About 260 were Vermont soldiers.

THE LONG MARCH TO GETTYSBURG

While the guns boomed in the distance at Chancellorsville, the Second Vermont Brigade had been on guard many miles up the Rappahannock, where butternut-clad soldiers could be seen on the river's far bank. On May 10, 1863 three black men, just escaped from a plantation at nearby Brandy Station, slipped into the 12th Vermont Regiment's camp. The plantation was owned by John Minor Botts, a self-proclaimed Union sympathizer. Botts showed up a few hours later and demanded that the slaves be turned over to him on the grounds that Abraham Lincoln's Emancipation Proclamation applied only to slaves owned by rebels, not to those owned by loyal Union people. The commander of the 12th, Col. Asa Blunt of St. Johnsbury, told Botts he could not follow his logic, but he did agree to let the Virginian speak with the three men. The youngest of the former slaves heard Botts out, then told him that if he was truly a Union man, he ought to respect Lincoln's proclamation, because it declared that all the slaves in any rebelling states were to be "thenceforward and forever free." Botts gave up the argument, left camp, and wrote a letter of protest to Abraham Lincoln. The three blacks eventually went north and settled in Vermont.

A soldier in the 16th Vermont, writing home to Cornwall, reported that most soldiers in the army wanted blacks allowed into the Union armies. He added, "None will dispute their fighting qualities; but I would to God that we could ever say this flag is a white one." His sentiments were not unique. Pvt. Wilbur Fisk summed up soldiers' feelings well before the Emancipation Proclamation was issued:

> The boys think it their duty to put down rebellion and nothing more, and they
> view the abolition of slavery in the present time as saddling so much additional

labor upon them before the present great work is accomplished. Negro prejudice is as strong here as anywhere and most of the boys would think it a humiliating compromise to the dignity of their work to have it declared that the object of their services was to free the repulsive creatures from slavery, and raise the negro to an equality with themselves. I verily believe if such a declaration was made today a majority would be inclined to lay down their arms and quit the service in disgust....

The most cordial reception by far that we have received since we left the free states was tendered us by this sable species of human property. As we were passing by the premises of one of the more wealthy farmers on our way here, a group of negroes, a score or more composed of men, women and children of all ages, climbed upon a fence by the roadside and greeted us in their earnest simple way "God bress you," "I's glad to see you," "I's glad you's come," "God bress you," and many similar exclamations as they bowed, and courtsied, and waved their hands to us, attesting their childish glee at seeing so many Union soldiers. They were dirty and ragged and probably as a perfectly natural result were ignorant and degraded, but they seemed to understand, as nearly all the negroes here do, that somehow all this commotion has a connection with them and will bring about their freedom in the end. They seem conscious of being at the bottom of all this trouble, and all the deceptions their masters could invent have failed to rob them of this knowledge.

On June 8, 1863 the cavalry of the Army of the Potomac and the Army of Northern Virginia clashed in the fields around Brandy Station, not far from the camp of the Second Vermont. The blue and gray horsemen rode back and forth across the Virginia meadows and fields with sabers swinging and guns blazing in the largest cavalry battle ever fought in the western hemisphere. Union horsemen had gone out looking for a fight, to beat up Jeb Stuart's cavalry and forestall a raid toward Washington. They discovered that Robert E. Lee, not resting on his masterful Chancellorsville victory, had his army on the move. Lee was determined to take the war out of his beloved Virginia onto Northern soil. He was moving west, soon to turn north.

When Lee began his march, the Vermont Brigade was still near Fredericksburg. On June 5 the brigade was ordered by John Sedgwick to recross the Rappahannock below Fredericksburg to see if Confederates were still there in strength. Though Lee was marching, he had left a corps behind to mask his movements. The Vermonters got into a fight.

"There was some sharp picket firing, but no advancing. Our pickets suffered severely. A great many were killed and wounded, some say as many as forty, mostly from the sixth regiment," Wilbur Fisk reported.

The fight below Fredericksburg cost the Vermonters less than Fisk feared. In the first wave of troops to move across the Rappahannock River were the men of the Fifth Vermont and the 26th New Jersey regiments. Some of the New Jersey soldiers had refused to cross, saying their terms of enlistment were too near an end to risk a fight.

Lee's vanguard crossed the Blue Ridge on June 12 and was in the Shenandoah

Valley, perhaps even aiming at Washington. Hooker got his scattered forces in motion and kept them between the Confederates and the capital day after day.

On June 13 orders came for the Vermont Brigade to march, and its five regiments started out in a rain that provided welcome relief from the increasingly oppressive heat. They went along the slippery country roads, singing and swearing, laughing and stumbling, through the Virginia villages of Stafford Court House and Dumfries. At Dumfries the brigade was drawn up into a hollow square, and 40 men of the 26th New Jersey were brought forward. The men had been court-martialed for refusing to cross the Rappahannock back at Fredericksburg. A band struck up the "Rogue's March," and the men were drummed out of camp in disgrace. Less than a week later, the nine-month enlistments of the 26th New Jersey expired, and the regiment left for home. The Vermont Brigade would be an exclusively Vermont outfit for the rest of the war.

The Sixth Corps forded the Occoquan River at Wolf Run Shoals. There the Vermont Brigade was allowed to rest and take a swim. Some units of the Second Vermont Brigade were nearby, and there in the fields along the lazy river the men got a chance to talk with some fellow Vermonters.

Next day the Old Brigade tramped on to Fairfax Station, where General Sedgwick ordered the Sixth Corps to take a full day's rest. The First Vermont Cavalry happened to be nearby. That evening, the Vermont infantrymen and horsemen got together around camp fires well into the night. The following morning the infantrymen shouldered arms and moved on, north and west, crossing the Potomac into Maryland on June 27. By the last day of the month the brigade had reached Manchester, just 30 miles from Gettysburg, Pennsylvania.

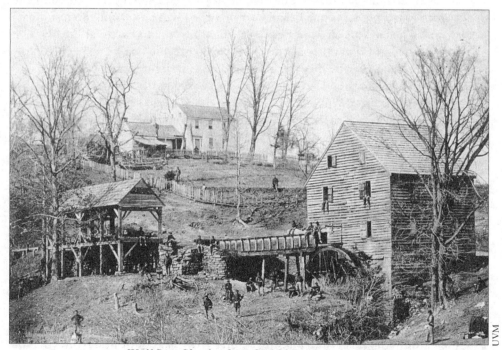

Wolf Run Shoals where the Old Brigade camped.

The Second Vermont Brigade broke camp and hit the roads on June 25, under orders from a new commander. With General Stoughton out of the army, the already fabled and fearless George J. Stannard, the first of all the Vermonters to enlist and now holding the rank of brigadier general, had been plucked from his command of the Ninth Vermont to lead the nine-month brigade. Stannard's new command was part of the First Corps of the Army of the Potomac, which had already gotten a start north when the Second Vermont Brigade, made up of the 12th, 13th, 14th, 15th, and 16th Vermont regiments, was ordered to follow.

The night before the march began, Pvt. William O. Doubleday sent a letter home to Sherburne. He had written several times since his outfit went south, most letters revealing his homesickness and longing for his wife, Asceneth, and his sons. From Wolf Run Shoals he wrote:

Dear Wife,
Well, Asceneth we have got our orders to march in the morning. We are to start at 7 and be at Union Mills at 11. Where we are to go from there, we are not allowed to know. Some say we are going to Harpers Ferry, some to Maryland, but we shall not know until we get to our stopping place. I think we shall go where we shall see rebs and perhaps some fighting, but I don't calculate to get killed now just before my time is out. I put an overcoat in a box to send home today. L[auriston] Manley [also of Sherburne] has some stuff in the same box. I was in hopes we should not have to move until after I got another letter from you, but I may get yours just as soon as I should here.

I am afraid I shall hear some bad news from home when I get a letter from you if there is anything in dreams. I dreamed that you and I stood up with a couple to be married last night. I hope I shall hear that Freddy is better and the rest of you are well. The boys are all wide awake for a fight here. I can't say that I really want to be in one but I don't dread it much. If we do get into one I shall try to do my duty. If I should get killed perhaps it would be as well for you. You would draw a pension of $8 a month and have a chance to get a younger and better husband. Kiss the boys for me, from Willie down to little Fred. Hoping I shall be spared to meet you all again in a few weeks. I wish you good night from your ever loving Husband,

Wм. O D

George Stannard was a hard driver; he had been told to march with the First Corps, which had a head start and was already in Maryland. Soon the men began to discard knapsacks and blankets, anything that did not seem absolutely essential. By June 28 the Second Brigade crossed the Potomac and the Monocacy rivers, and on the 29th it reached Frederick, Maryland.

The vast Army of the Potomac was marching on roads leading north. Lee had driven his divisions up the Shenandoah Valley, into Maryland, and now into Pennsylvania. The Confederates moved through small Union towns where the people stared in curiosity or hid behind shuttered windows in fear. The Union soldiers, however, received a warmer and warmer welcome as they moved north. The men stepped lively when passing through towns, regimental bands played a march or two, and flags were unfurled. The townspeople cheered, young women waved, and the young men of the armies, dust-covered and sweat-soaked, did their best to look military.

The First Vermont Cavalry regiment had left its northern Virginia camps on June 25. Now 840 strong, the Vermonters were part of a division under the command of Judson Kilpatrick, in a brigade led by an Illinois man, Elon J. Farnsworth. (The other brigade of the Army of the Potomac's cavalry corps was led by a Michigander, George Armstrong Custer.)

The Vermonters rode up through Maryland and into Pennsylvania, and on June 30 entered Hanover. Confederate horsemen under Jeb Stuart galloped into town, and a fight broke out that involved a company under Capt. John Woodward. One Vermonter was shot and sixteen were reported missing.

Young Captain Woodward and his men had been on the lookout for rebels day and night; the captain probably found time to ride by the side of his father, as the Fighting Chaplain kept up with the First Vermont Cavalry. The regiment camped the night of June 30 near Hanover, less than a day's ride east from Gettysburg.

Fighting began at Gettysburg on July 1. Federal cavalrymen under John Buford were there first, and early that morning Confederate infantry came in through the mist and shots were exchanged. Lee had no intention of fighting at Gettysburg. Nor did George Gordon Meade, the veteran officer from Pennsylvania who now commanded the Army of the Potomac. (Hooker had been relieved by Lincoln on the march toward Pennsylvania.)

Once the fighting started at Gettysburg it quickly got out of hand, and both Meade and Lee began massing men. Buford was hard-pressed but soon got help from fresh troops under John Reynolds. The fighting swelled on a ridge west of town, and soon Reynolds was killed and his men were forced back. For a time, command of the Union armies at Gettysburg fell on one-armed Oliver Otis Howard. Howard climbed a high building in Gettysburg and, seeing some hills and a long, low ridge to the east, decided that here was where the army should make its stand. The Union armies withdrew through the converging streets of Gettysburg to Cemetery Hill and Cemetery Ridge beyond. Maj. Gen. Winfield Scott Hancock soon arrived to take command from Howard, with Meade still en route. Assaults on Cemetery Hill were delayed, and at the bloody day's end, the Union army held a long fishhook-shaped line from Culp's Hill, around to Cemetery Hill, and down Cemetery Ridge toward rocky Little Round Top. Out on the roads, leading like the spokes of a wheel toward the hub that was Gettysburg, thousands on thousands of troops, including the Vermont units, were drawing closer.

The Second Vermont Brigade, not as used to marching as were the hardened veterans of the Old Brigade, were steadily tiring, but they made good time under the relentless direction of George Stannard. On June 30 the brigade was at Emmitsburg, two miles from the Pennsylvania line, having covered 120 miles in six days.

Stannard had been unmerciful. His orders to his brigade were explicit; to keep in ranks and not even to break for water along the hot and dusty roads. Capt. Stephen F. Brown, a Swanton man of the 13th Vermont, had finally seen enough of the suffering and ordered some of his men to hurry to a nearby stream and fill canteens. Stannard found out and promptly had Brown arrested. Though soon released, Brown was deprived of his sword, and he would go into battle without a weapon. Brown later wrote of that forced march:

Stephen Brown wielded a hatchet at Gettysburg.

This was the first summer beyond the cool breezes of our native mountains, and we were enervated by the semi-tropical heat of the south. Day after day, having already marched as far as seemed possible for us, we marched miles and miles further. Without food for days in that climate, in the hot summertime, clad in thick wool clothing, weighted with guns and 60 rounds of ammunition, upon blistered and bleeding feet, we had shortened the distance between our brigade and the veteran First Corps, also hurrying toward the invading foe....

As they marched, men fainted and fell, some with ghastly upturned faces, as if dead. Others struggled convulsively in the dust. They had no helpers. We were ordered to leave them in the dust where they fell.

I looked on the suffering men as martyrs of liberty, each bearing his cross from Gethsemane to his Golgotha, there to offer himself up to the good of others.

On the morning of July 1 the Second Vermont Brigade, at Emmitsburg, was back on the roads at about 6 A.M. Three miles down the road toward Gettysburg, orders came from Maj. Gen. Abner Doubleday to leave two regiments as guards for the First Corps wagon train, and to hurry the rest of the brigade on. The 12th and 15th regiments were left behind; the 13th, 14th, and 16th hurried on. Toward noon, after a brief shower that seemed only to make the blistering day hotter, a rider brought news from Gettysburg that Reynolds was dead and that the Vermonters were desperately needed. Stannard ordered the pace increased almost beyond endurance. But as the long columns crested a hill and began to hear the thunder of cannon, the ranks closed up, the pace somehow quickened, and no more men fell out. At 1 P.M. the brigade halted briefly just four miles from the battlefield, then moved on as the gunfire grew louder. At dusk the three regiments of the Second Vermont Brigade joined the main Union lines on

Cemetery Hill. The Old Brigade, however, was still far from the battlefield.

"Put the Vermonters in the lead and keep the column well closed." That command was given by John Sedgwick on the evening of July 1, as orders reached him from Meade to march his Sixth Corps, still in Maryland, the 30 remaining miles to Gettysburg. Speed was absolutely essential, so Sedgwick put his best marchers, the five regiments of the Vermont Brigade, in front of the 15,000-man corps to set the pace. All others were to keep up.

They hurried on along the Baltimore and Gettysburg Turnpike, at first in darkness, and then as July 2 dawned, in growing heat and gagging dust. But these farm boys were veterans, the Old Brigade, the best marchers in the Army of the Potomac. They kept on and on until noon, when a brief halt was called. Then they were back in ranks and moving again as the distant rumble turned to booming. The second day of Gettysburg was as bad as the first; the sound of battle carried for many miles on the sultry country air.

Near Littletown, 10 miles from Gettysburg, the brigade met carriages and wagons bearing wounded. Great clouds of smoke rose on the horizon like dark thunderheads. No stops were made; farm families came out with buckets and pitchers of water. By 6 P.M. the Vermonters crossed Rock Creek just outside Gettysburg. Wilbur Fisk wrote, "Weak and weary, stiff and sore, we plodded along....We called it that we had travelled 28 miles."

The great march to Gettysburg was all but complete. By then the Second Vermont Brigade had been bloodied along Cemetery Ridge. And the Vermont cavalry was at hand, ready to do battle amid the woods and fields of what would become America's greatest battlefield.

THE FURY OF GETTYSBURG

The stars were beginning to appear when the Second Vermont Brigade reached Cemetery Hill as the first day of fighting ended at Gettysburg. It had been a bloody day, though much worse was ahead; the Vermonters saw dead and wounded men everywhere. The march had been exhausting, and the men thought only of sleep. After waiting through an hour's dispute among army brass over where they should be assigned, the brigade was finally placed on the right of the Third Corps, in a field behind the crest of Cemetery Ridge. But slumber was not for all that warm night of July 1, 1863. A 200-man detachment from Wheelock Veazey's 16th regiment was sent on picket duty along the Emmitsburg Road, well forward of the Union lines. It was a fearful night for the Vermonters, halfway between the main Union and Confederate positions, in the darkness broken time and again by rifle shots and the cries of wounded. General Stannard was awake, having been appointed field officer in charge of the center. He spent the night riding along the Union positions on Cemetery Ridge and Cemetery Hill. Deep in the night, he exchanged greetings with the Army of the Potomac's new commander, George Gordon Meade.

Stannard's immediate command, the Second Brigade, was somewhat scattered. Though three regiments were on the battlefield, two were four miles away, guarding wagons. To Stannard's surprise, not long after the long night ended, Col. Redfield Proctor's 15th Vermont joined the rest of the brigade on the battlefield. On the previous afternoon Third Corps commander Maj. Gen. Daniel Sickles, spotting the Vermont wagon guards, was annoyed by the sight of what he considered good soldiers being wasted.

"I discovered," Sickles later said, "Stannard's Vermont Brigade guarding a wagon train. This was a duty those splendid soldiers did not much relish, so I took the responsibility of ordering them to join my command. You can hardly imagine their joy when they found they were going to join in battle."

184

Sickles told Colonel Proctor to follow one of his divisions to the battlefield "and bayonet any man that refuses to go forward." The 15th shouldered arms, bid the unhappy 12th Vermont adieu, and started for the fighting. It arrived in the morning, having crossed dangerously near enemy lines, and for a short time the regiment was on the battlefield with the rest of the Second Brigade. Not for long. Someone of higher rank than Sickles, perhaps Meade himself, ordered the 15th Vermont to go back and resume guarding the wagons. About noon on July 2 the 15th Regiment marched over the saddle between Big Round Top and Little Round Top and out of the Battle of Gettysburg.

As Thursday, July 2, dawned hot as the previous day, the remaining three regiments of the Second Vermont, some 1,500 men, came to realize that they were posted just behind the center of the Union battle line, near the little white cottage that was General Meade's headquarters. Those Vermonters must have wondered how fate had placed them, with only days remaining in their army service, directly at the front.

In early morning the Vermonters who had picketed along the Emmitsburg Road came in safely. Later in the morning, First Corps commander Maj. Gen. John Newton gave the men a boost as he was heard to say, on riding by, "Here are some boys that will fight when the time comes." The arrival of four wagons loaded with bread, pork, and coffee also cheered them. Toward midafternoon Confederate cannon began lobbing shells in the Vermonters' direction; one burst over a knot of men, killing two and wounding several others. The brigade was moved a bit closer under the hill for protection. Another shell hit close to General Stannard, knocking him flat, but he bounced up unharmed and brushed himself off. Stannard, on the crest near some cannon, in sight of Confederate gunners and sharpshooters, hardly seemed to notice the bullets, though one clipped a button off the coat of an officer with whom he was talking.

More Vermont troops were now ordered toward the Emmitsburg Road on picket duty, five companies of the 13th regiment. To the south near Little Round Top, about noon, Col. Hiram Berdan took about 100 men, 40 of them Vermonters, across the Emmitsburg Road on a scouting mission to find whether any Confederates had moved into the woods opposite the Union line's south end. With about 200 Maine infantrymen in support, the sharpshooters entered the trees and turned north, moving cautiously until rifle fire erupted in their front. The sharpshooters pressed on until Confederates were everywhere. Berdan had seen enough; he ordered a retreat. The sharpshooters had discovered that in front of the Union army, opposite Little Round Top, were thousands of Confederates. An attack could come at any time, Berdan reported to the high command.

The Union army lay in wait for what General Lee might do, division on division posted in a secure line on high ground from high Culp's Hill, along Cemetery Hill, and down Cemetery Ridge toward the Round Tops. It seemed a good defensive position. Then Dan Sickles marched his corps forward to the Emmitsburg Road, creating a great bulge in the Union line, vulnerable and unsupported. In midafternoon the Confederates blasted in against Sickles's salient. Bitter, bloody fighting developed in the Peach Orchard and Wheatfield, in a little valley along a stream named Plum Run, soon to be called the Valley of Death, and around a pile of massive boulders called Devil's Den. Thousands of butternut-clad Confederates, with the support of massed artillery, attacked Sickles's exposed corps, screaming the devilish rebel yell. Other Confederates swept in over the crest of Big Round Top and on toward Little Round Top, rugged hills that should have been firm anchors for the south end of the Union line but that were, remarkably, undefended. Meade's chief engineer, Gouverneur K. Warren, found out, just in time, that Little Round Top was unprotected, and called for the closest troops, Col. Strong Vincent's brigade that included a Maine regiment. Also in that portion of the battlefield were two companies of Vermont sharpshooters. Posted near the base of Round Top, the Vermonters of the Second US Sharpshooters got in the midst of the fighting early and were driven back, through woods and fields, firing all the way. Every bullet counted; up on the most southern slope of Little Round Top, Joshua Lawrence Chamberlain's 20th Maine, firing from behind trees and boulders, needed all the help it could get as the rebel assault surged uphill. Finally, with ammunition about exhausted, the Maine boys fixed bayonets and rushed downhill in a desperate charge. Little Round Top was held; the south end of the Union position was secure.

A little north, where Sickles's Third Corps was out front of everybody, things were not going so well. Sickles himself was down, a cannonball having blown away a leg. Men were dying by the hundreds in the Peach Orchard and Wheatfield. Finally, what was left of the Third Corps, although reinforced by one big Second Corps and two Fifth Corps divisions, was withdrawn back across the Valley of Death to the crest of Cemetery Ridge, whence it had come.

But Lee was not finished. As dusk came, so did more Confederates, toward the Union line's center on Cemetery Ridge. It was a thin blue line in places, the casualties having been heavy all day. Gen. Winfield Scott Hancock was in command in that part of the field where the Confederates surged in hardest and the defenders were fewest. He sent for reinforcements, which came up to the crest of the ridge and over the top and got hit hard. Suddenly Confederates were coming in toward the Union cannon. A little farther along the line, a Minnesota regiment was thrown against a mass of Confederates and lost four-fifths of its men.

At midpoint on Cemetery Ridge the Union line was threatening to break. General Meade came on the scene and immediately saw the need for more troops. "If you need troops, I saw a fine body of Vermonters a short distance from here, belonging to the First Corps, who are available," artillery captain John C. Tidball told him.

The Vermonters, still resting in the fields behind Cemetery Hill perhaps a mile to the north, were called to attention and formed in line of march. Off they went south, down the Taneytown Road, toward where the din of battle was now the loudest. Meade stayed near the critical point. Years later his son, Lt. Col. George Meade, recalled:

Directly in front of the general, a line of the enemy could be seen advancing between our ridge and the Emmitsburg Pike. I think it must have been [Ambrose] Wright's Georgia Brigade....

Just as we were making up our minds for the worst, someone shouted or rather yelled, "There they come, general." Looking around we saw a column of infantry come swinging down the Taneytown Road from the direction of Cemetery Hill, in close column of divisions, at a sharp double-quick, flags flying, arms at right shoulder, officers steadying their men with sharp commands. They came on as if on review. It was the most exciting and inspiriting moment I ever passed, and everyone yelled as if for dear life.

The three regiments of Stannard's brigade thus marched into their first battle, one of the most important of the war. General Meade rode with them to the crest of embattled Cemetery Ridge, where the Union line was about to snap. An officer rode up to Meade and observed that things were looking pretty desperate.

"Yes, but it is all right now, it is all right now," the commanding general replied. His son recalled: "This column of troops was [Abner] Doubleday's and [John C.] Robinson's divisions of the First Corps and I have always understood that at the head of the column was Stannard's Vermont Brigade. It has always been to me the most dramatic incident connected with General Meade on that field, and I have often wished that I could only command the power of description, so that I could give it as I saw it then and as I think on it now."

The 14th Vermont regiment led the way. Colonel Veazey's 16th Vermont came next, followed by the 13th. As the Vermonters crested the ridge, they were in the thick of battle, firing and taking fire. Also on the ridge was Maj. Gen. Winfield Scott Hancock, "Hancock the Magnificent," as he came to be known. As Colonel Randall and the 13th came up, Hancock pointed to some Confederates moving in among Union cannon and said, "Can't you save that battery, Colonel?"

"We can try. Forward boys," was Randall's reply. Four companies of the 13th Vermont took aim on the Confederates, and the guns were saved. Randall's men called for help in dragging the guns to safety, then they kept going, on down the ridge and all the way to the Emmitsburg Road, where they immediately came under cannon and small-arms fire. Confederate riflemen were in and around the Rogers House, on the east side of the road. The Vermonters rushed the place and, after a quick and bitter fight, captured 80 prisoners. It was almost dark when Stannard ordered these brave men's return to the main Union line. They came back across the bloody ground with prisoners in tow. When they reached the crest of the ridge, the rest of the Second Vermont Brigade was digging in. Under a starry sky some of the men fell asleep, but some were too exhausted for sleep. The bloody second day at Gettysburg was over and, just barely, the Union army still held its position on the high ground.

Several hours earlier, in late afternoon when the Confederates were attacking Little Round Top, a newspaper reporter named Charles C. Coffin was at

General Meade's headquarters. He recalled:

> It was nearly six o'clock. The sound of battle grew louder and nearer. [A. P.] Hill was threatening the center. A cloud of dust could be seen down the Baltimore Pike. Had Stuart gained our rear? There were anxious countenances around the cottage where the flag of the commander-in-chief was flying. Officers gazed with their field glasses. "It is not cavalry, but infantry," said one. "There is the flag. It is the Sixth Corps." We could see the advancing bayonets gleaming in the setting sun. Faces which a moment before were grave, became cheerful. It was an inspiring sight. The troops of that corps had marched 32 miles during the day. They crossed Rock Creek, filed into the field past the ammunition trains, threw themselves upon the ground, tossed aside their knapsacks and wiped the sweat from their sunburned cheeks.

The Vermonters were in the lead as the Sixth Corps completed its great march to Gettysburg. The Old Brigade soldiers immediately fell down to sleep but in a few minutes were roused up and marched more than a mile south to some fields behind the Round Tops. There the Vermont Brigade would stay, in support and ready for a call to action that never came. The Old Brigade would not fight in the Battle of Gettysburg.

The Army of the Potomac was assembled, strengthening its positions from Culp's Hill, around the fishhook curve to Cemetery Hill, and down Cemetery Ridge to the Round Tops, looming dark against the starry sky. Up on Cemetery Ridge, Colonel Veazey took his 16th Vermont and moved quietly in the darkness out beyond the lines and through the fields to the Emmitsburg Road, again to stand guard during a long and dreadful night.

"It was the saddest night on picket that I ever passed," said Veazey. "The line ran across the field that had been fought over the day before, and the dead and wounded of the two armies, lying side by side, thickly strewed the ground. The mingled imprecations and prayers of the wounded…were heart-rending. The stretcher-bearers of both armies were allowed to pass back and forth through the picket lines, but scores of wounded men died around us in the gloom, before anyone could bring relief or receive their dying messages."

One of the wounded was a Confederate general, William Barksdale of Mississippi, with bullets through his chest and both legs. A Vermonter brought him back to a tent hospital to the rear of Cemetery Ridge. "Tell my wife I fought like a man and died like one," he struggled to say before he died.

George Benedict, one day to be a historian, had joined the 12th Vermont as a private, now had a commission, and was a member of Stannard's staff. With a reporter's curiosity, Benedict was prowling about that night: "With the darkness, the firing ceased," he recalled, "and we heard from our front that sound which once heard will not be forgotten by any one—a low, steady, indescribable moan—the groans of wounded, lying by thousands on the battlefield. As the moon was rising I rode out upon the field in front of our lines. My horse started aside at every rod from the bodies of dead men or horses, and wounded men."

Later Benedict rode behind the lines, passing several Pennsylvania barns

*Two Confederates, in bronze, look toward the Clump of Trees
across fields Pickett's charge crossed.*

that had become hospitals. "By the door of one was a ghastly pile of amputated arms and legs," he recalled, "and around each of them lay multitudes of wounded men, covering the ground by the acre, wrapped in their blankets and waiting their turn under the knife. I was stopped hundreds of times by wounded men, sometimes accompanied by a comrade but often wandering alone, to be asked in faint tones the way to the hospital of their division."

In the little wooden cottage behind Cemetery Ridge that was Meade's headquarters, an evening council of war was called. As it ended and Meade dismissed his commanders, he stopped Maj. Gen. John Gibbon at the door to advise it was likely that General Lee would attack next day against the center of the Union army, Hancock's position.

Two miles away, along the Chambersburg Pike, in the yard of a stone house that was his headquarters, Robert E. Lee was also making plans for the next day. He would indeed attack the center of the long Union line. Next morning he would decide that a prominent clump of trees he saw along Cemetery Ridge would serve as a good guide for his advancing soldiers. Those trees would be the point of attack. As the men of the Second Vermont Brigade not out on picket duty tried to find sleep in the night of Thursday and Friday, July 2–3, some may have taken notice of a certain clump of trees about a quarter mile to the north that could be a good place to get some shade in the heat of the next day.

STANNARD'S VOLUNTEERS FACE PICKETT'S CHARGE

Friday, July 3, 1863, dawned hotter than the previous two days. As dawn was breaking, fighting began at the far right end of the Union line, around Culp's Hill, where the Confederates renewed efforts to achieve a breakthrough. The Second Vermont Brigade took sporadic cannon fire; one lucky Confederate shot hit a caisson loaded with ammunition and killed or wounded several men.

George Stannard led the Second Vermont Brigade at Gettysburg.

Stannard, up on Cemetery Ridge and the focal point of much attention as a brigade commander, paid scant attention to his safety. The activity around him drew fire from Confederate sharpshooters; one bullet slapped through the general's coat, another clipped the rim of his hat. Stannard finally asked that some men be sent forward to drive the snipers out of range.

Later in the morning the Confederates gave up the attack on Culp's Hill, and a quiet settled over the battlefield. Stannard's men had attempted to improve the position they held on Cemetery Ridge. They found more fence rails and tree limbs and, by adding stones and earth, made their crude breastwork two feet high in places. George Benedict of Stannard's staff described the positioning of the regiments: "The Sixteenth was on the skirmish line in front. The Fourteenth was moved forward to a line several rods in front where some trees and bushes offered a partial cover. The Thirteenth was placed to the right and a little to the rear of the Fourteenth."

During the lull, a soldier in the 14th Vermont, Cpl. Wesley Sturtevant, ambled over to the nearby 13th Vermont and found his cousin, Ralph Sturtevant. The two had grown up together in Swanton and been close friends. Ralph Sturtevant later recalled his cousin's sad words: "I shall never see home and dear friends again, something tells me I shall be slain in battle, and I cannot drive away the awful thought. I have come to tell you and

George Benedict, historian and Medal of Honor winner.

request that you tell father and mother, brother and sisters and dear friends for me and say good-bye."

Ralph Sturtevant did his best to reassure his cousin, saying he should not put much stock in such foreboding. But Wesley would have none of it. "With deep emotion he extended his hand and said 'Good-bye,' and hastily and deliberately walked back to his regiment nearby."

Noon passed; the day grew even hotter; the quiet held. Then a flurry of activity was seen across the mile-wide valley. Along Seminary Ridge, Confederate cannon were wheeled forward, shells rammed home. At about one o'clock a lone cannon sounded off near the town of Gettysburg. With that, more than 150 Confederate cannon along a two-mile line from the Peach Orchard to Oak Hill began to fire. Most shells seemed to be coming in toward the Vermonters near the Union center. "The air seemed to be literally filled with flying missiles," Benedict remembered. "Shells whizzed and popped on every side. Spherical case exploded over our heads and rained iron bullets upon us; the Whitworth solid shot, easily distinguished by their clear musical ring, flew singing by; ...[canister] hurtled around us or rattled in an iron storm against the low protection of rails, and round shot plowed up the ground before and behind us." Union guns from Cemetery Hill to Little Round Top responded: more than 275 rebel and Federal cannon were firing, the greatest artillery duel ever seen in the Western Hemisphere. "The thundering roar of all the accumulated battles ever fought upon earth rolled into one volume," a correspondent for the *London Times* recalled. The Vermonters stayed low. Wheelock Veazey remembered,

"Everyone clings to life with bated breath and gasps, as the very earth beneath us quivers with a tremulous jar."

Ralph Sturtevant said, "All this held us prostrate and fast to the ground anxiously watching and waiting for the guns to cease firing. The passing of each minute seemed a lifetime."

Though the cannon fire was coming in their direction, most of it passed well over the Vermonters' heads. The rebel cannoneers, in the smoke, were mistakenly lobbing most of their shells beyond the crest of Cemetery Ridge, missing the cannon and infantrymen they aimed for. Instead, support troops—the cooks and wagon drivers and supply sergeants—got the worst of it. In General Meade's headquarters behind the ridge, an orderly serving lunch was torn in half by a shell. Meade moved his operations to a hilltop a half

Ralph Sturtevant heard his cousin's dark premonition.

mile back. The Vermont troops began to relax. Veazey, with his 16th Vermont, observed: "The effect of this cannonade on my men, was the most astonishing thing I ever witnessed in any battle. Many of them, I think a majority, fell asleep, and it was with the greatest effort that I could keep awake myself, notwithstanding the fearful cries of my wounded men, and my anxiety in reference to the fearful scenes which I knew would follow."

The 14th regiment, a bit to the front, weathered the barrage best, save for the pickets of the 16th Vermont, far short of the impact zone, out by the Emmitsburg Road. The strange fact was that the closer the soldiers were to the Confederate lines, the less likely they were to be struck by cannon fire.

Toward 3 P.M. the Union artillery behind and to the sides of the Vermonters stopped firing. The Confederate shelling continued a few more minutes, then ceased. The silence was awesome. Men awoke and began to examine themselves, making sure they were still alive, still whole. Stretcher bearers retrieved the wounded. Officers checked the condition of their men. Generally, the Vermont troops seemed to be in good condition, save for a few who had been wounded or killed by a round that fell short.

As the smoke lifted, the slope of Cemetery Ridge down to the Emmitsburg Road, the fields across the road, the treeline on Seminary Ridge, and then the Confederate line a mile away could be seen. "There is a portentous hush," recalled one Vermont soldier, "and some one with a glass at his eye says, 'There they come,' and just emerging from the rebel lines you can see the long ranks of gray, the shimmer of steel in the July sun." The advancing Confederate lines stretched more than a mile from flank to flank. Battle flags were out; rifle barrels and bayonets gleamed in the severe July sun. Lee had ordered more than 12,000 men—11 brigades—to advance across a mile of open ground to attack, and breach if possible, the middle of the long Union line. Maj. Gen. George Pickett and his 5,000 soldiers from the Old Dominion were to lead the charge.

On Cemetery Ridge a good many Vermont soldiers must have been thinking of home: after all, if they could just get through this battle, they would be headed for the Green Mountains within the month. The Confederates' shouted orders reached them on the July air, as the Southern ranks moved at a steady pace from low Seminary Ridge through the summer wheat. Waiting to meet the men from Fredericksburg and Brandy Station, Richmond and Alexandria, the Shenandoah Valley and the Blue Ridge were men and boys from Montpelier and St. Johnsbury, Randolph and Bethel, Bridgewater and Burlington, Sherburne and Shrewsbury—farmers, store clerks, hired hands.

As the Confederate lines commenced their advance, Union cannon from Cemetery Hill to Little Round Top reopened. Holes were torn in the rebel ranks, yet they came on, at a pace of 100 yards per minute, toward the Emmitsburg Road, where pickets from the 16th Vermont were still on duty. Nobody had to tell them twice to get out of the way; they fired and beat it back up Cemetery Ridge, to rejoin the rest of their regiment. On the ridge Stannard gave orders to hold fire until the enemy was close in, then to give them the bayonet. The gray ranks crossed the Emmitsburg Road and began the plod up the gentle slope of Cemetery Ridge, where the thousands of Yankees waited. Fire from the Union cannons increased, Confederates fell in rows and clusters, but the attack came on. The Vermonters, off south of the clump of trees that was the focus of the Confederate attack, faced a largely unbroken Confederate mass. Benedict recalled:

> Preceded by their skirmishers, the long gray lines came on at common time, till they reached the lowest ground halfway across the open interval, when the Vermont Regiments, which it will be remembered, occupied a position advanced from the general front of the army, were ordered up into line by Gen. Stannard. The enemy's right was now aiming apparently directly upon the 14th Regiment; and the order was sent to Col. Nichols, by Gen. Stannard, to hold fire till the enemy was close upon him, then to give him a volley, and after that the bayonet.

Then unexpectedly, the Confederates changed direction; the attackers approaching the Vermonters veered north, toward the brigade's right. The Confederates were now coming in across the 14th regiment's front, and its men rose on command and let loose a volley. "It was a terribly costly movement for the enemy," Lieutenant Benedict remembered. "The 14th Regiment, upon its commencement, at once opened fire by battalion, and continued it by file, at about sixty rods distance, with very great effect. The 13th joined its fire with the 14th, and a line of dead rebels at the close showed distinctly where they marched across the front of the Vermonters."

The Confederate attack was now taking fire from thousands of rifles, with rebels falling by the score in the deafening, mournful roar. The Confederates penetrated the Union lines near the Clump of Trees, where rebels went over the wall and in among Union cannons. Union general Winfield Scott Hancock was there, ordering in more and more troops. Then he suddenly spurred his horse down the ridge toward Stannard's Vermonters.

The turning of the Confederate attack in front of the Vermonters had not escaped Hancock's attention. If Stannard could march his men out in front of their breastworks, Hancock reasoned, they could turn and fire directly into the flank of the butternut mass now piled in toward the Clump of Trees.

Apparently George Stannard got the same idea at about that time. Hancock sat his horse and told Stannard what he wanted him to do, to march his brigade out into the no-man's-land to the front. Stannard, no doubt, told him he had already begun it. Then a bullet hit Hancock's groin, a severe and painful wound, and the general slumped from his saddle, out of the battle, caught by two Vermont soldiers.

Stannard always insisted that the idea for the flank maneuver was his, that he'd already issued orders when General Hancock rode up. He later said:

> As soon as the change of the point of attack became evident, I ordered a flank attack upon the enemy's column. Forming in the open meadow in front of our lines, the 13th and 16th regiments marched down in column by the flank, changed front forward, at right angle to the main line of battle to the army, bringing them in line of battle upon the flank of the charging column of the enemy, and opened a destructive fire at short range.

Benedict wrote: "General Stannard ordered forward the Thirteenth and Sixteenth regiments to take the enemy on the flank. The Vermonters marched a few rods to the right, and then, changing front, swung out at right angles to the main line, close upon the flank of the charging column, and opened fire."

The 13th, followed by the 16th, marched north along the Union front about 200 yards and halted. Then the two regiments, one company at a time, swung like a great door out into no-man's-land, turning a full 45 degrees until facing directly at the mass of the Confederate attack now piled in front of the Clump of Trees. Acting as the hinge of the whole movement was the man at the head of the lead regiment, the 13th, Sgt. James Scully, until nine months previous a dry goods clerk in a Burlington store. In the words of the historian G. G. Benedict, Scully was "the pivot of the pivotal movement of the pivotal battle of the war." Colonel Veazey later said the difficult wheeling maneuver was executed "as if on parade." The Vermont battle line, hundreds of yards long and reaching almost to the Emmitsburg Road, came beautifully into line, and suddenly there were 900 Vermont riflemen aiming directly at the Confederates' exposed right flank. The bold advance did not go unnoticed, and more and more Confederates turned to fire into this most sudden and dire threat. "Our men are dropping all along our lines," said George Scott of the 13th regiment. "Our

*James Scully, the hinge of Stannard's
flank attack.*

gallant little Sergeant-Major [Henry] Smith came up to me, spaned his hands, and exclaimed, 'Scott, aren't we giving them hell?' in a moment he fell dead shot through by a cannon ball." Despite the heavy fire, the Vermonters took aim and loosed a volley, then another and another.

"The effect was resistless. The ground lay thickly covered with dead and wounded; hundreds, thousands threw down their arms," remembered one officer who saw it.

The Vermonters had blasted Pickett's flank to smithereens, slaughtered the brave men who had reached the Union center. Benedict wrote: "This was more than the rebels had counted on. They began to break and scatter from the rear in less than five minutes, and in ten more it was an utter rout."

"Glory to God, glory to God, see the Vermonters go at it," shouted Maj. Gen. Abner Doubleday on Cemetery Ridge.

According to Doubleday, Confederate prisoners said after the battle that "what ruined them was Stannard's brigade on their flank, as they found it impossible to contend with it in that position; and they drew off in a huddle to get away."

Any last dim Confederate hopes that Pickett's charge might succeed were dashed to sudden death by the Vermonters. The attack broke; Confederates streamed back toward Seminary Ridge. Hundreds of others surrendered to the nearest Union soldiers. Colonel Randall finally ran to the front of his men, ordering them to stop shooting at Confederates trying to surrender.

Out in the thick of it was Lt. Stephen Brown, the man Stannard had arrested for stopping to get water for his thirsty men on the long march to Gettysburg. Brown still hadn't got back his sword but had found a camp hatchet on the ground, which he waved while his comrades around him fired. When things died down, a Confederate officer came up to Brown and surrendered. Brown accepted the sword with hatchet held high.

Pickett's charge was broken, almost. But Florida and Alabama troops, the former led by Col. David Lang and the latter by Brig. Gen. Cadmus Wilcox, assigned to support and guard Pickett's flank, were now crossing the Emmitsburg Road, approaching the Union lines a bit south of the Vermonters. They were isolated, under heavy fire, and Wheelock Veazey saw an opportunity. He ordered the 16th Vermont to do an about-face, turning away from Pickett's massed troops, toward the new Confederate assault. Stannard came along and questioned the movement, for there were far more Confederates than members of the 16th Vermont. "Baldy" Smith, who knew both Stannard and Veazey but was not at Gettysburg, said the conversation went thusly:

"Why, you can't make your men go there, no men can do it," Stannard said. "I tell you, General, my men will do what I want them to," Veazey replied. Stannard: "If you won't do as I want you to do, do as you are a mind to." Veazey described what happened next:

The ground from our position toward the enemy was fairly smooth and a little descending; and upon receiving the order to charge the men cheered and rushed forward at a run without firing a shot. They quickly struck the rebel flank and followed it until the whole line had disappeared. The movement was so sudden and rapid that the enemy could not change front to oppose us. A great many prisoners were taken, but I cannot tell the number, as they were sent to the rear without a guard, as I had no men to spare for that purpose, and none were needed as the prisoners were quite willing to get within the shelter of our lines and away from the exposure to which they were then subjected as well as ourselves from the rebel artillery, which followed us with merciless vigor. As fast as they were captured they were told where to go and they went, and without standing on the order of their going. We took two stands of regimental colors and another standard from which the flag had been torn. This was the last effort of the infantry of the enemy.

George Benedict reported: "The Fourteenth met them with a hot fire in front, and Colonel Veazey with the Sixteenth, hurrying back on the double quick, took them at the flank and bagged about a brigade of them."

As Veazey's 16th was hammering the last vestige of the great charge, George Stannard was hit. In a last great shower of fire launched from Confederate artillery in a desperate attempt to aid Wilcox, a small iron ball took the Vermont general in a thigh and dug in deep. The pain was intense, but Stannard refused to leave the field until an hour later when a surgeon convinced him he needed care. He fainted just before being carried back to a farmhouse turned field hospital, well behind Cemetery Ridge. Next day he was started on his way to a military hospital in Baltimore, out of the war for months but not for good.

Pickett's charge was history. Of the more than 12,000 men who had started out as if on parade from Seminary Ridge, only about one-third returned to a disconsolate General Lee, who told them, "This has all been my fault."

Back on Cemetery Ridge, a mighty cheer went up along the Union line from the Round Tops to Cemetery Hill. Some chanted "Fredericksburg, Fredericksburg," feeling that the awful slaughter of the previous December, in front of Marye's Heights and the Sunken Road, had at last been avenged.

Pvt. Edwin Pierce of Shrewsbury stood up behind the rude breastworks and discovered that he was, after all, all right. Then he looked beside him and saw that his best buddy, Billy Cairns, from Middletown Springs, lay dead with a bullet hole in his forehead.

Out on the smoky ground where the Second Vermont Brigade had struck Pickett's flank, mangled men lay everywhere, some making piteous sounds. One of the wounded was William Doubleday of Sherburne, shot in a leg.

Ralph Sturtevant had come through it all unscathed. Reassured, he went off to make certain that his cousin Wesley had also survived, that his terrible premonition had not been fulfilled.

"Just before reaching his company," Ralph Sturtevant recalled, "I met some of his tentmates that were then on their way to find me. They took me only a few steps further and there on the ground as he fell was the mangled body of my cousin having been shot through the breast by a solid shot or shell. His comrades told me that he fell just as the regiment rose to take part in the advance against General Pickett's charge, being instantly killed."

The climax of the battle had, of course, been the repulse of Pickett's charge. A few days afterward the *New York Times* stated: "A Vermont brigade held the key of the position at Gettysburg and did more than any other body of men to gain the triumph which decided the fate of the Rebellion."

The Battle of Gettysburg was most convincingly decided, but the battle was not quite over, at least for some Vermont cavalrymen in the woods by Big Round Top.

"KILL CAVALRY"
KILPATRICK'S CHARGE

When the heavy cannonade lifted and Lee's infantry began the fateful march against Cemetery Ridge, a huge cavalry battle was underway well to the rear of the Union lines. Lee had sent Jeb Stuart to circle behind Cemetery Ridge and, Lee hoped, to gallop in as the Confederate infantry achieved the breakthrough he wanted. But Pickett's charge was broken, and in the farm fields east of Gettysburg the Confederate cavalry ran up against Union horsemen under George Custer. The fight there lasted nearly three hours; in the end, Stuart had to give up and trot back to Lee. As that fight ended, another cavalry attack was beginning.

It had taken the First Vermont Cavalry some time to finally reach the battlefield at Gettysburg. When the fighting began on July 1, the division containing the Vermonters, that commanded by Judson Kilpatrick (nicknamed "Kill Cavalry"), was still several miles from Gettysburg. Early on the morning of July 2 Kilpatrick was ordered to the field, and, approaching Gettysburg, the division was ordered northeast to keep an eye out for just such a cavalry movement as would be made by Stuart the next day. They met Confederates, and a long-range exchange of fire developed. When things quieted down, Kilpatrick's horsemen were ordered back toward Gettysburg, while Custer stayed and thus was in position to intercept Stuart.

The Vermonters, with Kilpatrick, rode most of the night, and on the morning of July 3 they came onto the battlefield, near the base of Big Round Top, close to the southern end of the Confederate line. The Vermonters exchanged sporadic fire with Confederate infantry, which lasted through the cannonade that preceded Pickett's charge and through the charge itself. Then the Vermonters heard the cheers from Cemetery Ridge that followed the repulse of Pickett.

About an hour later, Kilpatrick issued orders for a cavalry attack, a charge into enemy territory to be led by Elon Farnsworth, commander of the brigade to which the Vermonters were attached. Farnsworth was to ride against the nearest Confederate positions facing his command, in the woods and fields along Plum Run.

Farnsworth protested that the Confederates were too well entrenched and was quickly supported by Maj. William Wells of the Vermont cavalry, who had recently rejoined his outfit after spending three months in Libby Prison. Earlier in the day Wells had surveyed the landscape to his front and seen a lot of rocks, stone walls, and plenty of Confederates.

Kilpatrick relented to the extent that he would allow Farnsworth to make a reconnaisance. Capt. John Woodward, son of the regimental chaplain, quickly volunteered. He was back in a few minutes to lend support to Wells and Farnsworth, reporting that the Confederates were not only in considerable numbers and well dug in but also supported by artillery.

Kilpatrick listened but remained stubborn: the charge would be made, and if Farnsworth was unwilling to go, Kilpatrick would lead it himself. Farnsworth, insulted, replied that he was willing to go as far as any man and would take his men himself. Then he told Kilpatrick that if the charge were to proceed, Kilpatrick must take the responsibility. "Kill Cavalry" said he would, so Farnsworth wheeled his horse and gave the order to move out. It was nearing 5 P.M. when the attack began, Farnsworth and Wells trotting off toward the rebel guns at the head of a column of Vermonters and Western Virginians. One Vermonter said of the moment, "Each man felt, as he tightened his saber belt, that he was summoned to a ride to death." Behind, in close support, came regimental commander Addison Preston and other Vermont horsemen.

When the column reached the open ground of a farmer's field, Farnsworth and Wells spurred their horses and ordered the men to charge, sabers drawn and flashing in the afternoon sun. They hit the Confederate skirmish line and easily broke through, the shocked Southerners not expecting Yankee horsemen to come galloping out the side of Big Round Top. Some Confederates surrendered and were quickly taken back to the Union lines, but they were much in the minority. The Union cavalry had ridden in on Texas, Alabama, and Georgia troops, veterans all, who soon regained their composure. The advantage was quickly all theirs. The Yankees were galloping through a landscape where one would steer a horse most cautiously, even at a walk. Stone walls ran everywhere; boulders of various sizes were scattered amid woods and fields, as in a Vermont pasture. Streambeds cut across the patches of woods interspersed with small fields. For a third of a mile and more the cavalrymen galloped, deeper behind the Confederate front.

Sheltered by trees and rocks the Confederates took careful aim, and Yankee cavalrymen began to fall from their saddles. One rebel veteran was seen shooting at horses, not men. When asked why, he replied that he needed practice for deer hunting when he got home. An Alabama regiment let the head of the cavalry column pass, then moved out of the thick woods in which they were hiding to

Farnworth's futile charge at Gettysburg.

Howard Coffin Collection

unleash a savage flank fire. The Vermonters and western Virginians rode on, probably in something of a panic by now, into a field, across which they saw Confederate cannon aimed directly at them. The charge veered off as the guns exploded; still, men went down in a welter of dust and blood.

William Wells later wrote: "We charged over the rocks, over stone walls and fences....We charged about until we ran onto a brigade of infantry stationed behind a stone wall in the woods. They opened on us, killed some horses and captured some men."

At that moment, the charge failed: Farnsworth's column turned back toward where the Union lines should be. A Georgia officer described what he saw:

> The head of a line of...cavalry...emerged from the wood, galloping, hurrahing and waving their swords as if frantic. Our artillery, which had been thrown forward across the road, opened on them. They rode on. An infantry fire from a wood on their left opened on them. They then turned to their right to escape, turning down a lane. Some men of ours (cooking details) threw themselves behind the stone fence on the side of the lane and opened on them as they came down the lane. They then turned again to the right and entered the field and directed themselves back towards the point where they had first appeared to us. In doing so they had to pass a wood on their left. From this an infantry fire opened on them, and their direction was again changed to the right. The result was that they galloped round and round in the large field, finding a fire at every outlet, until most of them were killed or captured. Everything passed before our eyes on the mountainside as if in an amphitheater.

The officer also recalled:

> Some of the men engaged told me that the prisoners said it was General Farnsworth's brigade, and that they were all drunk. The same men told me that in going over the field for spoils they approached a fallen horse with his rider by his side, but not dead. They ordered him to surrender. He replied to wait a little, or something to that

effect, and put his hand to his pistol, drew it, and blew his brains out. This was General Farnsworth.

There was no evidence that the Vermonters were drunk. But the confusion may have led to that conclusion, for the charge, which never had any purpose, lost all order. Eventually, most of the 300 men got headed back in the general direction of the Union lines.

The reports that Farnsworth had shot himself persisted long after the battle. Along Plum Run, toward Big Round Top, Farnsworth had gotten himself surrounded; then his horse was shot. Major Wells was beside him and ordered another man to give Farnsworth his horse. Farnsworth mounted up and spurred his new mount up a knoll, only to find Alabama infantry waiting. Farnsworth ordered them to surrender, and they shot him. Later, a Union surgeon who examined his body said Farnsworth was hit by five bullets, four in the chest and abdomen and one in the upper thigh, but none in the head.

Major Wells made it back. But some 65 of the 300 men who started the charge were shot or captured, most of them Vermonters. Kilpatrick praised the men's bravery, particularly Farnsworth's. "Kill Cavalry" contended that the charge had military value, had presented the Union army with a chance to break through the southern end of the Confederate line. Many years later, the historian Edward Stackpole wrote: "With 300 men in the attacking echelon Farnsworth gallantly led a hell-for-leather mounted attack which reminds one of the Charge of the Light Brigade at Balaklava. As in the case of the British against the Russians, Farnsworth's attack was equally fruitless."

The Battle of Gettysburg had ended. Of the 170,000 men who fought, nearly a third were casualties; 50,000 killed, wounded, or missing. On the night of July 3 the exhausted armies slept on their arms. Saturday dawned rainy, the storm strengthening to a downpour by afternoon. The armies stood watch across the shallow, corpse-filled valley. There were no attacks. That night, Robert E. Lee headed his battered army toward old Virginia. Lee did not know it, but the Confederate cause had received another battering 1,000 miles to the west, along the Mississippi River, where more Vermont troops were fighting.

THE EIGHTH AT PORT HUDSON

July 4, 1863 was a great day for the Union. At Gettysburg, Meade's Army of the Potomac savored its victory over Lee. On the same day, a thousand miles to the southwest, after a 47-day siege, Ulysses S. Grant was accepting the surrender of Vicksburg, the major Confederate fortress on the Mississippi River.

But on that momentous day, some 250 winding river miles down the Mississippi, another fortified Confederate river town was still holding out against a superior Union army. The defenders of Port Hudson were reduced to eating their horses, and their time, like their rations, seemed about up. Watching the ramparts of the embattled fortress was a big Union force that included the Eighth Vermont, Stephen Thomas's regiment.

The Eighth, starting in late winter, had been on an expedition commanded by Maj. Gen. Nathaniel P. Banks, another Massachusetts politician who had maneuvered a high rank. Banks had won the derisive nickname of "Commissary" after he skedaddled his army out of the Shenandoah Valley as "Stonewall" Jackson's Valley Campaign unfolded, leaving tons of supplies behind for the grateful Confederates. Now Banks was out with a big army on a commissary raid of his own, up to the northeast corner of Louisiana and the Red River town of Alexandria. Along the way, he rounded up cattle, cotton, and other spoils of war with an estimated value of $5 million. Then the call came from the War Department to get his army back down to the Mississippi. Banks hastened along the Red River with his 18,000 men, and by the last week in May, his force increased to 30,000 by the advance of troops out from the Baton Rouge perimeter, he was facing fortified Port Hudson, on a high bluff overlooking the Mississippi. Within the little town's elaborate defenses were 7,000 Confederate soldiers, not about to surrender to an army even four times their number.

At first glance it was clear that Port Hudson would be no easy victory; it proved even tougher than it looked. With the help of slave labor, the Confederates had been fortifying for 10 months, and the results were impressive. The entire town, including the 80-foot-high bluffs on the river side, was surrounded by earthworks that connected forts at strategic points. Along those works were 50 cannon, 20 of which were heavy siege guns. Outside the works lay wooded ravines interspersed with swamps and gullies, or fields offering unobstructed aim for cannon and rifle.

The Confederate garrison was a tough bunch, as Rear Adm. David Farragut and a Union flotilla had found out in March. Farragut tried to run past Port Hudson's guns at night and had only partially made it. Of his seven ships, one sank and four retreated; 112 men were killed or wounded. On one of the ships that did not make it was a young Vermonter, a Norwich University graduate named George Dewey. Lieutenant Dewey's ship was hit, caught fire, and ran aground. Dewey, destined to command his own squadron many years later at Manila Bay, made heroic rescues of several crew members.

Brig. Gen. Godfrey Weitzel commanded a division that faced the Confederate works on the northeast. Stephen Thomas had moved up to the command of the brigade that Weitzel had led, and the command of the Eighth Vermont went to Lt. Col. Charles Dillingham, who had been practicing law in Waterbury when the war began. Near the Vermonters in the Union lines were two black regiments of Louisiana Native Guards, some of whose troops had almost gotten into battle with the Eighth Vermont some months back and now were to get their chance to fight. The 30,000-man Union army had Port Hudson ringed on three sides, with a river full of Union gunboats upstream and downstream. General Banks was bristling for a fight, and on May 27 he ordered an all-out assault on the Confederate fortifications.

The attack was preceded by a mighty artillery barrage, both from the Union positions and from gunboats, that seemed to turn Port Hudson into a mass of smoke and fire. Then the attack signal was given, and Weitzel's men rolled forward from the northeast. The Eighth Vermont was in the third wave. One observer wrote: "Over hillocks and ravines tangled with forests, through roaring, shrieking, whistling storms of great guns and musketry, amid the crash of gigantic beeches and magnolias cut asunder by shot, Weitzel's division drove in the enemy's sharpshooters, slackened its speed under the friction of obstacle after obstacle; passed in driblets through a vast abatis of felled trees, and spent itself in reaching the base of the earthworks." Clearly the attack was not going well.

VHS

Charles Dillingham fought with the Eighth at Port Hudson.

Before Thomas's brigade went forward, the two lead battle lines had advanced and taken heavy casualties. Now came the turn of Thomas's brigade. The Eighth Vermont led the way and immediately came under rifle fire from a partially completed trench up ahead. The Vermonters moved on, though men were falling fast, drove the enemy from the trench, and went on through a tangle of fallen timber cut to hinder the advance of infantry. Suddenly they were at the edge of open ground, being swept by rifle fire and canister from the main Confederate works. Several Vermont soldiers went down; Thomas, seeing the impossibility of the situation, called a halt. He and General Weitzel conferred and agreed that to continue the advance was futile. Through the rest of that long day of shot and shell, the Vermonters and the rest of Weitzel's division dug in where they were; their position became the new Union frontline. In truth, it had not been a good day for the Vermont troops. The men had halted where other units had moved on in the face of heavy fire. The best that can now be said, from afar, is that Vermont common sense had dictated that the thing was hopeless, so they halted.

Not far from where the Vermonters went in, the Louisiana Native Guards also attacked, black soldiers en masse at last given a chance at combat. And they did themselves proud, 1,000 men going forward under murderous fire, with one in four getting shot. Though their brave attempt ended in futility, they proved to the nation that black troops would fight as well as any.

The Union attacks that May 27 had been poorly coordinated; movements against Port Hudson from the southeast, meant to coincide with the attacks off to the north, came much later in the day. It was a bad show of generalship by Banks; the grim accounting showed that almost 2,000 Union soldiers had been cut down, while Confederate losses were little more than 200. A total of 88 Vermonters were hit. The siege of Port Hudson dragged on day after day as the Louisiana summer came on full hot blast and the Vermont lads began to get sick. Fred Smith of Montpelier was the Eighth's regimental quartermaster; in June he described conditions:

> Our officers and men lie quietly down, day and night, week after week, with hundreds of rifle balls whistling within a few feet, often a few inches, of their heads. And when from necessity, they must leave their posts, they have to crawl behind logs, and through ditches and ravines to get to the woods in the rear. Perhaps on the way they must cross a knoll or a ridge of land, when—whist! whist! whiz-z-z go a half dozen bullets from sharpshooters, who are constantly watching every such exposed place.
>
> The men of this command have been confined for more than a month to the ditches in which they live, sleep, eat and fight. In front are embankments of their own building, on the top of which are sandbags and logs, forming loopholes through which they watch the enemy, and shoot at the sight of anything that moves. These are in many places within 20 rods of the earthworks behind which lie the enemy, keeping as close watch of us as we do of them. A continued roar of musketry is kept up on both sides while the bullets clip the leaves and branches overhead almost

constantly. Along a large part of the line the men are obliged to approach the trenches crawling on their hands and knees. Here, too, they sleep, if they sleep at all, in such an inclined position that morning finds them several feet lower down the bank than when they lay down. If the night be ever so rainy, all they can do is lie or stand and take it.

When the ground gets very slippery, so that they slide too much, they must drive some stakes to brace their feet against. Many of the men have dug holes in the bank large enough to admit their whole bodies, so that they literally live in caves of the earth. The cooking has to be done half or three-quarters of a mile in the rear, out of range of the guns, and the food is carried in by cooks and negroes. You can easily imagine of necessity the men are very dirty and ragged, for their clothes soon get terribly filthy, or wear out. So much is their appearance altered that you would recognize but few of the men or officers of the old Eighth.

Occasionally, a few get out, stretch their legs and get washed, and those who are fortunate enough to possess a change of shirt, put on a clean one. But as a rule the poor boys are unshaven, their hair is long and frequently uncombed for a week or more; and if close inspection were made, it might surprise their wives or mothers to find vermin living on their heads and bodies. Their food is, of course, very plain and very poor. The water they get is very bad even for this country, and the best they are able to procure would be thought unfit for cattle in Vermont.

This preview of trench warfare in World War I came more than a half century ahead of its time, but it was working, for the Confederate garrison at Port Hudson was cut off, and few if any supplies were getting in. Time was on the Union side, but "Commissary" Banks wasn't about to wait. On June 11 he probed the rebel defenses, a fight the Eighth was spared from joining. Nevertheless, four men of the regiment were killed during the accompanying artillery barrage.

Two days later Banks, who had received grim reports of conditions within the fortress from southern prisoners, asked the Confederate commander whether he might care to surrender. No, not at all, replied Maj. Gen. Franklin Gardner. The next day, June 14, Banks launched another all-out infantry assault, preceded by a heavy artillery bombardment. He planned to move in close to the Confederate works under cover of darkness, then to surge forward at daylight. But the blue lines were cut down as they rose to charge. In the Eighth Vermont, 60 men were shot in five minutes as the regiment was driven back into a ravine. There it reformed and again went forward, though only a few steps. One who fell was Col. E. B. Smith, a New Yorker, who commanded Colonel Thomas's brigade that day because Thomas was ill. When the attacking stopped, another 2,000 Union soldiers had been hit. Only about 50 Confederates were casualties. The Eighth Vermont had suffered 90 men killed and wounded, including Lt. Stephen Spaulding of Montpelier, who had taken a rifle-musket from a fallen man and was aiming when a bullet entered his head, killing him instantly. Spaulding had told a friend the evening before the attack, "I shall not spend another night with you."

The siege went on. Francis W. Williams of Brattleboro, chaplain of the

Eighth Vermont, wrote a history of his regiment, which gave vivid accounts of life in the trenches around Port Hudson:

> For weeks the two hostile armies faced each other within hailing distance, and the rebels watched from the cover of their earthworks, while the besiegers, strongly entrenched, slowly laid the mines which at last resort would be fired beneath the enemy's walls. Under the laws of warfare, of course, no intercourse could be allowed between the armies, except through the mouths of shotted guns, or officially under a flag of truce. But it would be scarcely human for one body of men to be thus held close prisoners week after week by another body speaking a common language, and having so many interests in common, and no attempt be made by the former to get news from the outside world. As a matter of fact, therefore, signals were frequently passed between the privates of the two lines, and the blue and gray would pass over the fortifications and hold a friendly chat on neutral ground. Referring to this practice, Major Wickham Hoffman of General Banks's staff, writes:
>
> "It was curious to observe the sort of entente cordiale which the soldiers on both sides established during the siege. When they were tired of trying to pick each other off through the loop-holes, one of them would tie a white handkerchief to his bayonet and wave it above the parapet. Pretty soon a handkerchief, or its equivalent—for the rebs did not indulge in useless luxuries—would be seen waving on the other side. This meant truce. In a moment the men would swarm out on both sides, sitting with their legs dangling over the parapet, chaffing each other, and sometimes with pretty rough wit. They were as safe as if a regular flag were out. No man dared to violate this tacit truce. If he had done so, his own comrades would have dealt roughly with him. After a while, on one side or the other, some one would cry out, 'Get under cover now, Johnny,' or 'Look out now, Yank, we are going to fire,' and the fire would recommence."

One day Sgt. Lewis Child of Fairlee and three fellow infantrymen walked across no-man's-land and climbed into the Confederate trenches for a chat. A Confederate officer happened by and told the Yankees to "get out or get shot." They obeyed and returned to their trenches safely.

Chaplain Williams also quoted a fellow soldier in the Eighth:

> While in the rifle-pits…we were constantly on watch for a chance to make a sharp shot at anything which might appear inside the Confederate lines. Directly in front of the position occupied by Company B, but nearly over to the river, was a large round tent standing by itself, but so far off and so situated, that with the naked eye it was almost impossible to see if it was occupied, the opening being on the side. Corporal W. E. Halladay of Company B, had a small telescope, with which he used to amuse himself by watching anything which might attract his attention inside the enemy's lines. One day while in the pit with Samuel O. Horn, a movement at the opening of the tent attracted his attention, and he remarked to Horn that a man was standing just inside the tent at the opening, and he described to him the exact position. Horn, who was a good shot, immediately sighted his Enfield rifle to the

highest notch, and aiming at the part of the tent indicated, asked Halladay to tell him if the man made his appearance again. After waiting a few minutes the man came and stood in the same place where first seen, holding the flap of the tent back with his hand. At the word Horn fired, and in a very few seconds afterwards the flap of the tent suddenly closed. We never learned if the shot took effect on the man at whom it was fired, but in the course of fifteen or twenty minutes an ambulance displaying the hospital flag drove up to the tent, thus advertising that some one got hurt.

The siege dragged on. Chaplain Williams added:

Being under fire night and day for so long a time as we were at Port Hudson, some of the boys became reckless, and exposed themselves unnecessarily. In digging our rifle pits, we would dig a trench up the side to the brow of the hill, then run off to the right and left, throwing the dirt to the rear. This formed a bank on which a man sitting would show his head and about half of the body. On the morning of June 20th, Samuel O. Horn and Edward Belville [of Derby], after coming off duty, and having had a wash and their rations, went back into the pit without their equipments and in their shirt sleeves. After being there a short time talking with C. D. House [of Derby], who was on duty, both sat down on the earth bank in the rear, with their feet and legs hanging into the pit. Their white shirts made a conspicuous mark, which was soon seen by the Confederate sharpshooter, who sent a ball whizzing close to their heads. Horn immediately called out, "You are no sort of a shot. You couldn't hit the broad side of a barn. Try again." Apparently the same man did try, as soon as he could reload, and sent the bullet to the center of Horn's forehead, killing him instantly. After this Belville was less reckless of unnecessary exposure, but met his fate in a similar manner.

The isolation of the Confederate garrison at Port Hudson was taking its toll, according to Chaplain Williams:

So complete was the investment of Port Hudson, that it was utterly impossible for General Gardner and his army to hold any communication with the outside world, or convey any supplies within their stronghold. Consequently, the stock of provisions became so much reduced by the last of June, that the garrison were obliged to subsist on a small allowance of corn-meal, and an occasional ration of mule meat. Even this meal was obtained and prepared with great difficulty, for lack of a gristmill. They had a small portable mill, but no power, and to supply this they resorted to a curious device. There was within the garrison a small locomotive, which the ingenious Johnnies raised up on blocks, so that the driving-wheel could clear the rails. Round one of these was passed the belt of the corn-mill, and after the engineer had got up steam, he was able in this way to furnish meal at the rate of several miles an hour.

Union and Confederate artillery dueled, with far more shots coming from the Union guns, which had an open supply line to more ammunition. The First and Second Vermont Light Artillery batteries were at Port Hudson, the Second being the closest of all the Union batteries to the Confederate works.

The siege stretched on through June and into early July. To the north, Grant was tightening the noose on Vicksburg as the Confederate garrison neared starvation. Finally, on July 3, the day of Pickett's charge at Gettysbury, Confederate commander John Pemberton asked Grant for terms of surrender. Grant replied that there would be none, but he changed his mind. On July 4 the Vicksburg Confederates surrendered.

Down at Port Hudson the Union forces were unaware of the historic happenings upriver. Nevertheless, a Fourth of July celebration was held as a cannon salute was fired, with the Confederates as targets. Further downriver at New Orleans was Rufus Kinsley of the Eighth Vermont, who had so vividly described the regiment's long ship voyage to Louisiana. Spared the Port Hudson siege, but still a member of the regiment, Kinsley gave a grim assessment of things along the Mississippi on July 4: "Celebrated the 'Glorious Fourth' by staying in doors and keeping comfortable, and wondering how men could be so jubilant, and the country still so sick. Things in this department have never looked so dark as now; but I hope our case is near the turning point and that in a few days Drs. Banks and Grant may make us convalescent."

On July 7 Kinsley recorded in his diary: "Glorious news from Vicksburg. Pemberton surrendered on the 4th with 31,000 prisoners, 208 guns, and 50,000 new Enfield rifles, in boxes, besides all the small arms in use by the prisoners. Port Hudson must fall soon."

News of Vicksburg's surrender reached the Union troops in the lines around Port Hudson on July 7; day 46 of the siege. General Banks had, that day, planned another attack on the still-daunting Confederates works, but a hard rain interfered. While the troops waited in the storm, the Vicksburg news made the Union lines erupt in cheering.

Chaplain Williams recalled:

As the message passed along the lines, the troops hailed it with such loud and hearty shouts of joy that the Confederates knew that some important event had taken place, and called out, "What's the news, Yanks" and soon the Port Hudson garrison knew that another stronghold of the enemy had fallen.

Early next morning white flags were displayed above the invested works, and Gen. Gardner sent a messenger under a truce to inquire if the news of the Vicksburg surrender was official, and Gen. Banks returned answer that it was captured on the 4th. This was soon followed by a second message from the commander of the works, stating that he had appointed three commissioners to confer with three officers, whom Gen. Banks would detail, and arrange terms of capitulations. This was cheering news indeed, and in the course of a few hours the details of the surrender were completed and the garrison that had defied the Union army...voluntarily opened its arms to receive them....

On the morning of July 9th, the Union columns marched into Port Hudson and halted in front of the Confederate garrison, which was drawn up in line of battle. Gen. Gardner gave them his last order to ground arms, the Confederate flags were pulled down, and the stars and stripes rose in triumph, amid the exultant cheers of the victors. The surrender included between 6,000 and 7,000 men, with their arms and the armaments of the works. When Port Hudson fell, the last Confederate defence of the Mississippi was removed, and a free waterway was opened from Cairo to the Gulf.

In New Orleans, Rufus Kinsley wrote on July 10: "Gun boat came down this morning bringing official intelligence that Port Hudson fell to our hands yesterday, with 5,000 prisoners, 50 heavy guns, and all the small arms. The river is at last open."

When news of the triumphs along the Mississippi reached the White House, the president declared in words that still ring down the ages, "The Father of Waters again goes unvexed to the sea."

At Port Hudson today, little is left of the strategic village so fought over, just a collection of dilapidated houses and camps. Even the Mississippi River has turned away from the place, leaving the great bluff guarding nothing but a swampy lowland. Still the state of Louisiana has created a battlefield park and has preserved much of the fortifications, some of the best preserved on any battlefields. Rangers warn visitors to beware of poisonous snakes along the trails that wind through the deep ravines and up the steep bluffs. Clearly, it was a savage place to fight. The land across which the black units attacked, in the first major action for black troops of the Civil War, has just been purchased to be forever preserved. A museum at the visitor's center offers a display of battle artifacts, including several cartes de visite of Eighth Vermont soldiers, and artillery shells fired by the Vermont batteries.

DR. HENRY JANES TENDS THE GETTYSBURG WOUNDED

As Confederate control of the Mississippi ended with the capitulations at Vicksburg and Port Hudson, the great rainwashed battlefield at Gettysburg had turned into a sea of human misery. Wilbur Fisk marched with the Second Vermont Regiment through an area where hard fighting had occurred. He wrote: "I saw but a small portion of it, but I saw all I wished to. The rebel dead and ours lay thickly together, their thirst for blood forever quenched. Their bodies were swollen, black and hideously unnatural. Their eyes glared from their sockets, their tongues protruded from their mouths, and in almost every case, clots of blood and mangled flesh showed how they had died, and rendered a sight ghastly beyond description."

Fisk believed himself hardened by the war to almost anything, but "I cannot say I ever wish to see another sight like that I saw on the battlefield of Gettysburg."

The dead were everywhere, men, horses, mules. The stench was overwhelming as burial parties were unable to keep up, interring corpses fast

Dr. Henry Janes cared for Gettysburg's wounded.

as they could, where they'd fallen, in shallow graves. But the living carnage of the great battle was a more formidable challenge, for some 20,000 wounded men, all in need of care, overwhelmed the capabilities of the 2,500 Gettysburg townspeople and the army medical staff. Most of the casualties were Union soldiers, for General Lee had attempted to take his wounded with him back to Virginia. But several thousand Confederates were too badly hurt for the bumpy wagon ride and were left behind. Nearly every Gettysburg house, church, and barn became a makeshift hospital, and tent hospital cities were erected, especially along the banks of Rock Creek east of Cemetery Ridge. A Vermonter, Dr. Henry Janes, took charge of this most awesome medical challenge in the history of America.

Janes, a doctor in his hometown of Waterbury, had enlisted as the war began to become surgeon of the Third Vermont Regiment. One of his patients after the battle at Lee's Mills had been the famous Pvt. William Scott. Janes was no stranger to handling large numbers of wounded, for in the fall of 1862 he had supervised a Federal hospital at Frederick, Maryland, where he cared for casualties from the Antietam campaign. Then he headed a hospital for the Sixth Corps after Chancellorsville. But no American doctor had ever faced a challenge like Gettysburg. Dr. Janes, now holding the rank of major, set to work, and as he did so, he held to a firm medical principle he had adopted early in the war. The good doctor from Waterbury believed that far too many soldiers were losing arms and legs because of hasty amputations. At Gettysburg he set up a special 2,000-bed hospital for the most seriously wounded and instructed the staff to use the saw only as a last resort. Janes had 250 surgeons under his command; they listened and worked well, and as a result, a higher proportion of men kept their limbs than from any previous major battle. Janes also strove to see that Union and Confederate wounded were treated equally.

Lee and his Army of Northern Virginia slipped away from Seminary Ridge the night of July 4 while a 17-mile-long wagon train passed through Cashtown Gap headed for the Potomac River and the safety of Virginia. The Confederate lead lengthened, as General Meade was slow in ordering his army to pursue. The Sixth Corps and its Vermont Brigade, which had spent the battle behind Little Round Top, were finally moved forward on July 4 and got into a short firefight. The next morning, discovering that Lee was gone, the Sixth Corps was put on roads leading south, taking a roundabout way. It was not until July 10, almost a week later, that John Sedgwick's corps encountered Confederates. Lee's army was found drawn up in a wide semicircle, with both flanks anchored on the Potomac River near Williamsport, Maryland. There Lee and his battered legions sat, for the river was in flood. The defeated army was a ripe target for Meade's superior forces. Yet Meade, to Abraham Lincoln's consternation, never made a strong attack, and Lee got away. Before he escaped, however, the Vermonters got into a tough fight.

On July 10 Union cavalry under John Buford, in pursuit of Confederate horsemen, galloped into the village of Funkstown, Maryland, along Antietam Creek. Suddenly they collided with rebel infantry that happened to be passing through. Buford quickly got out of town, withdrew south to a long ridge, and suddenly found himself confronted with what appeared to be a Confederate battle line, supported by artillery, moving out from Funkstown through tall midsummer grass. Buford positioned his men and went looking for help, soon meeting Brig. Gen. Albion Howe, who ordered Lewis Grant and his Vermont Brigade forward. The Old Brigade got to the ridge top just in time, as Buford was nearly out of ammunition. The Vermonters, in a line that eventually was extended two miles, deployed to slow the enemy advance until the rest of the Sixth Corps could come up. But the rest of the corps never arrived: the Vermonters in their thin blue line stood on their low ridge alone and held their ground.

While history has all but forgotten the fight at Funkstown, it occupied a prominent place in the memories of Vermont soldiers. The Vermont Brigade always claimed to have fought off a Confederate infantry advance with a meager picket line. One Sixth Corps soldier described what happened:

> After the battle of Gettysburg, when Lee's army was in the vicinity of Hagerstown and the Antietam, the Vermont Brigade was deployed in a skirmishing line, covering a front of nearly three miles. The enemy here was in force in front, near Beaver Creek. The Sixth Corps was held in readiness in rear of the skirmish line, anticipating a general engagement. The enemy had evidently determined to attack. At last his line of battle came forward. The batteries opened at once, and the skirmishers delivered their fire. Our troops were on the alert, and stood waiting to receive the coming assault. But the skirmishers would not come in; and when the firing died away, it appeared that the Vermonters thus deployed as a skirmish had repulsed a full line of battle attack. Twice afterward the enemy advanced to carry the position, and were each time again driven back by this perverse skirmish line. The Vermonters, it is true, were strongly posted in a wood, and each man fired from behind a tree. But then everybody knows that the etiquette in such matters is for a skirmish line to come in as soon as they are satisfied that the enemy means business. Those simple-minded patriots of the Green Mountains, however, adopted a rule of their own on this occasion; and the enemy, disgusted with such stupidity, retired across the Beaver Creek.

Wilbur Fisk wrote: "Their officers tried to urge them on; they shamed and threatened them; they told them that there were but few of us, and we could easily be captured. Some turned on their heels and run, some rallied again to the charge. They came on a few rods further, when their ranks broke, and the whole battalion, officers and all, skedaddled for their very lives. They had discovered that they were blundering on a nest of Vermonters."

Some Confederates who came in from along the Antietam, trying to turn the Vermonters' flank, were beaten back when Colonel Grant shifted troops toward the creek. Another attack was broken in a cornfield near the center of the Vermont line; after it was sent reeling back, all assaults ended. When the Confederates moved back toward Funkstown, some of the Vermonters began taunting them, yelling that all they had faced was "some Yankee militia."

When the fight ended, 66 Vermonters had been shot, of whom 16 died. Colonel Grant estimated Confederate losses at 200 men. One of the Vermonters who got hit was Col. Charles Stoughton, commander of the Fourth Vermont and brother of Edwin Stoughton. Stoughton was up on the line with his regiment when a bullet took him in the head, blasting away one of his eyes. Believed to be mortally wounded, he was carried from the field, but Stoughton recovered to live a long life, though his days of service to the Vermont Brigade had ended. Colonel Stoughton is buried beside his brother in the Stoughton family lot behind the Episcopal church in Bellows Falls.

After the fight at Funkstown, General Sedgwick praised the Vermont Brigade for its "remarkable conduct." General Howe said, "It is believed that another instance of a skirmish line, extending over so great a distance, repeatedly repelling the assaults of strong lines of infantry at different points, cannot be found in the history of any war."

Just what happened at Funkstown is not entirely clear. Certainly the Vermonters made a remarkable stand against an assault by a Confederate force of considerably greater numbers and fought remarkably well. They held a ridge the Confederates set out to capture. But the Confederates were in a defensive posture at Funkstown generally, protecting Lee's bridgehead at Williamsport. Had they decided they

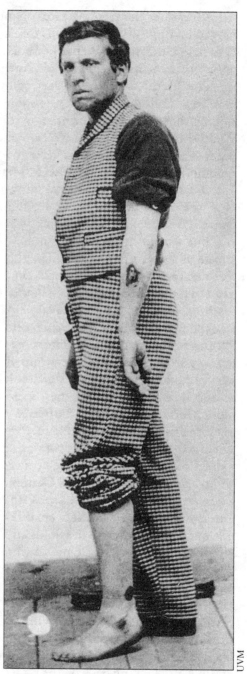

Wounded Levi Goddard, Sixth Vermont, by Dr. Janes.

must have the ridge, it is doubtful that a skirmish line, even of Vermonters, would have held it, and the rest of Howe's division would have had to come up. But they never did, as the Vermont Brigade stood firm against three Confederate advances.

A day later the Confederates abandoned Funkstown, and the Vermonters moved on through it and toward Lee's main force at Williamsport. By the time Meade decided to attack, the Potomac had receded to a point where Lee could put a bridge across; the Army of Northern Virginia was safely on home soil.

The First Vermont Cavalry regiment left the Gettysburg battlefield the morning of July 4. Kilpatrick was ordered to follow Lee south toward Maryland. Among those riding off the great battlefield were regimental chaplain John H. Woodward and his son John W. Both men rode with heavy hearts. In addition to the losses of the Vermonters, news had come from Vermont of the death from typhoid fever of young Woodward's fiancée in Cambridge. Thereafter Captain Woodward became reckless, seeming to care little for his life. He had, of course, volunteered for the dangerous scout into enemy territory that preceded Judson Kilpatrick's foolhardy charge on July 3.

The cavalry neared the Potomac ahead of Lee's army. But when the Vermonters reached Hagerstown, headed for Williamsport, they ran into a strong force of Stuart's cavalry. A spirited fight developed in the streets of the town, with the Vermonters giving way street by street. One group of 14 Vermonters was cut off and took refuge in a house, where they were hidden for nearly a week by the friendly owner until Union troops rode in. Pvt. Antipas Curtis from Chelsea got sick of hiding out, put on civilian clothing, and walked into the street as General Lee trotted by. Curtis saluted the Confederate commander and kept on walking, out of town and into the fields and hills, eventually finding a Union outfit.

UVM

Capt. John W. Woodward of the First Vermont Cavalry.

The rest of the Vermont cavalry had a hard time getting away from Hagerstown and were forced to fight a series of delaying engagements as the gray cavalry pressed in hard. Capt. William Beeman, a St. Albans man, found himself surrounded and was ordered to surrender. "I don't see it," he replied, spurred his horse, leaped a fence, and got away. The Vermonters finally reached safe ground, and looking back on the day, Addison Preston reflected: "The Vermont Cavalry fought most desperately, and I saw men shed tears that they could not do more. We were in a very dangerous position, with the rebel army on three sides, but we cut our way through.... You cannot imagine how desperately our boys will fight."

That day of charge and countercharge cost the Vermont regiment 76 casualties. In the end, their part in the attempt to cut Lee off from his Potomac crossing went for naught. Five men had been killed, including Captain Woodward. Just outside Hagerstown he and his men had been holding an advanced position while other Vermonters fell back. He got too close to the Confederate horsemen; bullets hit him in the heart and brain. Woodward, heartbroken and careless, had died the soldier's death he seemed to desire. His comrades recovered his body, which was promptly sent on its way back to the hills of home. With it went Chaplain Woodward, the spirit for war gone out of him. Back he went to Westford and then over the hill to Cambridge with his son's body. Then he was laid to rest in a Cambridge cemetery beside the grave of Hattie Chadwick, the young lady he would have married.

At Gettysburg the terms of enlistment for the five regiments of the Second Vermont Brigade were about to expire. Wounded General Stannard's place as brigade commander had been taken by Col. Francis Randall, of the 13th Vermont. His was a fast-diminishing new command. The 12th Vermont's nine-month enlistment had ended on July 4. Colonel Blunt's men, who had missed the battle by a narrow margin after General Sickles had ordered them to the field only to see the order reversed, began marching for home on July 5. On reaching Westminster, Maryland, they entrained for Baltimore, where they headed north, arriving in Brattleboro July 9. As they got there, word came of bloody draft riots in New York City. The field-grade officers and some 200 men of the regiment quickly volunteered to help put down the strife. Governor Holbrook was in Brattleboro and heard of the offer but said that, barring some desperate call from New York authorities, the men should proceed home and get on with their lives. They did.

On July 6 the remaining regiments of the Second Vermont Brigade began a slow pursuit of Lee's army. Two days later they had reached Middletown, Maryland, where the 13th Vermont was ordered to head home. The regiment started east toward Frederick to catch a train at Monocacy Junction. Near Frederick the brigade chanced to meet the veterans of the Old Brigade on the march to Funkstown. The men of the 13th boarded trains at Monocacy Junction on July 11 and, after chugging through Jersey City and New Haven, arrived in Brattleboro the evening of July 13. The 12th Vermont greeted them with torches; both outfits marched with a cheering crowd to the barracks at Brattleboro to be mustered out.

The three remaining regiments of the Second Vermont, now commanded by Wheelock Veazey, still had a few days of military service ahead. They came within two miles of the fighting at Funkstown, then marched on through that town to the outskirts of Williamsport, where the Army of the Potomac confronted Lee's Army of Northern Virginia. On July 13, 150 men of the 16th Vermont got in a long-range shooting match with some Confederates, and one Vermonter was wounded. It was the Second Vermont Brigade's last fight. That night Lee crossed the Potomac. The three Vermont regiments followed the Confederates for five more days. On July 18 they were put on trains for Baltimore, reached New York City on July 20, and stepped off the trains into a city torn by rioting. The regiments were held for a few hours at the south end of

Manhattan Island, along the Battery, where the commander of Federal troops in the city appealed to the Vermont commanders for help. The request was passed on to the men of the 14th; they quickly declined. At dusk the 14th boarded a ship to sail up Long Island Sound for New Haven. There it boarded trains again, and at 5 P.M. on July 21 the 14th Vermont Regiment reached Brattleboro.

Colonels Redfield Proctor and Wheelock Veazey of the 15th and 16th Vermont decided to forgo asking the opinions of their men about helping New York City and, instead, volunteered them. The disgruntled troops went into camp on the Battery for two days while their officers were regally entertained at the Union League Club uptown. Then the men were roused out of camp and they, too, were put on a ship to New Haven, where they boarded trains. On reaching Brattleboro, the men were sent home for a few days' furlough. They returned for formal mustering out. The Second Vermont Brigade, which saw action in only one battle—perhaps the biggest and most important of the war— was home.

Pvt. Edwin Pierce, of the 14th Vermont who had lived through Pickett's charge to find his best buddy dead beside him, reached Brattleboro on July 21. Next day he boarded another train, up the Connecticut Valley to Bellows Falls. There he changed trains and headed up the Williams River Valley to Chester and on up the Rutland Railroad tracks, finally arriving at Cuttingsville Station. There Private Pierce shouldered his gear and headed on foot toward North Shrewsbury, four miles uphill. He probably thought somebody would give him a ride, but it didn't happen and Pierce trudged to North Shrewsbury and then struck off down the Upper Cold River Road. In the days and weeks before, he had been on a long march, in a thunderous battle, had marched some more, and then had made a long journey home. Edwin Pierce was a tired young man, and the last miles of his long journey to the Pierce farmhouse must have been pure agony. He got there with the lights of home showing. As he stepped through the front door, Edwin Pierce collapsed from exhaustion.

Back in Gettysburg, the war had shifted south, but the long agony continued. Surgeon Henry Janes continued his care of thousands of wounded men, sometimes taking time to note the progress of significant cases in a large bound volume of notes. One of the men in his charge was homesick William O. Doubleday of the 14th Vermont, shot during Pickett's charge. Doubleday lingered several weeks in one of the army hospitals, his left leg smashed by a Confederate bullet. Three weeks after the battle, though his wound seemed to be healing well, he developed chronic diarrhea. On August 4 he was taking arrowroot soup for a condition that only worsened. Three days later, a prescription of brandy had been added to his medications. Still he weakened.

On August 10 Janes's surgeons did what their supervisor permitted only as a last resort. They removed Doubleday's leg. It did no good. At 6 P.M. on August 12, 1863 William Doubleday died. Not long before the end, Doubleday, now a corporal, wrote one last letter home to his wife, Asceneth. In it he noted that an uncle had come to his bedside from Vermont to help in his care.

A good letter you sent me—strawberries oh how good—taste to me. You don't know how glad I was to see Mr. Avery. He says he will stay with me until I can go home. He tend right to me. How I want to see you but don't make yourself sick worrying about me. We are expecting every day to be moved. We can't go to a worse place than this. Uncle Dan says I must not write any more, so good by. Kiss the boys for me. From your ever loveing William.

As the hot summer wore on, the governor of Pennsylvania, Andrew Curtin, directed that a fitting resting place be created for the fallen. A 17-acre plot was purchased on West Cemetery Hill and a soldiers' national cemetery laid out. The 3,500 Union dead, many lying where they had fallen, were exhumed, brought to the hill, and reburied in wedge-shaped plots arranged in a circle, state by state. Corporal Doubleday was unearthed and placed in the Vermont plot.

While the reburials went on, a local committee was at work planning a cemetery dedication. They set the date for November 19 and invited the noted orator Edward Everett to deliver the keynote speech. Later they extended the formality of an invitation to President Lincoln. To their surprise Lincoln accepted and set to work on his few appropriate remarks. The committee also developed a list of dignitaries who would sit with the president onstage at the cemetery; one of them was the surgeon in charge of the Gettysburg hospitals, Maj. Henry Janes of Waterbury.

On the day of the dedication, the orator Everett spoke on for more than two hours before Lincoln rose. The president proceeded to deliver, in his high-pitched voice with a frontier twang, 279 words, the finest statement in all the American experience. Dr. Janes left no record, that has come to light, of the great day.

Funkstown today is a sleepy little town that lies along historic Antietam Creek some 10 miles from the Antietam battlefield. In the midst of the little village is an old iron marker that reads: "After Gettysburg, in order to mask entrenching operations along the Potomac River by Robert E. Lee, Confederate troops led by J. E. B. Stuart engaged Union forces under Gen. John Buford. The day-long battle east of the road resulted in 479 casualties." No mention is made of a Vermont presence.

About a mile south of Funkstown, the Poffenberger Road branches west off Route 40, leading down to Antietam Creek and one of those elegant, arched stone bridges common to western Maryland. It's a tree-shaded place where the locals fish and swim. It was apparently just upstream from the bridge that the Vermonters anchored the left end of their line. The road seems to follow the low ridge the Vermonters held, but Interstate 70 cuts through the terrain between the ridge and Funkstown, through the battlefield's center. The scene of the fighting is irreparably damaged.

Far north along Waterbury's Main Street today stands the red-brick library, once the home of the town's beloved doctor, Henry Janes, who came home from war to again minister to the needs of his townspeople, as he had cared for the shot and bleeding of Gettysburg. He practiced medicine in Waterbury until shortly before his death in 1913. Part of the second floor of the library is a museum, where some of Dr. Janes's Civil War relics, including his military surgical tools, are displayed. On the wall is Henry Janes's treasured imprint of Lincoln's Gettysburg Address.

Americans have gone to Gettysburg more than to any other of the Civil War's great battlefields. Tourists daily come by the thousands to drive the national park roads and visit the still-famous places of the battle. The tourists come principally in silence to Little Round Top, Cemetery Ridge, the Angle, the Peach Orchard, the Wheatfield. Over the years, monuments have been erected to the men who fought, who hallowed, the fields of Gettysburg. There are so many monuments that some seem to have been forgotten; walking off into the woods and fields of lesser traveled portions of the field, one finds them in the leaves and bushes.

In 1972 a Vermonter named Newton Burdick wrote a strange, impressionistic little book about Gettysburg. "The view through the window from my desk corner is as old as the hills. The view looks like an oil painting with Ascutney, forty miles south, rising in the centre of it. Beyond that in the subdued twilight of reminiscence looms Gettysburg, five hundred miles further south, except that part of it lodged here." Gettysburg has become a distinct and honored part of the Vermont experience.

Behind the Round Tops along the Taneytown Road is a monument to the Vermont Brigade. Flanking the park road along the base of Big Round Top is a bronze statue of William Wells. And off in the woods up the road toward Little Round Top, where Elon Farnsworth was shot, is a monument to the Vermont cavalry. A soaring monument to the Second Vermont Brigade stands on Cemetery Ridge, a column topped by a statue of General Stannard. It stands in a long line of stone tributes to the men who held Cemetery Ridge and turned back Pickett's charge. A narrow path leads down from the ridge top across the park road from the Second Vermont Brigade monument. Following it, one comes to a low sign noting that men of the Second Brigade advanced there to fire into Pickett's flank. To stand on that spot, beyond the monuments where the main Union battle line once lay, is to have a true sense of the isolation Stannard's troops must have felt on that fateful July 3, 1863.

I have always preferred to walk Cemetery Ridge at sunset, looking west toward the low line of Pennsylvania hills to see the sun disappear. Through those hills Lee and his great army appeared, and from Cemetery Ridge they were turned away in smoke and blood and sent back to Virginia. The Army of Northern Virginia reached its zenith on the long, low rise of Cemetery Ridge and then went on to a long, agonizing death. Against the gathering darkness George Stannard stands in bronze, resolute as ever, determined that the Union shall not fail for want of anything undone by his nine-month boys from Vermont. Almost 50,000 sunsets have passed since the Vermonters fought at Gettysburg, yet something of what they did abides. Gettysburg makes us ponder the deepest meanings of the Civil War and what it has led to. Always, the words of Lincoln echo back: "It is for us the living...."

A FROZEN END TO BLOODY 1863

The Vermont Brigade marched through Maryland after its heroic performance at Funkstown and after Lee recrossed the Potomac on July 14. En route, the men got the cheering news that Vicksburg had fallen; they stepped lively when a band played "Carry Me Back to Old Virginny" as they returned to the Old Dominion. Then the Old Brigade was given a few days' rest near Warrenton, where it was hot but quiet and the blackberries were ripe.

One evening Wilbur Fisk and a friend went in search of fresh milk and came to the home of two elderly black men, an old house "pierced in several places with solid cannon shot and an almost endless number of bullets."

Fisk, who had once expressed a negative assessment of Southern blacks, now wrote:

Everything within this house had the appearance of scrupulous neatness. The walls, chairs, ceilings, and whatever furniture I noticed was cleanly kept and tidily arranged, evincing considerable taste, and refinement even, on the part of the occupants, 'niggers' though they were; that was apparent to the most casual observer....I couldn't help wondering, as I talked to this man—had I ought to say nigger?—so respectful and gentlemanly in his demeanor, and thought how universally he was avoided and despised, whether He who made his skin black and mine white, would endorse my title to exclusiveness in that other world where we conclude there are no such visible distinctions made, and where he was evidently much more fitted to enter than my humble self....

This man had never been a slave, and has consequently possessed many advantages that are denied to slaves; but if his superiority to the common negro is attributable mainly to freedom, it only furnishes an argument against this institution of bondage that all the sophistry of the infernal regions cannot overthrow. If the soul of the African has sufficient elasticity to rise to such a height, when released from the pressure of slavery, it must be a fearful responsibility for a nation to keep them down. This nation has run the risk, and is reaping the consequences. It is of no use to speak of the prejudice against that race; but when this prejudice leads to the revolting scenes that were enacted in New York during the late bloody riots, it throws off its mask and shows its hideous deformity. A hatred that leads men to murder women and children, burn orphan asylums, and makes it dangerous for a colored person, however innocent, to be seen abroad anywhere—and all this from no provocation whatever, except the crime of color—must be wholly wrong, unnatural and unjustifiable. What if Jehovah should espouse the cause of this despised race, and shift the inequality to the other side, where then, my negro-hating friend, would your arguments and your boasting be?

While the Vermonters rested and things were generally quiet in the war zone, the draft riots Fisk mentioned had erupted in New York, Boston, Jersey City, and other cities in response to Lincoln's most recent call for troops. City authorities asked Lincoln for help, and soldiers from the Army of the Potomac were sent north, including the troops of the Vermont Brigade.

Arriving in New York on July 20, the Vermonters found themselves part of a 12,000-man force ordered to cool down the embattled city. With so many armed and uniformed men around, the trouble making stopped. The Vermonters were assigned to three locations: Washington Square, Tompkins Square, and Madison Square. There they put up tents and proceeded to spend one of the easiest and most enjoyable periods of the war.

Wilbur Fisk reported from Washington Square:

We have a camp as usual, live in our little shelter tents as we always have, and sleep on our blankets now as has been our custom; but the rattling of carriages, the constant passing and repassing of well dressed ladies and gentlemen, and the busy hum of peaceful life, are things that we have long been strangers to…we are surrounded on all sides by the lofty, elegant mansions owned by men of large wealth…and which I notice differ most essentially from our simple tents in point of comfort and convenience.

Fisk spoke of a good life in the shade of the park trees, and indeed there was little duty for the Vermonters. Fisk also noted: "We have had to preserve a line of sentinels around the camp here to keep the men from straggling away without passes. Besides the sentinels, there is, to prevent this, an iron fence of good, lawful height, which it is considered a breach of good conduct to jump, but a great many of the boys are just breachy enough to do it."

Many soldiers' kin took trains from Vermont for visits, which were not always successful since the troops were under general orders limiting time on passes to two hours. The Fifth and Sixth Vermont regiments were then ordered up the Hudson River to Kingston, and Fisk's Second regiment was sent to Poughkeepsie. Away from New York City, unit commanders allowed a relaxation of the rules. Fisk wrote: "As our new A tents that we had received at New

York just in season to occupy for a day and night, were brought along here, some of the married soldiers pitched them just outside of the camp and gave their wives a practical instruction to a soldier's life in real camp style. We never have been in a camp that has seemed so cheerful and pleasant as this one."

Two soldiers were united with their fiancées in hasty marriage.

In mid-September the regiments of the Vermont Brigade reassembled in New York City, with the exception of a few men who succumbed to urban temptations and deserted. On September 16 the brigade was back in Virginia. The Vermonters took with them the official thanks of Brig. Gen. Edward R. S. Canby, who commanded in New York:

> The admirable conduct of the soldiers and officers of the army of occupation in this city has been remarked by all classes of our citizens. The brawls, drunkenness and scenes of violence, which are so common in European cities where large bodies of troops are quartered, we are happily free from. Nothing could be better than the behavior of the troops now in New York. If the soldiers now in this city are a fair sample of our armies, we can safely claim having the best, in a moral sense, as well as the bravest and most patient troops on earth.

The Vermonters marched out from Alexandria, taking 150 teams of mules and 1,000 beef cattle. En route, they passed the camp of the 10th Vermont Regiment, now a part of the Third Corps. On September 22 they tramped through Culpeper and by nightfall were back in camp with the Sixth Corps.

The Army of the Potomac, now 90,000 strong, was well down into Virginia, and General Lee, just across the Rapidan River, reacted. With his 60,000-man army, Lee moved north to threaten Meade's supply lines; Meade responded as Lee suspected and started north himself. Much hard marching, but little fighting, followed. In one 21-hour span the Vermont Brigade tramped nearly 30 miles, too much for some of the new recruits. By October 14 the brigade and the entire Sixth Corps had moved back to the vicinity of the old Bull Run battlefield. The Vermonters had marched through a railroad stop, Bristoe Station, as they neared Bull Run. Bringing up the rear of the army was the Fifth Corps under Gen. Gouverneur Warren. At Bristoe, Warren got his troops hidden behind a railroad embankment, with artillery in the woods on a hill behind, and waited until pugnacious Gen. Ambrose Powell Hill's force appeared. Hill ordered his men to attack. Warren's men rose up behind their embankment, and Union cannon wheeled out of the woods in as neat an ambush as the war produced. Lee gave up the pursuit of Meade and withdrew south.

The First Vermont Cavalry regiment had been active through the brief campaign that ended at Bristoe Station. Late in August the Vermont horsemen had been transferred to a cavalry brigade commanded by the flamboyant George Armstrong Custer. There had been a cavalry fight on the old Brandy Station battlefield, then a number of sharp little clashes as Meade withdrew from the Rapidan and up across Broad Run. Custer was always spoiling for a fight—a compulsion that would end his life along the Little Bighorn River 13 years later.

As Lee's army withdrew southwest, Custer's feistiness saved Brig. Gen. Henry E. Davies's brigade. The Confederate cavalry under Jeb Stuart was moving down the Warrenton Pike from Broad Run, a tempting target. A division of cavalry under "Kill Cavalry" Kilpatrick, with Custer's brigade in the lead, gave chase. Custer crossed Broad Run at Buckland Mills and positioned his brigade to face south, in the direction of Auburn. As it turned out, Kilpatrick was being led into a trap concocted by Stuart and Fitzhugh Lee. As Kilpatrick and Davies reached Chestnut Hill, Lee brought his troopers up the Auburn Road to hit the Union flank. Custer checkmated him. At the same time, Stuart's horsemen turned and charged Davies's onrushing Federals. Kilpatrick had no choice but to turn tail and ride hard.

The resulting five-mile gallop to Buckland Mills was known ever after by the Confederates as the "Buckland Races," ending when the Union riders reached Albion Howe's division of the Sixth Corps, waiting along Broad Run with the Sixth Vermont and Seventh Maine up front. The regiments opened their lines so first Davies's and then Custer's people could gallop through, then closed ranks and put an end to the Confederate pursuit with a couple of well-aimed volleys.

Meade moved the Army of the Potomac south again, to the banks of the Rappahannock River in the vicinity of Warrenton. Strongly urged by Lincoln to strike an effective blow against Lee, Meade in early November hit an exposed point on Lee's Rappahannock line, a fortified bridgehead on the Union side of the stream at Rappahannock Station. Meade attacked on November 7 with the Sixth Corps; the Confederate position collapsed.

The Vermont Brigade was held in reserve behind the crest of a hill from which the Federal artillery was firing. Wilbur Fisk noted:

> These cannon-balls as they came tearing along through the air almost exactly in our range, could often be distinctly seen although the batteries from which they were fired were over the hill out of sight. Some of them appeared to be oblong chunks of iron, and looked like a bird flying swiftly through the air, though they moved so very rapid as to appear to the eye a mere speck, utterly incompetent to make the shrieking noise that always followed them.
>
> We expected to be ordered forward every minute, but the regiments engaged needed none of our help, and we remained where we were until the firing had ceased.

Rappahannock Station was a tidy little victory but certainly not the decisive blow Lincoln had pressed for since Gettysburg. But chances for one seemed rather good, for now Lee had little more than half as many soldiers as Meade, about 45,000 to 85,000, and Meade knew it. Meade decided to have one more go at Lee before hard winter.

Lee's Army of Northern Virginia in mid-November was posted well out along the Rapidan River, its center some 30 miles west of Fredericksburg. Meade planned to come in around the east end of Lee's line, west of a woodsy stream called Mine Run, and he began marching on Thanksgiving Day. It was a clear and bracing late fall morning as the army moved out, led by Maj. Gen. William French's big three-division Third Corps. In that corps was the 10th Vermont Regiment, under Albert Jewett of Swanton, headed for its first real combat of the war. French was under orders to move fast across the Rapidan fords, down through the Wilderness seven miles west of the old Chancellorsville battlefield, and come in on Lee's right, before the rebel commander could shift enough troops to stop him.

French got his divisions close to the Rapidan and into a traffic jam. Once they were unsnarled and across the river, he called a halt. Next morning, November 28, French sent his forces on the wrong road and was forced to backtrack. Meanwhile, Lee was sending troops east to intercept the Yankees, and as French moved cautiously toward Mine Run, he met Confederates in the woods and fields of the Payne Farm. There the 600 men of the 10th Vermont made their first charge of the war. One of French's officers, New York Brig. Gen. William Morris, described the Vermonters' part in it:

> The enemy was holding a fence on the crest of the hill in our front, and I ordered the Tenth Vermont to charge and take it. While making preparations to execute this daring duty, I received the same orders from General [Joseph] Carr [another New Yorker]. The regiment advanced in gallant style and took the crest. The left wing in its enthusiasm having advanced too far beyond the fence, it was necessary to recall it. The colonel's order not being distinctly understood on account of the noise, the regiment fell back to its first position. It formed rapidly and again advanced to the fence, which it held until the Third was relieved by the First Division about sundown. I cannot speak of the conduct of the officers and men with too much praise....Though the regiment had never before been under sharp fire, they behaved with the determined bravery and steadiness of veterans.

Regimental chaplain Edwin M. Haynes of Wallingford recalled: "It was truly a baptism of fire, while it was a deluge of lead and iron that swept over us. The musketry was not in the least of a jerky or intermittent sort, but one continuous roll."

The green Vermont regiment paid a heavy price in its maiden battle: 17 killed, 58 wounded, and 1 missing. That night the Confederates withdrew to join the bulk of Lee's army behind Mine Run. By next day, November 29, the entire Army of the Potomac came up, including the Sixth Corps and the Vermont Brigade. It encountered seven miles of stout rebel entrenchment, sited on high ground across Mine Run's boggy lowland. The Sixth Corps was assigned to attack the north end of Lee's lines, and shortly after midnight the men of Sedgwick's corps moved two miles to jump-off positions. The march took the Vermonters past the hospital area, where army doctors could be seen readying surgical instruments. Once in position, the problem was to keep warm. Wilbur Fisk wrote: "It was very cold, but no fires were allowed to be built there. The Johnnies were having their nice comfortable fires, and they appeared to be but a short distance from us.…But we must keep back in the woods out of sight and keep warm the best way we could. By scuffling, knocking off hats, and running around a ring that we made a path for in the woods, we managed to keep from freezing."

Some men in other units who had slept were found frozen to death. Others had written their names on slips of paper and pinned them to their shirts. Awed by the look of the rebel fortifications, the veterans thought they would die and wanted to be sure their bodies would be sent home.

Morning came, and the scheduled hour of attack passed. About 8 A.M. an artillery bombardment shook the frozen woods and fields. The men fell into line on command, shouldered muskets, and grimly waited orders to cross Mine Run and move against the rebel line. "We expected to be ordered into action every minute," Fisk wrote. "The companies to be deployed were selected, but the order to advance did not come. The boys were tired of waiting. If they had got to charge on the enemy, they wanted to do it at once, and have it done with, and not stand there and dread it all day in the cold."

As the advance was about to start, an aide dashed up to General Howe ordering a cancellation, for Meade had concluded that the Confederate position was too strong to be carried. The troops stayed in position through the cold day; that night a withdrawal was ordered. It came just in time, for through the night Lee massed troops for an attack on the south end of the Union line, a thrust intended to be as devastating as "Stonewall" Jackson's surprise attack at Chancellorsville. But the Yankees were gone, back across the Rapidan River to safety. "I am too old to command this army," Lee said. "We never should have permitted those people to get away."

As Meade's forces retreated, a surgeon in the 10th Vermont, Almon Clark of Barre, stayed behind to care for 20 wounded soldiers in a cabin near Locust Grove. Clark recalled:

I told the men…that the army was gone and we must soon expect to be captured. They accepted the bad news as they did their wounds, without complaint. After doing what I could for their comfort, I began to take a little note of our situation. The old house was not so good as most pig-pens are in the north. It had only one room which was occupied by a very old and extremely ignorant man and woman, and so far as I could discover, there was nothing in the house for them to live on.

The men had a few days food in their haversacks, some of which they gave to the old couple, who went at it with a pleasure that showed that they were very hungry. I was restless, and every few minutes I went outside the hut to scan the edge of the woods, where every minute I expected to see the rebel cavalry coming to make us prisoners. I had retained my horse and my watch and I killed quite a few moments petting the former and nervously noting the slow movements of the hands of the face of the latter, glancing often at the surrounding woods at the same time. I wondered how and where we would spend the night, and had many other anxious thoughts, as men do in unpleasant situations. At last, after we had been there perhaps two hours, I caught a glimpse of a horseman in the thicket, south of the house, and with a heavy heart I went to tell my companions that the enemy were at hand. In a moment I found courage to go out and receive my visitors when, imagine my joy! Instead of troopers with revolvers in hand ready for use, there stood Lieutenant [Rufus] Tabor and four empty ambulances that had been found somehow and, at great risk of capture, sent back to save us.

Those men hustled aboard about as quickly as such a thing could be done by two men, and we made great haste to catch up with the troops, which we succeeded in doing without accident, just at dark.

The Mine Run campaign ended, and with it all fighting in the east in 1863. Thus began the long winter encampment for the Army of the Potomac, a winter most Vermont soldiers remembered as the most pleasant of the war. But before everyone got settled down in camp, there was an unpleasant task to be performed in the Vermont Brigade. On December 18 the troops were paraded to witness the death by firing squad of two deserters, Privates John Tague of Rouses Point, New York, and George Blowers of Arlington. Wilbur Fisk described the scene:

The band discoursed a dirge-like piece of music, when the prisoners were conducted to their coffins, on which they kneeled, and the guard filed around and took position in front of them, scarcely half a dozen yards distant. A sergeant put a circle around the neck of each, from which was suspended a white object over the breast, as a target for the executioners. The prisoners were not blindfolded, but looked straight into the muzzles of the guns that shot them to death. The guard were divided into two platoons, one firing at one prisoner, and the other platoon firing at the other prisoner, but there was no reserve to be ordered up in case of failure. Blowers had been sick, his head slightly drooped as if oppressed with a terrible sense of the fate he was about to meet. He had requested that he might see his brother in Co. A, but his brother was not there. He had no heart to see the execution, and had been excused from coming.

Tague was firm and erect till the last moment, and when the order was given to fire, he fell like a dead weight, his face resting on the ground, and his feet still remaining on the coffin.

The other lad did not die instantly. The spark of his young life burned just long enough to utter three words, which serve as an appropriate epitaph for 1863, a year of fire and blood that left the war still far from decided. Wilbur Fisk: "Blowers fell at the same time. He exclaimed, 'Oh dear me!' struggled for a moment, and was dead."

"BALDY" SMITH'S
GREATEST MOMENT

"He is a sandy complexioned, hard, wiry looking man with a short, stiff beard, and if physiognomy is good for anything is as obstinate as he is represented." So Lt. Col. Charles Cummings of Brattleboro recalled Ulysses Simpson Grant in the summer of 1864. One famous description of Grant held that he had the look of a man determined to drive his head through a wall and about to do it. Wilbur Fisk noted that the men had a nickname for Grant, calling him "Old Useless."

As 1864 began, Grant was about to come east to command all the Union armies but especially to put himself in personal charge of George Meade's Army of the Potomac. Grant was the superstar of the Northern military effort; Lincoln was determined to put the fate of the United States of America in his hands.

By the end of 1863 more than 25,000 Vermonters had gone to war, and more than 1 in 10 had died in uniform. But to what end? In the East, Lee's two northern invasions had been turned back, at Gettysburg and Antietam; inept Union commanders failed to exploit the victories. The cost and suffering of nearly three war years by the Army of the Potomac had been too much in vain.

Out West it was a different story. If the Seventh and Eighth Vermont regiments had suffered terrible hardships and losses in the malarial lowlands along the Mississippi, at least the great river was now in Union control. The victory at Port Hudson had been part of a grand strategy that included the taking of mighty Vicksburg, successfully accomplished by General Grant. Not long afterward, Grant was promoted to major general in the regular army and given command of the Military Division of the Mississippi. His immediate challenge lay at Chattanooga, where 40,000 Federal soldiers were trapped along the Tennessee River under Confederate guns on Missionary Ridge and Lookout Mountain. The army was in danger of starvation, as its only supply route, 60 miles of bad road through territory rife with Confederate raiders, was too long and difficult to keep that many men alive.

William F. "Baldy" Smith, first commander of the Vermont Brigade, former Sixth Corps commander who now was in Chattanooga as chief engineer of the beleaguered army, had been studying the situation. One day he rode out to the picket lines along the river, and many years later he wrote:

> The officer in command informed me they were stationed there to prevent a crossing at Brown's Ferry, the road leading down to the river directly opposite. I found that friendly relations existed between the pickets on the two sides and leaving my horse I walked down to the bank and sat there for an hour scanning the hills, the gap, the road through it and the smoke of the picket guard campfires, which were some distance back from the river.

Smith devised a bold plan for a nighttime waterborne operation aimed at opening a much shorter and safer supply route to Chattanooga. Grant reviewed the idea and approved it. He later wrote, "General W. F. Smith had been so instrumental in preparing for the move which I was now about to make, and so clear in his judgment about the manner of making it, that I deemed it but just to him that he should have command of the troops detailed to execute the design, although he was then acting as a staff officer and was not in command of troops."

In the small hours of October 27, 1,300 men boarded pontoons and rafts to float from Chattanooga around a loop in the Tennessee River. Just before dawn they came silently bobbing in on a key Confederate position several miles down the Tennessee. The Yankees struck fast and soon took Brown's Ferry. Then a relief column under Joseph Hooker arrived from Bridgeport and reinforced the bridgehead. The Tennessee River was quickly spanned by a pontoon bridge. A Confederate counterattack was turned back; the Union army at Chattanooga had a new supply route, half the length of the old one and far faster because it was mainly a water route. And it was well out of range of the rebel gunners on high and steep Lookout Mountain. Tons of supplies poured into Chattanooga, and the grateful soldiers dubbed "Baldy" Smith's route the "Cracker Line." Now they were getting all the hardtack, or crackers, they wanted, and more. Thanks in great part to "Baldy" Smith, the army at Chattanooga was saved.

Grant wasted no time savoring a triumph but quickly strengthened the once near-starving Chattanooga army. Soon 60,000 well-fed troopers were in and around the city, and in late November Grant sent them into action. They first took Orchard Knob, then Lookout Mountain in what became known as the Battle above the Clouds; then on November 25 the other high-rise Confederate strongpoint, Missionary Ridge, fell in a thunderous infantry attack up its steep slopes.

The key to Grant's latest successes in the west was the opening of the Cracker Line, as conceived by "Baldy" Smith. It was Smith's greatest moment in the Civil War. (Later, the artist Julian Scott painted a formal portrait of Smith, in full uniform and looking impressive. In the painting's background looms Lookout Mountain, with Union army tents in its shadow. That painting today divides its time between the Vermont State House and the Julian Scott Gallery at Johnson State College.)

John Gregory Smith, the last Civil War governor.

While "Baldy" Smith was enjoying accolades for his Cracker Line, his cousin, John Gregory Smith, had been elected governor. Smith, a St. Albans native and University of Vermont graduate, had studied law at Yale and gone into the family law practice in his hometown. Involved in the family's prosperous Vermont Central Railroad business, he entered politics in 1858 and by the first year of the war had been chosen Speaker of the House. The voters picked Smith as governor by a margin of 29,228 to 11,917 over Democrat Timothy Redfield of Montpelier. Smith assumed office in October 1863 and said: "The progress of events within the past year, in the struggle which now involves the country, has been such as to call forth our devout gratitude to Him who controls the affairs and destinies of nations."

The governorship had become vacant on the retirement of Frederick Holbrook after serving two one-year terms. Holbrook went back to Brattleboro, to his banking, his agricultural writings, his inventing, and his beloved music. He had left an important war record: raising, equipping, and paying new regiments and caring for Vermont's wounded. By the time Holbrook left the governorship in the fall of 1863, 16 regiments had been organized and sent to war. In August 1863 Holbrook ordered formation of the last Vermont regiment, the 17th. There were hopes the unit would be filled by members of the Second Vermont Brigade, but the Gettysburg veterans were less than eager to get back into the fray; when the new year of 1864 rolled round, the 17th Vermont was still far short of a full quota. In late January Governor Smith declared:

> The Seventeenth Regiment must be filled. The men already enlisted are idle, waiting for the completion of the organization; large expense to the state has already been incurred, which must be lost unless the regiment is filled; and the honor of the state is involved, that the work be speedily completed. Every man in the state should feel it to be part of his duty....The failure to complete the Seventeenth Regiment...will be a neglect of duty for which no excuse can be made, and which will admit no apology.

Strong language failed to spur enlistments; but in February Smith appointed Col. Francis V. Randall, former commander of the 13th Vermont, to lead the 17th. He named Lt. Col. Charles Cummings of Brattleboro, editor of the *Brattleboro Phoenix*, second in command. The 17th went into camp at Burlington in early March, with just three companies totaling 249 men. The unit finally departed for the war zone on April 18, still at less than half strength. On April 25, at Alexandria, it joined the Second Brigade of the Second Division of the Ninth Army Corps, commanded by the luckless Ambrose Burnside. By then the Army of the Potomac was under the firm control of Grant, who, before boarding a train for Washington, had put the US forces in the Military Division of the Mississippi in the most capable hands of his old friend William Tecumseh Sherman.

Fresh troops were coming from Vermont to fill gaps in the older regi-

VHS

Francis Randall led the 13th at Gettysburg.

ments. One new trooper was a cavalryman from the Canadian border town of Derby, Eri Woodbury. Woodbury, a Dartmouth College graduate and Cheshire, New Hampshire, native, had come to Vermont in 1863 to serve as principal of Derby Academy, but he held the post only a few months before enlisting. He kept a diary from the time he left Vermont until he returned at war's end. The following are excerpts from his diary:

Wednesday, Jan. 20: Started for front. Went on open platform cars. Cold, barren, desolate country. Encampments all the way along. Here and there were villages, i.e. an old barn, or a chimney left standing to mark the site of some place inhabited before the war. Poor, foolish, deluded Virginia. Reached Brandy Station at 7 eve.

January 22: Our work consists chiefly of care of horses. I am in a little log tent with three others, not very companionable fellows owing to their profanity, etc. Mud thou art a nuisance.

February 13: Five "Johnnies" came over on raft last night. Several more wished to, but could not get on raft. These desertions are frequent all along our line. One of our boys carried coffee down to them…in exchange for tobacco which the Rebs seem to have in abundance.

March 23: Clear, cool, snow nearly a foot deep, but fast setting away. Ordered to be ready for grand review by Lieut. Gen. U. S. Grant in few days to have hair and beard neatly cut and trimmed.

Before Grant arrived, "Kilpatrick's Raid" occurred. In midwinter "Kill Cavalry" Kilpatrick, last encountered at the "Buckland Races," went over the heads of superiors with a plan for a cavalry raid on Richmond. Kilpatrick got Secretary of War Edwin Stanton and President Lincoln to hear his bold proposal; they liked what they heard and quickly approved. Despite protestations from some military superiors, "Kill Cavalry" equipped some 4,000 Union horse soldiers for a strike at Richmond. Along the way, Kilpatrick promised, his men would distribute copies of a proclamation recently issued by Lincoln offering amnesty to any citizen of the Confederacy who would again pledge allegiance to the Federal government. The project reeked of the sort of favor-currying, command-bucking confusion the Army of the Potomac had seen too much of, and it is doubtful that General Grant would have approved.

Kilpatrick got his go-ahead just in time, and on the moonlit night of February 28 took his little army, including the men and horses of the First Vermont Cavalry, splashing across the Rapidan River bound for Richmond. To help surprise the Confederate capital's defenses, George Custer lunged deep into enemy territory, to the very outskirts of Charlottesville, away from the direction in which Kilpatrick was headed. In advance of Kilpatrick's main column were 500 troopers under the one-legged cavalryman Ulric Dahlgren, wounded in the Gettysburg aftermath.

The way led past the Army of Northern Virginia's eastern flank and on down through Spotsylvania Court House. As the big column approached Richmond, the skies opened in a downpour. Everything got wet and heavy, especially the bundles of Lincoln proclamations, and they were dumped by the roadside. Dahlgren and his 500 had swung off west and got lost in the rain. To make matters worse, the countryside was awakened to the presence of Yankee cavalry, and some local snipers took potshots. On March 1 Kilpatrick nevertheless brought his men within sight of the Richmond fortifications, little more than six miles from city center. That night Kilpatrick summoned Addison Preston and told him to take the Vermont cavalry and some other handpicked men and dash into Richmond next morning to free Union soldiers in Libby Prison. Though the task must have looked daunting, Preston quickly readied his command. But at the last minute Kilpatrick changed his mind. If anyone could have gotten into Richmond and freed the Libby prisoners, it probably was Preston, but he never got the chance, for Kilpatrick lost his nerve.

Kilpatrick, having lost touch with Dahlgren and believing the Richmond defenses too strong, called off the raid and headed for Union-held Yorktown. As he departed, rebels attacked; the Vermont cavalry got into a hot rearguard action.

Meanwhile, young Dahlgren was having an equally bad time, having gotten his directions confused. He was accompanied by a local black man who promised to take the Yankees to a safe place for crossing the swollen James River, preparatory to attacking Richmond. But the river was found to be impassable, and a disgusted Dahlgren hung the luckless man from a riverside tree.

Kilpatrick reached Union lines near Yorktown on March 4 after a tedious ride, hounded by Confederate militia, angry locals, and regular cavalry. Dahlgren's troops were far less lucky; the young commander got killed. The raid cost some 350 Union cavalrymen shot or captured. The First Vermont Cavalry had 12 men wounded and 59 men reported missing, probably captured after taking wrong turns in the darkness and rain.

Writing to his parents in Waterbury on March 15, William Wells noted that Kilpatrick's men "came close to getting into Libby." Wells knew the prison well, having been confined there for a time.

The Wells home in Waterbury stands today, a red-brick house with a columned door on the main street and a motel added on the back. It is obviously a very substantial house, and the Wellses were a most prominent Waterbury family. Among their neighbors was Paul Dillingham, who would one day represent Vermont in the US Senate. The Dillinghams had two sons in the army. One, Edwin, who had left law school to enlist, was now a prisoner in Libby.

When William Wells's mother received his letter of March 15, she replied, "They [the Dillinghams] had a letter from Edwin Saturday. He had just received the two boxes they sent the first of the winter there is another on the way....What a glorious thing if you could have opened those prison doors." Edwin Dillingham would soon be released anyway and rejoin his 10th Vermont Regiment.

The Vermont Brigade's winter encampment was livened with occasional snowball fights between units, well-attended religious services, and competition among debating societies. Many officers' wives came down for visits, as did the new governor, John Gregory Smith.

On March 23 the new commander of all the armies ordered a major reorganization of the Army of the Potomac. Grant decreed that the five corps of the army be consolidated into three. The Second Corps would be headed by Winfield Scott Hancock, the Fifth Corps by Gouverneur K. Warren, and the Sixth Corps by John Sedgwick. The Sixth Corps would consist of three divisions, to be commanded by Generals Horatio Gouverneur Wright, George Getty, and James B. Ricketts. Getty headed the division that included the Vermont Brigade, General Howe having been sent to take charge of Washington's defenses. Getty was a Washington, D.C., native and a West Pointer, who had been promoted for bravery during the Mexican War. Though married to a Southern woman, Getty's loyalty was unquestioned, and he had fought well in charge of a division in the Ninth Corps.

Getty had five brigades in his new division, one the Vermont Brigade, commanded by another Grant, Lewis. Two of the regiments of the Old Brigade were now under new commanders. Col. Newton Stone, a Bennington lawyer and son of a Readsboro minister, led the Second Vermont, having replaced Colonel Walbridge, forced to resign by rheumatism. Col. George Foster, of Walden, had taken over the Fourth Vermont from Charles Stoughton, who had been shot at Funkstown. Thomas Seaver remained in command of the Third,

John Lewis still led the Fifth, and Elisha Barney the Sixth.

The Union cavalry also got a thoroughgoing shake-up. At the top was Philip Sheridan, replacing Alfred Pleasanton. "Kill Cavalry" Kilpatrick was sent west to join Sherman, and James H. Wilson was named to succeed him as commander of the Third Division. The Second Brigade of that division, to which the First Vermont Cavalry was assigned, was led by George Custer. On April 28 Col. Edward Sawyer resigned as commander of the Vermont regiment and went home to Hyde Park. Addison Preston was named his replacement. Sawyer had never been popular with his men, and one Vermont horse soldier wrote in his diary: "Col. Sawyer of my regiment has finally resigned and gone home. He is fit for command of home guards. Lt. Col. Preston, one of the most brave and dashing cavalry officers in the army is to be Col."

Grant was now in charge of an army that had his personal stamp all over it. Spring came to the Virginia countryside, the roads were drying nicely, and a Vermont soldier noted in his diary that all traces of snow had disappeared from the Blue Ridge. The time was fast approaching for campaigning under Grant.

TERRIBLE LOSSES
IN THE WILDERNESS

On the night of May 3, 1864 a private in the Second Vermont Regiment wrote a letter to his mother in East Barnet.

> Dear Mother,
> We have got orders to march tomorrow morning at 4 o'clock with 50 rounds of cartridges and six days of rations. I can't write any more this time for I have got a lot of things to do, besides tending to my guard.
>
> Good bye
from your son
>
> PETER M. ABBOTT

In the darkness of early May 4, 1864, exactly one year after it retreated across the Rappahannock River from the disaster at Chancellorsville, Ulysses S. Grant set the Army of the Potomac in motion. Three days later, far to the south and west, Grant's old friend, William Tecumseh Sherman, marched south from Chattanooga, bound for Atlanta. Grant moved at night for Ely's and Germanna fords on the Rapidan River. Beyond the river was a second-growth forest, a vast thicket a dozen miles across and an equal distance east to west. Grant planned to march quickly through the Wilderness before Lee could hit him, then to do battle on open fields and woods to the southeast.

"On the morning of the 4th of May we left our old camp at early dawn," Wilbur Fisk wrote, "and took the war path once more. The morning was bright and clear, the air cool and refreshing, as we bid adieu to our winter's home, and started on what we knew to be the most perilous campaign of the war. We took the same line of march that we did last fall, marching direct to Germanna Ford,

Grant's army crossing the Rapidan, Wilderness bound.

Howard Coffin Collection

and halting for the night two or three miles beyond."

As the Vermont Brigade stepped along with the Sixth Corps, General Grant rode by and the men gave him a loud cheer. Before dark the brigade made camp in the ghostly woods of the Wilderness, miles short of the open fields. Some of the men found themselves bedding down in places where the dead of Chancellorsville had been hastily buried. Moving south a few days later, Harlan Closson, a Thetford man serving in the Third Vermont Artillery, camped in the cellar of the Chancellor House. He wrote in his journal: "It is but a few rods from where the rebels buried some of our dead a year ago. Many of them simply had earth thrown over them where they lay. Their bones are now scattered over the ground."

Trying to sleep, some men could hear a rumbling to the west, as Lee's Army of Northern Virginia moved toward the Wilderness. The Vermont Brigade's daylight route led south along the Brock Road, the principal north-south way through the Wilderness. Two roads intersected the Brock Road in the Wilderness, the east-west Orange Plank Road and the Orange Turnpike. Lee sent troops moving east along both roads to strike the marching Union columns, and the collision came about noon on May 5 as the Confederates roared in shooting. The Union troops swung off the Brock and Germanna Ford roads and formed lines of battle as best they could in the tangled woods.

Grant set up headquarters on a knoll near Ellwood, the Lacy family farm, and there he sat, dispensing orders and whittling sticks. As the fighting developed, the Union command suddenly realized that the key Brock–Orange Plank roads intersection was unprotected. Moving toward it from the west were battle-hardened Confederates under the pugnacious Lt. Gen. A. P. Hill. Bruce Catton, in his *Centennial History of the Civil War*, described what happened next:

> Back on his knoll, Grant read his dispatches and he reached for the nearest troops. These happened to be Brigadier General George Getty's division of the VI Corps— 6,000 soldiers as cool and tough as any, including in their number a Vermont Brigade which is still remembered as one of the two or three best in the army. Getty was told to get his men over to the Plank Road at top speed and clear the Southerners out of there.

Getty and his staff arrived ahead of the troops; for a few anxious minutes the general and his aides were all that protected the crossroads. The foot soldiers got there just in time, and the Vermonters were dispersed south of the Plank Road, holding the front rank.

"After a little skirmishing, the rebels fell back," Wilbur Fisk wrote.

> Here was a high point of land where the roads cross at right angles, and it is in the midst of an endless wilderness—"a wilderness of woe," as the boys call it. The troops massed here in considerable numbers, and after some moments got into working order. Our regiment crossed the Fredericksburg road, and filed into the woods with other troops in line in our rear and front. Pretty soon the order came to advance. We marched in line of battle on the left side of the Fredericksburg Road, in the same direction that the road runs, and we soon came upon the enemy. There was one line ahead of us. We followed close to them, and were equally exposed. The rebels gave us a warm reception. They poured their bullets into us so fast that we had to lie down to load and fire. The front line gave way, and we were obliged to take their places. We were under their fire over three hours, before we were relieved. We were close onto them, and their fire was terribly effective. Our regiment lost 264 killed and wounded.
>
> Just a little to the rear of where our line was formed, where the bullets swept close to the ground, every bush and twig was cut and splintered by the leaden balls. The woods was a dense thicket of small trees about the size of hop poles, and they stood three times as numerous as they usually set in a hop yard, but along the whole length of the line I doubt if a single tree could have been found that had not been pierced several times with bullets, and all were hit about breast high. Had the rebels fired a little lower, they would have annihilated the whole line; they nearly did it as it was.

Private Fisk came out of it almost unharmed. "I had a bullet pass through my clothes on each side, one of them giving me a pretty smart rap, and one ball split the crown of my cap into two, knocking it off my head as neatly as it could have been done by the most scientific boxer."

In Fisk's Second Vermont, regimental commander Newton Stone, the minister's son, just 25, was in the frontline when a bullet hit him in the fleshy part of the leg. He was taken back to an aid station, where the wound was quickly dressed. Stone hobbled back to his horse and rode back into the thick of things, where his men greeted him with a cheer.

"Well, boys, this is rough work; but I have done as I told you I wished you to do, not to leave for a slight wound, but to remain just as long as you can do any good. I am here to stay as long as I can do any good," he said. As Stone rode up to his Company B, a bullet hit him in the head; he was dead as he hit the ground. His body would be taken to Bennington for burial, and Vermont Brigade commander Lewis Grant would send along the message, "He was beloved by his command, and by all who knew him."

Command of the Second Regiment fell upon another minister's son, James S. Tyler of Brattleboro. Tyler, too, was moving along the frontline, giving encouragement to his men, when a Confederate bullet took him in a thigh and he had to be carried away bleeding heavily. He was transported back to a hospital at Fredericksburg, where he asked to be taken home to Vermont. He died on the way, in a New York City hotel.

Command of the Second Vermont passed to Samuel E. Pingree of Hartford, who had been wounded at Lee's Mills in the spring of 1862. The fighting swelled through the long afternoon. Musket fire of an intensity never before heard ripped through the Wilderness: some men likened its sound to the tearing of a sheet. The woods were too thick for cannon, so many big guns on both sides stood idle. Some soldiers remembered the battle as massive bushwhacking. Usually, neither side could see the other, so men fired at sounds and shadows, at smoke and flame. Two great armies groped, advanced, and retreated in confusion, yet in unrelenting determination. In places the dry leaves of the previous fall caught fire and wounded men stranded between the battle lines burned to death. But as Bruce Catton wrote: "The Vermont Brigade hung on with a thousand of its men killed or wounded, and the terrible little flames came snaking forward through the dead leaves and dry pine thickets."

In the Second Vermont, a rebel bullet felled big Pvt. George Flagg. Before the war Flagg had gone from his family's Braintree farm to become wrestling champion of the Champlain Valley and now was the reigning champion of the Army of the Potomac. The tough Flagg would be back with the regiment in a month, survive the war to become a nationally famous wrestler, and one summer day in Bethel whip 10 of the best wrestlers in the country. His secret? "Brought up on salt pork, corned beef, boiled potatoes and maple sugar and seasoned by four years service in the Civil War."

In the Third Vermont, Henry Houghton of Woodstock said of the fighting:

We marched in on the left of the Orange Plank Road with scrub oak so thick that we could not keep any formation and the first we knew of the enemy we received a volley from a line of battle within a stone's throw. One man at my left fell dead, and a bullet went so near the face of the man in my rear that it took an eye out, two bullets went through my haversack and one through my canteen and another passsed so near my neck that it burned the skin then entered my blanket and when I unrolled it I found 19 holes in it.

Getty's division held its position at the vital crossroads, fighting virtually alone for three hours in front of the Union lines, such as they were.

In the Fourth Vermont, Col. George Foster was shot in the leg and gave up command to Maj. John Pratt of Bennington. The commander of the Fifth Vermont, John Lewis of Burlington, had an arm smashed by a bullet. In the Sixth Vermont, a bullet to the head killed Col. Elisha Barney. Maj. Charles Dudley of Manchester took over.

The historian G. G. Benedict wrote:

Of the company officers, one after another fell not to rise again, or were borne bleeding to the rear. The men's faces grew powder-grimed, and their mouths black from biting cartridges. The musketry silenced all other sounds; and the air in the woods was hot and heavy with sulphurous vapor. The tops of the bushes were cut away by the leaden showers which swept through them; and when the smoke lifted occasional glimpses could be got of gray forms crouching under the battle-cloud which hung low upon the slope in front. For two hours this went on, and the ammunition of the men was nearly exhausted, when General [David] Birney, having got into position, sent a brigade to the support of the Vermont regiments. By this time, also, the other divisions of Hancock's corps arrived within supporting distance, and were posted along the Brock Road.

Though relief had arrived, Lewis Grant faced the problem of how to get his men safely away. Grant ordered Major Dudley and the Fifth Vermont to make a charge, to drive the enemy back and buy a little space and time for the withdrawal. The Fifth rose up and went forward, yelling and firing as it went. Rebel fire not only from the front but from the left flank caught the regiment, and men fell fast. Dudley saw it was hopeless and halted. The Vermont Brigade finally withdrew, with the rest of Getty's division, to the Brock Road. They went as best they could, some crawling, some running. When the Vermonters got back to the road, they expended their last energy in throwing up rough breastworks. The Brock–Orange Plank roads intersection had been held, at least for the day, as welcome night fell on the smoking Wilderness. By the time May 5 ended, 1,000 Vermonters were casualties.

The sufferings of Vermonters were not confined only to the Old Brigade. The 10th Vermont had moved into the Wilderness, as a unit in Brig. Gen. William H. Morris's brigade, James Rickett's division, of John Sedgwick's Sixth Corps, the morning of May 5. The Vermonters were commanded by Lt. Col. William W. Henry of Waterbury. Henry had recently replaced Lt. Col. Albert Jewett, forced to resign because of sickness. The role of the 10th in the Wilderness was mainly in reserve, but the regiment came under occasional artillery fire. Maj. Lemuel A. Abbott of Barre wrote in his diary:

Before Captain H. R. Steele had hardly finished dressing his company after forming line a shell…exploded in the ranks of Company K, killing a private and wounding others. The shell had burst actually inside the man completely disemboweling and throwing him high in the air in a rapidly whirling motion above our heads with arms and legs extended until his body fell heavily to the ground with a sickening thud.

I was in the line of file closers hardly two paces away and just behind the man killed. We were covered with blood, fine pieces of flesh, entrails, etc., which makes me cringe and shudder whenever I think of it. The concussion stunned me. I was whirled about in the air like a feather, thrown to the ground on my hands and knees—or at least was in that position with my head from the enemy when I became fully conscious—face cut with flying gravel or something else, eyes, mouth and ears filled with dirt, and feeling most nauseated from the shake-up.

Next day Abbott noted, "It is also rumored that the Vermont Brigade...was badly cut up yesterday afternoon, but I hope it's not true."

The Vermont Brigade had indeed been badly cut up, and the First Vermont Cavalry, now assigned to George H. Chapman's brigade in James H. Wilson's division, had also been engaged. Sheridan had the Union horsemen in action west of the big infantry fight in the Wilderness. Near the scene of the Mine Run confrontation of the previous November, the Vermont cavalry ran into Confederate horsemen commanded by Thomas Rosser, West Point friend of George Custer. It was a sharp fight, and the Confederates were driven back. The battle that the Vermonters called Craig's Meeting House cost the Vermont regiment 4 killed and 31 wounded, with 14 men reported missing.

Derby schoolmaster Eri Woodbury wrote home:

At about 8 a.m. we were met by a strong force of cavalry and infantry...[several miles east of] Mine Run. This company and another were dismounted and placed behind fences and in woods as skirmishers. I had taken position behind a rail fence when one of our company came up on my right and I moved about a foot and a half to the left, he taking my place. In half a minute a ball hit him in temple and without a groan even he was "mustered out." His warm blood formed a little pool in which my knees were steeped. Several balls cut through the rails in that very spot, throwing dirt into my face, but I was unharmed.

Back in the Wilderness, a reporter for the *New York Herald* wrote: "The sun went down red...[smoke] hung in the lurid haze all around the horizon." The night brought relief, but by no means a cessation, of the fighting of May 5, the most costly day in all the war for the state of Vermont. In the terrible Wilderness the shooting kept on through the darkness and increased with the first trace of dawn. Men were isolated and afraid, unsure where theirs or the enemy's lines might be, and fired at sounds and shadows. There was no way to bring in most of the wounded, some of whom screamed and cried and crawled as best they could in terror from the flaming leaves and undergrowth.

Pvt. Peter S. Chase of Weston and the Second Vermont was wounded three times and left between the lines. That night four of his comrades found him. Chase recalled: "The corporal had a short piece of candle which he lit to help on the way, but as soon as the rebels saw the light they began to fire on it. The balls whistled so near us it made us feel rather uncomfortable, and he was obliged to conceal the light under his coat. They soon had me out on the plank road."

Fighting on May 6 resumed before sunrise, with both Lee and Grant determined to attack first. Lee got things started a little before 5 A.M., but then Grant ordered an all-out assault to be spearheaded by Winfield Scott Hancock's Corps and supported by two brigades of Getty's division, one the Vermont Brigade. The Old Brigade moved out from its low breastworks along the Brock Road and surged west along the Plank Road in support of the big Union advance. That advance rolled down the road for more than a mile, halting only when it reached an open field, where Lee himself was in the midst of the action. Texas and Arkansas soldiers came up shouting, "Lee to the rear, Lee to the rear," and when Lee turned his horse Traveller from the front, and only then, did his men go in against Hancock, bringing the Yankee assault to a halt.

During a lull in the fighting both sides brought in fresh troops. Unbeknownst to the Union, James Longstreet was massing 7,000 Confederates to the south for an attack on the Union's left flank, once again aiming to grab the Brock–Orange Plank roads intersection. What happened to the Vermont Brigade was described by Gen. Lewis Grant:

> The tide of battle had turned. The front line was broken, and men came disorganized to the rear. The brigade, at the time, happened to occupy a slightly elevated or rolling ground, where the enemy had, for his own use, thrown together two irregular lines of old logs and decayed timber. The Vermont regiments took position behind these logs and rubbish and awaited the progress of the battle.
>
> In less than half an hour the four lines in our front were swept away, and heavy lines of the advancing enemy came upon us with great force. They were received with a bold front and galling fire, and their advance was completely checked and thrown back in confusion. Still determined, the enemy reformed his lines, and again advanced to the attack and again went back. The attack was many times repeated, and as many times repulsed.

As Confederate pressure increased, units to the left and right of the Old Brigade began to give way. The Vermont troops found themselves increasingly isolated, with Confederates to the front and coming around both flanks. "Perhaps the valor of Vermont troops and the steadiness and unbroken front of these noble regiments, were never more signally displayed," Lewis Grant said. "They stood out in the very midst of the enemy, unyieldingly dealing death and slaughter in front and flank. Only the day before, one-third of their number and many of their beloved leaders had fallen; but not disheartened, the brave men living seemed determined to avenge the fallen....For more than three hours did the brigade hold this advanced position, repelling every attack."

Wilbur Fisk recalled: "One of my comrades was shot dead there. I was lying at the time as close to the ground as I could to load and fire, while he, less timid than myself, had raised himself up, and was loading and firing as fast as possible.

The ball struck near his heart. He exclaimed, 'I am killed,' and attempted to step to the rear, but fell on me and immediately died."

With Confederates moving toward the Vermonters' rear, Getty ordered a withdrawal to the Brock Road breastworks. "There was no chance for us when the left gave away but to run or be taken prisoner," Wilbur Fisk wrote. "We were between two fires, and the enemy had every advantage....Every man that had good legs was duty bound to use them."

The Vermonters rallied at their Brock Road breastworks, and a strong line was formed. It held. Wrote Fisk: "No serious attack...was made in our front, but to the left, where we advanced in the first place, they tried to break our lines and they tried it hard. They charged clear up to the breastwork, and fairly planted the colors on the top of it, but they did not live to hold them there long. The ground in front of the works was literally covered with the rebel dead after they left."

Also in action that grim day was the brand-new 17th Vermont Regiment, 313 strong, just down from the home state and assigned to the Ninth Corps division led by Brig. Gen. Robert B. Porter. The 17th received its baptism of fire near the center of the Union line, around the Chewning Farm, fighting in woods so thick the men had to crawl to get anywhere. Then the regiment was shifted to the south, near where the Vermont Brigade was fighting. Lieutenant Colonel Cummings described the fighting in a letter home to Brattleboro:

> In the afternoon we were moved further to the left and about 2 p.m. we were hotly engaged with Longstreet's troops. It was in the woods where artillery could not be used, so the engagement was close and the musketry firing fearful. We made one charge on our own hook and carried one rifle pit but not being supported could not hold it so we were forced to withdraw two rods. Soon after, while on one knee the better to discern the enemy and direct the fire of my men (smoking my pipe meanwhile) a minie ball struck me on the right side of my head against my hatband. It cut a hole four inches long backwards and upwards as my head was pitched forward at the time and almost two and one half inches long in my scalp. The blow did not make me reel but it bled with such profuseness from a breaking of a branch of the temporal artery, that I concluded to go to the rear.

At day's end, Colonel Cummings was but one of 74 men in the 17th Vermont who had become casualties on that second day of the Wilderness.

When the long day of May 6, 1864 finally ended, 250 more members of the Vermont Brigade had been cut down. But again, the Brock–Orange Plank roads intersection was in Union hands. The Battle of the Wilderness neared its end. The Old Brigade remained in position through the night and into the afternoon of May 7, when it was withdrawn from its frontline breastworks, moving back from the bloody intersection to safer ground.

The cost had been terrible. A total of 1,234 members of the brigade had become casualties, with 191 killed, 947 wounded, and 96 missing. In the days ahead, 151 of the wounded died. One in eight of the casualties sustained by the

Army of the Potomac in the Wilderness had been suffered by but 1 of its 32 brigades, the Vermont Brigade. Twenty-one Vermont officers had been killed or would die of wounds, while 29 more were shot.

Grant's army had taken a beating. Both its flanks were battered in, and the final casualty count put the Army of the Potomac's losses at 17,000, while Lee lost less than 8,000 men. Former Union commanders would have retreated beyond the Rapidan, or Rappahannock, as fast as possible, but not so Grant. In the darkness of May 7 he rode southeast with his staff, and as he reached the Brock–Orange Plank roads intersection, where he could have turned east and back toward Fredericksburg and safety, Grant kept his horse trotting southeast down the road toward Spotsylvania Court House. The soldiers saw it and cheered what it meant. All the blood and dying of the past two days had not been in vain.

The Sixth Corps was moving south also, and at one point John Sedgwick sat his horse by the road to watch his battered men pass; as the Vermont Brigade went by, they cheered him. "Uncle John" blushed like a schoolgirl. And the Vermonters were cheered as they passed other units along the road. News of the Vermonters' stand had spread through the ranks of the army, and battle-hardened fellow soldiers saluted them in a rare display of admiration for fellow soldiers.

Seth Eastman, a soldier in the Sixth Vermont who fought in the Wilderness, wrote many years later: "Where ever we went the army recognized us and they would stand along the sides of the roads as we passed and cheer and shout for the Green Mountain Boys."

With the Wilderness's carnage, the war was now about to come home to Vermont as never before. One regiment of the five in the Vermont Brigade, one of seven Vermont regiments fighting in the Wilderness, lost the following men killed in the horrible woods. Many bear the names of families who still live in the state of Vermont. Killed in the Fourth Vermont Regiment were:

Obadiah Barnes of Eden	Silas Webber of Calais
George Bracey of Bennington	William Aiken of Corinth
Lewis Bryant of Chester	William Heath of Newbury
Arunah Burt of Sutton	Louis Paquette of Newbury
Joel Streeter of Brownington	Daniel Perry of Cambridge
Franklin Eastman of Vershire	Anson Snow of Bridgewater
Luther Spencer of Rochester	Byron Wilson of Bradford
Stephen Capron of Bridgewater	John Campbell of Putney
Myron Chapman of Grafton	Darling Jones of Topsham
William Haradon of Putney	John Streeter of Townshend
Luke Kendall of Brattleboro	Jonathan Webster of Jamaica
William Roberts of Putney	Jerome Chadwick of Braintree
Henry Dunton of Concord	Albert Eastman of Hyde Park
Elhanan Ormsby of East Montpelier	Thomas Lowler of West Fairlee
Patrick Sullivan, hometown unknown	Adin Smith of Northfield

Harry Fales of Pomfret
Henry Woodworth of Shaftsbury
Hiram York of Rutland
Henry Smith of Williamstown
Joseph Blanchard, hometown
  unknown
Luther Carpenter of Johnson
Thomas Eagan of Weathersfield
Leighton Griswold of Springfield
Jerome Larrabee of Irasburg
John Miller of Springfield
Rollin Wickware of Chester
Joel Ball of Sutton
William Cutting of Barton
John Edson of Greensboro
Thomas Griffin of Greensboro
James Hulburt of Woodstock
Robert Rogers of Greensboro
Nathaniel Walker of Woodstock
Silas Barnard, hometown unknown
William Jones of Rochester

Ira Stevens of Rochester
George Hill of Guilford
Joseph Huntington of Rochester
Henry Magoon of Middlesex
William Marsh of Calais
William Parrish of St. Johnsbury
Nathaniel Bailey of Cabot
Frank Cudworth of Woodbury
Samuel Leighton of Danville
Edward Robinson of Danville
James Ryder of Weathersfield
Daniel Skinner of Bradford
John Wilmot of Thetford
Napoleon Amlaw, hometown
  unknown
Edward Carpenter of Putney
Leroy Kellogg of Jamaica
Justin Montgomery, hometown
  unknown
Henry Amidon of Pownal
Perry Pierce of Stockbridge

In the fighting around the Brock–Orange Plank roads intersection had been a father and two sons from a family with its roots in Stowe. The father was shot in a leg on May 5 and died 11 days afterward. One son came through the battle unscathed. His brother was hit in the chest and died on May 12. The father's name was Samuel Allen, the surviving son was Ethan Allen, the dead son Ira Allen.

Lewis Grant, in his report on the battle, said: "The flag of each regiment, though pierced and tattered, still flaunts in the face of the foe, and the noble bands of veterans, with thinned ranks and but few officers to command, still stand by them and seem determined to stand so long as there is a man to bear their flag aloft, or an enemy in the field."

A soldier wounded in the Wilderness came to the office of the *Rutland Daily Herald* not long after the battle to report: "All previous battles, not excepting Savage's Station and Gettysburg, were mere skirmishes compared with the Battle of the Wilderness."

Today the Brock–Orange Plank roads intersection is a part of the Fredericksburg and Spotsylvania National Military Park. Two monuments honor Pennsylvania troops, and three interpretive signs explain the battle action, though none mentions the Vermont soldiers. Yet it is to the Wilderness that one must go to find the place where the soldiers from Vermont made their greatest sacrifice for the cause of the American Union. Around that historic and unlovely place where two country roads still meet,

Vermonters by the hundreds fell bleeding to keep Meade's Army of the Potomac from being sundered. It is a place for all Vermonters to spend a few quiet moments by the remnants of earthworks the Vermont boys threw up on those fateful days in a May of long ago. They fought Confederates in the front and on the flanks, stood and fought because that is what they had been ordered to do. Vermont farm boys grew up starting a day knowing that certain things had to be done, chores had to be faced and got done before dark, or pretty soon the farm would fail and, besides, the old man would have none of shirking. So the Vermonters held firm in the Wilderness and did their awful duty, stood to defend a country crossroads that had suddenly become the most important place on the earth.

The Brock–Orange Plank roads intersection is Vermont's great Civil War battle scene.

SPOTSYLVANIA COURT HOUSE AND THE BLOODY ANGLE

On the night of May 7, 1864 what was left of the Vermont Brigade went tramping east to the Chancellorsville crossroads before turning south to join the general flow of the Army of the Potomac. Both Lee and Grant aimed to occupy the key crossroads village of Spotsylvania Court House, a dozen miles southeast of the Wilderness. Lee got there first, just barely, after Union cavalry got tangled around a road juncture at Todd's Tavern. As a result, the Army of the Potomac's route of march was blocked for precious hours. When the blue infantry at last came rolling in toward Spotsylvania in the morning of May 8, it was met by Confederate infantry already digging in on a rise to the front. Lee won the race.

The Confederates soon produced a broad loop of trenches surrounding Spotsylvania, strong earthworks topped with head logs. Every few feet an earthen wall extended backward as protection should any portion of the trenches be captured. It was a daunting obstacle, one Grant resolved to crack. In the woods and fields around Spotsylvania Court House some of the worst fighting of the entire Civil War occurred. For a time, it may have exceeded the fiery fury of the Wilderness.

The Vermont Brigade, down to about 1,600 men, reached the lengthening Union lines at Spotsylvania deep in the night of May 8–9. Next morning, Sixth Corps commander John Sedgwick went forward to a point where the enemy lines were dangerously close. Sedgwick was in a typically bright mood as he stood among artillery pieces despite warnings of rebel sharpshooters.

"They couldn't hit an elephant at this range," said the general. A minute later, a bullet hit him in the face, passing out the back of his head. The man the Sixth Corps affectionately called "Uncle John" was dead before he fell into the arms of the officer beside him. The sad news spread through the Sixth Corps in minutes; when it reached U. S. Grant, the Union commander twice asked for confirmation. Col. A. T. McMahon, adjutant general of the Sixth Corps, declared:

> Sedgwick's compliments many times cost the soldiers from Vermont very dear; for they were the high compliments of placing them on many battlefields in the foremost position of danger—of placing on them the whole reliance of the corps. On many a day he watched them, as the troops moved out of camp in the morning, or closed the long dusty march of the day;—and when, on one occasion, in the Wilderness, when the Vermont Brigade, returning, after heavy losses, from their march to the assistance of the Second Corps, saw the general ride along the lines as they were coming into bivouac, they burst forth in a hearty spontaneous cheer that touched him to the very heart. And when the cheers subsided one of them stepped to the front and called out with a comic and yet touching emphasis: "Three more for old Uncle John!" The general's bronzed face flushed like a girl's; and as his staff laughed at his embarrassment, the laugh spread along the lines and the whole brigade laughed and cheered as if just returning from a summer's picnic, and not from a bloody field, weary, worn and with decimated ranks. He could appreciate their humor, knowing that no thought of disrespect ever entered it; and a single smile from him went like a sunbeam through long columns of tired men, until it broadened into a laugh and culminated in cheers from the true hearts of as gallant soldiers as ever served the patriot cause.

"Uncle" John Sedgwick led the Sixth Corps.

Sedgwick, wounded at Antietam, had been several months recovering at his home in Cornwall Hollow, Connecticut. Back at war, the bachelor Sedgwick, who shared the family home with his sister, longed for the day he could return to his home. Sedgwick thought Cornwall Hollow the loveliest place on earth. His body was taken from the front by wagon, then by train, and then by wagon again to Cornwall Hollow for a funeral in the backyard of the home place. Then it was borne down to an old cemetery at the crossroads in the hollow, where Sedgwick lies today, his grave marked by an imposing stone monument that bears the Greek Cross of the Sixth Corps. Just up the hill is the Sedgwick house, looking much as it did the day the general's body came home. In the years after the Civil War, Cornwall Hollow was often visited by soldiers who had fought under "Uncle John."

The man named to succeed Sedgwick was Horatio Gouverneur Wright, like Sedgwick a Connecticut native and a West Pointer. Wright had attended

Norwich University in Vermont from 1832 until 1836 before entering the Point. He got off to a shaky start in his Civil War career, having been captured and released, then having led a division to defeat in South Carolina. But the heavy-set, bearded career soldier had performed capably as head of a Sixth Corps division at Mine Run, Second Fredericksburg, Rappahannock Station, and in the Wilderness, and now he had Sedgwick's corps. It was, in some ways, an impossible job: nobody was going to replace John Sedgwick, but Wright was a capable commander and earned the respect of his soldiers, if not their hearts.

In the woods and fields around Spotsylvania, skirmishing was continuous for two days. The 10th Vermont, fighting with Burnside's Ninth Corps, had gone into position well to the left of the Vermont Brigade. Maj. Lemuel Abbott wrote in his journal on May 10:

> Warm and sultry. The stench from the dead between the lines is terrible. There has been hard fighting on our right all day. As for the Tenth Vermont it has been supporting a battery most of the time. According to rumor we have captured a large number of prisoners and several pieces of artillery. About 6 o'clock p.m. our batteries opened a tremendous fire on the enemy's works, and kept it up for two hours, but with what result I do not know, except that the guns in our front are silenced. It was a fine artillery duel and the roar appalling even to a practiced ear. We are getting the best of Lee in this battle but it's stubborn fighting on both sides.
>
> The accuracy with which our gunners fire is wonderful. I have seen one piece of the enemy's artillery opposite me turned completely over backwards carriage and all, by a solid shot from one of our guns in front of our regiment; it evidently hit the enemy's cannon square in the muzzle. It is awe-inspiring to see the regularity, the determined set look and precision with which our begrimed artillerymen stick to their work; shot and shell screeching close by don't seem to disturb them. I was spellbound and speechless with awe and admiration for their splendid pluck and nerve....I think I can face anything in a charge without flinching after this splendid exhibition of nerve.

Major Abbott was right: there had been a battle further down the lines, with a considerable number of Confederate prisoners taken. The Vermont Brigade, once again, was involved. It happened because a young officer named Emory Upton, a 25-year-old New York brigade commander in David A. Russell's Sixth Corps division, surveyed the strong Confederate lines and came up with a plan for breaking through. North of Spotsylvania Court House the Confederate trenches made a northward bulge, following a low ridge, nicknamed "Mule Shoe Salient" for its shape, that commanded open fields. It was on this ridge, well below the tip of the shoe and along the west side, that Upton proposed to attack. He planned to hit hard and fast at a point where the nearest of a double line of rebel trenches was only about 200 yards from a wood line on the Union side. His aim was to send men running across the open ground, with uncapped muskets in the front ranks so they need not stop to fire. Once the trenches were reached, the men would range along them left and right and create a big hole in the rebel defenses. It was a plan not unlike John Sedgwick's that carried the Sunken Road and the heights at Fredericksburg. Grant and Meade heard Upton out and gave him 4,000 men to attempt the job, a force to include the Third, Fifth, and Sixth Vermont regiments.

It was 6 P.M. before the attack was ready, the men assigned all lying low in the woods under a steady fire of muskets from the nervous Confederates. Over their heads came a thunderous barrage of artillery, from Sixth Corps guns trying to weaken the enemy defenses. The signal was given, and the soldiers rushed forward with a cheer, bullets taking their toll as the open ground was crossed. But the plan worked like a charm; within minutes a hole had been punched in both of Lee's lines.

"The Rebels mowed down the men with awful effect," Wilbur Fisk noted, "but the advancing line was not checked. We drove the enemy out of his first line of works, and captured over 2000 prisoners. Another brigade that was to follow on our left broke and run before they reached the works. Of course this made our position untenable, and spoiled our victory which we had so nearly won."

Lee rushed up reinforcements, something the Union command failed to do. Upton's men, under increasingly severe fire, did their best to hold on. But it was hopeless; the Union attackers began to fall back across the field—all except some of the Vermonters, who hunkered down in their captured trenches and refused to go. Even Colonel Upton could see that the attack was a failure, and he ordered the Vermont soldiers to retreat.

"We don't want to go. Send us ammunition and rations, and we can stay here six months," came one reply. The Vermonters held as Confederate fire increased and more and more Yankees went back to their own lines. They held for two reasons: For one, they thought capturing the Confederate lines ought to be exploited. For another, there may have been reluctance to recross open ground to the rear, which was in the range of a good many Confederate rifles. A correspondent for the *New York Herald* wrote: "The blood of the Green Mountain Boys was up and they absolutely refused to budge a single hair from the field they had wrested from the enemy."

As the stubborn Vermonters clung to their dear-bought entrenchments, General Wright found Lewis Grant and told him of the situation. Grant quickly backed his troops with the words, "Pile in the men and hold it." Wright apparently was intent on doing just that when he learned that, at long last, the Vermonters had decided to come back to the safety of the woods and the Union lines. The fighting cost the Vermonters 88 men: 6 killed, 66 wounded, and 16 captured. Among the casualties was Maj. Charles P. Dudley of Manchester, the last field-grade officer left in the Fifth Vermont. In Upton's attack, the major was rallying his men when a bullet hit the fleshy part of his upraised right arm. He died a few days later.

So Upton's attack had ended in failure. But it had interested Ulysses Grant. If 4,000 men could capture two lines of rebel trenches, maybe six or seven times that many could really bust up Lee's army. Grant would try, 36 hours later.

That huge attack was massed in the woods and fields beyond the tip of the Confederate Mule Shoe Salient in the rainy darkness of May 11–12. Nearly 30,000 men, most of Winfield Scott Hancock's corps, were grouped on a narrow front many ranks deep. The rebels, expecting something to be mounted against the salient, had massed cannon near its apex; but in the night before the big attack the cannon had been moved elsewhere. In the first light of day Hancock gave the order to advance. The Confederate works were overrun; thousands of Union soldiers were suddenly within the Confederate lines and rushing down the salient.

Lee reacted quickly, riding nearly to the front with support troops, and since the Union attack lacked cohesion, the Confederates quickly stopped it. At stake was the main rebel line, the salvation of the Army of Northern Virginia. Lee's men fought accordingly, gradually moving Hancock's regiments back north. The blue-clad troops gave ground grudgingly but soon found themselves rallying on the trenches they had overrun a short time before. There the Union boys held, in their captured trenches, as Hancock sent in reinforcements to hold the breach in Lee's lines. Around the tip of the Mule Shoe and down its west face, the Yankees were forced back to the outside of the earthworks, firing back at the Confederate masses moving ever closer. Lee had to hold, to buy time to build a new line across the base of the salient, and, like Hancock, he kept piling in troops. In the rain and the mud, the Army of Northern Virginia and the Army of the Potomac fought from early morning until past midnight. At a place along the west side of the salient, where the trench lines made an almost imperceptible turn, soldiers were lined up nearly 30 ranks deep, the front ranks separated only by a breastwork. If the Wilderness was not the worst of the entire war, surely the fighting at "Bloody Angle" was.

The Vermont Brigade went into action about 8 A.M.—the remnants of the brigade, that is, for after Upton's May 10 attack there were scarcely 1,500 men in the five regiments. Yet they came in bravely, as part of the reinforcements that Hancock ordered up along the west side of the salient, in the area of the Bloody Angle. At times and in places, Vermont troops were at the very front, flush up against the outside of the Confederate works, with rebels on the far side, scarcely a rifle-musket's length away.

Wilbur Fisk called it "the most singular and obstinate fighting that I have seen during the war, or ever heard or dreamed of in my life." Fisk wrote:

> Hancock had charged and driven the enemy from their breastworks, and from their camps, but the enemy rallied and regained all but the first line of works, and in one place they got a portion of that. The rebels were on one side of the breastwork, we on the other. We could touch their guns to ours. They would load, jump up and fire into us, and we did the same to them. Almost every shot that was made took effect. Some of our boys would jump clear up on to the breastwork and fire, then down, reload and fire again, until they were themselves picked off. If ancient or modern history contains instances of more determined bravery than was shown here, I can hardly conceive in what way it could have been exhibited.

Spotsylvania's Bloody Angle, the war's worst fighting.

Brig. Gen. Lewis Grant also described the action:

> It was literally a hand to hand fight. Nothing but the piled up logs of the breastworks separated the combatants. Our men would reach over the logs and fire into the faces of the enemy, and stab over with their bayonets. Many were shot and stabbed through crevices and holes in the logs. Scores were shot down within a few feet of the death-dealing muskets. Men mounted the works, and with muskets rapidly handed up, kept up a continuous fire until they were shot down, when others would take their places and continue the deadly work. Some men clubbed their muskets, others used clubs and rails.

One private named William Noyes of the Second Vermont and Montpelier stood on the parapet firing into the Confederates with loaded muskets passed up by his comrades. Though his cap was shot off, he got off 30 shots before he jumped down unhurt. He was awarded the Medal of Honor.

The Old Brigade was apparently fighting just north of the Bloody Angle when some of the men mounted the breastworks. At the Bloody Angle itself, just yards away, a tree 22 inches in diameter, on the Confederate side of the works, was cut down by rifle fire. Pvt. Henry Houghton of Woodstock said, "Very soon it became so that we could not stir without treading upon the dead and wounded men, and the brush was literally riddled with bullets."

Lewis Grant said of Bloody Angle: "The brush and logs were cut to pieces and whipped into basket stuff; [it was] there that fallen men's flesh was torn from their bones and the bones shattered; there that the rebel ditches and cross-sections were filled with dead men several deep. Some of the wounded were almost entirely buried by the dead bodies of their companions that had fallen upon them. In this way the Vermont Brigade was engaged for about eight hours."

The brigade was withdrawn about sunset. The cost had, once again, been fearful. The casualty count in the five regiments totaled 254, of whom 42 had been killed, 186 wounded, with 26 men missing. Though the Vermonters were out of the horror of the Mule Shoe just before dark, the fighting went on in the steady rain until near dawn of May 13. In the end, Lee got a new line built and withdrew his men to it. The cost, to both sides, had been some 15,000 men shot or captured.

Lemuel Abbott of the 10th Vermont wrote the day after the battle:

The breastwork is filled with dead and wounded where they fell, several deep nearly to the top in front, extending for 40 feet more or less back gradually sloping from front to rear, to one deep before the ground can be seen. The dead as a whole as they lie in their works are like an immense wedge with its head toward the works. Think of such a mass of dead! hundreds and hundreds piled on top of each other! At the usual distance in rear of these breastworks, about 90 feet, are two more complete dead lines of battle about one hundred feet apart the dead bodies lying where the men fell in line of battle shot in their tracks. The lines are perfectly defined by dead men so close they touch each other. Many of the bodies have turned black, the stench is terrible, and the sight shocking beyond description. I saw several wounded men in the breastworks buried under their dead, just move a hand a little as it stuck up through the interstices above the dead bodies that buried the live ones otherwise completely from sight.

Abbott concluded, "Could anything in Hades be any worse?"

Another Vermont soldier, Tabor Parcher of Waterbury and the 10th Regiment, wrote the day after the battle: "We are having a hard time and we have been under fire for 8 days and am liable to be as many more before we whip Lee's forces but we are gaining a little the balls are flying over my head as I write but I have been lucky so far."

Before the great attack on the Mule Shoe, Ulysses Grant telegraphed Washington that he would fight it out on the lines at Spotsylvania all summer if need be. As it was, the fighting went on there for nine long days after the great battle of the Bloody Angle. The Vermont Brigade, which had boasted five full regiments of nearly 1,000 men each, was now down to less than 1,300 fit for duty. But help was coming. The night before the attack on the Mule Shoe, orders had reached headquarters of the 11th Vermont Regiment in the forts around Washington to prepare to march immediately. Next morning the infantrymen turned artillerymen said farewell to their long months of easy duty. Officers said goodbye to wives quartered with them in Washington. Some enlisted men had managed to have their wives employed as laundresses, and thus those wives were on hand to bid the men Godspeed. On May 15 the regiment marched in along the bloody, reeking lines at Spotsylvania. The 1,550 fresh men were a welcome sight. In command of the new regiment was Col. James Warner of Middlebury, the young West Pointer who had served on the western frontier with John Sedgwick.

The fighting at Spotsylvania was continuous. Dr. Joseph Rutherford of Newport, an army surgeon, wrote home on May 17: "This morning I rode around our breastworks where the 6th and 9th Corps are stationed. I could see the Reb sharpshooters in the trees in front of our line and our sharpshooters occasionally bring one down faster than he went up. I wanted to pick off one this morning but the Col. would not let me. I did want to draw a bead on the shark, I can tell you."

And echoing U. S. Grant, Rutherford added, "We are going to Richmond this time if it takes all summer to do it."

On May 17 the Vermont Brigade was part of an assault on the far, or eastern, side of the Mule Shoe Salient. It amounted to little, though 37 more Vermonters were hit, still it was the combat debut of the 11th Vermont. During the fighting, Colonel Warner was shot through the neck and was sent back to Middlebury for a long recuperation.

As the stalemate continued and casualties increased, Grant decided to abandon the Spotsylvania lines and move southeast around Lee's army, by his own left flank. A 200-man detail of the 11th Vermont was posted as part of a rear guard to screen the army's movement. The new frontline soldiers faced a host of Confederates, who at one point surged over the top of a trench held by the Vermonters. But the heavies stood their ground and in the early morning hours of May 22 were withdrawn south, away from Spotsylvania Court House. The battle named for the little crossroads village ended.

While Grant's and Lee's infantry had fought for nearly two weeks around Spotsylvania, rebel and Yankee cavalry had also been in action. Sheridan had ridden south with nearly 12,000 horsemen on a raid that took him, in three days, to the outskirts of Richmond. The biggest fight occurred north of the capital city on Telegraph Road at Yellow Tavern. Stuart's horsemen had ridden out to confront the Union raiders, and a spirited fight developed. At one point George Custer rode up to Addison Preston, commanding the First Vermont Cavalry, and asked him if he would care to join in a charge. Preston, like Custer, was always willing to get into a fight. Union horsemen went off in a long line across the level fields in an attack on the outnumbered Confederates. The blue horsemen came storming through a rebel artillery position but were met by a sharp counterattack directed by Stuart. The Confederate commander, encouraging his men, rode forward to a fence line behind which dismounted Confederate cavalry were firing. There a bullet from a Michigan horse soldier's pistol hit him in the stomach, and Stuart died the next day, May 12, as the fighting raged at Bloody Angle.

At Spotsylvania Court House the scars of war remain. The trench lines are now all soft and covered with grass and leaves with, here and there, old trees growing in their midst. The Bloody Angle, indeed the entire Mule Shoe Salient, is part of the Spotsylvania and Fredericksburg National Military Park. Perhaps no other Civil War place so moves people who have looked long and hard at the Civil War. One morning at Spotsylvania I talked with William Matter, the only person who has written a comprehensive book on the long battle there. I was curious, were those stories of Vermonters jumping up on the parapets true? He assured me that they were, for he had read of it in Confederate accounts.

The Bloody Angle today is much like a great lawn interspersed with trees and surrounded by high woods. It is a place that never seems to stay quite the same, the play of light through the trees strangely changing its look and feel from day to day. The trenches, once almost head high, are now settled to perhaps three feet, grassy and gentle. One early morning with sunlight slanting through a mist down on the fields, I walked out toward the Angle. Water from a night rain stood in the trenches as it had the day of the battle. As I approached Bloody Angle, I was met by the estimable Civil War historian Gary Gallagher who said: "Welcome to one of the points of the cross."

He spoke well for the feeling one gets at the Bloody Angle, an almost mystical place where people walk quietly and speak in hushed tones. One evening by the Angle I heard a man trying to explain to his young daughter what had happened there. The only words I caught were, "because they thought people should be free."

A marker shows where stood that 22-inch tree felled by bullets. Out at the park entrance is a monument to "Uncle John" Sedgwick, on the spot where his life ended. The trenches go on and on for miles. Spotsylvania Court House and its battlefield is a place to visit slowly, to allow time to try, always failing, to comprehend what horror once transpired in what is now so peaceful a place. Bloody Angle may be the loveliest of all Civil War places, the spot where the worst of the Civil War may have happened. Walk slowly, hear the whispers of the wind, and inhale the fragrance of the Virginia woods and fields. And note, as I have 50 times or more, that some feeling from that long-ago day of horror abides there.

Up a rough dirt road that ends back against a mountainside in the southern Vermont town of Stratton is a small, ancient graveyard, surrounded by stone walls and thick woods. Off in a corner is a new gravestone set above the earthly remains of the writer Robert Penn Warren. Warren was born in Guthrie, Kentucky, as the stone notes. His grandfather had fought for the Confederacy. Later in life Warren passed much of his time in Vermont, dying at his Stratton home in 1989.

In 1961, on the occasion of the 100th anniversary of the Civil War's beginning, Warren published a small book he called *The Legacy of the Civil War*. It was a time of high drama in the south as the Civil Rights movement was gaining momentum. I first read Warren's book in the mid-1970s; some of these words have often come back as I've walked the Spotsylvania battlefield: "Does the man who, in the relative safety of mob anonymity, stands howling vituperation at a little Negro girl being conducted into a school building, feel himself at one with those gaunt, barefoot, whiskery scarecrows who fought it out, breast to breast, to the death, at the Bloody Angle at Spotsylvania, in May, 1864? Can the man howling in the mob imagine General R. E. Lee, CSA, shaking hands with Orval Faubus, Governor of Arkansas?"

SLAUGHTER AT COLD HARBOR

The Vermont troops marching away from the terrible battlefield at Spotsylvania Court House were bound for another of the Civil War's slaughter pens—another previously obscure crossroads—Cold Harbor. The Army of the Potomac marched south and by the left flank from Spotsylvania, moving past the right of Lee's army. Skirmishing all the way, the two big armies first clashed on May 23 along the North Anna River, which cut across the line of march and behind which Robert E. Lee's army had thrown up earthworks on high ground. On May 23 and 24 Ulysses Grant attacked the strong Confederate defenses and was repulsed.

The Vermonters generally stayed out of this action. Maj. Charles Cummings of the 11th Vermont said:

> After crossing we lay in line of battle near the stream until 11 o'clock p.m., a drenching rain falling....We were put in front and directed to commence entrenching. Just as our breastwork was complete we were ordered to establish a new line farther in front. This we built with now and then a stray ball whistling by us. The men were now quite tired and were in hopes after breakfast to rest a little, but another line in advance was ordered, so we built, Wednesday morning, our third line. Here we lay without fires sending out skirmishers and watching the progress of events. Of the skirmishers sent out one was shot through the lungs and will probably not recover. Another man was slightly wounded.

On May 26 Grant again moved south and east. George Chamberlin, a St. Johnsbury lawyer and major of the 11th, sent a letter home to his father, mother, and sister:

> If Grant can beat Lee by maneuvering, and thus save slaughter, it will suit the army and country much better. The slaughter and suffering in this campaign have been

awful. The marching has been very severe, especially on our men, who are in a measure raw. Our manner of life is very rough and anything but agreeable. Nothing but the most solemn sense of duty could keep me here. When we stop at night we are generally too tired to put up even the poor shelter of our little tents, and we lie down under the open sky—sometimes in the rain.

Writing to his mother on May 29, Cummings said:

Thursday night we marched all night and all day Friday. Yesterday morning we crossed the Pamunkey on a pontoon bridge, and at noon encamped on the heights, about two miles from the river. We are about four miles northwest of Hanover Town, and about fifteen from Richmond. This second great flank movement has been very successfully accomplished, and we are satisfied that we are under a skillful leader. The march was very severe, and through it all I was near dropping down with fatigue.

Sheridan and his cavalry, having come full circle back to Union lines from their raid toward Richmond via Yellow Tavern, were the first Yankees to reach Cold Harbor, and on the last day of May they quickly grappled with superior Confederate forces. Sheridan needed support, which came on June 1 from the Sixth Corps, the Vermont Brigade leading the way in a long and dusty march.

The advance units found the hard-pressed cavalry relieved to see them, and Custer's band played "Hail Columbia" in welcome. The Vermont Brigade was put in position at the southern end of the lengthening Union line, facing Lee's forces to the west. Generals Meade and Grant wanted an immediate attack: the task was assigned General Wright's Sixth Corps and a force of some 10,000 soldiers just arrived from the 18th and 10 corps under Vermonter "Baldy" Smith. True to form, the Vermont Brigade was placed in the first line of battle in the rather small length of the Union front it occupied. But just before jump-off, set for late afternoon, Lewis Grant received information indicating a Confederate attack could come in on his southern flank. Consequently, he faced the Fourth and Sixth Vermont regiments and about a third of the 11th Vermont to the south, taking them out of the assault. The Fifth Vermont was sent to protect artillery, so when the Union line moved, only the Second Vermont and one of the 11th Vermont's three battalions rolled forward. To the north, the 10th Vermont of Rickett's division attacked near the Union center.

The 10th Vermont regimental chaplain, Edwin Haynes, also a historian, recalled:

The advance was made through the best of pine woods…over a plowed field, where the Confederate skirmishers had erected temporary breastworks of fence rails, through a shallow ravine and swamp, and into thick woods where their entrenchments were found and carried. Sergeant, afterwards Captain, [Silas] Lewis, of the Tenth, sprang over the works capturing single-handed a major, a lieutenant, and several men. The rest of this line extended out of the woods into an open field, and was much annoyed by an enfilading fire from the enemy's batteries to which the

Yellow Tavern, where Jeb Stuart fell.

men were exposed by the failure of the First Division, and besides being weakened by the lengthening of the line caused by keeping up the connection, were unable to carry the whole line of Confederate works, nor did they take the battery that caused them most annoyance; still they nobly stood their ground. It was now nine o'clock and nearly dark, and there was a lull in the storm of battle. The captured works were strengthened, and others thrown up. This business was not attended to a moment too soon, for an hour afterwards the enemy made a desperate attempt to regain their lost works and capture ours. In this attempt they were fearfully repulsed; repeating it several times during the night.

Among those shot was the 10th Vermont's Lt. Charles G. Newton. The 26-year-old Rochester native had worked as a schoolteacher in his hometown before enrolling at Middlebury College, which he left in his first year, 1862, to enlist. He was at the front, and Chaplain Haynes wrote that during a brief halt in the advance, Newton was seen to look toward the flank and then heard to exclaim, "I see the scamps! I see them!"

"In that instant," Haynes noted, "his throat was cut by a minie ball. It was instantaneously fatal. We gave him the rites of Christian burial, amid the thunder of the next day's battle, a short distance from the place where he fell."

In the Vermont Brigade's newest regiment, the 11th, Capt. Charles Gould of Windham wrote home of his men:

When they gained the crest of the hill they were received by a perfect sheet of flame which fairly mowed our boys down, but they kept their line perfect until ordered to retreat....We have gained ourselves a high reputation in our brigade. When we first joined the Corps we were called "white kids" or "soft breads" but our boys said

The doomed Union attack at Cold Harbor.

nothing but when opportunity occurred we showed them that we were from the same Green Mountain State as themselves.

Gould also wrote:

A poor fellow of my Regt. was shot through the head and killed instantly within a few feet of me—We were under heavy fire of case and shell, and laying flat on the ground with our knapsacks in front of our heads for protection, when he and others raised his head to look over a minute. At that instant a case shot burst when we all ducked for it—I saw him drop his head on his arm....A ball from the case shot had struck him through the brain and killed him. It did not even knock off his cap.

The attack had come very close to carrying the Confederate works, and it put the Union lines in what the high command saw as a good jumping-off spot for a bigger attack. It had been bloody work. The 11th Vermont got hit hardest, losing 13 men killed and 107 wounded. Nine men were wounded in the veteran Second Vermont Regiment. Before the fighting at Cold Harbor ended, the 10th Vermont's cost would be 181 men hit, 30 fatally.

Grant decided to make a full-scale attack next morning on the entire Confederate front, stretching six miles from Totopotomy Creek to the Chickahominy River. But there were delays; the Union command was far from its best at Cold Harbor. The assault was postponed by a full day, to early morning, June 3. Years later, Ulysses Grant confessed that the attack was the greatest mistake of his military career. The Confederates had used the extra day to improve their defenses, veteran battle-toughened soldiers digging in not only to hold their positions but to kill as many Yankees as possible. They constructed on their slightly elevated ground six miles of rather innocent-looking earthworks that proved to be some of the most formidable positions of the war. By the morning of June 3 they occupied double and triple trenches laid out to pour crossfires over the flat and mostly open ground to the front. At key points, artillery was moved up and sighted.

A soldier in the 10th Vermont said: "On the front every device of engineering skill had been lavished, in order to render the works impregnable; and received additional protection everywhere from batteries so placed as to guard every approach, both with their direct and enfilading fire. Here were six miles of mortality."

In the hours before dawn Union soldiers were once again seen to pin names on their uniforms so that their bodies might be properly identified. Daylight brought a thunderous cannon barrage from the Union guns. Then the three-mile-long battle line, 40,000 strong, advanced across the flat ground toward those low and deadly rebel entrenchments. It was over quickly.

The advance was made by the Sixth, Second, and 18th corps, commanded by Wright, Hancock, and "Baldy" Smith. Their soldiers were slaughtered. Chaplain Haynes recalled:

> Promptly at the hour these corps advanced to attack under heavy rifle fire and carried the enemy's advanced rifle pits. With this initial success the Confederate artillery especially from flanking batteries, increased both in volume and effectiveness sweeping the attacking column from right to left and left to right....Our brave men swept on, notwithstanding this fearful deluge of iron missiles, until in some places they were within 30 yards of the enemy's main line of entrenchments. Seeing the improbability of carrying them, they stopped and secured the position they had taken and held it until the night of the twelfth when the army moved away from this part of Virginia. In covering themselves, the men used bayonets, tin cups, plates and for this purpose split canteens.

In less than 40 minutes more than 7,000 of Grant's soldiers were shot, most in the first 10 minutes. The fighting lingered all day, the attackers lying low and digging in as best they could. The Vermont Brigade, in the second line of the Sixth Corps' advance, was not as badly chewed up as others; but of 800 casualties in the corps, 104 belonged to the Old Brigade, most to the Third and Fifth regiments. Seventeen were mortally wounded. The 10th Vermont again took heavy casualties, though far fewer than two days previous.

Also involved in the desperate charge had been another familiar Vermont figure, George Stannard, back in uniform after recovering from his Gettysburg wound. Stannard led a brigade in "Baldy" Smith's command that made three advances, twice coming within yards of entering the Confederate works. Stannard drove his men relentlessly, as he had driven the Second Vermont Brigade toward Gettysburg. But with more than half of his men cut down, and after being shot in the leg, Stannard had to withdraw.

Despite the defeat, the Union commanders immediately began preparing for a second big assault as troops were shifted and reserves brought up. But in the end, Grant and Meade were persuaded that the thing was hopeless. The two armies dug in dangerously close together; Cold Harbor became trench warfare.

"Hundreds of dead men and many wounded and helpless, beyond the reach of friends, by night and day, lay stretched between these lines....Some had lain here since they fell, six days before, but now swollen and torn by the lead and iron tempest that had twice swept over and beaten around them. Many were scarcely recognizable by friends who eagerly sought for them," wrote Chaplain Haynes of the 10th Vermont.

Captain Gould of the 11th Vermont wrote home to Windham:

Our boys got in one of the wounded men while I was with them that had been shot through both legs and the shoulder. One of his legs was broken and he was wasted almost to a skeleton. He felt chipper as could be and talked and laughed with the boys. He had an eye as bright as any one, and on hearing it mentioned, said that it would bright anyone's eye to get among friends again after giving up in despair all hopes of anything but a miserable death of hunger, thirst, and wounds, in the burning sun.

The boys in the Third Vermont got one inside the works in the following manner. They took several tent ropes, tied them together, tied a canteen of water to the end, and threw it over the works to him. After drinking he revived so that he tied the rope around his body and was hauled to the works.

Major Chamberlin of the 11th Vermont wrote home on June 6:

I am literally in a hole in the ground. Last evening we moved forward into the very front line of trenches, only two hundred yards from the enemy....The bullets generally pass above our heads, though the sound is anything but pleasant.

On June 7 Jonathan Blaisdell wrote home to Cambridge:

We have been within 60 rods of the Rebel rifle pits the pickets have kept up firing all of the time. The firing was stopped. Some of the boys exchanged papers with them. The flag was up about an hour and a half. They buried their dead and then the flag was taken down and they went to fighting another again. I understand that it is not but 10 miles to Richmond....I should be glad when we get out of this place.

On June 8 George Chamberlin wrote:

All firing has ceased, and the flag went out on the front of my battalion. Two officers from each side, at six o'clock, were seen to start from their respective line of works. Our flag consisted of a white handkerchief simply held up in the hand. They approached, touched caps, talked five minutes and separated. Parties were out immediately on our front to complete the burial of our dead, and the troops from both sides rose up from their works, shook out their blankets, stretched themselves, looked, talked, and rested from strife. I could not help wishing, as the two flags approached each other, that the good men of both sections might come together und, by reason, put an end to this fraternal slaughter. At eight o'clock all retired behind the works, to watch and wait the opportunity of destroying each other's lives.

The confrontation at Cold Harbor dragged on until June 12. Wilbur Fisk wrote:

> The earth is like a pile of dust, and it dances before every breeze like Vermont snow in midwinter. A man may spread down his rubber blanket for a seat, and one puff of wind will cover it so completely with dust that it will be difficult to distinguish it from the ground around it. Our clothes are filled with dust, and our coffee and everything else we cook is sure to get a clever sprinkling of this fine sand. This dirt goes everywhere.

Col. Addison Preston of the Vermont cavalry.

While the infantry marched to their deaths at Cold Harbor on June 3, Wilson's cavalry fought rebel cavalry under Brig. Gen. Rufus Barringer at nearby Haw's Shop. The men of the First Vermont Cavalry dismounted and moved forward through some woods. Col. Addison Preston was, as usual, to the front, and, seeing a line of men out beyond his position, moved toward it, apparently thinking them Union soldiers. They were Confederates, as a blast of musketry proved. Preston fell with a bullet through his chest. William Wells, who succeeded Preston as commander of the regiment, wrote home to Waterbury:

> He was killed on the skirmish line. He had just ordered me to put my battalion in line on our left. He says Major don't allow your men to fire for our men [from the other regiment] are in your front. I saw nothing more of him until I was informed that he was wounded in front of my line. Several times I attempted to advance my lines to get his body but was driven back, but the third time I got his body off. He was just alive, not conscious. Died about 15 minutes after we got possession of him. He was shot in the left side near the heart.

Preston, who had once been willing to charge Richmond itself, who had been twice wounded, and who had survived untold narrow escapes, was now out of everything. It was hard to believe that, in younger days, ill health had forced him to withdraw from Brown University and go to the sea for fresh air. Then he'd gone to Australia, then California, living the life of the adventurer until war broke out and he hurried home to the Caledonia County hills to enlist. As he rode out to Haw's Shop on the hot morning of June 3, word in the ranks had it that he was about to be made a brigadier general.

Just after Preston died, George Custer rode by, dismounted, knelt by the body, rose, and as he turned away said, "There lies the best fighting colonel in the Cavalry Corps."

Preston's body came north to his hometown of Danville for burial in the cemetery just south of the village. Danville people today tell how folks came from all over the county for the funeral and how the procession stretched from the village to the grave. Addison Preston's body lies beside those of his wife and a young child in the shade of old oaks.

In Virginia, on the night of June 12, the long ordeal at Cold Harbor ended as Ulysses Grant started his battered army southeast, to steal a march on Robert E. Lee. Wilbur Fisk noted that Union soldiers used to say that four men perished from disease on a campaign to one from the enemy's bullets. "But Grant reverses the order, and kills four men on the battlefield, to one that perishes from disease."

Near the top of the road up from Prosper, in the hills of North Bridgewater, is a country cemetery surrounded by an old stone wall. Off in a corner in the shade of aged maples is the memorial stone of Isaiah Maxham, beside which a bouquet of lilacs and a new flag are placed each Memorial Day. Maxham was 22 years old when captured on the battlefield at Cold Habor. He died three months later in the worst of all Confederate prison camps, the stockade at Andersonville. For many years I assumed Maxham's stone was a gravestone, but one day I spoke of it while walking a Virginia battlefield with the historian Edwin Bearss. Bearss suggested, and later confirmed, that Maxham was buried in the national cemetery at Andersonville; thus his North Bridgewater marker is a memorial stone.

For me, the Maxham stone has long symbolized what was lost by the Vermonters who left home to fight in the Civil War. Captured on one of the Civil War's worst battlefields, then taken to die in the hellhole at Andersonville, Isaiah Maxham never even in death came home to his green hills of Vermont. His stone, beside that of his father who died five years later, lies among green hills and farm fields where cattle often come grazing up to the cemetery wall and deer come softly to feed at evening. Birds sing in the trees, a little brook rushes nearby, and maples, which take color as September becomes October, climb the high hills. Nearby is an old farmhouse and barns weathered by a hundred winters and more, and up the hill is a small red schoolhouse.

STALEMATE AT PETERSBURG

On June 2, 1864, as the Army of the Potomac prepared to assault the impregnable Confederate works at Cold Harbor, a South Reading woman sent the following letter to her sister:

> He is dead. I never shall see him again. Oh I cannot have it so all my hopes in life are oer. There is nothing but disappointment and trials in this world. He was shot in the head and died instantly, oh how like a knell it rings in my ears. I lay in a fainting condition most all night and am so weak in body and mind, have pity on me. He lays in the battle field far away without one moment's warning and could not send no message to the wife he loved so well. My poor mother is almost beside herself they all loved him so well.
>
> I can't write any more
>
> MARGARET

The husband, Erastus Scott, a private in the Third Vermont, was killed May 12 near the Bloody Angle at Spotsylvania. Word reached South Reading only on June 2, the eve of the last great bloodletting of what history would record as "The Forty Days." It was the bloodiest time in the history of the American nation. By the time Grant broke off the hopeless confrontation at Cold Harbor and marched southeast, 40 days had passed since the Army of the Potomac moved across the Rapidan and into the Wilderness. Along the way the army had suffered an average of 1,500 men killed, wounded, captured, or missing each day.

No one was more acutely aware of the bloodshed than President Lincoln, spending day after day in the War Department telegraph office reading dispatches in the company of Vermonter Albert Chandler. Lincoln always managed to summon a bit of humor, Chandler recalled, once greeting Secretary of War Stanton with "Good evening, Mars." But the war was telling on the president, who spent sleepless nights walking the White House halls, sometimes reading from Shakespeare's tragedies. On one particularly dark day Lincoln invited his friend Jacob Collamer, the senator from Vermont, to the White House. The two men spent 12 uninterrupted hours together. Collamer, the man Charles Sumner called "the Green Mountain Socrates," never disclosed what they discussed.

In no state had the toll been more terrible, on a per capita basis, than in Vermont. By the middle of June letters filled with despair, such as that written by Margaret Scott, were being penned by the hundreds in the Green Mountains. En route to Cold Harbor, the Vermont Brigade had suffered losses since the Battle of the Wilderness began that stood at 249 killed, 1,231 wounded, and 170 missing. Of the wounded, 190 would soon die. Some 400 more men either had been discharged or sent to Northern hospitals, having broken under the strain. Almost two-thirds of the men who had crossed the Rapidan on that sunny morning in early May were now gone from the Old Brigade's five original regiments. Even in the new regiment, the 11th, 175 men had been knocked from the ranks by the end of the fighting at Cold Harbor—and they had missed the worst of Spotsylvania and all of the Wilderness. In Ambrose Burnside's Ninth Corps, the 10th Vermont Regiment, mustered into service with 1,016 men, marched away from Cold Harbor with 364 able to fight.

At home, news of the horrible casualties at the Wilderness and Spotsylvania prompted fast action. Governor Smith, along with the man he had recently appointed state surgeon general, Dr. Samuel Thayer of Burlington, and some 20 other Vermont doctors, set off south to help. So too went dozens of Vermont wives and mothers to care for their loved ones at Fredericksburg, where most of the Federal wounded had been taken, the roads directly north from the battlefields toward Washington being too vulnerable to Confederate raiders. The wounded went in wagons along the rough backcountry roads, descending on a war-torn town in no way prepared—or of a mind—to receive a host of shot and bleeding Yankees.

A Vermont soldier recorded: "The sufferings of our wounded at Fredericksburg, from lack of beds, supplies and medical care, have been dreadful. When Doctor Thayer arrived there, thousands were lying in their bloody garments on the bare floors, and some had not had their wounds dressed for days."

A New York doctor wrote:

We are almost worked to death. All day yesterday I worked at the operating table. That was the fourth day at the tables, besides two whole nights and part of another. It does not seem as though I could take a knife in my hand today. Yet there are a hundred cases of amputations waiting for me. It is a scene of horror such as I never saw. Hundreds of ambulances are coming in now, and it is almost midnight. So they come every night.

More than 1,000 Vermont wounded were in Fredericksburg, and with a corps of home folks to assist, they received better care than most men from other states. A correspondent from the *Boston Journal* wrote of Governor Smith that he spent his time "directing his assistants, laboring with his own hands, hunting up the sick and wounded, giving up his own cot, sleeping on the bare floor or not sleeping at all, cheering the despondent, writing sympathetic letters to fathers and mothers whose sons were in the hospitals, or had given up their lives for their country."

The facilities at Fredericksburg were far from adequate; in late May the wounded were moved to hospitals in Washington. Since a new wave of wounded was about to reach Vermont, a third Vermont military hospital was constructed on a hilltop overlooking downtown Montpelier (in the area where Vermont College now stands). Dr. Henry Janes returned home to run the 600-bed facility. Military hospitals were now operating on the drill field at Brattleboro, near the Burlington lakefront, and on a rise overlooking the State House. By September the total number of Vermonters in these hospitals reached 2,251. Some 600 soldiers from other states would also be treated there.

Henry Janes's Sloan Army Hospital at Montpelier.

In the battle zone around Cold Harbor, despite the appalling casualties, Grant was preparing still another major offensive. Since the assaults of June 1 and 3 the Vermont Brigade had suffered an additional 48 casualties in the hot and horrid trench warfare that lasted until the night of June 12. That night the Army of the Potomac disappeared from its trenches and outfoxed Robert E. Lee.

Grant's strategy was to move his army directly southeast, bypassing Richmond and coming in on Petersburg, through which ran the capital city's main rail lines. The trick was to steal a march on Lee, so the army would not be attacked while vulnerably strung out and moving south. The way led across the Virginia Peninsula and down to the James River, where army engineers constructed one of the longest pontoon bridges in the history of warfare. The Vermont Brigade moved in the night of the 12th. After reaching and crossing the

James on June 15, Private Blaisdell wrote home: "We have had another tough march. I came as near giving out as I ever did in my life. We crossed the James River last Thursday night on the pontoon bridge. It was the longest pontoon bridge that has been built. For some time we are about two miles from Petersburg. We can see the steeples of the meeting houses."

Before crossing the big river, the Vermont Brigade had stood guard at the north end of the bridge for two days. George Chamberlin wrote home: "Encamped on a wide plain on the left bank of the James River. It is half a mile wide here, and filled with boats of all descriptions, and it was very cheering to come in sight of a scene so lively and homelike."

The fortunes of war now presented one Union general officer with a golden opportunity to take Petersburg and perhaps hasten the end of the war by months. Governor Smith's cousin, "Baldy" Smith, and 15,000 men had been sent not south but northeast, out of the Cold Harbor lines to White House Landing on the Peninsula to catch steamboats. They steamed around the Peninsula and up the James River to disembark at Bermuda Hundred, where old "Beast" Butler was in command of troops hopelessly bottled up by a smaller Confederate force. Smith's orders were to grab Petersburg, if he could. The opportunity certainly was there, for General Lee had been caught off guard by Grant's well-conceived and screened southeastward shift. When Smith on June 15 got his troops up to face the entrenchments around Petersburg, only about 2,500 Confederates under old Bull Run hero P. G. T. Beauregard faced him. Smith reconnoitered the Confederate defenses and, as night came on, ordered an attack. A white brigade under George Stannard and a black brigade led by Brig. Gen. Edward W. Hincks quickly captured more than a mile of the undermanned rebel works. But there they stalled, and in the darkness Smith called off the attack. The Confederates dug a new line during the night, as tough looking as it was hastily dug. During the next two days, with reinforcements coming steadily to him, Smith faltered and hesitated, giving Lee time to move enough troops into the entrenchments to stop an all-out June 18 attack. Smith's great opportunity disappeared.

"Baldy" Smith had been appalled by what he had seen of the Union slaughter at Cold Harbor. He later said, "I lost too many good men ever to forget the battle." When he next confronted Confederate entrenchments at Petersburg, daunting in appearance if thinly defended, he feared another Cold Harbor slaughter. He later said that he was most careful in scouting the Confederate defenses so that "when I did make the blow I might make no failure and murder no men." He also wrote: "The lives of the soldiers were intrusted to me with the command of them and were not to be wasted uselessly. During the war I made it a rule never to order soldiers into a fight without knowing what it was in front of them."

The Confederate commander, General Beauregard, later said, "Petersburg was clearly at the mercy of the Federal commander, who had all but captured it, and only failed of final success because he could not realize the fact of the unparalleled disparity between the two contending forces."

Grant, who had suffered more than 65,000 casualties to develop the opportunity at Petersburg, was furious with "Baldy" Smith, who also got into one of his familiar quarrels with a superior, the eminently criticizable Benjamin Butler; Smith also had some less than kind words to say about George Meade. On July 19 Grant removed Smith from command.

Because of "Baldy" Smith's hesitation, the fight to capture Petersburg would now be a very long one—indeed, the longest of the war. As Lee got his men down into the earthworks around the place, Grant massed his tens of thousands. The lines lengthened; grim and bloody trench warfare developed. By June 20 the Vermont Brigade was posted in the frontline of Union works and the long siege of Petersburg was under way.

A Vermont soldier noted in his diary the next day: "Within a mile of the city [Petersburg] and within less than half a mile of the rebel lines. We can see them plainly."

George Chamberlin wrote from "south of Petersburg" on July 5: "The men are cleaning up their muskets, and we are generally endeavoring to repair, to some extent, the wear and tear of the past fifty days of terrible labor. My wall tent is up, and I have a little table and seat extemporized, and am quite comfortable." Later he wrote:

> We dig up to the very teeth of the enemy, and then watch him. It is not safe to expose one's head above the embankment, as a few sharpshooters keep up their murderous work through the little loopholes in the parapet; otherwise there is not much firing. Living under ground is very dirty work, as you can imagine. One night, I remember to have been awakened by something on my neck, which I discovered to be a medium sized toad. Bugs and worms crawl over us promiscuously.

While the armies dug in at Petersburg, the Vermont cavalry was on the move, under Sheridan. William Wells was in command as the Vermonters screened the movements to Petersburg of Grant's infantry. From near Petersburg, on June 22, the Vermonters were dispatched as part of a 5,000-man force commanded by Brig. Gen. James Wilson on a raid south and west to tear up track on the railroad lines supplying Petersburg. The raiders hit the Weldon Railroad, then moved on to the Southside Railroad, then rode far west to the Richmond and Danville line. More than 60 miles of track were destroyed, and Lee was not about to let anyone play such havoc with his communications. Confederate forces far outnumbering Wilson's troopers were sent in pursuit, and in the end most of Wilson's men had a hard time getting back to friendly lines. Eri Woodbury summed things up in a letter written from the safety of City Point on July 3: "Our raid, in some respects disastrous, came to a close last Sat. here on the James....11 days we were out. The Rebs had us surrounded for 2 or 3 days, but after burning wagons and leaving ambulances full of wounded to the enemy and losing our artillery, we made good our retreat."

Meanwhile, outside Petersburg, Wilbur Fisk wrote from his new surroundings:

The weather has been for the last few weeks of the hottest kind, and the temperature is daily increasing. It seems already to have reached about as high a point as human nature can stand. There has been one or two attempts at rain, but since the first of June, I have not seen enough to lay the dust. The sun only mocks at our little shelter tents. With the hot sand underneath, and the burning sun overhead, our little tents are so many little ovens, and a fellow is well nigh roasted alive in one of them.

Another Vermonter wrote home: "It may be days, and even weeks, before Petersburg falls, but that it must fall, as surely as results follow causes, I have not the shadow of a doubt....Grant, like truth, is mighty and will prevail."

The Army of the Potomac would occupy the frying pan around Petersburg for nearly 10 months.

THE WAR COMES HOME

A South Royalton man, Leslie Sherlock, recalled many years after the Civil War:

> My father, about 12 years old, with his dad sometimes used to drive down of an afternoon to see the 2:30 northbound train pull in. From four to 10 wounded soldiers might get off, all bandaged, sometimes minus arms or legs.
>
> Elisha Beedle was escorted off the train and to the hotel with two railroad men, with the top part of his head shot off....
>
> Father asked if he could see the wound.
>
> "Oh my God Lish," [he said,] for he could see the pulse beating in his brain.
>
> Mr. Beedle was so angry about the war he said he was going to get fixed up and go back in. He did, as a Union sniper, and came home alive.

The passenger trains don't stop at South Royalton any more. But the brick station is still there, now a savings bank, by the tracks along the west side of the village green. And on the green is a Civil War memorial, a stone soldier with rifle, doing honor to the soldiers from South Royalton. The statue, like Private Beedle, has a part of its head knocked away.

In the summer of 1864 the war was coming home to Vermont as never before. Of course, since Lee's Mills more than two years before, mangled and broken men had been returning home, some able to walk, some carried, some in boxes. But the home folks had seen nothing before like the results of Grant's 1864 drive to Petersburg.

Drive Route 15 today into the hamlet of Noyesville in the Caledonia County town of Walden, turn right up a dirt road past the old white church, and two and a quarter miles along on the right side of the road is a weedy, wild-looking tree-lined pond, a favorite of ducks and an occasional moose. Up the rough dirt road along the north side, once amid farm fields, was the farm home of Freeman Capron and Sophronia Gould Capron.

The Caprons had two daughters, Clarissa and Sarah, and four sons, Marshall, Hiram, Nathaniel, and Henry, to help work their upland farm, where the views reached Canada and the winter winds seemed to come from the North Pole. The Caprons had a side means of livelihood, a sawmill on the little brook that flows from the millpond. The mill's stone foundations are still visible where the brook passes through a culvert. The Caprons ran what they called "a thunder shower mill"; only when it rained hard did enough water flow from the pond to turn the mill wheel and run the saws. When the sky suddenly darkened, Freeman Capron and his four boys would run for the mill to saw logs while the runoff lasted. When war came Freeman Capron, age 50, and his oldest son, Hiram, joined the army, leaving the farm and mill in the charge of Sophronia, the two daughters, and the remaining three boys.

Freeman Capron served only briefly, coming home sometime in 1862 in poor health. Soon sons Henry and Nathaniel enlisted, with their parents' perhaps reluctant permission. After all, father Capron had seen the reality of uniforms and flying flags. On June 27, 1862 Hiram Capron, a member of the Fourth Vermont, was shot in fighting on the Virginia Peninsula. He was taken prisoner and, though exchanged just a month later, died of his wounds.

Henry and Nathaniel served together in the Third Light Artillery Battery and in the summer of 1864 were in the sweltering earthworks outside Petersburg. In early July Nathaniel, sick, was transported toward home. He died in a military hospital in Brooklyn. Henry got sick about the same time, was shipped to an army hospital in Washington, and died August 16. He was borne across the Potomac River and buried on the lawn of a place the Union command had decided to make uninhabitable, Robert E. Lee's former home. It became Arlington Cemetery.

So three sons of Sophronia and Freeman Capron went to war and never returned, leaving only son Marshall and the two daughters to help with the farm and mill. One summer day I walked the old Capron land with Marshall's grandson, Earl Capron of Chester, another Capron gone to war, as a bomber pilot in World War II. Earl Capron showed me the millpond, the mill ruins, and the Capron cellar hole. In the underbrush we found the Capron doorstep, where it's likely the three sons had said their good-byes. Down the road we found an old spring still running, where we imagined the sons might have stopped for a drink on their way to the train and perhaps, out of sight of the house, to wash away tears. Another summer evening, just as I arrived at the pond, a thunderstorm suddenly exploded out of the Northeast Kingdom skies, and water rushed from the pond through the ruins of the thundershower mill, enough to saw logs.

In 1857, 17-year-old Alonzo Hiram Rice, a bright lad, received a certificate to teach in Grafton's Eastman School District. On the first day a young pupil, Minerva Hazen, warned him that some boys were planning trouble. Teacher Rice dealt with them one at a time. Two years later the young teacher married Minerva. The new couple had two children by 1862, the year Alonzo enlisted in the new Ninth Vermont Regiment.

Writing home, Alonzo Rice told his wife that her idea of buying a home was a good one. Buy "a good place to bring up our children," he said. Rice came home to the new house on a brief furlough, and he and his wife conceived a third child. Back at war, he marched into Maryland, was captured with the Ninth Vermont at Harpers Ferry, and went to Camp Douglas at Chicago. In January 1863 his wife was notified that her husband was ill in the Brattleboro military hospital.

Minerva Rice left her three children, one three months old, with a neighbor and hurried to Brattleboro. She arrived too late; her husband had died the day before. Alonzo Rice left her a poem that read:

> *My partner through life, sure no one can tell*
> *The pangs I feel when I bid you farewell.*
> *Will you meet me in glory when this life shall cease?*
> *If so, I'm resigned and can now die in peace.*
> *Yes, I'll meet you in glory in the bright courts of bliss*
> *No more to be parted in a vain world like this.*
> *For I'm sure that Jehovah will never divide*
> *Two hearts that in union so strongly are tied.*
> *I must now bid farewell, yes, a long one, 'twill be,*
> *A place upon earth is no longer for me.*
> *Remember Alonzo wherever you go,*
> *And think of my final and lasting adieu.*

Upon returning to Grafton with her husband's body, Minerva Rice found her little girl, Minnie Maria, dead of diphtheria. Father and daughter were buried side by side in the Grafton Village Cemetery. A year later the new baby died of the same disease. Minerva Rice and her only surviving child, Alonzo, lived long lives, and in 1876 Minerva began receiving a military pension of eight dollars a month. The house she bought for her young family still stands on Chester Hill Road. The sad story of the Rice family is well told in a display at the Grafton Historical Society on the town's main street.

From the family farm outside Cuttingsville, in Rutland County, Carroll Duane Barney went in 1862 to enlist in the Seventh Vermont Regiment, bound for hard duty along the Mississippi River. Private Barney, raised in the fresh air of the Green Mountains, got sick in the Mississippi heat. Barney was hospitalized in New Orleans, where a doctor said he wouldn't live through the night, and he overheard an orderly order a coffin for him. Yet he survived many sickly nights and was finally put on a ship home. Years later the Barney family genealogist, Gertrude Ludens, wrote: "It was a long hard voyage. The ship was unseaworthy, undermanned, and overloaded with sick and dying soldiers. One stormy night when the miseries of sea-sickness were added to their other woes, the soldier who shared Duane's bunk with him was in worse condition than he. When Duane awoke the next morning, his companion was dead beside him."

Duane Barney disembarked at New York City, where he met a Vermont

Telegram informed the family of Elisha Mead that Charles had died at Gettysburg.

man who took him to a restaurant for a good meal, then to the train station. Ludens wrote:

> It was a fine July afternoon that Duane Barney looked up his brother John in Rutland and John put him on the 4 o'clock train for Cuttingsville and home. His oldest brother Allen was station agent in Cuttingsville and he hitched up his horse and drove him home.
>
> It was a happy homecoming. Jeffrey A. Barney told later that, "one morning when I took the milk pails to the barn I said, 'I will pray for Duane's return.' I set down the pails and kneeled down on the hay and asked God to bring him home. That evening after the chores were done, Mother and I stood in the doorway looking down the road and we could see quite a ways. We saw a horse and buggy coming. I said, 'that's Allen's horse' and as they came nearer I said, 'It is Allen and Duane!'"
>
> Yes, it was a happy homecoming. Duane Barney was home among the Green Mountains where he could rest and get well. And for supper that night, Grandmother Barney had a strawberry shortcake made with wild strawberries from the Shrewsbury pasture. Duane said that he never quite forgot that strawberry shortcake.

In the hillside cemetery in Barnet village, three identical gravestones stand side by side with carvings of a hand pointing skyward. Brothers Seth, Hiram, and Warner Somers, sons of Alexander and Sarah Janes Eames Somers, lie beneath the stones. Neither parent saw their three sons off to war, for Alexander Somers died in 1847, his wife three years later.

The youngest of the orphaned boys, Hiram Somers, was working as a hired hand in 1861 when, at 18, he said farewell to his young wife and joined the Second Vermont. Hiram served until February 1863, when he died of typhoid fever at White Oak Church, Virginia.

Warren Somers, unmarried and listed as a farmer, joined the Third Vermont in the summer of 1862. Soon he too was sick, transferred to the Brattleboro hospital, where he died of typhus on February 16, 1864. According to army records, he had $1.65 in his pocket.

Seth Somers, a bachelor and a mechanic, was 19 when he signed up with the Second Regiment. Shot at Savage's Station and left on the field, he was captured and sent to Richmond. When exchanged a month later Seth Somers was very ill. Discharged the following year, young Somers came home to Barnet, where he died on January 16, 1863.

The Somers boys had a sister, Clara, who married a blacksmith, Edwin Dewey. They had two children by the time Edwin, 29, joined the 11th Vermont in August 1862. He served at first as an artilleryman at Washington, then went south with his regiment to join the Vermont Brigade at Spotsylvania. He was hit by canister at Cold Harbor on June 30 and sent to a Union hospital, where a leg was amputated. Gangrene set in, and Dewey died on August 7, 1864, after having suffered, according to his records, "most excruciating pain."

On August 23, 1864 the surgeon Joseph Case Rutherford sent a letter home to his wife, Hannah Chase Rutherford, in Newport:

> I read your sad letter announcing the death of our darling little boy. The blow was more than I could bear...to have our fond hopes be suddenly blasted. Oh God it is hard. And if it is hard for me, God only knows how you can endure such a loss. I can't write now. I can't realize the awful fact. It has made me sick both body and mind. I can't do anything nor think anything and I almost envy the brave soldiers who are giving up their lives in our front this morning.

In St. Johnsbury the body of a young soldier who had enlisted was brought home for burial. He too had died in the military hospital at Brattleboro, taken sick before he could leave the state. His mother had been notified and she hurried to Brattleboro, where her son died in her arms. Henry Herrick, a former Vermont Brigade bandsman, remembered the smell of fresh flowers in the crowded church and the young man's cap upon the casket. Later Herrick wrote, "In the last sad weeks the reaper has gathered a terrible harvest, we look wearily down the long lists of that noble army of martyrs who have given their lives to the country, and sometimes a familiar name [ap-

Surgeon/letter writer Joseph Rutherford.

271

pears]—perhaps a dear friend...like a sword thrust to our hearts."

As the Civil War began, a carpenter and former schoolteacher named Oliver Plaisted of East Barnard wanted nothing of fighting. So Plaisted removed himself from his home along Broad Brook Road to a cave high on nearby Ellis Mountain. Later he got a railroad jack in Woodstock, hauled it to the hills, and erected a stone shelter topped by a massive single slab. Plaisted lived through the war in hiding, then returned to East Barnard to live a hermit's life in a shack along Broad Brook, until he died at age 58, 15 years after the war ended.

People in Royalton and Barnard give directions to what has become known as "Oliver's Cave." It's a healthy hike into the deep woods where, close beside one another, are Oliver's little cave and the stone structure that replaced it as his hidden home. Scratched in the cave walls are the words of a cold and lonely man, another kind of casualty of the Civil War: "This is hell."

LUTHER HARRIS SURVIVES ANDERSONVILLE

One of Vermont's oddest pieces of public sculpture stands at Lyndon Center, a fountain in the shape of a huge boar that spouts water from its mouth. Given to the community by Luther Harris, for years president of the Lyndonville Bank and an amateur sculptor, Harris once saw a similar statue while touring Italy. Exactly why he chose to put a spitting pig in the middle of his town is unknown, but the statue portrays bounty (all that pork pouring forth an endless supply of clear cool water); could it not be the vision of plenty of a man long deprived of food and water? Luther Harris lived for many months with very little to eat or drink within the squalid confines of the Confederate prison at Andersonville. He survived, just barely, and came home to live a long and prosperous life. Not all Vermonters sent to Andersonville came home, including many of the 401 members of the Vermont Brigade captured June 23, 1864 in fighting near the Weldon Railroad south of Petersburg, one of the saddest of all days for Vermont in the Civil War.

It occurred because Ulysses Grant would not sit around and let the Confederate forces entrenched around Petersburg wither and die. Soon after the two armies squared off at Petersburg, after "Baldy" Smith failed to break the rebel lines, Grant on June 15 launched a frontal assault on the Confederate defenses. The Union attack was thrown back, with the Vermonters, for once, kept out of the fighting. Grant employed another strategy, extending his lines below Petersburg to the west to cut the important Weldon Railroad. The operation began toward midnight on June 21 and ended on June 24. Grant sent the Sixth Corps to seize the railroad, and he deployed Winfield Scott Hancock's Second Corps (absent Hancock, whose Gettysburg wound had flared up) in support. The assault ended in disaster as Lee quickly perceived Grant's intentions and, attacking with troops under Billy Mahone, a rapidly rising Confederate star, got his men between the Union corps, some even coming in behind the Union line. In defeat, 1,600 Union soldiers were sent to Southern prisons.

The Vermont Brigade got a dangerous assignment in the Union advance, as guard of the far end of the entire line. The Third Vermont Regiment and one of the 11th's three battalions formed a skirmish line out by themselves toward the railroad. The Vermonters advanced within a mile of the tracks, then 90 men of the Third Vermont under Capt. Alexander Beattie of Maidstone were sent the rest of the way to the rail line. To prove he had reached his objective, Beattie sent a piece of severed telegraph line back to headquarters. An additional 250 men under Lt. Col. Samuel Pingree were moved forward in support. All the while, Vermont Brigade commander Lewis Grant was concerned for his men. A key rise of ground to the Vermont Brigade's front was conspicuously undefended; rebel soldiers could be seen moving ever closer. Grant summoned Sixth Corps commander Horatio Wright, who surveyed the scene and declared that, should the need arise, the Vermonters could withdraw through some trees to their rear.

It was not enough. The Confederates began closing in from front and flank, and soon were behind the Vermonters. The men of the Fourth and 11th regiments, out toward the railroad, were hit the worst. They put up brief fights but, with no orders to withdraw, held their ground.

Luther Harris, then a private in the Fourth Vermont, remembered:

We did our work on the railroad well, tore it up, burned the station and a bridge or two, threw the rails on the fire so as to warp them, they could not be used again, and about noon were ready to retire. Our regiment was on the skirmish line that day, in the center....Our commanding officer was Col. Pingree of the 3d Vt. Infty, who was officer of the day. Before the movement to the rear began I saw him go to the rear. This seems to me to have been about one o'clock but it may have been later which left us without a commander, as the senior captain (our regiment had lost all its field officers) was not informed of the state of affairs, and the lines on our right, and on our left were withdrawn leaving us an easy capture. It was apparent before three o'clock what must come about.

The great mistake was that we did not all go without orders, but we had been in so many hard places and been true to our soldierly principles, that no one thought of such a thing.

According to Luther Harris, the Vermonters put up a good fight. "If we fell back we fell into their hands so we had a double incentive to maintain our ground, the little hillock and the trees furnished us better protection than any artificial breastwork. We had sixty rounds of ammunition each, and the campaigns of the Wilderness had taken out the unskilled and all were experts with the rifle. Without orders we had deployed almost as skirmishers, in fact orders were unknown that afternoon."

In the fighting, Pvt. Patrick Howard of the 11th Vermont was shot; he survived just two days. Howard was 14 years old, the youngest soldier who went to war from St. Johnsbury. His parents got the bad news of his death about the same time they learned that Patrick's brother, John, had been captured that same day. John would die at Andersonville in early November.

The fighting had been in vain. Harris recalled:

> The work of capture was begun at the extreme left of the regiment, it was on lower ground. One by one the men were overpowered. We were on the extreme right....I had a gun that I had carried through the war, a good one, and I was determined that no one else should ever use it. Instead of giving up my arms I struck a half grown tree with all my might and the flexible barrel doubled up like an oxbow around it, and we were prisoners of war.

Just before the capture, 50 of the Vermont troops lit out for some distant woods and got safely back within the Union lines. But 401 prisoners marched away under tight Confederate guard. They were held in downtown Richmond for several days, then were transported to another well-known Confederate prison, Belle Isle, in the middle of the James River. The Green Mountain boys were finally placed aboard trains for a long journey south, once interrupted by a forced 60-mile march between railheads. But the men eventually arrived at their grim destination.

Private Harris recorded his capture and imprisonment in a book he wrote 20 years after the war, a handwritten manuscript now at the University of Vermont. Harris described the prison, which he says the Confederates called "Prison Sumter," as follows:

> The prison as it seems to me was in an immense forest of pines. For fifty miles before reaching it we saw nothing but pine trees. It is in the county of...[Sumter], Georgia, about a quarter of a mile from the railroad at a station called Andersonville or Anderson and I do not know which. There was maybe a house or two beside the railroad station but there is no village. It cannot be far from the Florida line. I believe it would be healthy enough under ordinary circumstances. The prison was said by some to contain seventeen acres and by others thirty three acres. I am inclined to think that it was nearer the former figure.
>
> A creek runs through it a little south of the centre. The bluffs on each side of the creek were quite prominent, making the most of the prison high land. Two or three acres of swamps along the creek made that part of the prison untenantable.
>
> The whole was enclosed by a stout stockade made of the trunks of pine trees hewn square and set upright side by side in trenches eight feet deep thus forming a solid wood wall from fifteen to twenty feet in height, with a smooth surface. At regular intervals, sentry boxes were placed on top of the stockade with rough stairs leading to them from the ground....About fifteen feet from the stockade on the inside was the dead line, a sort of fence, made by driving posts into the ground and nailing a narrow board to them about waist high. This dead line extended entirely around the prison and no one was allowed to pass this under any circumstances. The sentinel had orders to shoot anyone that could be seen outside....

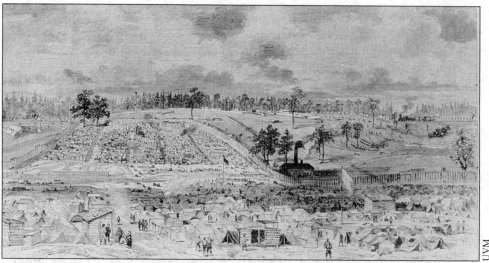

The Confederate prison at Andersonville, Georgia.

The dead were brought into the street every morning before being carried into the dead house.... The custom was to take all the clothing from the dead body, tie the great toes together, and if any knew the name lay a piece of paper, or a chip of wood, upon the breast, with name, company and regiment written thereon. It became an everyday occurance, the habit of tying the toes together brought it about, for a weak one to say to his comrade, "it won't be long before you can tie my toes together and swap me for a stick of wood," for the men were allowed to bring in a stick of wood on their return from taking out a dead man. There was a hospital outside at the southeast corner of the enclosure, but it was entirely incompetent to attend to the needs of the camp, in fact I never knew of any one being treated there. They had no medicine, if they had had the room and attendants.

Conditions in the Andersonville prison were horrible. Water was polluted, sanitary facilities nonexistent, shelter consisted principally of caves dug in the clay earth. Food was poor and scarce, distributed at a starvation rate. The searing Georgia sun scorched the earth in summer, while the damp cold of winter cut to the bones of men clad in the ragged remnants of uniforms.

Harris recalled:

The soldier who got mad, and the soldier who made the best of everything, lived until long into the winter. He who constantly complained of his lot, and saw nothing except through doleful eyes, soon began to grow weak, then looked sallow, the teeth grew loose, little by little the legs refused to do their duty, it was found that they could not be quite straightened at the knees and as the days rolled on, that difficulty increased until the knees almost touched the chin, then an ugly sore would break out on the side of the calf, seemingly to show resentment at being thwarted in that it could not further cramp and double up its victim. Those sores never got better, day by day they opened wider down the side of the leg. It was a slow fight, but the outcome was never in doubt, and when at last the struggle was over with this monster, that clung like some great serpent in whose coils the victim was powerless to do nought but think, and struggle, when the time came the end was easy enough, many died in their sleep.

The disease arising from insufficient and poorly balanced food enters into the case, and frequently death comes from a disease brought on by slow starvation. Scurvy and chronic diarrhea were the diseases most common, all or nearly all had the former, very few escaped the latter....

As I walked about, that which impressed me most was the absence of care or attention between the men. The dying man got no attention from a comrade although perhaps they touched as they lay. There were men who spent their time among the sick, and did what they could, but they were few. The bones had little covering of flesh. Scurvy made the skin unhealthy, therefore when one was compelled to lay on the ground, sores soon came on the exposed joints of the body, shoulders, hips, knees, and ankles. The very earth seemed poisoned with the many thousands that never moved from where they lay and had no care. Taking into account the time of year and the terrible heat, it is wonderful that the air was not so poisoned that one breath would kill. The stench was something indescribable.

George Crosby of Brattleboro, captured in the Wilderness and confined at Andersonville with Harris, kept a diary now in the Vermont Historical Society. The following entries were recorded in Crosby's first days of capture:

Wednesday, June 8: A very hot day....I cannot stand the hot sun have to stay in the shade it makes my head ache and dizzy. Drew very small rations did not get them til after dark.

Thursday, June 9: Showery, men are dying at the rate of 60 every 24 hours mostly of scurvy and diareah thousands not even a blanket for cover. Water is poor and dirty, fighting occurs several times every day, alas for human depravity.

Friday, June 10: Every day is very hot this is the first day this month that we have not had a shower. If our government lets us remain here through the summer I have little hope of ever seeing home again.

Crosby survived Andersonville and returned to Brattleboro a year later.

Luther Harris noted that vermin were everywhere:

When the sun came up these pests would crawl into the porous, filth filled ground....In the swamp along the creek, nothing but maggots could be seen, even in the scorching sun, they were in constant motion like the waves of the sea. The flies liberated from this mass seemed a constant swarm, as they took on their wings and completed their change from a maggot to a fly. The annoyance of these flies was great, filling the sick ones mouths and nostrils.

Under such suffering at Andersonville and at Columbia, South Carolina, it is not surprising that of the 401 Vermonters captured at the Weldon Railroad, more than half died within six months. The historian G. G. Benedict estimated that 70 percent died either in prison or as a result of their imprisonment. But Luther Harris kept on living. He wrote that he became involved in efforts to tunnel out of the stockade, in holes disguised as attempts to create wells. "The mind was pleasantly occupied, the division of labor was such that the work was no more than should be taken for exercise, but above all the contact with the pure earth while at work, the fresh smell, the purity as compared with the putrid conditions that surrounded one at all times on the surface, was helpful to a great degree."

Harris wrote that he escaped one dark night, using a rope made from bits of cloth and leather to climb the stockade wall:

> It stopped raining as I got away and there was little water standing on the ground therefore one of the helps I had depended upon to cover up my trail in water failed me. At daylight my cord dangling from the stockade informed the guards that some one had gone and the hounds were put on my track, at about eleven o'clock I heard them and in a few minutes they were in sight. I took refuge in a small tree. As the dogs came up they formed in a circle around the tree, about twenty feet from it, and began to howl.

The treed Harris was returned to Andersonville. He was much more fortunate than Lt. Edward B. Parker of Middlebury. Captured at Weldon Railroad, he was taken to the prison pen at Columbia, South Carolina. In October he too escaped. Parker was hunted down by dogs and torn to pieces.

Private Harris was taken before the notorious commandant of Andersonville, Capt. Henry Wirz. Harris remembered: "The captain gave me quite a lecture on the shortcomings of our government. He spoke english with some difficulty and, I believe, used the expression for which he afterward became famous, for the first time, 'That when he first came to this country he thought the American Eagle one fine bird, but now he thought it one d——d buzzard.' I was returned to prison, and I quietly took my place again."

At long last, as William Tecumseh Sherman's forces advanced through Georgia, Private Harris and the thousands of other prisoners were moved from Andersonville. "I looked back at that terrible pen with something almost like attachment for it," Harris recalled. "Many of my comrades were there, in the trenches, with no marks to their graves. I could remember them as they were before the capture, strong true men, tried in the furnace of battle. My step was joyous, but I felt a sort of desire to stay, it seemed as though the dead were looking on in dismay at our going, as though we were deserting them."

Harris was sent to other prison camps little better than Andersonville, and despite a cold winter with scant heat or clothing, he lived on. Finally he was exchanged and returned to the Union army. He wrote of that day:

> On the twenty eighth day of February A.D. eighteen hundred and sixty five, on the Cape Fear River, a few miles north from Wilmington, North Carolina, was enacted a quiet scene that, to its actors, or participants, was the one great day of

their lives. There were some thousands of men...who walked or were carried through a line of soldiers, who counted each soul as they passed through, the soldiers, a handful, stood in two ranks facing in, one rank composed of northern troops and the other of southern, the former in blue the latter in gray rags....The men passing through this to the gateway to freedom and home, were prisoners of war from the prison pens of the south....

Not a word of exultation, or joy, or even satisfaction was heard, there was not the strength for that, there was only a quiet, steady air of home in the men.

When Luther Harris and the Vermonters entered Andersonville, the prison population had reached about 30,000. Today at the prison site, preserved as a national historic site, a national cemetery contains the graves of 12,912 Union soldiers. Vermonters lie in 76 of those graves. Confederate prisons claimed the lives of 302 members of the Vermont Brigade.

THE HOME FRONT

In May 1864, as the Army of the Potomac prepared to march south from Spotsylvania Court House, the family of Pvt. Jonathan Blaisdell, in Cambridge, opened a letter that began: "I have got about sick of writing without getting any answer." About the same time Charles Cummings wrote home:

> My dear wife,
>
> I have not received a line from you since yours of the 29th [a month before] but knowing your usual punctuality I lay the delay to the mail arrangements. Yet it was a disappointment to me yesterday when the mail arrived with letters from Vermont as late a date as June 10th and not one for me.

Soldiers' letters often complained of unanswered mail. It seems surprising, but in fact the home folks—particularly the women, with thousands of the most fit men constantly gone away from the time of Bull Run to Appomattox—were often busier than the men in uniform. War then, though not as true as in modern times, meant long periods of boredom punctuated by moments of sheer terror.

The burdens of everyday life, of keeping up with farm chores, fell to the people left behind, younger brothers and grandfathers, but most particularly on mothers, wives, and sisters. In one of the great injustices of the Civil War period in Vermont, the *Manchester Journal* editorialized soon after many local soldiers had been killed at Savage's Station: "One great hinderance to enlistments is the women. They do not seem animated by the spirit of the Spartan mother, who counselled her son to return with his shield or on it. It is thus that mothers, sisters, wives, daughters of the North counsel? The time has come, if ever, when sacrifices have got to be made, when mother must tell her darling and wife her noble husband to go and do his duty."

Without the women of Vermont keeping things going on the home front, there would hardly have been a war effort. In 1864, when the Ladies Aid Society of Cornwall shipped a box of hospital stoves to the war zone, a member stated, "Our ladies have enlisted for the war." Indeed, as T. D. Bassett noted a century later, Vermont women "enlisted for the duration." Even in the criticism of the Manchester newspaper is an implied tribute: less affected by the flag waving and patriotic songs, with no chance of going to war, Vermont women took a more realistic view of things and anticipated the horrible cost both on the battlefield and at home.

Some soldiers seemed to have forgotten that their absence was felt back on the farm. Capt. Charles Gould of Windham and the 11th Vermont wrote to his parents in 1864:

> If you can get a bottle of cough medicine, put it in the box where it will come safely I would like it. Mother you want to know how my shirts wear. They are firstrate now. There is not a hole in them but perhaps you had better send some cloth like them as you are sending a box and I have a chance for probably they will wear to mending before spring. I would like the box to start as soon as is convenient but still I don't want you to hurry or overdo for I can wait very well. I have wrote my things all along in my letter and don't know as you can pick them up and put them together. Pack the box as snug as possible and stick in something in every corner. Make me 2 or 3 little cloth bags and send them for they come very handy to put little things in. I will close now till morning for I may think of something else in the night I want. I want some sealing wax and ginger. I don't think of anything more now. Write often as you can.

The war hit especially hard in Brattleboro, with its military hospital and encampment. Soldiers, well and wounded, going to and from the front, hospitalized or drilling, were always in the community. Many years after, a Brattleboro woman, Mrs. Levi K. Estey Fuller, reminisced in a talk before the local woman's club. The text has been preserved:

> Brattleboro, at the beginning of the war, had business interests in the South. Ira Miller's carriages and wagons were sold to Southern planters on account of their thorough workmanship and durability. Our Water Cures were patronized largely by people of Southern wealth. They brought some of their slaves with them; gay-turbaned black nurses were a common sight on our streets in my childhood. The Zyragars, the Eustaces, the Buckners from Louisiana, the Stoddards from Savannah, and many from Charleston, South Carolina, summered here. They worshipped with us in our churches on the Sabbath; they loved our hills and streams; they helped to keep the beautiful gardener's path in order, and some stayed late in the autumn to see the reds and yellows of our maples that shaded our streets. Two families built lovely homes here. But after the war came, the Water Cures felt the loss of Southern patronage.
>
> I think I shall never forget the day that the news came that Sumter had been fired on. Upon my return from school at noon I noticed my mother's face and asked

what dreadful thing had happened, and she told me that Sumter had been fired upon and President Lincoln had called for seventy-five thousand troops for three months.

Mrs. Fuller continued: "I think but a few weeks passed when in my early home we did not have as guests there those who came to say 'goodbye' to some son or brother or husband who was going off with his regiment. Many were from farms and were unaccustomed to going away from home. Some one would recommend them to come to our house, and they would come and say 'You are our kind of folks, and will take us in.'"

One day a minister and his family from northern Vermont came to stay.

The minister and part of the group came back late, and every bed was occupied, so I took the young girl with me up into the unfinished attic, where mother had an old bed all arranged for me to sleep in whenever the house was full; and I shall never forget the sorrow of that poor girl, and her tears, for she had a lover as well as a brother who was going to war the next day. We wept and prayed together.

Mrs. Fuller noted that whenever a regiment left for war, the women of Brattleboro made hot coffee and served food to the soldiers.

And they were busy indeed, after the first battles of the war, sewing, knitting, rolling bandages and scraping lint. The Sanitary Commission and the Christian Commission received the goods and distributed them in army and field hospitals as they were needed.

The art of canning fruit had not become so general in those days, but we had jellies of all kinds and dried fruits in sugar which were sent at regular periods to the front.

Women's organizations were formed to support the troops. "We learned to knit socks, and it was considered a disgrace to attend a concert or lecture without taking a soldier's sock for knitting work," said Mrs. Fuller.

One wounded soldier, she said, wrote to his mother of the arrival of a box of garments from home and how a nurse removed one that seemed made for a four-legged animal. "In those days sewing machines were not very common, and most of the sewing was done by hand."

The opening of the military hospital at Brattleboro was a great relief to the residents of South Main and Canal streets (near the encampment), Mrs. Fulller recalled, "for…nearly every house had a sick soldier in it to care for, and many of them died. People were allowed to visit the wards, and carry things to entertain the convalescents. How they did enjoy looking over our photograph albums, and books of prints. Some did so want home cooking."

War drove prices up, particularly those of cloth.

Yard wide cotton was thirty-five, forty and even forty-five cents a yard. If you thought it dear, you knew it would be dearer tomorrow. Nothing counted in those days but how to keep up until the Rebels were conquered....Fast days were frequent; there was never a prayer offered in church or at home that our President and his soldiers were not prayed for; dependence upon God was realized fully. One day at high school, our class in United States History had recited and returned to our seats, when our teacher slapped the history down upon his desk and said, "Scholars, this history of the Revolution is pretty tame compared with what is going on today. You are LIVING history at the rate of thirteen pages a day."

Mrs. Fuller stated that many of her classmates were married or became engaged just before their boyfriends left for war, noting that one particular friend had been secretly married. "How I pitied her. Her parents disliked the young man. It is hard to study of the doings of Aeneas and Dido in Virgil when your mind was upon your own love affairs, and you never could tell but you might be a widow any day."

News of a battle brought a call for old linen, cotton bandages, and money for supplies. "The young women were the ones to solicit in different parts of the village, and we all had our beats. One friend, a school mate, and I, had part of our side of the brook, and I remember we collected $100 in an hour and a half after the Gettysburg battle, and we had been over the same ground before."

One day a train brought men released from Andersonville, and a friend of Mrs. Fuller's saw them. "Some were on mattresses as they could not sit up. They were nothing but skin and bones. Some were just ready to die, and all so feeble and thin."

She also noted: "The games of the children on the streets during those war days partook of the war spirit. Amputating arms and legs; carrying each other about on an improvised stretcher, and in case of a difference of opinion, battles were fought between 'The Yankees and the Secesh.'"

People from other states came to Brattleboro to visit soldiers confined in the hospital. Mrs. Fuller remembered a Pennsylvania woman who came to retrieve the body of a brother and was taken to his grave.

Looking up, with her eyes full of tears, she said, "At last my search is ended....The mountains and rivers seem so much like our own Pennsylvania. I shall leave him here to rest till the morning of the Resurrection."

The memory of those four awful years seems to those who lived through them like a dreadful dream. How often some of our own dead were brought back here for burial. The military funeral, the flag-draped coffin, the muffled drum, will long be remembered by us who were born in the 40's.

Bassett, in his dissertation "Urban Penetration of Rural Vermont, 1840–1880," noted: "The most important facts in the conscious lives of Vermonters during the war years were the heroic fighting of their volunteers and their willing sacrifice at home."

While Vermonters by the thousands fought for freedom hundreds of miles away, back on the home front the basic freedoms were not always respected.

Bricks and stones were thrown through the windows of a newspaper office in Montpelier because the editor was not thought to be adequately supportive of the war effort. But that was the exception; Vermont newspapers devoted much of their space to war news and associated stories. Battle accounts were reprinted from metropolitan papers, supplemented by reports from soldiers, such as Wilbur Fisk, who served as correspondents. Also, families passed on interesting letters sent by loved ones for publication.

News easily reached railroad towns like Brattleboro, with fresh deliveries of papers and the comings and goings of soldiers. In many small towns, however (including Rochester, as a town historian noted), "A daily paper was subscribed for to be read publically at the town hall, read nightly to large crowds." In even smaller towns, there were only once-a-week readings of newspapers from the steps of the town hall or perhaps the local store. A Groton man recalled:

> There was no radio in Groton then, or telephone, or telegraph. News came slowly but whatever came through was eagerly sought. Every evening except Sunday a large portion of the male population would gather at the store of Hosea Welch II to await the arrival of the daily stage from Wells River, bringing in the mail and one copy of the daily newspaper. After the mail was sorted and distributed Mr. Welch, the storekeeper and postmaster, would take a vantage position, adjust the kerosene lamp, and read from the Boston Journal the news of the day to a most eager and attentive audience. Sometimes it was "All quiet along the Potomac"; at other times it told of the carnage at Bull Run, Cedar Creek, Gettysburg, or the Wilderness. It made men wonder whether any Groton boy was killed or injured in the fight, or taken prisoner, as rarely were individuals mentioned.

As the war dragged on, more and more calls for volunteers reached Vermont. Each town was given a quota to fill; to make sure it was met, towns paid bounties

Highgate paid George Bradley a $1,000 bounty.

to those who enlisted. The price went up as men became more scarce, with bounties reaching $500 and more. As Bassett has noted, the larger towns, with more resources, exceeded their quotas more easily than the small towns, and men came from neighboring communities, even down from Canada and from neighboring states, to claim the larger bounty payments. At the same time, eligible men could pay substitutes to go to war in their place, and 816 did so. A total of 1,917 Vermont lads paid $300 commutation fees to avoid service.

The Vermont Legislature voted to supplement each private's $13.00 monthly pay with an additonal $7.00, and the state paid nearly $3.5 million in soldier pay by war's end. Governor Holbrook went to Boston to secure favorable loans from some large banks, later calling it his proudest achievement. Towns contributed more than $4 million in bounty payments.

William Herrick of St. Johnsbury, early in the war a member of the Third Vermont band, was discharged in 1862 because of ill health. He returned to work at the Fairbanks factories and noted in his diary on April 12, 1863 that the military draft had come to Vermont:

> The draft is the subject of conversation and discussion today, and much to the neglect of ordinary occupation and usual labor. It seems to come particularly hard in the shops, taking 44 from those connected with the Fairbanks works, but all seem to take it as a matter of course....Of course it must come hard in some cases and is so with the Carpenters, a wife and two children only previously able to get along by hard scratching and unable to furnish a substitute.

The previous day Herrick, who had seen the reality of battle on the Virginia Peninsula, had noted: "My heart is full of gratitude and thankfulness. The draft, long expected and much dreaded has come and I am spared. I have room for no other feeling tonight but complete thankfullness and mercy."

Several wealthy Vermonters sent sons to private schools in Canada to escape. Exemptions from the draft were allowed for physical disabilities, but some newspapers carried lists of those exempted. A few men reportedly pulled teeth and even cut off fingers to avoid serving. There was one instance of organized draft resistance, in the marble quarries of West Rutland. Local authorities moved in to restore order, and at least one arrest was made. Still, in the end, every town in Vermont met its draft quota.

More than 100,000 rifles for the Union armies were manufactured in the brick and stone Robbins Building in Windsor (now the American Precision Museum). Gunpowder was produced by the Bennington Powder Company. Material for uniforms was spun at the Prosper Mill in Felchville. Tailors in Rutland and Brattleboro turned the cloth into uniforms. Woolen mills in Winooski and North Pownal did big war business.

In St. Johnsbury, Amos Belnap, a blacksmith who had experimented for years with steel, learned how to temper it to an unusually light, thin, strong, and sharp blade. He passed the secret on to his son John, who during the Civil War operated a factory that turned out 100 of the expensive knife blades per week.

(Purchasers supplied their own handles.) The blades were popular with Union soldiers who could afford them; George Custer was presented with one after the war and may have carried it to the Little Big Horn. John Belnap kept the secret of his blades with him until he died, drowned while installing a waterwheel at his mill where Sleeper's River meets the Passumpsic, now the site of a slaughterhouse.

Grocers and innkeepers prospered in towns where the troops encamped, particularly Brattleboro and St. Johnsbury. During the war years new streets, business blocks, and churches opened in Rutland and Burlington, the latter introducing gas street lighting in 1862. In Brattleboro those who dealt in stoves, iron, tinware, dry goods, and lumber thrived. A Burlington company made prefabricated barracks to house troops. The hospital at Montpelier was built, cleverly, so that the wards could be disassembled when no longer needed and used for houses. Around Vermont College today where the Montpelier hospital once stood, there are many wooden story-and-a-half homes, with identical basic structures, that were once part of the medical complex presided over by Henry Janes. Though the hospitals contributed to the local economies, there were complaints in Montpelier that some of the men from the hospital were seen frequenting establishments with a low reputation located at the foot of the hill.

Gov. Erastus Fairbanks profited. When sales of scales from the family factory lagged, it began turning out harness hardware for army mounts. Copper mines in Orange County prospered, as did ironworks in Pittsford and Bennington. Wages throughout the state went up. Farmers found no shortage of outlets for their goods, but times were tough on the farm with the boys gone. Bassett has noted that the sale of mowing machines increased during the war years, as those left at home struggled to fill in for the laborers lost to uniforms.

Railroads thrived, as did express and telegraph companies. Resorts also prospered, especially those on lakes or mountains. New steamships plied Lake Memphremagog; railroads added luxury cars for the increasing tourist business. The proprietor of the hotel in South Royalton across from the railroad station gave a free night's lodging to soldiers going to, or coming from, the war zone.

Many Vermonters boycotted goods produced by slave labor. William Lloyd Garrison noted that the Robinsons of Ferrisburg did without cotton and used no sugar, substituting maple sugar.

Suppers, shoots, and rallies raised money to support the war effort; some communities even allowed gambling for the same purpose. In the winter months some of Vermont's more famous military leaders came home to participate in patriotic meetings. On a December night in 1863 William Herrick noted in his diary: "There was a war meeting at the Town Hall this evening....The hall was packed full. Lt. Clarke sang 'The Song of the Vermonters' with much spirit. Then Lt. Col. Grant got up to speak for half an hour rather swell-heady."

Earlier in the war, enthusiasm had not always come easily. In response to Lincoln's July 1, 1862 call for 300,000 more men, the people of Pittsfield gathered, faced with filling a quota of eight nine-month enlistees. The *Rutland Herald*'s account noted that the meeting began with stirring remarks "by several of our townsmen which gave the assembly the feel that men were needed and men must be had." It continued: "But the wheel moves slow. There were but two ready to offer themselves on the altar of southern rebellion and those were of doubtful physical ability. The ship seemed about ready to ride her anchor and dash on the shore of disappointment."

The meeting was adjourned until the following evening. Upon reconvening: "The fire of patriotism began to burn…each heart commenced swelling with patriotic emotions which seemed ready to burst, when 8 of our best young men came forward. Thus has Pittsfield shown that her patriotism is yet alive."

With preachers and teachers away at war, church services and school classes suffered. In St. Johnsbury, Herrick wrote: "The people are getting to be strangers to me here and in the congregations I saw few familiar faces. I feel very sad at the thought of the many who used to be there that I shall see no more forever.…The preaching was poor enough and the singing horrible."

List of items sent south, compiled by women of the Burlington Relief Association.

"Intemperance prospered," Bassett observed. A Montpelier woman complained in a letter to the local newspaper, "Our streets are almost daily disgraced by some soldier or citizen in a state of Beastly intoxication." Bassett summed it up: "The war could not fail to transform mores and institutions, but social changes came slowly. While submerged in the fog of battle, Vermonters dreamed only in terms of conditions they knew before. They could see that times were fast and good, that cash came easy, but prices were high and money had wings. When this cruel war was over, the lasting would emerge from the chaff of passing fashion and temporary luck."

In Washington, D.C., the wife of Vermont Senator Justin Smith Morrill worked tirelessly, accepting shipments from Vermont and making sure they reached the troops in the field. In Burlington the minutes of a single Ladies Relief Association meeting recorded that its membership assembled at the town hall had completed:

80 haversacks
164 woolen shirts
168 drawers
185 towels

80 kits with needles, pins, thread, buttons, and a New Testament
30 sheets
21 bed gowns
12 pillow cases
12 bed ticks
12 pillow ticks
12 ring pads
10 surgeons pin cushions
2 sacks of bandages

According to Bassett:

For the first time, individualistic Vermonters were cooperating in a huge, public collective enterprise, which proved its merit by helping win a great war. The immensity of the resources focused to this end, the complicated, extensive, and large-scale logistics and the size of the labor force, dwarfed all previous Vermont private enterprise, even the building and operation of the railroads. Although the Civil War was far from total war, the state and local authorities spent…eight or nine million dollars for Vermont's share of war costs, not to mention uncounted private contributions. The people of Vermont never had been and never would be so unanimous about anything.

Although times were profitable, the trains ever came north bearing their somber cargoes of broken and lifeless men. Prayers for peace came from pulpits and from dark bedsides on the narrow side streets of towns and from lonely farmhouses in the ancient hills and hollows.
Mrs. Fuller, in Brattleboro, concluded: "God grant that the present generation may never know what my generation and the one before endured during those four awful years."

WASHINGTON DEFENDED

West of Washington the Maryland landscape breaks against the Appalachians in a series of long ridge lines that even a Vermonter would call hills. Beyond the easternmost sizable ridge, the Monocacy River meanders down to join the Potomac. There in July 1864 a battle was fought to save the capital of the United States.

By late June Robert E. Lee was in considerable trouble as Ulysses Grant had the shrinking Army of Northern Virginia pinned under fire in the entrenchments stretching long miles from north of Richmond down to and beyond Petersburg. There, it appeared, Grant could hold until Lee ran out of men and material. But Lee, ever resourceful, wasn't one to sit and starve, and he sent orders to Gen. Jubal Early in the Shenandoah Valley to move north. Early was glad to oblige; after an errant Union commander shirked his duty of keeping Early's army under close watch, 15,000 Confederates were loose and moving toward Washington. It was a serious threat, for the stout fortifications that ringed the capital were thinly manned, principally by inexperienced militia.

Union commands reacted slowly at first, save for a general stationed in Baltimore—Lew Wallace. Wallace, a rising star early in the war who had ended up out of the fighting after a poor performance at Shiloh, had languished in an administrative position. Quickly perceiving the threat Early posed, Wallace assembled a ragtag force of 2,300 militia and 100-day men, braced by the veteran Eighth Illinois Cavalry and the Baltimore Artillery, and moved out to Frederick, into the path of the approaching Confederates. On July 6 Grant reacted, withdrew a division of the Sixth Corps from the Petersburg lines, and put it on steamships. James Ricketts's division, which included the 10th Vermont Regiment, was transported to Baltimore and then hurried west, where it joined Wallace on July 8. That brought the Union force to some 5,800 men, hardly more than one-third Early's numbers. Wallace drew up his little army along the east bank of the Monocacy River.

The Union defenses extended nearly three miles, from the National Road bridge on the north, down past a railroad bridge and another bridge carrying the Georgetown Pike, then through cornfields and meadows following the Monocacy south past a stately brick house owned by the Thomas family. On the river's west bank Wallace posted a skirmish line of 275 men, green militia save for 75 members of the 10th Vermont. All was quiet through the night of July 8–9. Not long after sunrise, the 10th Vermont's chaplain, Edwin Haynes, and two Vermont surgeons took a leisurely ride west along the Georgetown–Frederick Road. Rifles suddenly cracked ahead, and the three Vermonters wheeled their horses and galloped back to the Union line. The rebel army approached.

Jubal Early's battle plan was to make a demonstration against the north and center of Wallace's line, while swinging the bulk of his men downriver to ford the Monocacy and hit the south end of the Federal line. Fighting began about 9 A.M. as Confederates, in blue uniforms, advanced against the skirmish line on the far side of the Monocacy. The highest ranking of the Vermonters, Lt. George Davis of Burlington, told a militia captain to order a volley fired at the men in blue. But the captain refused to give the order, thinking the oncoming soldiers to be Union men: he refused until bullets began whistling in from the advancing bluecoats. At that point the captain, disgusted with himself, turned command of the skirmishers over to Lieutenant Davis; before the day ended Davis had qualified for a Medal of Honor. Meanwhile, a rebel cavalry brigade dismounted, forded the Monocacy and formed for an assault on General Wallace's left flank. The rebels surged forward and were repulsed by Yankee skirmishers. They reformed and came on again only to be again beaten back. By 2 P.M. John Brown Gordon's three-brigade division had waded the Monocacy. Thus three brigades of Southerners faced a brigade and a half of Yankees, including most of the 10th Vermont, posted along a fence line that ran between two farmhouses, the Worthington House to the front and the Thomas House to the rear.

The Confederates on Brooks Hill confronted the thin Union line across a 700-yard-wide field. In the initial attack, only a single rebel line advanced. The Confederates emerged from high corn and shocks of wheat and were met by a furious volley. They held but a moment, then went staggering back. An hour passed; again the Confederates attacked, this time in three battle lines. Lemuel Abbott, a Barre man, remembered:

> The long swaying lines of grey in perfect cadence with glistening guns and brasses, and above all the proudly borne but to us hated banner of the Confederacy with its stars and bars, was a spectacle rarely surpassed in the bright sunlight of a perfect summer day....As soon as they first appeared on the hill all firing largely ceased in my front on the skirmish lines and everything was as hushed save the indistinct distant battle cry of the enemy as on a Sabbath day even the men looking at the spectacle in silent awe for apparently the enemy which greatly outnumbered us, was making directly for our part of the line....On they came, swaying first one way and then another.

The collision came, and around the Thomas House the battle wavered, one side holding the house, then the other, with the frightened Thomas family huddled in the cellar. The attack was stopped, and the battle developed into a deadly rifle duel at perhaps 200 yards. General Early sent more men across the Monocacy to increase pressure on the Union left, and the blue line gradually began to give. The Vermonters moved back to the Baker Valley Road adjoining the Thomas property and there, bareheaded, stayed low and fired fast as they could, holding a vital position, the left end of the Union line. All the while, rebel artillery across the Monocacy raked their position from the flank. The Confederate line soon extended well beyond the Vermonters, and the Union position began to dissolve.

To the north, Jubal Early moved to break the Union center. Lieutenant Davis and his Vermonters hung on, though most of the accompanying militia had drifted across the river to safety. Davis wrote later, "The enemy pressed us so hard at one time that for a few moments we sought refuge in a railroad cut a few rods to the rear, but quickly regained our position and held it."

They held for more than an hour, under hot fire, in a most precarious position, since General Wallace had burned the highway bridge connecting them with the main Union line. The only way back would be the narrow railroad bridge. Davis recalled:

> It was now time for us to leave or be taken prisoners. We crossed the iron bridge, stepping upon the ties, there being no floor. The enemy came in upon us, upon both flanks, firing at our backs at a range of ten to 20 rods, and calling upon us to surrender. Some of our men were killed, others were wounded and fell through the bridge to the Monocacy river, 40 feet below. Five of my own company marching near me were taken prisoners upon or near the bridge, one of whom died in Andersonville prison. One-third of my picket detail were killed, wounded or captured. It has always been a mystery how any of us escaped the bullet or capture.

At the same time, the Union line to the south was giving way. The Green Mountain boys turned and ran for their lives with the rest of the Union soldiers. They reached safety only after racing uphill through a large open field, clear targets for the oncoming Confederates. The Battle of the Monocacy was over. Wallace's small army had suffered more than 1,500 casualties, 71 of them Vermonters, and been soundly defeated. But Early's advance on Washington had been delayed by a full and costly day.

Soon after the battle General Wallace, who had a flair for writing and after the war wrote the novel *Ben Hur*, scribed his official report. A copy, handwritten by an aide and signed by Wallace, resides in the University of Vermont's Special Collections, and it concludes: "Orders have been given to collect the bodies of our dead in a burial ground on the battlefield, suitable for a monument, upon which I propose to write, THESE MEN DIED TO SAVE THE NATIONAL CAPITOL—AND THEY DID."

Despite the bloodshed along the Monocacy, Jubal Early advanced on

Washington under the burning July sun. Washington was in a state of panic; a rebel army was closing in from the northwest and there were no regular army units to man the defenses. But help was on the way, the Sixth Corps coming up the Potomac in a long line of transports. The first ship putting in at the Potomac docks at noon on July 11 was a small steamer bearing division commander George Getty and other Sixth Corps officers. Abraham Lincoln, looking tired and worried, was there with his secretary of war, Edwin Stanton, to greet the troops. Surgeon Samuel J. Allen of Hartford later described what happened.

"What troops does this steamer bring?" the president inquired of one of the first uniformed men to step ashore.

"It brings Major General Getty and his staff, but no troops," was the answer.

As Lincoln turned away, obviously disappointed, he said, "I do not care to see any major generals: I came here to see the Vermont Brigade."

Lincoln was also present, chewing on hardtack given him by a soldier, when the Vermont Brigade and the rest of the Sixth Corps came ashore. Their arrival was timely, for that morning Jubal Early had closed within sight of the Capitol dome, some five miles to its north. After long-range firing he allowed his exhausted troops to fall out for a night's rest. But now, with his men somewhat refreshed, Early was preparing a try at breaking the Washington defenses, in the area of Fort Stevens, one of the strong points in the miles of fortifications that protected Washington. Manning the fort and the surrounding earthworks were 100-day enlistees and some inexperienced artillerymen, less than eager for their first fight.

Back on the Potomac, the Sixth Corps troops shouldered arms, moved up from the riverfront, and marched through the city along Seventh Street. This was a rare moment for the veterans of the old Sixth Corps, used to soldiering in unfriendly territory. Maj. Aldace Walker of Middlebury and the 11th Vermont said: "The sight of the veterans of the Sixth Corps was an intense relief to the constitutionally timid Washingtonians. We passed through crowded streets; cheers, good wishes, and fervent God-speeds were heard on every side. Citizens ran through the lines with buckets of ice-water, for the morning was sultry; newspapers and eatables were handed into the column, and our welcome had a heartiness that showed how intense had been the fear."

As John Sedgwick's, and now Horatio Wright's, old corps swung up the street with the easy long strides of veteran infantry, words such as "It's the Sixth Corps" and "Hurrah for the men who stormed Marye's Heights" were heard. They covered the miles quickly and, after spending the night of July 11 near the Soldiers' Home, filed into the works around Fort Stevens. General Early, through binoculars, saw to his dismay the arrival of troops that looked far more like veterans than the lads he had previously scanned on the Union parapets. "Old Jube" must have known his grand try for Washington was at an end, but he wasn't yet ready to go home.

Fort Stevens was familiar to the men of the 11th Vermont who had helped construct the place during their days as Washington artillerymen. Some of the veteran cannoneers expressed a wish to man the artillery as they watched their successors struggle to handle the big guns. The Third and Fourth regiments were posted in rifle pits to the left of Fort Stevens, while the remainder of the brigade and other Sixth Corps units were massed in woods behind the fort, awaiting a signal to attack.

Presently 80 handpicked marksmen were sent forward under command of the Third Vermont's Capt. Alexander Beattie of Maidstone. Confederates were waiting; a long-range but deadly exchange of fire commenced, with six Vermont men hit, one fatally. Somewhat later 50 men of the Sixth Vermont were sent out to reinforce the skirmishers.

As the afternoon wore on, President Lincoln, Secretary Stanton, and other cabinet officials arrived. The president mounted the fort's parapet to get a good look at the battlefield. At about 4 P.M. several thousand Union soldiers moved to the front of Fort Stevens. Aldace Walker commented, "The pseudo-soldiers who filled trenches around the fort were astounded at the temerity displayed by these war-worn veterans in going out before the breastworks, and benevolently volunteered most earnest words of caution."

The veterans, including the Vermont marksmen previously moved forward, lined up and, under the eyes of their commander in chief, moved to close with the Confederates. For a time the fighting was brisk, with wounded men borne back past the president. As Lincoln stood on the ramparts, by far the tallest figure, Confederate bullets whizzed by, and an officer several feet from him was wounded. Only then did Lincoln heed General Wright's pleadings and step down, though he kept peering over the top.

The Confederates were driven back a mile, at a cost of 280 men shot on the Union side. Toward dark the Vermont Brigade relieved the attackers, but the fighting died without a major assault. In the night Jubal Early turned his army west and moved away from Washington, a great chance at true military glory lost. At noon next day the Sixth Corps started after him; the Vermonters marched 20 miles before they got a rest.

If Grant had been a bit slow to react to the Washington threat, he now made sure the capital was in no danger. Not far behind the Sixth Corps on the Potomac River were transports carrying other veteran Union troops, men of the 19th Corps who had done their service thus far in Louisiana. Among them was the Eighth Vermont Regiment, some 700 soldiers under the command of Col. Stephen Thomas. The regiment had been transferred from the Deep South to join the Army of the Potomac in the siege of Petersburg, but at the last minute was diverted to Washington. As the advance guard of the 19th Corps, the regiment arrived on July 13, the day after Early's repulse, and marched by itself past the White House. Lincoln came out to watch, and the men cheered as the president lifted his stovepipe hat to them. The Eighth went through the city and into the Maryland countryside, coming up behind the Sixth Corps, to join in the pursuit of Early's army.

The Vermont troops faced marching strenuous enough to rival that of the Gettysburg campaign. Wilbur Fisk wrote:

It is a rare thing now-a-days that a soldier in the Sixth Corps gets a leisure moment to write a letter, or to do anything else. If anyone tries to keep track of us they need not expect to hear from us twice in the same place. We are on the march almost every day, and very often we march all night and all day too. It has been continual marching ever since we came into Maryland and from present appearances I see but faint reasons to hope that our task is completed.

He added: "It is terrible hot marching now. The men cannot endure it. Many fell out in our march yesterday, and several died from sunstroke."

Two weeks later Fisk wrote: "Whoever may have been the first to propose the theory of perpetual motion, I believe the Sixth Corps have been the first to demonstrate its possibility by actual practice."

The Vermont troops moved into western Maryland, then into Virginia, crossing the Blue Ridge Mountains to the Shenandoah Valley, then across the Blue Ridge and all the way back near Washington. Unbelievably, they were then turned around and ordered back over the mountains to the Shenandoah Valley, then back to Frederick, and on to Harpers Ferry, covering some 75 miles in one 48-hour stretch.

Julius Lewis wrote home to Poultney from near Frederick: "We get green corn potatoes watermelons and most everything we want. I should like to soldier here if they did not march us so to hell."

Early was raising hell in the valley and then sent a raid into Pennsylvania; the raiders burned Chambersburg on July 30. Union commanders did their best to counter him despite conflicting orders from Washington.

On August 7 Ulysses Grant had enough of this wasted effort and ordered his cavalry commander Philip Sheridan to take charge of things. Sheridan was told to follow Jubal Early's army "to the death." At the same time, Grant instructed Sheridan to lay waste the beautiful Shenandoah Valley, to the extent that a crow flying over it would have to carry its own provender. Those harsh words would be followed to the letter.

So a new army, under Sheridan, was officially formed consisting of the Sixth Corps, the 19th Corps, and remnants of the Union forces in the Shenandoah Valley that had let Early get away for his move on Washington. Also reporting to Sheridan were three cavalry divisions. Sheridan commanded more than 35,000 men. In that army was the Vermont Brigade's Second, Third, Fourth, Fifth, Sixth, and 11th regiments; the Eighth Vermont as part of William Emory's 19th Corps; the 10th Vermont in James Ricketts's division of the Sixth Corps; and the First Vermont Cavalry. This unprecedented conjunction of Vermont fighting men was taking place in western Maryland, to constitute nearly one-fifth of the army destined for hard service in the Shenandoah.

At first the Vermont troops were suspicious of their new commander. Sheridan was the latest in a string of leaders who had been serious disappointments. This short, muscular, bow-legged man with intense black eyes was an unknown quantity, though a considerable reputation preceded him. Soon the soldiers began to see things they liked: his unostentatious style, his Spartan headquarters, his riding with the troops. But they soon would see him at his very best—in battle.

A 1930s reconstruction of the west half of Fort Stevens stands in a small park on the north side of Washington, surrounded by streets and buildings, the battlefield long gone. Along the Monocacy a new national battlefield has been opened, its headquarters in a stone mill that stood during the battle. Nearby is a high railroad bridge that has replaced the one the Vermonters ran across to safety. It stands on the abutments that carried the ties and rails in 1864. To the south the broad field the grand Confederate attack crossed has grown in considerably but is publicly owned and thus will be preserved. The Thomas House remains, in private ownership, all bullet-scarred in a great grove of trees. The Worthington House is now part of the park and will one day be opened to the public. And if you know where to look, a line of trees denotes the location of the fence where the Vermonters and their fellow outnumbered Union soldiers shattered the first Confederate attack.

Along the sunken road where the 10th Vermont made its final stand, on a little plot of ground owned by the state, stands a monument to the Vermonters. Dedicated in 1914, it overlooks the Thomas Farm and the fields across which came the Confederate attacks. On the monument is the Greek cross of the Sixth Corps and the words: "During the battle fought here on the ninth day of July 1864 to save Washington, and we saved it, seven companies occupied the Washington Pike."

Traces of the road cut can still be seen where the bareheaded Vermonters stayed low and fired like fury—to save Washington.

VICTORY AT WINCHESTER

Soon after Sheridan took command of what was officially designated the Army of the Shenandoah, he marched into its namesake valley. Chaplain Edwin Haynes of the 10th Vermont recalled:

> At eight o'clock we reached Charles Town, the place made famous as the scene of the imprisonment, trial and execution of John Brown. The soldiers had not forgotten this thrilling page of history, perhaps the introductory chapter to the annals of the rebellion....As they marched through the streets, it seemed as if every soul was touched with the memory of the old hero, and ten thousand voices broke forth singing "John Brown's body lies mouldering in the ground."
>
> A dozen bands played the air to which these words were set; and what with the music, the singing, the measured tread of thirty thousand men, with their very muscles, as well as their vocal organs, in time and tune, afforded a spectacle that time cannot erase from the memory of the participant or the beholder.

It was late summer in Virginia, the nights beginning to cool a bit, and hope was in the air. Lee was at bay at Petersburg, and Jubal Early had been driven from Washington; far to the south, Uncle Billy Sherman and his army group had captured Atlanta. The end of the long war seemed, if not in sight, at least just beyond some near horizon, so much so that a Union army including most of the Vermont troops could burst into song for the man who, some would say, had started it all.

As the Vermont Brigade moved into the valley, it was down to less than 2,500 fighting men, the five old regiments numbering less than 400 men each. The three-year enlistments of the Old Brigade's veterans were fast expiring, and most were choosing to go home. On August 16, for instance, 150 men left the Third Vermont and started north. Among them were the commander, Lt. Col.

Tom Seaver, and the second in command, Maj. Samuel Pingree. Both had been in all the fighting since long-ago Lee's Mills.

By August 10 Sheridan had marched his 35,000 men all the way south of Cedar Creek to Strasburg, where Jubal Early was found well entrenched on high, steep Fisher's Hill. Shots were exchanged before Sheridan withdrew three miles north behind Cedar Creek. Then he moved way back to Charles Town and dug in southeast of town. Early followed and on August 21 he moved to attack, an assault that never fully materialized. But the Vermont Brigade had a sharp fight; though most history books fail to mention the "Engagement at Charles Town," a name proudly added to the Old Brigade's list of battles.

The action started when Early probed the Union picket line posted three miles south of Charles Town. The pickets were quickly driven in, and the Vermont Brigade was roused from morning coffee to be sent into the open fields in their place. The Third, Fourth, and Sixth regiments formed the frontline, with the Second, Fifth, and 11th in close support. The Vermont troops first pushed into a field of tall corn, driving out concealed Confederate riflemen. The Vermont Brigade kept on, moving a half mile south to regain the position held in early morning by the Union pickets. General Getty was with the Vermonters; a bullet took his horse from under him. The general found that his men had gone too far, almost coming in on the main Confederate position. Getty ordered his troops back to a long, low ridge, where the Vermonters formed a mile-long front, a position they would hold all day.

Commanding the 11th Vermont was Lt. Col. George Chamberlin of St. Johnsbury. Chamberlin was a prolific letter writer who often expressed to his loved ones a fervent hope for peace. As his regiment moved toward the Shenandoah Valley, he wrote to an aunt and uncle about how much he missed his wife:

> My great trial is the separation from her whom I love so much better than all else on earth. It is cruel and very hard to bear, I assure you, and I long for its close and pray for our reunion soon....You can know nothing of what a horrible thing war is; who have never been on a battlefield or in a field hospital; and I cannot write it. This war is a stupendous work. I believe we shall succeed, and pray God it may be soon over.

On the morning of the fight at Charles Town, he wrote:

> My dear, precious wife:
> We are in God's hands, and His will is better and wiser than our will; we love and trust him, and be satisfied. Orders to strike tents and pack up immediately. Picket firing in front is quite sharp, increasing for the last half hour, and it seems nearer, as though our pickets were falling back.

Those were the last words he ever wrote. About an hour later, as the Vermont Brigade moved against that Confederate-filled cornfield, George Chamberlin was shot in the stomach. He fell into the arms of a fellow soldier, was carried to the rear, but lived only a few painful hours. Maj. Aldace Walker assumed command of the regiment.

The fight south of Charles Town got worse, with the Vermont soldiers holding their line, the Confederates pressing in, bullets flying fast, and more men getting hit. In the midst of the Vermont line was an old brick mansion owned by a family named Packett, direct descendants of George Washington. "Men were soon put into the house, and fired from windows, doing good execution," one Vermont soldier recalled. "The enemy could not stand this, and commenced shelling the house with great fury and accuracy....The men were so anxious to fire that as soon as a shell pierced the brick wall, immediately thrust out two or three muskets."

The fight became something of a metaphor for the dilemma of the nation George Washington was said to have fathered. In the basement of the house, people with the blood of the founding father in their veins cowered while bullets from Americans north and south tore through their home. Cannonballs blasted through the walls; a bureau once owned by Washington was reduced to splinters. Eventually some Vermonters went into the basement and escorted the terrified Packett family to safety.

The fight went on until dark, and by one estimate the Old Brigade used 56,000 rounds. Local legend in Charles Town holds that the Vermont soldiers, lacking horses and mules, used cows to haul ammunition. Residents also claim that some Vermont soldiers, firing from the windows of the Packett House, donned dresses so it would appear that the Packett women were in the house.

After dark Sheridan withdrew his army five miles north to Halltown, though the Vermonters remained in position until 3 A.M. The day had been a costly one for the Green Mountain State: 24 men lay dead and 100 wounded, 16 of whom later died of wounds.

Colonel Chamberlin's body was sent home to St. Johnsbury, where a funeral service was held. A family member noted: "The black bier stood under the evergreens in the edge of the garden. We followed it to the church. Dr. Goodwin, who loved him too, spoke the last words. Forest trees bend over his grave, the birds sing there; kindest hands administer to make it beautiful, but when all is done, it is still GEORGE'S GRAVE."

Not long after the fight Early took his Confederates south to occupy high ground beyond the Opequon Creek. Several weeks of relative inactivity followed, during which the Vermont troops voted absentee in their state elections, casting a lopsided vote in favor of a second term for John Gregory Smith. On September 16 Ulysses Grant suddenly appeared at Sheridan's headquarters, concerned about a lack of decisive action in the Shenandoah Valley. The visit created a great stir among the troops, who knew that with Grant around, action was soon to follow. Three days after his departure, Sheridan moved to attack Early's army posted behind Opequon Creek.

The Battle of the Opequon, or Third Winchester, began in the predawn of September 19 as Union horse soldiers, including the First Vermont Cavalry, moved out to lead the advance of Sheridan's army. Sheridan had chosen as the principal route toward Early's lines a long, narrow defile known as Berryville Canyon. Well before dawn, James Wilson's cavalry splashed across the Opequon and into the canyon, riding easily through to higher ground, where it began to come under the fire of Confederate artillery.

As the infantry moved along the canyon, a traffic jam developed: wounded cavalrymen had come back to seek shelter, the place was not wide enough for an army anyway, and everything got tangled. As a result, the big infantry attack, planned for early morning, was delayed; it was nearly noon before Sheridan got the Sixth and 19th corps, 20,000 infantry, up on high ground and in line of battle.

Sgt. George Carpenter of Northfield, with the Eighth Vermont, described the early action:

> At the appointed time the march was begun under cover of the darkness, and as we filed out of camp the column turned toward Winchester. While halting for a little rest just after daybreak, we heard that sound which I believe strikes a chill through the bravest man that lives, and causes him to feel that his heart is sinking down, down, till it seems to drop into his boots. I mean the dull rustling of air which is hardly more than a vibration, but which to the experienced listener betokens artillery firing at a distance.
>
> Pressing forward at a rapid march we entered a deep, wooded gorge, and while there got the order to quick-step and then double-quick, while the noise of fierce strife beyond and out of the woods gave a fearful meaning to the haste with which we were urged forward. In this defile was established a hospital; and as the regiment passed, we saw surgeons taking out and examining the bright, keen knives; laid on a table was a victim undergoing amputation of the leg, which with other mangled men, and pools of blood, showed too plainly what was going on at the front.

Major Walker recalled, "As we filed out of the ravine which toward the last was lined with wounded cavalrymen, we found Sheridan, his headquarters fixed on a conspicuous elevation.... It was with great satisfaction that we found him in this early twilight at the very front, and under the fire of the enemy, carefully attending to details which we had been accustomed to see more celebrated commanders entrust to their staff."

Sheridan finally got his army formed, and at midday he moved toward the well-prepared, though outnumbered, Confederate defenders. The Vermont Brigade, under the command of Col. James Warner, with Lewis Grant on leave, was on the left end of the main Union line. From the first, the attack did not go well. Confederate artillery broke up the Union center, while on the left, units attacked without coordination. The Vermont Brigade moved under fire along a country road that led toward a rise of ground. Fronting it was a swampy area, which the Vermonters aimed to cross and gain some protection behind the rise. Major Walker noted:

> As we reached its swampy bottom, we saw at our right, at short pistol range, at least a full regiment of the enemy drawn up in line near the point where the road crosses

the hollow, in anticipation of our taking precisely the course we did, and firing coolly, as rapidly as they could load, directly along our line, thus enfilading us completely....The slaughter was for a few moments murderous....We therefore floundered on, our coherence entirely lost, entered the clusters of evergreens through which the cruel bullets whistled fearfully, and at last, a confused mass at best, those of us who escaped unhurt reached comparative safety under the very crest of the hill, and high above the deadly hollow.

On reaching the hilltop, the Vermonters looked to their right, expecting to see the long sweep of the rest of the Union battle line. Instead they saw Confederates and, realizing they were isolated, beat a quick retreat over much of the ground they had gained at high cost. The first Union assault at Third Winchester had failed; now the Confederates took the offensive.

Off to the right, where the Eighth Vermont was fighting, Pvt. Herbert E. Hill, a 19-year-old soldier from Marlboro, noted:

Our fresh volleys come none too soon, but they are heeded, and the enemy's advance is checked in our front. A tall man near me receives a bad gash in his forehead; the crimson blood flows down his face and bosom. Another has his chin shot away, leaving his tongue dangling exposed over his throat. Both must probably die; but life is dear, and with a beseeching, parting look, they crawl back to the rear and from my sight forever, but their faces are imprinted in my memory.

We are in an open field. The enemy are strongly posted in the woods only a few rods in front, and nothing between them and us but thin Virginia grass....in grim silence the men load their guns while lying on their backs, rise quickly to their feet, glance across the gleaming barrel, and fire. The first man to die on this spot is Walter Pierce, who had the strange presentiment of his fate last night. A minie bullet strikes his face as he rises to fire for the third or fourth time. Not a word escapes his lips as he falls lifeless to the earth....

A desolating fire of musketry sweeps across the exposed ground we occupy, the bullets sounding like angry hornets, as they cut the air so close to the face as to be felt....Now word is along passed that Charles Blood is killed. Another is wounded, and we wonder who will be the next, when Corporal James Black settles slowly to the ground. And still the ugly work goes on. Colonel Thomas sits like a statue on his horse, refusing to dismount, encouraging the men within sound of his voice.

Sergent Francis E. Warren is at my side, and has partly risen to watch the rebel movements, when a bullet enters the socket of his eye, and comes out his ear. With a groan he bows his head between his knees, and drops at my feet. Next to fall is Edmund Fisher, a man past fifty years of age, and never yet absent from his post of duty....Our rifles become so hot and foul from constant and rapid use that we are forced to abandon them and take others from the dead soldiers lying within reach.

The little Eighth held its position; it was late afternoon before Sheridan could get his lines squared for another assault. Sheridan was everywhere, seeming to ignore the heavy artillery fire. "He personally inspected the rest of his army and the enemy's position, riding at a terrible speed along the whole of our extended skirmish line," said Aldace Walker.

Those who fought at the Opequon never forgot the majesty of the final Federal assault, Sheridan's army in a long line moving in unison with flags flying and bayonets gleaming in the autumn sunshine. Major Walker recalled: "The order to advance was soon received, and the line moved forward; not with the promiscuous disorderly rush of the former charge, but steadily and deliberately, aligning carefully by brigades and by divisions, we swept forward into battle."

Maj. Edwin Dillingham died at Winchester.

The Vermont Brigade advanced through a field of tall corn, coming to a rail fence on the far side. Walker noted: "Behind this fence we had halted when we opened fire. The enemy was in plain sight but a short distance before us and the men worked at their guns with the diligence of desperation."

The 10th Vermont was fighting off to the right, under command of one of Vermont's fine soldiers, Maj. Edwin Dillingham of Waterbury. Dillingham, once confined in Libby Prison, was suddenly struck by an artillery round that nearly tore off a leg. Bleeding terribly, he was borne to the rear, where he died three hours later. A man who fought with Dillingham remembered him as "young, handsome, brilliant, brave amid trials, cheerful under discouragements, upright, and with the kindness of heart which characterizes all the true gentleman, combined with firmness and energy as a commander; respected by all of his command, and loved by his companions." Before he died Dillingham said, "I am willing to give my life for my country and I am not afraid to die."

Off where the Eighth Vermont was fighting, the advance of the 19th Corps had come to a halt. Now Colonel Thomas, out of the high hills of Bethel, took charge. Thomas rode to the front of his battered brigade, turned, and in the thunderous voice he had used on the battlefields of the Deep South, called: "Boys, if you ever pray, the time to pray has come. Pray now, remember Ethan Allen and old Vermont, and we'll drive them to hell. Come on, old Vermont."

With that, Thomas turned his horse toward the enemy battle line and began to ride deliberately forward. His men, with bayonets fixed, gave a cheer. They soon had passed him and went rolling on into the rebel-held woods ahead. So too moved the 19th Corps, the Vermont Brigade, the whole Federal battle line. Now Eighth Corps troops Sheridan had posted beyond the left flank of the Confederates came pushing down from the north. As the Union line came to a crest, soldiers saw a wondrous sight. Trotting in from the right was the Union cavalry, sabres flashing in the brilliant September afternoon sunlight.

Lemuel Abbott of the 10th Vermont remembered the cavalry as "proudly and majestically en masse in perfect order and cadence, line and bearing, coolly confident as though at parade."

Aldace Walker in the Vermont Brigade said:

Presently the line of enemy before us was seen to waver and melt away; many had fallen, others could not endure the deadly fire....The whole left of the enemy rushed past us toward our left in the wildest disorder.... The Brigade rose as one man, rushed at the fence that had partially protected us, and as it fell, passed over it into the open plain. The whole army was seized with the same impulse and strode joyfully forward, a huge crescent, with waving flags and wild hurrahs.

Abbott saw it all as "an immense graceful waving ribbon along the surface of the ground, caused by that enchantingly swinging, billowy motion characteristic of regulars when marching in large bodies, its fluttering banners, glittering arms, equipments and blue uniforms looking prettier than ever in the bright September sunlight under a bright blue sky specked with fleecy clouds."

Sheridan, Abbott wrote, "dashed back and forth the line on horseback like a restless lion."

It was not all beauty and splendor. In the Eighth Vermont, a piece of shell laid open the side of Pvt. Ransom Coalbeth, tearing out two ribs and exposing the contents of his chest. Somehow he lived, and he was back doing light duty before the war ended. Edward Belville, also in the Eighth, was not so fortunate. An artillery shell bounced toward him and struck a fence rail, which smashed into Belville, knocking him several feet. Belville got up and walked away, but in a few minutes fell dead.

The attack went on, the infantry marching in a resistless wave, cavalry moving from walk to a gallop. The Confederates, badly outnumbered and overlapped, wavered, then broke altogether. One soldier recalled:

The cheers of the Union boys rose clear and strong above the roar of artillery and the harsh rattle of musketry, and Early's demoralized divisions were rushing through Winchester in unutterable confusion. Frightened teamsters were lashing their animals through the streets in greatest alarm; and riderless horses were galloping here and there. Some streets became entirely blocked by the disordered mass, and even footmen could not pass through. A squad of cavalry coming to one of these obstructions leaped from their horses and made their escape on foot. Our cavalry rushed among the panic-stricken fugitives and gathered hundreds of them.

Third Winchester ended in a rout, though the numbers did not show it; much of Early's army got away as night fell. Sheridan's army suffered nearly 5,000 casualties, while Early lost about 3,500 men. Some 350 Vermonters were shot in the battle, with about 80 dead on the field or later dying of wounds.

Colonel Warner's magnificent handling of the Vermont Brigade brought him a promotion to command of a brigade. Since Col. Lewis Grant had still not returned to the army, command of the Old Brigade was given to Col. George Foster of the Fourth Vermont.

The Confederate retreat led 15 miles south, back to the impressive rise of Fisher's Hill. There the remains of Early's army, still numbering 10,000 men, dug in. Sheridan brought his army down on September 21 to face the Confederates across Tumbling Run, with the steep hill beyond. Early had always felt safe at Fisher's Hill, recalling that Sheridan had faced him and then turned away in the recent past. Not this time.

Sheridan prepared for attack by ordering troops under Colonel Warner to seize Flint Hill, with its commanding view of Fisher's Hill. This Warner did with a bayonet charge, heard but not seen by the Vermont Brigade nearby. The Old Brigade then moved to the summit of Flint Hill and thus had a clear view of the Confederate entrenchments on the heights ahead. Brigade commander Foster, more than six feet of him, was walking along the brigade's lines with his color bearer, Cpl. Tom Miller of Barnet. A Confederate sharpshooter took aim, probably at the colonel, and young Miller fell dead. He was the only Vermonter to fall at Fisher's Hill.

The prospects for the frontal assault the Vermonters expected were daunting, with well-entrenched Confederates on the heights supported by cannon. But about 4 P.M. on September 22 a commotion began on the far left flank of the Confederate line. Unbeknownst to most of the army, Maj. Gen. George Crook's Eighth Corps had been marching along the side of wooded Little North Mountain, around the flank of Early's line. He attacked and rolled up the Confederates, driving them from the crest of Fisher's Hill. When the Vermonters went forward, across Tumbling Run and up the steep hill, Sheridan was with their division and was heard to shout, "Run boys, run. Don't wait to form. Don't let them stop."

Early's men ran, with the Yankees in hot pursuit, until dark. When the fight was over, Early had suffered 1,200 casualties to only about 500 for Sheridan. The Confederates' valley army was once again in retreat.

While in the Shenandoah Valley the Vermont Brigade did its part in following General Grant's grim laying-waste orders. Abel Gilbert, of the Sixth Vermont, wrote a letter home to Copperas Hill in Thetford that read in part:

Foraging…well I will tell you what it means. It is taking up all the beaves [beef cattle] that we could find. Kill and eat all the sheep we came acrost. Go into a man's barn and carry off all his hay and grain….Drive off their cows and make ourselves to home in general. I have known boys to go into a man's house and take all the flour and meal that they could find. Even take their table cloths and tear them up and use them for towels.

Among the civilians roughly treated by war was Mrs. Betty VanMetre, who lived on a farm near Berryville, not far from the Winchester battlefield. Her house had been spared, but her cattle had been run off and fences flattened. Her husband was a Confederate officer, then in the Union prison at Fort Delaware, south of Philadelphia.

To her home, after some of the skirmishing that preceded the Battle of the Opequon, was brought a terribly wounded Vermont soldier, Henry E. Bedell of Westfield. Bedell had lost a leg, two fingers, and much blood; he was unable to ride in a rough ambulance and follow his army. Mrs. VanMetre concealed him, cared for him, and several times went in a wagon past Confederate outposts to Union lines and brought back food and medicine. She also brought Union commissary whiskey to buy the silence of a few old men, neighbors of the VanMetre farm, who knew Bedell was being concealed.

Gradually her once strapping young patient began to regain his health, with her careful care. Word never reached local Confederate partisans, always looking for stray Union soldiers who had torn up their beloved valley. Finally, Bedell was healed enough to travel. Betty VanMetre hid him in a wagon and set off toward the Union camp at Harpers Ferry. They arrived safely, and the next day Bedell and Mrs. VanMetre, their story preceding them, headed by train for Washington, where they were admitted to the office of the secretary of war. Edwin Stanton wrote out a special order for Bedell and Mrs. VanMetre to take to Fort Delaware, where they found Mrs. VanMetre's emaciated husband and set him free. The VanMetres accompanied Bedell to his home in Westfield, to spend the winter while the husband recovered. "If on the face of the earth there is a region where man with every breath draws in a new supply of health and strength and glorious vigor of body and mind, it is Vermont on a winter's morning," wrote Lucius Chittenden in a book about the Bedell–VanMetre ordeal. Colonel VanMetre recovered; at war's end the Virginians returned to the Shenandoah Valley and rebuilt their lives.

Betty VanMetre cared for the wounded Bedell.

Vermonter Henry Bedell, hidden by a Confederate.

Much of the battlefield of Third Winchester has been consumed by development. Yet the heart of the field, several hundred acres, remains untouched and lovely and includes some of the land, alternately woods and fields, where the Ninth Vermont took and returned heavy fire, then rose and charged. Herbert E. Hill, who wrote of the Eighth's grim fight, returned to Winchester years later and erected on the battlefield a monument to his old regiment. Many years ago it was moved to the national cemetery in Winchester, where it stands today, in the southeast corner of the stone-walled burying ground with its thousands of Union graves. The monument's inscription notes that the Vermont dead are "committed to the care of those once brave foes, now our generous friends." I counted 94 Vermont headstones in the Winchester National Cemetery.

Near Charles Town the Packett House, which down the years became known as Locust Hill, was patched up and lived in. But it has long stood abandoned, and all that's now left are its four thick brick walls. A housing development is enveloping the ruin, which now stands beside a golf green. I visited crumbling Locust Hill on a November day with a very Vermont-like November wind whistling through the vine-covered brick walls, the roof open to the sky. Bullet holes still pockmark the south wall, the one that faced the Confederates.

CEDAR CREEK: "DON'T RUN, MEN, TILL THE VERMONTERS DO"

Virginia's Shenandoah Valley nowhere more resembles Vermont than where Cedar Creek flows into the Shenandoah River's North Fork. There the north end of Massanutten Mountain, a long, high ridge that divides the valley, dominates the surrounding farmlands. To the east rise the Blue Ridge Mountains, to the west are the Alleghenies, and in between the Massanutten soars 1,600 feet above the valley floor. No place in Vermont looks so much like it as the Champlain Valley around the apple orchard towns of Addison and Shoreham: the mighty Adirondacks to one side, the lofty Green Mountains on the other, and down the middle runs Snake Mountain. Without Lake Champlain, the place is almost a twin of the Shenandoah Valley at the Cedar Creek–North Fork confluence. Otter Creek winds its way along the flank of Snake Mountain, much as the North Fork hugs the Massanutten.

As October passed its midpoint and the leaves colored, the Vermont Brigade went into camp with Sheridan's army on the high fields above the north bank of Cedar Creek, getting a well-earned rest after the battles at Winchester and Fisher's Hill. In their aftermath Early had been pursued 50 miles southeast to the vicinity of Waynesboro, before Sheridan withdrew back down the valley. As he went, the army set fire to crops and barns and drove off cattle in the thorough ruination of the Shenandoah Valley that Grant had ordered. Dr. Joseph Rutherford, with the 10th Vermont, wrote home: "When we fell back from Harrisonburg we destroyed everything that fire would burn and left the country one desert waste. The people will have to leave the valley or starve."

Early, still unbeaten, had his cavalry nipping at the Federals' heels, and on October 7 there was a fight, with the Confederates getting the upper hand. Next day Sheridan visited his cavalry's encampment and found his commanders, especially George Custer, enraged by their orders to keep moving north instead of turning to smash at the Confederate horsemen. Custer was particularly angry, because the opposing cavalry was led by old West Point classmate and rival Thomas Rosser. Sheridan heard his commanders out and responded, "Start out at daybreak and whip the rebel cavalry or get whipped yourself."

The fight developed the next day, October 9, along Tom's Brook, a stream that joins the Shenandoah's North Fork south of Fisher's Hill, five miles from Cedar Creek. The sudden about-face of the Union cavalry caught Rosser by surprise. The Federals, with William Wells's First Vermont Cavalry on the right end of a long line of attack, struck with a powerful charge. Rosser rallied his men, but the Union cavalry regrouped and attacked again. When it ended, Rosser's horsemen had been driven 12 miles down the valley. Three Vermonters were killed.

The victory at Tom's Brook made Sheridan's army rest even easier, drawn up behind Cedar Creek in the hazy sunshine and the cool nights of a Shenandoah Valley autumn. Sheridan himself felt so good about things that he departed for Washington to confer with superiors about his next move. He cautioned the man he left in charge, Sixth Corps commander Horatio Wright, to stay on guard and keep a close watch on Early, not to rest easy.

Abraham Lincoln, never much of a sleeper, was now worried not only about the war but also about his chances in the approaching November elections. His Democratic opponent, the politically ambitious former general George McClellan, was attempting to seduce the American voters with a peace platform. Though great victories had been won—Sheridan's at Winchester and Fisher's Hill, Sherman's capture of Atlanta—Sherman was now stalled, and Early's army was still not totally defeated. A Union defeat could be a political disaster for Lincoln and for his intent to pursue the war to victory, while one more military success would likely sew up his reelection.

About mid-October election officials arrived in the Union camps, ready to record the soldiers' votes for president—for either their commander in chief or their former commander. Wilbur Fisk, encamped with the Vermont Brigade, noted a keen interest among residents of the Shenandoah Valley: "I haven't talked with a single citizen that did not deplore the probability of Lincoln's reelection. That, they think, shuts out any hope."

While the Union soldiers rested and talked politics, Confederates were looking down from the peak of the Massanutten. Jubal Early, reinforced, now with an army of some 20,000 men, was intent on one more try at whipping Sheridan. His subordinates on the mountain surveyed the Union camps and earthworks, searching for weakness. Certainly it was not to the west, where the powerful Union cavalry guarded the right flank. Nor was it along the main Union line east of the cavalry, where the tough Sixth Corps rested. Further east was Gen. William Emory's 19th Corps, on high ground sloping away to the front, a good defensive position. But on the eastern, left flank of the Union army, where Cedar Creek joined the Shenandoah at the foot of the Massanutten, the Union line held by George Crook's Eighth Corps did not quite extend to the river. The

The Battle of Cedar Creek, October 19, 1864.

Union flank seemed vulnerable, not unlike Hooker's fatal oversight at Chancellorsville.

On the night of October 18 Early sent 7,000 men single file along a pig track that skirted the mountain's base, leaving behind canteens and cups, anything that would rattle but rifle-muskets. They moved noiselessly through the night, quietly overwhelmed the Union pickets along the river, and before daylight on the 19th were in attack position, lined up opposite the left flank of the Union line.

Stephen Thomas had been ill at ease all through the night, while serving as officer-of-the-day for the 19th Corps. His nervousness began the previous afternoon when he spotted two men in civilian clothes, out beyond the Union lines, who seemed to be reconnoitering the Federal positions. Thomas reported it to Generals Wright and Emory, who paid little heed. In the dark morning hours of October 19 the uneasy Thomas rode down the Valley Pike, the valley's main north-south route, which cut through the center of the Union position. He walked his horse across the Cedar Creek bridge and up the slope beyond when "Surrender you damn Yankee" was shouted from a group of horsemen barely visible just ahead.

"Not just yet. It's too early in the morning," hollered Thomas as he galloped away, bullets whistling by. The colonel headed toward headquarters to report the alarming nearness of rebels, but before he got there, Thomas heard rifle fire to the east. The Confederate surprise attack had begun.

Early morning fog often lies along the low fields where Cedar Creek meets the North Fork; it was unusually heavy on the fateful morning of October 19. Suddenly George Crook's Eighth Corps heard shots, and thousands of screaming Confederates were swarming out of the fog and first light to overrun their positions.

Wilbur Fisk recalled:

> The Eighth and Nineteenth Corps, it appears, had no warning of their approach whatever. It is said the rebels entered a sutler's shanty before the sutler was awake, inquired the price of whiskey and tobacco, and then they coolly informed him that they would relieve him of what little he had, and before the sutler had hardly got his eyes open to perceive the condition of affairs, he found himself minus a stock of goods and a prisoner in the enemy's hands.

The Eighth Corps was routed. The dazed soldiers who managed to get away streamed through the 19th Corps camps. It was a Union disaster, the Army of the Shenandoah's left wing rolled up and running away. Clearly the army was in jeopardy. The great gray wave next hit Emory's 19th Corps. Emory reacted fast. He sent for his nearest troops, some New York, Connecticut, and Pennsylvania troops, along with the battered Eighth Vermont Regiment (less than 400 men fit for duty after Winchester). For the moment, all were under the command of Stephen Thomas, and they were camped in a field near the stone Belle Grove mansion along the Valley Pike. Thomas had no more than 800 troops all told, of whom only 166 were Vermonters, some 200 of the Eighth Vermont being elsewhere on picket duty. General Emory told Thomas to take his men across the pike and make a stand as long as he could.

Years later Thomas and Emory met on the Cedar Creek battlefield. Emory said, "I never gave an order that caused me more pain than the one I gave you that morning. I knew it was sending you into the jaws of death, and I never expected to see you again."

Time had to be bought so a heavy defensive line could be formed. The Eighth Vermont moved with Thomas's 800 across the pike, through a shallow pasture ravine, and up a low wooded ridge. There they stood and fought for a half hour, buying time for the rest of the army. Later a veteran of the Union army would say, "I never on any battlefield saw so much blood as this. The firm limestone soil would not receive it."

Pvt. Herbert Hill, who so vividly described the Eighth Vermont at Third Winchester, was again in the midst of things at Cedar Creek: "The Eighth Vermont, under Major [John B.] Mead [in command because Thomas was leading the entire force], occupied the most exposed position in the brigade, as the enemy, with deafening yells, were moving swiftly in from front and flank. As the great drops of rain and hail preceded the hurricane, so now the leaden hail filled the air, seemingly from all directions, while bursting shell from the enemy's cannon on the opposite hill created havoc."

The small regiments making up Thomas's command were forced to fight individually as Confederates got in between the units. "The Eighth Vermont was practically alone for a time, as the swarming enemy broke upon it with almost resistless fury," said Hill.

The heaviest fighting developed around the Eighth Vermont's battle flags, as a mass of rebels stormed in demanding their surrender. Hill:

Men seemed more like demons than human beings, as they struck fiercely at each other with clubbed muskets and bayonets. A rebel of powerful build, but short in stature, attempted to bayonet Corporal Worden of the colorguard. Worden, a tall, sinewy man, who had no bayonet on his musket, parried his enemy's thrusts until some one, I think Sergeant Brown, shot the rebel dead. A rebel soldier then leveled his musket and shot Corporal Petrie, who held the colors, in the thigh,—a terrible wound, from which he died that night. He cried out: "Boys, leave me; take care of yourselves and the flag!"

But in that vortex of hell men did not forget the colors; and as Petrie fell and crawled away to die, they were instantly seized and borne aloft by Corporal Perham, and were as quickly demanded again by a rebel who eagerly attempted to grasp them; but Sergeant Shores of the guard placed his musket at the man's breast and fired, instantly killing him.

Then Corporal Perham was shot dead, the fallen flag grasped by Corporal Blanchard. Capt. Squire Howard of Jamaica remembered, "Bayonets dripped blood and skulls were broken, but the little band held on."
Private Hill recalled:

Lieutenant [Aaron] Cooper was seen to raise his arm in the air; and shouting, "Give it to them boys!" he too was stricken with a death wound, and his white, sad, dead face is one of the living memories of the spot. Lieutenant Cooper's death was instantly avenged, however, by Sergeant Hill of Company A, who shot the rebel. Hill then turned to assist a wounded companion who had fallen at his side, when an excited enemy made a lunge at him, his bayonet gliding between the body and arm.

Sergeant Hill clubbed the man with his musket but was quickly surrounded by Confederates and shot in the side. He escaped later in the day and rejoined the Eighth.
"A rebel discharged his rifle within a foot of Corporal Bemis of the color guard, and wounded him," Hill recalled, "but was in turn shot dead by one of our men. A little later, Sergeant Shores and Sewall Simpson were standing together by the flags, when three rebels attacked and ordered them to surrender; but as they (the enemy) had just discharged their pieces, Simpson immediately fired and shot one while Shores bayoneted the other."
Private Hill was ordered to surrender but refused. Meanwhile, Sergeant Lamb was shot through the lungs, Captain Howard was twice wounded, Captain Hall was mortally wounded, Captain Ford was shot through both legs, Captain Smith was hit, and Major Mead was shot in the side. Mead gave command of the Eighth to Maj. Moses McFarland of Hyde Park, who had led the assault on the rebel boat *Cotton* in a Louisiania bayou when the war was much younger. Lieutenant Chaney was fatally wounded. Lieutenant Bruce swung his sword at a rebel and at the same time was shot. Private Austin was killed when brained by a clubbed musket, and Lieutenants Sargent and Carpenter were shot.
Hill recalled:

Over one-half the regiment was wounded or killed when the third color bearer, Corporal Blanchard, was also killed, and the silken colors, their soft folds pierced with bullets and their bearer weltering in his blood, bowed low to the earth amidst triumphant yells of the enemy; but to their chagrin in a few seconds it was again flaunting in their faces. Bleeding, stunned and being literally cut to pieces, but refusing to surrender colors or men, falling back only to prevent being completely encircled, the noble regiment had accomplished its mission.

What was left of the Eighth Vermont retreated, with more than 100 of the 159 men who had gone into action either shot or captured. The remnants of Stephen Thomas's little force kept some order and, on reaching Belle Grove, rallied and fired a few more rounds. Valuable time had been bought, but by now most of the Federal army was in retreat.

North of Belle Grove, once army headquarters, the 10th Vermont stood its ground as a wave of frightened soldiers swept through and around it. Out in the fire and smoke to the front were three heavy Union cannon deserted by their cannoneers. Up rode General Ricketts. "Are you not going to leave McKnight's guns there? About face, and draw them off," he shouted.

The 10th Vermont moved forward just in time, as rebel infantry rushed in around the guns. The Vermont troops stopped and fired, then fired again. The Confederates dispersed. The 10th's commander, Col. William Henry of Waterbury said, "Sergeant William Mahoney…was the first to reach the guns, planting the colors upon one of them. The rebels gave way in confusion, and fled across the valley and over the ridge beyond. The recaptured guns were drawn off."

The Confederates regrouped and poured deadly fire into the Vermonters, who held to the cannons, pulling two by hand back within the Union lines.

And what of the Vermont Brigade?

The Old Brigade had been farthest from the Confederate flank attack, camped on the right, the west end of the Union line. Rosser's Confederate cavalry had probed there before the surprise attack, and 30 startled men of the 11th and Sixth Vermont regiments were taken prisoner. Fourth Vermont commander George Foster was nearly one of them. Like Stephen Thomas, Foster was serving as a corps officer-of-the-day, for the Sixth Corps. Lewis Grant was back from leave, so Foster had relinquished his brief command of the brigade. When Rosser's men appeared, Foster happened to be out on the Union line, among the pickets. He helped stabilize the line, and after Rosser's initial success the rebel cavalry was held in check. That firing was heard by the veterans of the Vermont Brigade, who paid little attention and rolled over for a little more sleep. But heavier firing, when it erupted around 5 A.M. to the southeast, roused the entire Sixth Corps. The troops calmly struck tents, shouldered knapsacks, and prepared to move out as the sound of battle grew. Then the corps was marched to the north and east, toward the village of Middletown, astride the Valley Pike about three miles north of Cedar Creek. As Getty's division, including the Vermont Brigade, neared the pike they saw, in the words of Aldace Walker:

Wagons and ambulances lumbering hither and thither in disorder; pack horses led by frightened bummers, or wandering at their own free will; crowds of officers and men, some shod and some barefoot, many of them coatless and hatless, few without their rifles, but all rushing wildly to the rear, oaths and blows alike powerless to halt them; a cavalry regiment stretched across the field, unable to stem the torrent; and added to the confusion and consternation the frequent sight of blood, ambulances, wagons, men, stained and dripping, with here and there a corpse; while the whistling bullets and the shrieking shells told that the enemy knew their advantage and their ground. It was a sight that might have demoralized the Old Guard of the first Napoleon.

Despite the panic, the Sixth Corps maintained order. Getty's division posted itself along Meadow Brook, facing the village of Middletown and the advancing Confederates. The division was taking considerable fire from a woods to the front, so Lewis Grant was told to deploy skirmishers and move forward. The Fifth and Sixth regiments and a battalion of the 11th soon cleared the trees of Confederates. Getty now moved the rest of his division up in support, and held his position under increasing fire, with Federal artillery hitting dangerously close from the rear, until General Crook rode up and told him, for his own safety, to move back.

Getty's veterans withdrew across Meadow Run with Confederates in close pursuit. They did not retreat far, settling down on the first defensible ground found, a curving ridge with a small cemetery on top, commanding the fields to the south and east. There Getty aligned his men, with the Vermont Brigade at the center of the position. The men loaded their rifle-muskets, lay down on the crest of the ridge, and awaited the Confederate onslaught. Lewis Grant was in command of his Vermont Brigade that day, steadying his men as Confederate veterans under Stephen Dodson Ramseur and John Pegram advanced within 30 yards of the Vermonters' rifles. Then the Old Brigade raised up and let loose a staggering volley. The Confederates reeled down the slope and back across Meadow Brook, then "retired into the fog, which from this time began to disappear," Aldace Walker said. The Vermonters, along with the rest of Getty's division, waiting for the next assault, knew they had to hold. Somebody, sometime that day, had to stop the rebel advance and, if possible, save Sheridan's Army of the Shenandoah.

The Confederates brought artillery forward and for half an hour blasted the Union-held ridge. The Vermonters hugged the ground, some behind tomb-stones. The rebel battle line came forward again. Fighting beside the Vermont-ers was a brigade of New York troops, commanded by Gen. Daniel Bidwell. Walker recalled:

On the rebels came, through the woods, straight against Bidwell's line and the left of Grant's, with a vigor that promised success. As they pressed us harder and harder, the lines being but a few yards apart, Bidwell's brigade began doggedly to give way, gradually retreating step by step almost to the foot of our little hill, of which the rebels occupied the summit, while the left regiments of Grant swung back, without confusion, to maintain the continuity of the line. A panic for the moment seemed to threaten the Sixth and 11th Vermont, but the bravery of the officers at once restored the courage of the men, and they gave and took without further flinching, though the struggle was deadly.

General Bidwell was at the front, on horseback, when a bullet hit him in the chest, fatally damaging both lungs. He fell from his horse, bleeding horribly, and died. The sight was unnerving, to say the least, and the New Yorkers began to show signs of panic. Bidwell's replacement, Colonel French, jumped to the front of his men and uttered one of the memorable commands of the entire war.

"Don't run, men, till the Vermonters do," French shouted.

The rivalry between Vermonters and New Yorkers has its roots in the feuds between Ethan Allen's Green Mountain Boys and the Yorkers. No Vermonter, or Yorker, for that matter, was about to be the first to run away from anything in the presence of the other. So they held to that grim ridge top against more and more Confederates, with perhaps the ghost of Old Ethan steadying them. "With a cheer of desperation [the New York] troops sprang forward reaching the first position on the crest. The astonished rebels formed in rows behind the trees for protection," one Vermonter recalled. The assault was broken, the slopes of the ridge now strewn with dead and wounded. As the rebels went, Lewis Grant ordered a skirmish line forward to receive the next charge. By this time Getty's division had held its position for a full hour. More artillery fire hit the ridge, and more Confederate troops were coming up for another try. Getty ordered a retreat. The Vermonters and their comrades went not in panic but in orderly withdrawal north through the woods and fields. As they went, the Confederates quickly took position on the cemetery ridge.

Henry Houghton summed up the desperate fight succinctly: "We took our position at the top of a hill, in the open ground without as much as a bush to shield us, where we held our lines until ordered back."

The Vermonters moved north for a mile and a half, at last coming into line on another ridge where other Union soldiers were gathered, men of the Eighth and 19th Corps, with more and more Sixth Corps soldiers arriving all the while. It was 10 A.M. The Union army had been driven more than four miles since the predawn surprise attack. A thin line was formed facing south; the worst was expected, a final massive Confederate assault. The tired soldiers settled down to await it; some fell asleep.

A mile south, Jubal Early was expressing satisfaction with a job well done, telling subordinates it was only a matter of time before the Union line dissolved and his foe marched away. "But that is the Sixth Corps," an aide protested, saying they would not go unless attacked. Still Early hesitated as the sun rose higher over the bloody fields, the battered Union army waited for the last attack, and the Confederates waited for orders to deliver the coup de grace. They never came.

Philip Sheridan had spent the previous night in Winchester, a dozen miles north of Cedar Creek, on his way back from Washington. He had wakened to the distant rumbling of guns and thought it likely that General Wright was doing some minor probing. As the noise persisted, Sheridan mounted his black charger Rienzi and started down the Valley Pike. Just south of Kernstown he met Union soldiers fleeing from the battle, men who told him breathlessly of the disaster along Cedar Creek. Sheridan put spurs to Rienzi, leaving most of his staff in a cloud of white dust. As he rode, Sheridan came on more soldiers, and he stopped

Howard Coffin Collection

Sheridan's ride on his black horse Rienzi.

just long enough to urge them to go back. Some did turn and start toward the smoke and thunder, and soon a stream of blue soldiers was moving south.

Had the officer been Ambrose Burnside or Joe Hooker, even George Meade, the men probably would have kept plodding north. But Sheridan had that mysterious quality possessed by the truly great combat commanders, men like "Stonewall" Jackson, Robert E. Lee, Ulysses Grant, Bedford Forrest, and William T. Sherman. His 12-mile journey, mostly at a gallop, would be known as "Sheridan's ride," one of the great dramatic events of the entire war; the powerful little black-haired man on his charging black horse pounding down the Valley Pike, ordering, imploring the soldiers he met to face about and return to battle.

Wilbur Fisk was on the pike as a wagon guard. "We met him on his way up," he recalled. "There was a look of confidence and stern determination in his eye that inspired the men with more hope and courage, I believe, than a whole corps of reinforcements would have done."

On the low ridge where the battered Union army was reforming, the Vermont Brigade still rested. Aldace Walker recalled:

> While thus waiting for the complete reformation of the army, sulkily and it is to be feared profanely growling over the defeat in detail which we had experienced, though not in the least disposed to admit that our division had been whipped, in fact a little proud of what we had already done, and expecting the rebel charge which we grew more and more confident we should repulse, we heard cheers behind us on the pike. We were astounded. There we stood, driven four miles already, quietly waiting for what might be further and immediate disaster, while far in the rear we heard the stragglers and hospital bummers, and the gunless artillerymen actually cheering as though a victory had been won. We could hardly believe our ears.
>
> The explanation soon came….As the sturdy, fiery Sheridan, on his sturdy, fiery steed, flaked with foam from his two hours mad galloping, wheeled from the pike and dashed down the line, our division also broke forth into the most tumultuous applause.

Sheridan halted in front of the Vermont Brigade, and Pvt. Henry Houghton of Woodstock and the Third Vermont was within hearing:

> When Sheridan met General Getty he asked, "What troops are on the skirmish line?" General Getty replied, "The whole of the Vermont Brigade."
> "We are all right," says Sheridan. "We'll have our old camps back tonight."

Sheridan spurred Rienzi on down the long line of his battered army and the cheers echoed across the fields and off toward the Blue Ridge. He took his time getting things lined up just as he wanted. More and more stragglers were returning, taking their places, sheepishly getting reacquainted with their comrades who had not run. Getty's divison and the Vermont Brigade were in the middle of the line; off to the right were the remnants of the battered 19th Corps, including what remained of Stephen Thomas's Eighth Vermont; and still farther to the right, on the west end of the line, was George Custer's cavalry, including the First Vermont's horsemen.

About 4 P.M. Sheridan ordered his troops to advance. When the tattered battle flags went forward through the smoking, dying afternoon, their momentum was relentless as the slanting sunlight. The Confederates fought gallantly, their artillery dealing death and havoc most effectively. Maj. Gen. Stephen Dodson Ramseur was on his horse trying to steady his men, the Confederacy's youngest major general. A Yankee bullet took him in the belly, knocking him from his horse. His men picked him up and got him painfully into a wagon and headed south.

Herbert Hill of the Eighth Vermont remembered the great counterattack:

There was a continuous line along our entire front, and as far as we could see to the left and some distance beyond our right flank we had driven this line back, but as yet were unable to pierce it. Every inch of the ground was stubbornly contested....Thomas's own regiment gained a decided advance, pierced the enemy like an arrowhead, and had the fortune to witness the first break in their line. We emerged from the woods, and to our front was an open field for a quarter of a mile, unobstructed save by the tall dried grass and fragments of a zigzag rail fence....Just as the rebel line was reached it broke and with wild shouts the brigade dashed ahead. We pierced the enemy's line of battle, and from that moment, his doom was sealed.

Stephen Thomas was urging his men on when a bullet took his horse from beneath him. Thomas got quickly up and, with sword aloft, went forward on foot with his men. Remarkably, the Eighth Vermont Regiment, so shot up in its desperate stand in the morning fog, became the first Union regiment to break the Confederate line.

Sheridan's army recrossed the ground given up earlier on that fateful day. The general was always among his men, driving them. Major Walker recalled, "We saw the flag that followed Sheridan, a white star on the red above a red star on the white, flashing in the front and centre of the army, literally leading it to victory."

Once it seemed that Jubal Early's veterans might stop the advance before nightfall and save a part of the field so brilliantly won at first light. Then from the north and west came a rumble, soon the ground began to shake, and out of the twilight pounded the 12,000 hoofs of Custer's cavalry, including William Wells's Vermonters. It was more than the Confederates could withstand. The Battle of Cedar Creek became a rout. As Wells later said, "We pressed them back to the creek charging several times....We charged the enemy through Strasburg a distance of about 4 miles capturing prisoners, artillery, wagons....It is the biggest thing of the war."

As darkness fell, a traffic jam of retreating Confederates developed where a bridge south of Strasburg had collapsed along the Valley Pike. Union cavalry rode in among the rebels, shooting and stabbing, demanding surrender. Cpl. Frederick Lyon of Burlington rode to the front of a Confederate ambulance and told it to halt. The driver testily replied that he had no business issuing orders to General Ramseur's ambulance.

Lyon replied that he guessed the

William Wells rose from private to general.

general was the very man he was looking for. So a Vermont corporal captured General Ramseur, who was taken back to Belle Grove a weak and bleeding prisoner. Before he died the next day, his old friend from West Point days, George Custer, spent a few quiet moments by his side.

Eri Woodbury, the Derby schoolmaster, rode down on four Confederate infantrymen and told them to surrender. One of the men, Woodbury noticed, seemed to be trying to hide his weapon behind him. Woodbury ordered him to hand it over and it proved to be not a rifle but the battle flag of the 12th North Carolina Infantry. After the battle, Woodbury, Lyon, and Pvt. James Sweeney of Essex, who had also captured a flag—Vermont cavalrymen all—went with General Custer to Washington to be personally congratulated by Secretary of War Edwin Stanton.

The fighting at Cedar Creek ended. Capt. Squire Howard of Jamaica and the Eighth Vermont boasted, "Never since the world was created was such a crushing defeat turned into such a splendid victory." Looking back, it is hard to see how that victory would have been possible without the soldiers from Vermont. The price was high: more than 500 Vermonters killed, wounded, or missing.

News of the great Union comeback and of Sheridan's wonderful ride electrified the North. Abraham Lincoln suddenly had no need to worry about reelection. Wilbur Fisk reported from the front: "The election returns are coming in; the Brigade will stand two for Lincoln and one for McClellan; the whole vote at the latest was 1,114. There was 764 for Lincoln, and 350 for McClellan....Soldiers don't generally believe in fighting to put down treason, and voting to let it live."

Back in St. Johnsbury, William Herrick wrote in his diary: "Well, the great day is over and the crisis to the nation is passed. The presidential elections came off today and enough has come by telegraph tonight to make Lincoln's reelection sure. So the people didn't endorse the Chicago surrenderer and have given their emphatic voice for a prosecution of the war."

The Shenandoah Valley countryside around the Cedar Creek–North Fork confluence today remains mostly rural, though development is beginning to take its toll and an interstate highway cuts through. Little Middletown village is expanding, yet one can still get a good idea of what the Cedar Creek battlefield was like in 1864. Belle Grove stands and is open as a museum. If one knows where to look, there are the remnants of trenches dug by the 19th Corps and overrun the morning of October 19. A mile north of Belle Grove, west of Middletown, is the curving ridge with the cemetery where the Vermont Brigade made its valiant stand. As one drives along the Valley Pike, now Route 11, passing the entrance to Belle Grove, a stone monument surrounded by an iron fence is visible to the east on the nearest ridge line. Placed there by the state of Vermont, it honors Stephen Thomas's Eighth Vermont Regiment on the site of its heroic stand. In a patch of trees in a pasture, it's on private land; yet the kindly lady who owns it usually gives permission when a Vermonter asks to walk to the head of the little ravine, on the low ridge. Stephen Thomas was present for the monument's dedication 20 years after the battle. He was in his grave by October 19, 1914, the 50th anniversary of Cedar Creek, when a monument was erected at the site of his birth, high in the hills above Bethel Gilead.

THE CONFEDERATE ATTACK
ON ST. ALBANS

On a day in mid-October 1864, with the remnants of autumn's colors still in the maples 550 miles north of Cedar Creek, Vermont's First Lady, Anna Smith, entertained a guest at her St. Albans mansion. He was new in town, 21 years old, tall and handsome, with perhaps the slightest trace of a Southern accent. The Kentuckian's name was Bennett Young, though it is doubtful he used it that day, and he was most interested in the Smiths' horses. Mrs. Smith gladly showed him around the grounds of her grand house, for word had got around St. Albans that the young man was a theology student from Montreal. She probably knew that some of the local ladies had invited him to speak at church. Though Governor Smith was away tending to business in Montpelier, there seemed no harm in entertaining a young gentleman of such upstanding character.

Anna Smith was unaware that her guest was an escaped Confederate soldier who had come to St. Albans to rob its banks and, if he could, burn the town. Not only was the daring plot the dream of this adventurous young man, but it also had the blessings of the highest levels of the rebel government in Richmond.

Since the war began, the Confederacy hoped that Great Britain could be lured into the war on its side. The hope lived even in the fall of 1864, and a raid on St. Albans near the border of the British Empire would be one last try at stirring up the English. At the same time, some badly needed money might be delivered to the Confederate treasury. A little revenge for Yankee depredations in the South also would be nice.

On October 12 Governor Smith addressed the legislature on the need to organize and equip an effective state militia. "Vermont stands today utterly destitute of any arm of defense or any effective power to resist or prevent invasion," he said. "The dangers to our frontiers are by no means inconsiderable."

Bennett Young assembled in Montreal a force of young men who, like himself, had fled to Canada from Yankee prison pens. The lads, 19 in all and none older than 23, began arriving in St. Albans on October 10. They came in twos and threes, getting off the train at the local station and taking hotel rooms. St. Albans, a community of 4,000, was a busy railroad center where strangers came and went every day. When one of the raiders told a desk clerk his name was Jefferson Davis, the remark drew only laughter.

Young, who reached St. Albans first, spent his time leisurely riding the roads toward Canada, scouting escape routes, and reading the Bible. Young's unit was assembled on October 18. He considered launching the raid then, but it was market day, with streets and stores crowded, a bad time for robbing banks. Young gathered his band in a hotel room, announced they would strike the next day, on Wednesday, October 19, and gave each man several hand grenades containing a new substance called Greek Fire, supposed to set ablaze anything they shattered against. As the raiders met, Jubal Early was assembling soldiers 550 miles south to launch his surprise attack along Cedar Creek.

In midafternoon on Wednesday, a heavily overcast day that promised rain, raiders moved onto St. Albans's Main Street and toward the town's three banks. Others stood guard at key intersections, particularly concerned that the hundreds of workers at the railroad yards not learn of the goings on. The young men, some wearing parts of Confederate uniforms, brandishing long cavalry pistols and talking tough, entered the three banks simultaneously. The employees' first reaction was disbelief, but as pistols were cocked and pointed, reality set in.

At the St. Albans Bank a raider some locals thought smelled of liquor announced, "Not a word, we are Confederate soldiers, have come to take your town, have a large force. We shall take your money, and if you resist, will blow your brains out. We are going to do by you as Sheridan has been doing in the Shenandoah Valley."

From the first the raiders encountered the ingrained Yankee regard for money, an attitude that held a bank's assets about as dear as life itself. Martin Seymour, a clerk in the St. Albans Bank, met the demand for money with a demand of his own for a thorough inventory of anything taken so that Federal reimbursement might be sought.

"God damn your government, hold up your hands," was the response. Though the robbers left that bank with $12,000, they did not take the $50,000 that Seymour, though staring down the barrel of a gun, never admitted was in the vault. The raiders had more success at the other two banks.

"We are Confederate soldiers. There are hundreds of us. We have come to rob your banks and burn your town," the rebels announced to the startled staff and patrons of the Franklin County Bank. "We want all your greenbacks, bills, and property of every description." The demand was obeyed.

As the robbers prepared to leave, they ordered the cashier, Marcus Beardsley, into the safe. Beardsley protested strenuously that the vault was airtight and that he could roast when the town burned. Twenty minutes later he was set free by fellow workers.

Confederate raiders steal St. Albans horses.

At the First National Bank the cashier, Albert Sowles, confronted a man wielding a pistol who declared, "You are my prisoner." Sowles was warned he would be shot if he caused trouble. The man's trembling hands caused the cashier added anxiety, as other raiders jumped behind the counter to clear out drawers. They entered the safe and, seeing coin bags, asked about the contents. Though the bank clerk insisted they contained pennies, a disbelieving Confederate slashed one open. Pennies poured out. A bag of gold was never checked. During the robbery, a 90-year-old veteran of the War of 1812, John Nason, sat in a chair reading his newspaper, hard of hearing and oblivious to the new war going on around him.

While the First National Bank was plundered, William Blaisdell wandered in and inquired what was happening. Seeing the holdup, Blaisdell headed out the door, only to be confronted by a Confederate. Blaisdell shoved the man to the ground and pounced on him, but another rebel pointed a pistol at Blaisdell's head and ordered that his comrade be released. Blaisdell complied and was ordered across the street to Taylor Park, the town green. There a considerable crowd had assembled; all passersby were directed there by the raiders to be kept under surveillance. But St. Albans was proving a tough town to control.

Word of the robberies was spreading, and some townspeople raced home to get firearms and began taking position in windows and around corners to shoot at the raiders. As the robbery proceeded, the raiders heard gunshots on the street. Collins Huntington, walking down Main Street, ignored an order from a man he presumed to be drunk to cross the street and go to the park. Huntington was shot in the back, but the bullet hit a rib, leaving only a nasty flesh wound.

Meanwhile, Bennett Young entered the livery stable to appropriate horses for the getaway. When the owner resisted, Young cocked his pistol and fired. The bullet went through the man's hat, but did no other harm.

Leonard Bingham, another resident, dashed toward Young and was met with a volley of fire from other raiders. Bingham, slightly wounded in the stomach, got away. The shooting intensified, but with amazingly little effect: a considerable number of the bullets proved to be duds, and the excitement of the hour spoiled both sides' aims.

Meeting more opposition than expected, the Confederates climbed on stolen horses, saddlebags and pockets bulging with more than 200,000 Yankee dollars, and galloped north along Main Street. As they rode, bottles of Greek Fire were tossed into and against buildings. Bennett Young and his men tried to start a Yankee conflagration, for this was war, and if a peaceful community in Vermont had to go up in smoke, even with locals shot or roasting in a locked safe, war was hell in the Shenandoah Valley, too. But the grenades only smoldered; no fires broke out.

"As we looked down the street, we saw armed horsemen shooting their guns with the greatest impunity," one St. Albans resident wrote. "Our citizens stood silent and almost speechless. A man came running up the street exclaiming, 'All the banks are robbed, what shall we do?' 'What can we do?' was the universal answer."

Up along Main Street, a New Hampshire man, Elinus J. Morrison, was overseeing construction of a new brick hotel. Descending the staging, Morrison got shot in the stomach as he tried to enter the local millinery store to take cover. He was taken to the Dutcher & Sons drugstore across the street, where his wound was judged mortal. Then he was carried to his room at the American House, where he died two days later.

A message was telegraphed to Governor Smith in Montpelier: "There is a party of rebels here shooting and killing citizens. Have stolen as many as fifteen horses, and robbed all the banks."

Hearing gunfire, the governor's wife stood guard on the front porch of her mansion with an unloaded pistol. But Bennett Young did not return.

Children in the town school, which overlooked Taylor Park and Main Street, were attending an assembly on the third floor when the excitement began. The teacher hurried the children downstairs to their classrooms, in the rear of the building. On their descent, the students looked out the window at the scene of confusion in their normally quiet town.

The raid had taken less than half an hour. Around 3 P.M., as Sheridan dressed his lines for the great counterattack at Cedar Creek, the robbers thundered out of town, under increasing fire. One raider took a bullet in the back, a serious wound, and his eventual recovery was considered a miracle.

A 50-man posse was hastily organized by Capt. George Conger, a veteran of the First Vermont Cavalry. Within minutes armed and angry men were following Young's route up Main Street to the north end of town, veering right onto the road to Sheldon. They rode past farms and fields, under a dark gray sky, past

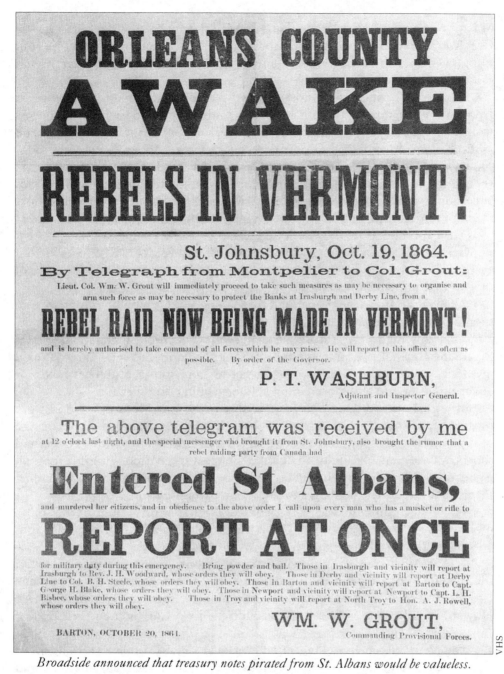

ORLEANS COUNTY
AWAKE
REBELS IN VERMONT!

St. Johnsbury, Oct. 19, 1864.
By Telegraph from Montpelier to Col. Grout:

Lieut. Col. Wm. W. Grout will immediately proceed to take such measures as may be necessary to organise and arm such force as may be necessary to protect the Banks at Irasburgh and Derby Line, from a

REBEL RAID NOW BEING MADE IN VERMONT!

and is hereby authorised to take command of all forces which he may raise. He will report to this office as often as possible.   By order of the Governor.

P. T. WASHBURN,
Adjutant and Inspector General.

The above telegram was received by me
at 12 o'clock last night, and the special messenger who brought it from St. Johnsbury, also brought the rumor that a rebel raiding party from Canada had

Entered St. Albans,

and murdered her citizens, and in obedience to the above order I call upon every man who has a musket or rifle to

REPORT AT ONCE

for military duty during this emergency.   Bring powder and ball. Those in Irasburgh and vicinity will report at Irasburgh to Rev. J. H. Woodward, whose orders they will obey.   Those in Derby and vicinity will report at Derby Line to Col. B. H. Steele, whose orders they will obey. Those in Barton and vicinity will report at Barton to Capt. George H. Blake, whose orders they will obey. Those in Newport and vicinity will report at Newport to Capt. L. H. Bisbee, whose orders they will obey.   Those in Troy and vicinity will report at North Troy to Hon. A. J. Rowell, whose orders they will obey.

WM. W. GROUT,
Commanding Provisional Forces.

BARTON, OCTOBER 20, 1864.

VHS

Broadside announced that treasury notes pirated from St. Albans would be valueless.

trees still showing a good deal of foliage. About halfway to Sheldon the Confederates encountered a farmer riding a fine, fresh horse and took it, leaving the Vermonter with one of the stolen mounts. The startled man was still beside the road when the posse came in sight. Seeing the previously stolen horse, Conger's men assumed the farmer was a Confederate and began shooting. The man saved himself by running across a field and into a wooded swamp.

Reaching the village of Sheldon in gathering darkness, and aware that pursuit was not far behind, the raiders crossed the covered bridge, then tossed Greek Fire on a hay wagon within the bridge. The structure was charred, but Captain Conger and the boys were able to get across and continue their pursuit as raindrops began falling.

In darkness the raiders crossed the Missisquoi River on the bridge at Enosburg Falls, then kept on going north to the border and what they hoped would be the safety of Canadian soil. As Captain Conger neared the line, he asked how many of his men would follow him across. About 20 volunteered.

The raiders' hope that they would be safe in Canada proved, at least in the short term, to be vain. Conger pounded through the little border communities and soon rounded up several raiders. Bennett Young was captured the next morning, after putting up a spirited struggle with his fists. Canadian authorities were also apprehending the Confederates.

Conger and his men had no way of knowing that an order had gone forth from eastern military headquarters in New York City ordering pursuit and capture of the raiders north of the border. Thus, when Captain Conger was met by Canadian authorities who demanded that Young and his men be turned over to them, Conger reluctantly agreed. Had he been aware of the order from New York, Conger might have refused, causing a grave incident with Great Britain. President Lincoln, learning of the events and fearing a major international incident, soon issued orders requiring permission from the highest levels of government before any more Union soldiers could enter Canada.

In all, 14 raiders were apprehended and taken to Montreal. None were returned to St. Albans, where they might well have been hanged. An exchange of diplomatic correspondence between US and British authorities concerned the fate of the men. Naturally, the United States wanted them returned for trial. A hearing was held in Montreal, before a packed courtroom; a Canadian magistrate ruled that the men should not be extradited.

The raiders thus got away with their feat, though little or none of the stolen money every reached Richmond. Eventually, the Canadian government sent $88,000 to the St. Albans banks.

The St. Albans raid caused an uproar in Vermont. Governor Smith called out the invalid corps to guard the border and the St. Albans area. Also, Norwich University cadets hastened to the north country, some to Newport, where Howard F. Hill, one of the cadets, recalled the following incident:

The Newport people had organized a company most fearfully and wonderfully armed....We were met by this array at the depot. There was good, untutored stuff in these bodies. On alighting from the cars, we were ordered to load our Springfields with ball cartridge, and marched to the wharf to receive an incoming steamer, then visible in the dusk, as the possible carrier of raiders. We formed with the Newporters as support. The first few minutes were big with possibilities, but nothing happened. Captain Kent was on the left with the company's youngest members. As the boat came in, some one cried out, "Fire." But not a shot was heard; for we knew better than to fire from "the ready." It was owing to good drill that nobody let go in the excitement. If that little company had fired, somebody, or more, would have been "hurted."

Five days after the raid, a letter appeared in a Burlington paper reporting on the state of things in St. Albans:

The excitement in the borough has by no means subsided. Revolvers are the most saleable articles of hardware, and rumors of all sorts of coming horrors keep prudent people on the alert and nervous persons in a state of chronic perspiration. The rumors of to-day are that Plattsburg was invaded yesterday and the banks robbed by a party of raiders, and that authentic advices have been received by Governor Smith that two thousands armed and organized rebels in Canada are about to invade St. Albans and complete the devastation which the rebels left unfinished.

Brig. Gen. George Stannard, somewhat recovered from the loss of an arm in fighting near Richmond, was sent north to take command of troops assigned to patrol the Canadian border. In Irasburg, militia guarded road junctions, and one night at the Brewster farm, where roads from Coventry and Lowell met, a jumpy part-time soldier aimed and fired at a racket that suddenly sprung up in the darkness. Fortunately, neither Mrs. Brewster nor her geese were hurt.

As the years passed, the raid became the stuff of legend, North and South. In 1911 Bennett Young visited Montreal, and a group of leading citizens of St. Albans went to the Ritz Carlton Hotel there to pay him their respects. Their journey had to be made, for an attempt to bring Young to St. Albans as an honored guest at a celebration marking the 300th anniversary of Lake Champlain's discovery had failed. Though Mayor Warren Austin (later America's first representative to the United Nations) issued Young an official invitation, veteran's groups throughout the state protested. In the end, Young was disinvited and never did return to the scene of his triumph.

But he became a considerable figure in the South, as evidenced by the letter a Kentucky woman wrote to the St. Albans newspaper in 1948, describing an event held in Louisville in 1905: "At the national reunion of the Confederate soldiers at Louisville, I saw the raiders in a parade. They rode fine horses, carried a large banner marked, 'St. Albans Raiders,' and were cheered by thousands of people. Some of them wore Confederate uniforms....In the parade the raiders received as much applause as General Stephen D. Lee, Mrs. Stonewall Jackson, and other noted Confederates."

Hollywood made a movie in the 1950s called *The Raid*, starring Van Heflin.

In 1964, on the 100th anniversary of the raid, Bennett Young's daughter visited St. Albans and was warmly welcomed at an official ceremony.

St. Albans retains much from the time of the raid. Taylor Park, where the raiders herded the townspeople, is still the great open green space in the city's center. The county historical society is located in the school building from which children got a glimpse of the raid. Several dollar bills stolen by the rebels are displayed there. The robbed banks are gone, though a modern bank is built on the site of the old Franklin County Bank. The hotels where the raiders stayed still stand: the American House, much altered, is at the corner of Main and Lake streets; the St. Albans House is down Lake Street, catercorner from the railroad station. On Main Street, the building to which the dying Elinus Morrison was taken is now a branch of Vermont Community College.

To follow the raiders' escape route, drive north up Main Street and go right onto Route 105 toward Sheldon. Approaching the Missisquoi, turn right and go over the hill into Sheldon village, bearing left and down the hill to the concrete bridge in the center of town, built on the site of the covered bridge the raiders tried to burn. Then staying on the south bank of the river, proceed to Enosburg Falls. The raiders split up north of the village to confuse their pursuers and reached Canada in small groups.

PETERSBURG UNDER SIEGE

In the Noyesville Cemetery high in the Walden hills, a granite monument bears the inscription:

John T. Cole
Co. A 10th Vermont Vols
Lost Both Eyes in
The Battle of Petersburg

Earl Capron of Chester, who took me one day to the John Cole stone, told me his father said that Cole often talked of his soldier days and how he had been cautioned, on arriving in the trenches before Petersburg, not to peek over the parapet or through the firing slits. But Cole was young and curious and could not resist a quick look. When he did, a bullet took away both eyes and the bridge of his nose. He went home to Walden and lived 30 sightless years, never tiring of telling the story of his last moment of light.

On December 9, five months after departing the Petersburg trenches to head off Jubal Early, the Sixth Corps and the Vermont Brigade left the Shenandoah Valley and headed back to the same trenches. So too went the 10th Vermont, leaving what was left of the Eighth Vermont as the only Green Mountain State infantry unit in the Valley. The First Vermont Cavalry also stayed behind. The Vermont Brigade came east by railroad, a slow ride in severe winter weather. Wilbur Fisk wrote: "Night came on and the storm came with it. It is impossible to convey any sort of an idea of the misery we suffered during that miserable night. I doubt if real physical torture was ever reduced to a more concentrated form, or ever was doled out in a manner more excruciating."

Jonathan Blaisdell wrote home to his father in Cambridge on December 17: "We left the valley the 9th of Dec and got to City Point the 12th and went up in the front line of the breast works the next day in front near Petersburg. I am a picket to day. I can see the rebel camp and hear them talk and laugh. All is quiet in our camps, but there is booming of cannon off to the right and they keep firing day and night. I was in hopes never to see Petersburg again."

Wilbur Fisk said he would sooner have stayed in the Shenandoah Valley and fought Jubal Early "as often as he could have raised an army big enough to make it pay, than to have come back into these dirty trenches again." He added, "I suppose those that are braver have a keener relish for this continual skirmishing and picket firing, but I own I haven't."

Back home on November 20, as the Vermont troops prepared to leave the Shenandoah Valley, William Herrick was attending church in St. Johnsbury. He remembered:

> Mr. Cummings began his sermon this morning by an allusion to the sickness and apparent near approach of death of Gov. Fairbanks and while he was yet speaking, word was brought to him and announced to the congregation that he was dead. Mr. Cummings stopped a while quite overcome by his emotions and there were many tears shed in the congregation for the good old governor was much loved in the church of which he had so long been a deacon.

Funeral services were held in the same church, and at their close the congregation filed by Fairbanks's open casket to say a final farewell. At the graveside, the Reverend Cummings said as the casket was lowered into the chill Vermont soil, "A good man has gone home, like a shock of corn fully ripe for the harvest."

The man who first sent Vermont sons off to the Civil War had not lived to see the end, though he did know of the great Shenandoah Valley victories and of the reelection of the man to whom he had pledged Vermont's utmost war effort. Certainly, Fairbanks knew victory was in sight, and for the men down around Petersburg, there were strong signs of it. Jonathan Blaisdell wrote on December 27, "Deserters come in about daily. There was 600 come in the night of the 24th."

There was reason to be thinking hopefully of home. Blaisdell began his first letter of the new year of 1865: "I guess it is going to storm. Well Frank do you skate any this winter on the creek? There is no snow or ice here how would you like to live in such a place. I had rather live up home."

Later he described his living quarters: "The shanty...is about 10 feet long and eight wide and it is made of round logs about six inches wide in diameter and it is 7 logs high and covered with four half tents...there is no floor to it there is a very good fireplace two bunks there is six of us....Pretty small space for a family of six but we get along pretty well."

In another letter he reported, "Went down where the rebs was chopping wood and exchanged papers with them and swapped,..for tobacco....There was 75 rebs [surrendered] yesterday and last night."

Men were constantly being killed at Petersburg by sharpshooters and artillery. Lee's army was shrinking: the Confederacy had been bled out of its supply of able young men. More and more older men and young boys filled the rebel trenches. As Lee's men hungered, mountains of supplies piled wharves at the Federals' City Point supply base. And for every killed or wounded Union soldier, there was usually a replacement.

Grant did not sit idle, and he had not waited for the Sixth Corps's return to smash at the Confederate lines. When he did, Lee lashed back. The most dramatic attack came on July 30 while the Vermont Brigade was chasing Jubal Early. The Battle of the Crater happened because some Pennsylvania soldiers, former coal miners, got permission to dig a tunnel underneath the Confederate works at a point where the entrenchments were unusually close.

Charles Cummings, commander of the 17th Vermont, which was destined to fight in the Battle of the Crater, wrote to his wife in Brattleboro on July 18, "Our big mine will, I understand, be ready for explosion in a day or two when we shall probably have some hard fighting to do."(Such a letter would have been censored beyond recognition in a modern army.)

Barrels of gunpowder were placed under the rebel entrenchments, and thousands of Union troops under Ambrose E. Burnside were massed for an attack. The mine was exploded in the predawn hours of July 30, tearing a great hole in the Confederate lines. For a moment the way again lay open to Petersburg. But the Union attack was bungled, and the Confederates rushed in reinforcements.

A lieutenant in the 17th, Frank Kenfield of Morrisville, remembered the mine explosion:

> The whole earth seemed to sink beneath our feet. The air was literally filled with men, timbers, dirt and everything the fort contained. The scene was beyond description! No words of mine can give you an idea of the terrible sight! Nothing in my whole life can begin to equal this experience and to increase the trying ordeal, 100 pieces of artillery in our rear opened with all their fury upon the rebel works. It seemed as if hell was let loose for our benefit, but the worst was yet to come. As soon as the air had cleared away, the order came to fix bayonets and charge. On we went up the hill, over the dead and dying in the crater. Here we saw a terrible sight, a sight that beggars description. Here was a hole in the ground 250 feet long, 50 feet wide, and 25 feet deep literally filled with dead and dying men torn and mangled in every form and those that were alive begged for mercy.

Kenfield described how rebel cannon opened on the Crater, and continued: "The rebels with that tremendous yell known to all old soldiers made their charge upon us, and those that were behind our line retreated and got back but we that were in the front had to succumb to the cruel fate of man, throw down our arms and beg for mercy at the hands of the rebels."

Lieutenant Kenfield was taken to Andersonville, and he remained a prisoner until March 1, 1865.

Maj. William Reynolds, a Milton native doing a law clerkship in Burlington when the war began, led the 17th Vermont in the battle, the only Vermont regiment then at Petersburg. The attack was later described by Brig. Gen. Simon Griffin, commander of the brigade in which the 17th fought:

> At first a heavy column of earth, dust and smoke rose in the air to an estimated height of eighty feet or more. Then came a dull, heavy thud, which I should say might have been heard, or felt, or both, for miles around, if the conditions were favorable. The troops moved at once, but [Brig. Gen. James] Ledlie's men plunged into the crater and they were stuck. They packed it full, in one solid mass, as thick as they could stand. They would not go through, and were powerless to do anything where they were. The enemy quickly gathered their wits and turned all fire upon that spot. Ledlie's men refused to leave that excellent cover, and my troops could not get through or over that mass of humanity, nor could any others, as none could pass on either side, for the enemy's lines to the right and left were still intact, protected by abatis, and as tenaciously held as ever by their troops. My men made gallant and desperate attempts to push forward in all directions on our side, got through their abatis and over their works, into their traverses and covered ways, and succeeded in getting farther to the front than any other troops,—the Seventeenth Vermont as far as any—but the difficulties were so great, and the fire so destructive it was impossible to make much headway in that desultory manner, without regular formations.

Lt. Worthing Pierce of Woodstock and the 17th said, "Our advance was checked by a murderous fire from the enemy on each flank, and from a battery in our front, shielded by a house, through the broad hall of which, running from side to side, a gun throwing grape and cannister raked the crest of the crater and trenches in front."

Colonel Cummings wrote home after the battle: "The 17th went out with 8 officers including Maj. [William B.] Reynolds commanding and not one returned to the regiment including Maj. Reynolds. The major and two lieutenants were killed, one wounded and four taken prisoners. Out of about 100 men we have lost 41 tonight."

Major Reynolds, who had survived Confederate captivity after Savage's Station, took a bullet through his body. In a whisper, he asked for water and pointed to a ring on his finger; then he was gone.

The battle ended in failure; it was back to trench warfare for the 17th. Colonel Cummings wrote home:

> There is not much vanity or romance about this condition of things, although it is easier than marching it is not as healthy. We have not had five minutes rain in any place where I have been since the night of the 2nd of June, and oh how dusty it is. The air is filled with this palpable powder which covers the earth from one inch to one foot, and we breathe, eat and drink it. We are a dirty, lousy set of men. The heavens are brass and the earth as molten iron.

On August 18 and again on September 30 Ulysses Grant extended his lines still farther west, and on the latter day a battle developed several miles west of the Weldon Railroad, where so many Vermonters had been captured three months before. In the fight, known as Peebles Farm or Poplar Spring Church, about 2,000 Federals became casualties, 75 of them members of the 17th Vermont. Colonel Cummings had by then recovered from the illness that kept him out of the fighting around the Crater. On the morning of the battle he wrote his wife that he rather expected orders to march, but added, "they may not come at all." A few lines later he closed his letter:

> My Dear Wife,
> Love to all the family. It looks as if orders would come in a minute.
> > Your loving husband,
> > CHARLES

Later that day, on the battlefield, General Griffin wrote the following letter to Mrs. Cummings:

> My friend,
> With sincere regret I have to inform you that your husband was wounded and captured by the enemy in the action of the 30th.
> His wound was in the hip but we hope it was not serious. He fell but a few steps from the enemy, who were pressing us so closely at the time it was impossible for his men to bring him off.
> Knowing how anxious you must be to hear from him, I take the first opportunity to send you a line which I am compelled to do in pencil.

The wound had been serious; Confederate pickets passed the news on to the Union lines that Charles Cummings had died and was buried within their lines. Later, the body of the editor of the *Brattleboro Phoenix* was sent home to wife, children, and friends for a formal burial with Masonic rites.

While the battle raged at Peebles Farm, at the far end of the long Petersburg lines north of the James River, a powerful Union assault was also underway. Grant had directed Ben Butler to storm New Market Heights and attack two prominent Confederate strongpoints outside Richmond, Forts Gilmer and Harrison. In the attack, launched by nearly 20,000 Union soldiers, were the men of the Ninth Vermont Regiment.

When last observed, the Ninth Vermont had ended its arduous confinement at Camp Douglas and come east by train to Fort Monroe. Edward Hastings Ripley soon rose to command the regiment, and it came under fire for the first time since Harpers Ferry while doing battle with James Longstreet in April around Suffolk. Later the Ninth participated in a half-hearted and badly failed attempt to capture Richmond via the Virginia Peninsula. For a time the Ninth camped in a swampy area where fever ran rampant through the ranks. Governor Smith and US Senator Solomon Foot of Vermont finally interceded to get the Vermonters moved.

The Ninth was then dispatched to North Carolina and in the spring of 1864 was engaged around New Berne with rebel troops under Maj. Gen. George Pickett. But generally the Ninth had been off the war's center stage. Then suddenly it received orders to report to the long lines around Richmond and Petersburg. The Ninth Vermont joined the 18th Corps, part of General Butler's Army of the James, based on Bermuda Hundred between the James and Appomattox rivers near Richmond. Colonel Ripley was promoted to command of the brigade to which the Ninth was assigned. Brig. Gen. George Stannard was also a part of the 18th Corps, commanding a division.

The Ninth Vermont reached Butler with 1,129 men, a very big regiment for that time of the war. It was soon in action, attacking Forts Harrison and Gilmer. Troops under George Stannard were ordered on September 29 to lead the charge on Fort Harrison, a big earthen citadel that could be attacked only across a wide expanse of open ground. Stannard's men had suffered fearfully in their gallant attack at Cold Harbor and in the early assaults on Petersburg, and Stannard thought it unfair that they should lead this dangerous assault. He protested in person to Ulysses Grant, who replied, "General Stannard, we must carry Fort Harrison and I know you will do it."

Stannard obeyed. About one-third of his men got shot, but Fort Harrison came into Union hands. Meanwhile, the Ninth Vermont was moving on Battery Morris, an artillery position supporting the fort. The earthwork battery fell, but a later attack on big Fort Gilmer failed. Seven Vermont men were killed, forty-seven wounded, and thirteen missing. In the try for Gilmer, Edward Ripley had stopped to survey the fort when, as he recalled:

> I was standing, field-glass in hand, watching the movements of the enemy. Major Brooks, Lieutenant Peck and two or three others were in the group. The shelling was noisy. The men were lying thickly near my feet: and almost under me was a private of a Massachusetts battery who had strayed into the ranks of the Ninth Vermont. He was frightened by the heavy explosions around and at each one would jump upon his feet and stare around as though crazy. I had told him three or four times to keep down; but in a moment, after a louder crash, he sprang to his feet before me. As he did so, I was dashed in the face with a streaming mass of something horrible, which closed my eyes, nose and mouth. I thought my own head had gone. I was helped to sit down and Captain Hart, of Heckman's staff, who had just come up, happening to have a towel in his pocket, they cleaned away the disgusting mass from my face with it, and I opened my eyes. Unbuttoning my sabrebelt, and throwing open my blouse, I threw out of it a mass of brains, skull, hair and blood. The headless trunk of the artillery-man lay between my feet, with the blood gurgling out with the pulsations of the heart not yet stopped.

During the night General Stannard ordered a dirt wall constructed across the Confederate side of Fort Harrison—just in time. On the afternoon of September 30 General Lee sent 7,000 troops against the fort in three assaults. The fighting was some of the most desperate of the war. At one point a Confederate colonel was captured and brought before Stannard. "Well, you had better get out of this for General Lee is over there," said the colonel, "and he says he will retake these works if it takes half his army."

Stannard replied that he would be "happy to see General Lee whenever he chose to call."

At times it must have seemed as if half of Lee's army was coming in on Fort Harrison, but at day's end it held. Edward Ripley recalled: "I have often said that General Stannard held Fort Harrison against desperate odds, of men fighting under the inspiration of Lee's own presence, by the sheer force of personal character. And there was not another division or another general of the Army of the James that could have done it. He was an army in himself in such supreme moments."

In the second Confederate assault, as Stannard was prowling the ramparts, sword in hand, a bullet shattered his right arm. Word spread through the ranks that he was dead, but Stannard was tough, and he survived a jolting trip to a field hospital. There his right arm was amputated. In time he recovered, but Stannard, the first Vermonter to enlist and one of the true heroes of Gettysburg, was out of action for good, although he was assigned to Canadian border duty.

In late October the Ninth Vermont took part in another attack on the Confederate defenses of Richmond. It amounted to very little; the rebel defenses were not breached. The fight, on an old battlefield of the Peninsula Campaign, was known both as Fair Oaks and as Seven Pines. In the fight was a private from South Pomfret, a farmer named Elba Jillson. He had stayed out of the early war, instead tending to his little farm across the valley from a steep pastured hill that one day would be known as Suicide Six. He and his wife, Mary, had a young family growing toward 12 children, so the pressure was intense for the head of the household to stay home. But on August 31, 1864 he left the farm and signed on for a year. Fair Oaks was the only battle in which Private Jillson fought, and he seldom spoke of it or any part of the Civil War through the remainder of a life that lasted until 1923. He did allow, once, that during the battle he was standing beside a man who had his head blown away by a cannonball. Only one Vermonter was killed at Fair Oaks, Pvt. Alonzo Grover of Rupert, apparently the man standing by Jillson.

The siege of Petersburg wore on through the fall and into winter, when the Vermont Brigade came back to the long trenches. As the new year arrived, Wilbur Fisk summed things up:

> We have no fears, a revolution against such a government as ours is too foul a thing for God to permit. The Confederacy is doomed. Cut asunder now in two vital points, their armies pent up, they can only struggle and die. Their victories, if they have any more, will be few and feeble, and may possibly lengthen out the contest a short time, but not long. Trusting in God we know the issue cannot be doubtful, and we commence the new year with the firmest determination and the highest hopes.

On March 13 Private Fisk wrote: "We are having genuine March weather here just now, and its drying winds are having a salutary effect in relieving us of mud and the surplus water with which the ground is abundantly saturated. The wind is blowing in a very becoming manner today, considering what it has to do, and the sun 'pours his full radiance far,' as if to help in the benevolent work."

Nine days earlier Lee had sent a message through the lines to Grant, proposing a meeting to discuss peace. Grant rejected the offer; the siege went on. Lee launched a heavy attack on March 25 that captured one of the major Union strongholds, Fort Steadman. But a heavier counterattack by Grant brought the fort back under Union control with frightful loss to the Confederates. As part of the resulting action, some units of the Sixth Corps that included the Vermont Brigade attacked Confederate rifle pits near Fort Fisher. The Vermonters bagged more than 500 Confederate prisoners and, in all, a mile and a half of rifle positions. At the time it did not seem like strategic territory, but eight days later it would be used as the jumping-off point for a massive Sixth Corps attack.

On March 26 Frederick Gale assessed the situation in a letter to his wife in Barre:

> It will be sure death for them to remain in Richmond and if they evacuate they cannot come north at this season of the year. What they will do must be decided before many weeks for our armies are fast closing in on them.
>
> We have news today of another victory. The rebels attempted to break our lines at…[Fort Stedman] Hatcher's Run and were repulsed, as the telegraph reports, with a loss of 3,000 killed and wounded left on the field and some 2,000 prisoners. Our loss was reported at 800 in all—small by comparison—but oh! how many hearts will it cause to mourn and how many homes will be desolate.

A mighty Union host was now gathering for a final battering of Lee's long and ever more thinly held defenses. Sheridan was now in from the Shenandoah Valley—in for the final kill—and he brought a magnificent cavalry force of 10,000 men that included William Wells's First Vermont Cavalry. On April 1 Sheridan launched a thunderous attack on the western end of Lee's lines, at a place where many roads met—Five Forks. Lt. Eri Woodbury was in the fight with the Vermont cavalry: "Charged with Custer's whole division. Had my 'Little Rebel' shot…another charge….I was taken by 2 rebs with muskets at my breast. Up my sabre and struck spurs to horse and left for woods. 'Stop that Yank, shoot him,' rang after me and one shot instantly killed my horse. I up and gave leg bail and escaped."

Capt. Horace Ide of Barnet recalled:

> We saw the Fifteenth New York charge, and supposing we were to follow, advanced carbines and drew sabres and started, but were ordered back and came into line under shelter of a little ridge. Custer stationed his band on the top of the ridge in front and ordered them to play. The rebels shelled us, dropping the branches of the pine trees upon us, but inflicting no damage. The Fifteenth New York was

repulsed, and returning took position beside us. Custer made a short speech to us; the bugle sounded a charge, and away we went.

The enemy fought well; but soon gave way all along the line. A column of the enemy's cavalry came toward us. The Fifteenth New York was on their right, our infantry on their left and we in front of them; but as they came right down toward us as cool and in as good order as if on dress parade, until they were within pistol-shot, when they broke and fled, we after them, helter-skelter, until we struck a road which we followed a short distance; then across the fields to another road leading to the right. We captured several prisoners, but as it was getting dark, we went slow. We soon saw before us some mounted men who asked, "Who are you?"

Some one answering: "We are Vermonters."

They replied, "We are Carolinians," and fired. But it was so dark and they were in such a hurry that no one on our side was hurt. But it threw us into some confusion; and when we got straightened out they were gone. We pursued them some distance, but hearing Custer's bugle on the other road, which showed that we were too far in advance, we returned to the column, which marched back a mile or so and went into bivouac. In this battle the usual order had been changed, the infantry doing the flanking, while the cavalry charged the enemy's works in front.

Five Forks was an overwhelming Union victory. Clearly things had much changed since the dashing days of Jeb Stuart, when the Confederate cavalry had been invincible. At Five Forks the remnants of a beaten army were badly trounced by Sheridan's hard-driving cavalry and Maj. Gen. G. K. Warren's Fifth Corps soldiers that were present in superior numbers. Grant issued orders for an all-out assault the length of the Richmond–Petersburg lines the next day.

RICHMOND FALLS,
LEE SURRENDERS

When Charles Gould was two years old, he climbed onto his grandparents' stove in the kitchen of their Windham farm home, lured by the aroma of cooking applesauce. The child lost his balance and fell into a big pot of applesauce just taken from the fire. Terribly burned, Gould could not walk until he was six years old. As he recovered, his mother taught him needlework. When Gould regained normal strength, he became something of a daredevil among the Windham children. As the war began, although his parents were much against his enlisting, Gould walked from Windham to Bellows Falls and signed up. He became an excellent soldier, a captain in the Fifth Vermont Regiment, despite his boyish looks and scarred body. In the pre-

VHS

Capt. Charles Gould's face bore bayonet scar.

dawn hours of April 2, 1865 Gould was in the front rank of a mass of 14,000 Sixth Corps soldiers waiting for the order to move against Robert E. Lee's lines around Petersburg.

The Sixth Corps attack on March 25 had captured more than a mile of Confederate rifle pits between the Union and Confederate lines. Along those pits, in the night of April 1–2, Horatio Wright aligned his soldiers in a great wedge-shaped formation poised to attack. At the narrow, forward point was the Vermont Brigade, with 2,209 men. General Wright had told Lewis Grant, "If the corps does as well as I expect, we will have broken through the Rebel lines in 15 minutes."

"I heartily approve," Grant said.

The 10th Vermont was also part of the assault, and the historian G. G. Benedict wrote:

> Coffee was served to the troops at midnight, and as the moon went down, the regiments, in light marching order, filed outside the breastworks, and moved silently into position without attracting the attention of the enemy's pickets, 200 yards in front. The position of the Tenth was a short distance in rear of the entrenched picket line, and about half a mile to the left of that of the First Vermont brigade. The men lay shivering in the darkness for three hours....As the earliest streak of approaching daylight crept along the horizon, the parapets of a Confederate earthwork became dimly visible a few hundred yards in front of them. At half-past four o'clock, upon the firing of the signal-gun from Fort Fisher, the men sprang up and started forward.

The Third Vermont Battery, the last of the three artillery units formed in Vermont, had been heavily involved in fighting the previous day near Petersburg. Now, in the night, the battery was shifted west to support the Sixth Corps and given the honor of firing the signal gun to start the advance. The object was to smash the long Confederate line at a marshy spot where there was a break in the earthworks. Only about 100 feet wide and well protected, the breach still presented a tempting target, and just before dawn, when the signal gun boomed, the Sixth Corps started toward it.

The massed assault nearly reached the rifle pits before the first shots were fired. The Sixth Corps broke into a run with a loud cheer. The rebel trenches erupted in fire but not as concentrated as the men had feared. By this time no more than 30,000 soldiers manned the long Confederate trenches stretching more than 30 miles from north of Richmond to far southwest of Petersburg. The mighty attack rolled forward, with the Vermonters in the lead. Charles Gould found himself, in the dim first daylight, confronting the high, mounded Confederate main line. It must have been an awesome sight, with flashes and bangs of rifle fire coming from over the top, but he kept on running, bounding up and over the earthwork and down into the rebel trench. He later wrote home: "Have got a bayonet wound through the cheek, another between my shoulders and a sabre cut on my head....I am sorry that I was wounded before I got to Richmond."

Although he did not realize it at first, this farm boy from Windham was the first Union soldier to breach the Confederate defenses of Petersburg; a Medal of Honor would follow. Thus the great 10-month siege of Petersburg ended. Later, at Benedict's request, Gould produced a more thorough account of his great moment:

My appearance on the parapet was met with a leveled musket, which fortunately missed fire. I immediately jumped into the work, and my part in the engagement was soon over. I was scarcely inside before a bayonet was thrust through my face and a sword-thrust returned for it that fully repaid the wound given me, as I was subsequently informed that it killed my assailant. At almost the same breath an officer—or some one armed with a sword—gave me a severe cut in the head. The remainder of my brief stay in the work was a confused scramble, from which, had my assailants been fewer in number, I should scarcely have escaped. As it was, firing on their part would have been dangerous for their own men; consequently their efforts were apparently restricted to the use of bayonets and clubbed muskets. During the struggle I was once seized and my overcoat partially pulled off, and probably at this time another bayonet wound was given me in the back, as the bayonet passed through my inner coat between the shoulders, while my overcoat remained intact. This was the most severe wound of the three, the bayonet entering the spine and penetrating nearly to the spinal cord. I have no distinct recollection of what followed, until I found myself at the parapet, trying to climb out of the work, but unable to do so. At this time, Private Henry H. Rector, Company A, Fifth Vermont, appeared upon the parapet at that point. The brave fellow recognized the situation, and notwithstanding the danger incurred in doing so, pulled me upon the parapet, receiving a gunshot wound himself while saving me. This terminated my part in the assault upon the lines at Petersburg.

While Gould was the first Union soldier into the Confederate works, the 10th Vermont claimed the honor of being the first regiment to plant its colors in the rebel works. "Pile in, boys, don't give them time to load," one officer of the 10th shouted as the Confederate line cracked.

The Sixth Corps assault was watched from the Union's Fort Welch by the surgeon Samuel J. Allen of Hartford. Allen could "hear the muffled tramp and rustle of the moving host but could discover nothing." Then he saw flashes of the first volley, "heard the mighty shout of 10,000 throats, and then saw stretching across the front for half a mile, a line of flashing fires, crackling, blazing and sparkling in the darkness, more vividly lighted up by the heavier flashes of artillery, while shells, with their fiery trails, sped forward through the gloom in every direction."

Bullets were whipping over Fort Welch, but Allen stood his ground, transfixed by that "line of deadly fire." He recalled, "Suddenly in the middle of it there appeared a tiny black spot, a narrow gap, which spread and widened, moment by moment, to the right and left." Allen knew the Petersburg line had been broken "even before the exultant cheers of our troops proclaimed the fact."

After 10 months of siege, begun after "Baldy" Smith had missed his golden chance, the Petersburg lines were broken and forever smashed. The Sixth Corps rolled into the breach, spreading along the Confederate works to the left and right. The break widened, with Confederates by the hundreds shot or surrendering. Again the Sixth Corps moved forward, halted beyond the works to get its lines dressed, and rolled on. The Vermonters were still to the front, overrunning rebel artillery positions, capturing guns and caissons, turning the guns on the fleeing Confederates, and firing them by shooting down vents.

The attack surged past a house that had until the previous day been Robert E. Lee's headquarters; it was soon in flames. The Union juggernaut surged on in the smoky light of midmorning until the spires of Petersburg could be seen. Before the day of Union triumph ended, Getty's division of the Sixth Corps claimed that it alone had taken 2,100 prisoners, 20 cannon, and nine battle flags. The rebel lines were breaking everywhere as the Confederacy collapsed by the minute.

The Vermont Brigade did not know it, but here was its last hard fighting, a glorious, smashing climax to three and a half years of war. The end of the agonizing trail through Lee's Mills, Fredericksburg, Antietam, Marye's Heights, Gettysburg, the Wilderness, Spotsylvania, Cedar Creek, and all the other slaughter fields had come in sight. The last Confederate defenses, built to protect the capital and its supply lines, had been pulverized and overrun. Up ahead, Lee and what was left of his army were fleeing Petersburg and the capital city of Richmond, moving west in a last try to live and fight a few days more. As night came on April 2, the great Confederate bastion of Richmond and Petersburg lay open to the Union army. The day had been costly for the Vermont Brigade; 25 men killed and 161 wounded. Eight men later died of wounds.

Well to the north and east, as the Sixth Corps and other units assaulted the Petersburg defenses on April 2, men of the 24th Corps, including the Ninth Vermont Regiment, heard the distant thunder of the assaults and saw battle smoke rise. They were ordered to prepare to attack the defenses of Richmond in the morning. In the darkness of April 2–3 they heard distant explosions, which later proved to be the rebels blowing up their own gunboats on the James River. Then a deserter came through the lines with word that the Confederates were abandoning the city's defenses. When the Union forces advanced in the morning, well after a foggy dawn, no fire came from the rebel entrenchments and the troops walked right up and over them. The Ninth Vermont was in the front rank and moving steadily until a halt was called for lunch. When men from another unit began to move forward, the Vermonters, wanting no other outfit to beat them into Richmond, resumed the advance. On they moved, reaching the inner lines of the Confederate defenses, also undefended. A general officer rode by and told the Vermonters to halt. He could have saved his words, for the troops paid no attention and marched ever closer to the city that had troubled their dreams for so long.

Dark clouds of smoke arose from the rebel capital, set afire by looters and retreating soldiers. Brig. Gen. Edward Hastings Ripley was at the head of the advance, commanding a brigade in the 24th Corps. His old Ninth Vermont was with him. Ripley paused only long enough to move the three brass bands in the column to the front. Then he walked his horse in behind the bands, at the head of his former regiment, up in front where it had been since the advance started. At that moment an aide to Maj. Gen. Godfrey Weitzel informed Ripley that "you are in luck today" and officially ordered him to do what he was about to do anyway, lead the Union army into Richmond.

Ripley remembered:

> While this was going on an iron-clad which was yet lying in the stream abreast of us, the last of all the river fleet, blew up with a terrific concussion, nearly knocking us off our feet and overwhelming us with a tempest of black smoke, cinders and debris. I do not remember that any one was injured, though part of it went over our heads into the field beyond. The roar of exploding arsenals, magazines and warehouses filled with the explosives of the Ordnance Bureau was deafening and awe-inspiring.

Ripley gave the command "Forward," and his bands began to play as the Vermont troops stepped off. And so it was, at long last, not only "on to Richmond" but *into* Richmond. Ripley wrote:

> The bands had arranged a succession of Union airs which had not been heard for many days in the streets of the Confederate capital, and had arranged to relieve each other so that there should be no break in the exultant strain of patriotic music during any portion of the march. The route was up Broad Street to the Exchange Hotel, then across to Main to Capitol Square. The city was packed with a surging mob of Confederate stragglers and negroes, and mob rule had been supreme from the moment [Lt. Gen. Richard] Ewell crossed the James and burned the long bridge behind him. The air was darkened by the thick tempest of black smoke and cinders which swept through the streets, and as we penetrated deeper into the city the bands were almost drowned by the crashing of buildings, the roar of the flames and the terrific explosions of shells in the burning warehouses.

One Vermonter recalled: "The entrance to the city was more like an ovation to returned heroes than the surrender of a conquered city. The streets were lined with inhabitants, both black and white, and the cheers and songs and gladness from the sidewalks drowned the shouts of joy from the soldiers."

Edward Ripley said:

> Densely packed on either side of the street were thousands upon thousands of blacks, till that moment slaves, down upon their knees, throwing their hands wildly in the air, while floods of tears poured down their wild faces, and shouting "Glory to God! Glory to God! the day of Jubilee hab come! Massa Linkim am here! Massa Linkum am here!" They threw themselves on their faces almost under our horses' feet to pray and give thanks in the wild delirium of their sudden deliverance.

The column moved uphill to the Virginia Statehouse, for the past four years capitol of the Confederate States of America. Ripley rode into the capitol square, thronged with Union troops and terrified Richmond citizens gathered in the nearest open space to escape the fire. He dismounted and ascended the steps of the capitol, where he was met by General Weitzel, who informed Ripley that he

UVM

Edward Ripley's men enter Richmond.

was to take command of the conquered city. Ripley accepted and selected the Richmond City Hall across the street as his headquarters. He immediately dispatched orders for Union troops to fan out through the city, to stop looting, but also to join Richmond firemen in putting out the fires. Ripley recalled:

> The troops quickly marched to their assigned places, and I opened my headquarters in the City Hall, and posted a placard throughout the city commanding all good citizens to assist the military authorities in restoring order by retiring to their houses, keeping closely within doors, and threatening with arrest any citizen who should be found on the streets after nightfall.
>
> Officers were quickly sent to Libby prison to liberate the Union prisoners there, and the place was used to confine the Confederate stragglers, who were captured to the number of over 7,000. It was so crowded that when on the next morning I had time to ride by, on an inspection of the city, they had boiled up through the roof and were sitting crowded all over it.

Ripley later brought home the key to Libby Prison; it now is displayed at the Bennington Museum.

Slowly, steadily, order was restored; the fires controlled. Ripley wrote:

> It was after midnight on April 3 when I got sufficient respite from the exertions of the day to get into my saddle and make an inspection of my command....For hours we passed up and down the streets which echoed to the clatter of our horses' hoofs and the jingle of our sabres, astonished at the discipline that had been established in so few hours. It was near morning when we gave ourselves up to rest, in the house

we had selected for headquarters, and enjoyed the novel and delicious intoxication of rest in beds with mattresses and fresh linen. So ended the first day of the occupation of the Confederate capital.

Ripley would command Richmond for two full weeks.

With Petersburg and Richmond doomed, General Lee ordered a full retreat to the west, with the faint hope of linking up with Joseph E. Johnston's army somewhere to the south in North Carolina. Grant lost no time setting his army in pursuit along the Appomattox River.

Everywhere the Confederacy was disintegrating. William Tecumseh Sherman, his long march to the sea having ended at Savannah, was driving hard up the Atlantic Seaboard in pursuit of Johnston. Far to the south the Seventh Vermont Regiment was part of a big Union force at the gates of Mobile; that key Southern city was about to fall. The last, best hope of the Confederacy lay with Lee, his shrunken army moving west from Richmond and Petersburg. Grant and Sheridan pursued him relentlessly, men in the ranks ever willing to take the punishment of hard marches because each could be the last.

The Vermont Brigade, with the Sixth Corps, left Petersburg on April 3 and tramped 14 miles that day to Whipponock Creek. The brigade then marched 12 miles to Deep Creek, and 16 more the next day, reaching Jetersville Station. On April 6 George Custer's cavalry overtook the rear of Lee's retreating army in lowlands along Sayler's Creek. A vicious battle developed, the day to be known to Confederates as "Black Thursday." Robert E. Lee watched from a hilltop and exclaimed, "My God. Has the army dissolved?"

Nearly 8,000 rebel soldiers surrendered at Sayler's Creek. The 10th Vermont was briefly in the day's fighting, firing its last shots of the war. The Vermont Brigade stood in line of battle through much of the day but did not fight. With darkness gathering in the smoky Virginia sky, the Second Vermont Regiment encountered Confederate skirmishers along the west branch of Sayler's Creek. A hot exchange of fire developed; after a few minutes, the Confederates moved away. Pvt. Henry Houghton wrote, "Soon after crossing the creek we had a slight skirmish and there was the last time I heard the song of the rebel's bullet."

The next day, April 7, the Vermont Brigade pressed on 14 miles to Farmville and crossed the Appomattox River. It moved on in the morning, but soon received orders to return to Farmville and guard supply trains. Thus it did not approach Appomattox Court House with the rest of the Union army.

But the First Vermont Cavalry did, William Wells's men getting in a fight on April 8 and helping to capture several cannons and a wagon train. In that fight Lt. Eri Woodbury got shot. He wrote home from a hospital at City Point a few days later:

I can write only a few lines and that with my left hand. On the 8th at Appomattox Station a fragment of shell struck me slightly wounding me in the breast and left side, severely in the left arm and taking off the 2 left fingers of the right hand, also took nearly half the palm of the hand. I was rather roughly handled to be sure but many a brave fellow fared worse so I have still much to be grateful for.

Woodbury may have been the last Vermont cavalryman wounded in the war. The next day, April 9, General Sheridan cut off Lee's retreat near Appomattox Court House. The First Vermont Cavalry was there as Sheridan aligned his legions for one last devastating assault on Lee's thin ranks. There in the fields ahead were Lee's veterans with their tattered battle flags held high and rifle-muskets at the ready, awaiting the last, deadly assault. The First Vermont Cavalry trotted along between the Union and Confederate lines, moving to take its place for the onslaught. "Never did the regiment, even on dress parade, keep in better line than it did then," cavalryman Horace Ide remembered.

It was sure to be a slaughter. Custer was there and gave the order to move forward. The Union horsemen, at a walk, began their advance on Lee's tired soldiers, still defiant, still ready to fight. Suddenly a colonel from Custer's staff came riding along the lines shouting, "Lower your carbines, men, lower your carbines. You will never have to raise them again in this war."

The lines halted; men threw their caps in the air and shouted. Then a silence descended on the field. At about 5 P.M. Custer arrived from Appomattox Court House and rode along the lines announcing that terms of surrender had been agreed to by Ulysses Grant and Robert E. Lee. It was April 9, Palm Sunday. During that lull Lee and Grant had met in the parlor of Wilmer McLean's house in the village nearby.

William Wells got himself to the McLean house as fast as he could, where he joined the souvenir-hunting spree. He came away with a strip of red cloth that had covered some furniture in the surrender room. He sent it home to his parents. (It is now at the University of Vermont, his alma mater.) Wells was also about to receive promotion to brigadier general, a rank he had ambitiously sought and come to expect. When it arrived, a month after Appomattox, it reflected one of the extraordinary metamorphoses of the war: Wells had risen from private to general. In the ranks of the Vermont soldiers on April 9 there was many a quiet prayer of thanksgiving that the war had ended. But for Wells, the war had been going well, and he sent a note home with the piece of cloth that read: "The war is over. We have no enemy to fight. What shall we do?"

Wilbur Fisk more accurately caught the spirit of most Vermont troops when he wrote, "Men have been busy putting up tents and fixing things up as nice as they can, for they are old soldiers the most of them, and they know that the nicer they fix up things here the surer they will be to leave, and to leave now means to go home."

From a hospital bed Charles Gould wrote on April 10, "Yesterday our misguided brother Bob Lee turned over the command of his army to old Useless."

West of Petersburg, the Confederate works first penetrated that fateful April 2 by the Vermonters still stand in a somewhat swampy woods. I found them one hot summer day, looming through brush and timber. The land on which they stand, including the earthworks Captain Gould became the first to cross, is about to become a park and should be open to the public in 1994. Fort Welch, from whose ramparts Samuel Allen watched the twinkling rifles, is preserved on national park land, deep in a woods. I reached it after a walk down a narrow road crisscrossed with cobwebs as though I were the first to walk that way in a very long time. The Saylers Creek battlefield, near where the Vermont Brigade fired its last shots, is a Virginia state park. Appomattox Court House is preserved as a national park—a shrine, really, its fabled "stillness" seldom broken.

LINCOLN'S LAST DAYS

Abraham Lincoln went from Washington to join Grant at his headquarters for the final days of the Petersburg campaign. There he met his son Robert Lincoln, who had recently secured an appointment (with his father's help) as a captain on Grant's staff. Young Robert, fresh out of Harvard, spent most of his time escorting dignitaries about headquarters. The president visited an army hospital at City Point where Wilbur Fisk was detailed as an orderly:

> President Lincoln was here at the hospital to-day to visit the boys, and shake hands with them. It was an unexpected honor, coming from the man upon whom the world is looking with so much interest, and the boys were pleased with it beyond measure. Everything passed off in a very quiet manner; there was no crowding or disorder of any kind. When the president came all the men that were able arranged themselves by common consent into line, on the edge of the walk that runs by the door of the stockades, and Mr. Lincoln passed along in front, paying personal respect to each man.
>
> "Are you well, sir?" "How do you do to-day?" "How are you, sir?" looking each man in the face, and giving him a word and a shake of the hand as he passed. He went into each of the stockades and tents, to see those that were not able to be out. "Is this Father Abraham?" says one very sick man to Mr. Lincoln. The President assured him, good naturedly, that it was. Mr. Lincoln presides over millions of people, and each individual share of his attention must necessarily be very small, and yet he wouldn't slight the humblest of them all. His wife, accompanied by [Massachusetts] Senator [Charles] Sumner, and other ladies, officers and eminent men were with him. The men not only reverence and admire Mr. Lincoln, but they love him. May God bless him, and spare his life to us for many years.

After the occupation of Richmond, Lincoln on April 4 took a boat up the

James River to the waterfront of the still-smoking city. Edward Ripley was in charge there, and the presidential appearance, while a great honor, presented a security nightmare for the Vermont general. He recalled:

> The streets were crowded during the day-time with excited throngs of negroes and whites, and we were very uneasy at Mr. Lincoln's insistence upon visiting all interesting points. We tried to make him consent to an escort, but he would not allow it, and strolled through the city like a private citizen, followed by crowds of people, white and black. We were obliged, unknown to him, to surround him with a crowd of detectives in citizen's dress, heavily armed.

Vermonter Lucius Chittenden, who knew Lincoln, wrote long after the war:

> Multitudes of the emancipated crowd around and seek to touch the garments of the benefactor, as with streaming eyes they shout their thanksgivings. Truly, as he said, "it is a great thing to be responsible for the freedom of a race." Note the historic picture as he removes his hat and bows in silence to the old negro who exclaimed, "May de good Lord bless you, President Linkum." Truthfully did one write at the time: "That bow upset the forms, customs, and ceremonies of centuries."

The next day Ripley was visited by a Confederate soldier who warned that Lincoln's life might be in great danger. The man claimed that rebel agents had been dispatched on a secret mission and that the assassination of Lincoln might be their aim. Though the report proved false, Ripley didn't know it at the time. Ripley:

> I wrote the President a note asking an interview at his earliest leisure. It was about 10 o'clock in the evening. In reply he wrote me a personal note, saying he would see me at 9 o'clock the next morning. I was promptly on hand, taking the Confederate soldier and his statement with me.
> The President received me most cordially in the Admiral's cabin, and then sat down on the long cushioned seat running along the side of the ship behind the dining table, I taking my seat opposite him. Little Tad, who was then a small and very restless boy, amused himself by running up and down the length of the sofa behind his father and jumping over his back in passing. As I progressed in my errand, the President let his head drop upon his hands as his elbows rested on the table, his hands supporting his chin and clasping either cheek in an expression of the most heart-breaking weariness. I read the paper; I urged upon him the reasonableness of the warning, the good faith and apparent integrity of the man. I begged him to let me bring him in and talk with him, but it was all to no purpose. Finally he lifted his head, and said,—"No, Gen. Ripley, it is impossible for me to adopt and follow your suggestions. I deeply appreciate the feeling which has led you to urge them on me, but I must go on as I have begun in the course marked for me, for I cannot bring myself to believe that any human being lives who would do me any harm."
> The interview then ended. He was so worn, emaciated and pallid that he looked

more like a disembodied spirit than the successful leader of a great nation in its hour of supreme triumph. I never saw him again.

In Vermont, on March 30, Gov. John Gregory Smith had issued a proclamation, anticipating Good Friday, that began:

The return of the springtime, and the lengthening rays of the sun warming the earth into beauty and life and giving promise of a fruitful harvest, should remind us of our dependence upon HIM who maketh the world and who giveth freely, and witholdest not from those who seek HIM in the faith.

In accordance with the custom of our fathers, which commends itself to every Christian heart, and in order that the people of this State may unitedly humble themselves before God and devoutly implore HIS favor, I do hereby appoint Friday, the 14th day of April next, to be publically observed as a day of HUMILIATION, FASTING and PRAYER, by the people of the state.

Lincoln departed the war zone for Washington on April 8, the day before Lee's surrender. On the evening of the day proclaimed in Vermont as one of thanks, April 14, the president and his wife, Mary; a young army officer, Maj. Henry Rathbone; and his fiancée, Clara Harris, went to Ford's Theater for a performance of *Our American Cousin.* Robert Lincoln, just returned from Appomattox with the gift of a picture of Lee for his father, declined his parents' invitation to join the theater party. Robert Lincoln never forgave himself, thinking throughout his long life that somehow, that night, he could have prevented that single shot from John Wilkes Booth's derringer. Abraham Lincoln was dead.

When the terrible news reached City Point, Wilbur Fisk wrote:

Never had sadder news been brought to us than this. It seemed as if we had lost a father....When he was here a week ago last Saturday, some of the surgeons told him that to attempt to shake hands with so many thousand men would be more than he ought to

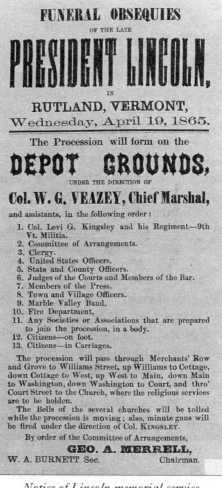

FUNERAL OBSEQUIES
OF THE LATE
PRESIDENT LINCOLN,
IN
RUTLAND, VERMONT,
Wednesday, April 19, 1865.

The Procession will form on the

DEPOT GROUNDS,
UNDER THE DIRECTION OF
Col. W. G. VEAZEY, Chief Marshal,

and assistants, in the following order:

1. Col. Levi G. Kingsley and his Regiment—9th Vt. Militia.
2. Committee of Arrangements.
3. Clergy.
4. United States Officers.
5. State and County Officers.
6. Judges of the Courts and Members of the Bar.
7. Members of the Press.
8. Town and Village Officers.
9. Marble Valley Band.
10. Fire Department,
11. Any Societies or Associations that are prepared to join the procession, in a body.
12. Citizens—on foot.
13. Citizens—in Carriages.

The procession will pass through Merchants' Row and Grove to Williams Street, up Williams to Cottage, down Cottage to West, up West to Main, down Main to Washington, down Washington to Court, and thro' Court Street to the Church, where the religious services are to be holden.

The Bells of the several churches will be tolled while the procession is moving; also, minute guns will be fired under the direction of Col. KINGSLEY.

By order of the Committee of Arrangements,

GEO. A. MERRELL,

W. A. BURNETT, Sec.   Chairman.

Notice of Lincoln memorial service in Rutland.

endure, but he overruled them, for he said he wanted to shake hands with the brave boys who had won the great victories which gave him, with all the rest of the nation, so much cause to rejoice, and had been wounded, many of them, in so doing. I believe he took almost as much pleasure in honoring the boys, as the boys did in receiving the honor from him. But Abraham Lincoln is dead.

Fisk went on to question why God had allowed such a thing to happen, and he concluded, "But we must quote, in view of this event, the same words that Mr. Lincoln quoted in his second inaugural, 'The judgments of the Lord are true and righteous altogether.'"

Word of the assassination reached Frederick Gale of the Eighth Vermont at Summit Point in the Shenandoah Valley. He sent a letter home to Barre around which he drew a border of black ink: "I have not heart to write today for my soul is filled with sadness. I cannot tell you what a gloom has fallen over our camps....The flags in each regiment are at half mast."

William Wells wrote: "Most of the officers wear a badge of crepe on their left arm...since the president was murdered. A letter from home says the people are feeling very badly, at the same time quite revengeful. It is the same here in the army."

G. G. Benedict wrote: "On the 15th the news of the assassination of President Lincoln was received, with indescribable grief and indignation. The men of the Vermont Brigade, especially, knew that they had attracted his interest and stood second to no brigade in the army in his confidence, and they mourned for him with a deep personal sorrow."

The sad tidings reached St. Johnsbury on April 15, and William Herrick recorded in his diary: "The president died this morning about 7 o'clock....It has weighed on my mind like a terrible load all day, everybody has looked very sad. He was like one of our friends. Dark and rainy tonight."

The next day, Sunday, Herrick attended church as usual and noted that "the service was solemn this morning, the church was draped in mourning. Chanted the old psalm 'Lord thou has been our dwelling place in all generations.' Hymn, 'Lord, How Mysterious are Thy Ways.'"

In Manchester a funeral service was held for Abraham Lincoln that ended with the singing of "America." The people of Manchester felt especially close to the tragedy, for First Lady Mary Todd Lincoln and Robert Lincoln had visited their village the two previous summers, seeking respite from the Washington heat and the stresses of the war. John Hay, Abraham Lincoln's secretary, however, once said that Robert went to Manchester because he was so upset by a recent wedding that "he rushed madly off to sympathize with nature in her sternest aspects." They stayed two weeks, Mary Lincoln enjoying carriage rides through the countryside around Manchester. As she left Vermont in 1864, Mrs. Lincoln made reservations for herself and for the president at the Equinox House for the following summer.

Mary Lincoln never returned to Manchester. But Robert Lincoln often came back, first as a guest at the home of his law partner, Edward Isham, and years later with his wife, Mary Harlan Lincoln, to build a home. By then he was a wealthy man, serving as president and chairman of the board of the Pullman Company. He also was appointed secretary of war by James Garfield and minister to Great Britain by Benjamin Harrison. The Lincolns built their "summer cottage" on the point of a ridge south of the village. "Hildene" commanded a view down the long valley between the Green and Taconic mountain ranges. Robert Lincoln spent 22 consecutive summers at Hildene, playing much golf and entertaining important friends. He died there in his sleep on July 26, 1926, six days shy of his 83rd birthday.

Hildene remained in the Lincoln family through several generations of descendants, until acquired by the Friends of Hildene in 1978, 412 acres and 27 buildings. The estate is now a museum and displays two of Robert Lincoln's treasured mementos of his father: a black stovepipe hat (could it be the one Lincoln lifted to the Eighth Vermont?) and an oval mirror. The mirror, set in an old wood frame, was in the White House, and according to family legend, the president looked into it as he left for Ford's Theater the night of April 14, 1865.

Surely that mirror must have recalled for Robert Lincoln another fateful time, from his college days, in the wartime summer of either 1863 or 1864. He wasn't sure which. He was a student at Harvard, en route to his parents' home in Washington, and was standing on a crowded platform in the Jersey City railway station. Jostled by the crowd, young Lincoln lost his balance and fell to the tracks, beneath the wheels of a train about to depart. He thought himself doomed, but suddenly a strong hand grasped his collar and pulled him to safety. Lincoln got only a glimpse of his savior's face. But he always swore he recognized the man as the famed Shakespearean actor Edwin Booth, brother of John Wilkes Booth.

HOMECOMINGS

One hundred years after Lee's surrender and Lincoln's death, a Vermont historian spent several weeks in Richmond conducting research in the Confederate archives. One bright morning he walked down the long hill from the city's center to the bank of the James River and stood several minutes watching the historic river flow by. He happened to glance back up the hill at the Virginia Statehouse, Thomas Jefferson's great columned building, once the capitol of the Confederate States of America. Atop it an American flag flapped, it seemed to him, "in a rather careless way." The thought occurred to the Vermonter how inappropriate that carefree motion seemed, considering the thousands of lives once sacrificed to place the Stars and Stripes there.

News of Lee's surrender reached St. Johnsbury on April 10. William Herrick, who worked in the Fairbanks factories, recorded: "It has been a great day in St. Johnsbury. The first intimation was from the clerks in the store counting room who came in swinging their hats and shouting. When it got down to the shops, work was quite out of the question so the bell rung and the machinery stopped and everybody went outdoors."

That night a candlelight parade wound through the streets of St. Johnsbury. The theme was "a funeral for the Confederacy," and a coffin draped with a Confederate flag was carried at the procession's head. When it reached the grave that had been dug for it, a large crowd sang "The Star-Spangled Banner" and "John Brown's Body." Then the casket was lowered into the Vermont earth, minus its flag, which was tossed in the street for everyone to trample.

In Burlington four barbers set to work on a man who had sworn in 1861 never to cut his hair until the Union flag should fly again over Fort Sumter.

In Manchester a Mrs. Wickham noted in the local paper: "The intense joy of the land uttered itself, now in praise, now in shouts. Our bells rang their loudest peals, banners were held up amid processions formed in haste, and the echoes of the cannon's roar from our stable mountains was a voice proclaiming the fullfilment of our hopes, the end of our fears. John had leave to ring the bell all day."

Church bells rang throughout Vermont as celebrations erupted. Lee's surrender and Union victory were proclaimed, crowds cheered and rejoiced at the imminent return of the Vermont regiments. But for some there would be a disappointingly long delay.

Though Lee and his Army of Northern Virginia had capitulated, Gen. Joseph Johnston and some 30,000 Confederates were still on the loose in North Carolina. It was not until April 26 that Johnston and William Tecumseh Sherman agreed on surrender terms, meeting in a log cabin near Durham Station.

The Sixth Corps left for North Carolina immediately after the surrender at Appomattox. Soldiers of the Vermont Brigade remembered the next four days as some of their toughest marching. "We left Burkville Junction a week ago last Sunday and marched to Danville in 4 days," Pvt. Jonathan Blaisdell wrote. "Maj. Gen. Wright was in command. I would as leaf see him shot as a rebel, it is all he knows to march troops to death when there is no need of it & then make his brags about it."

The brigade covered 100 miles to Danville, where it went into camp. Not until May 16 did the Vermont regiments begin to board trains and head north. At Richmond the brigade got four days of rest and took time to tour the fallen capital. Then General Wright ordered the Sixth Corps to march from Richmond to the Washington area, another order the troops abhorred. But the men set out, it being the way toward home, and trudged up through familiar country, passing some of the old battlegrounds, and arrived in the vicinity of old Camp Griffin the first week in June. There the Vermont Brigade went into camp with members of the Eighth and 10th Vermont regiments and the First Vermont Cavalry. Those three outfits had been formally made a part of the Vermont Brigade to close out their service.

The Eighth Vermont had, since Cedar Creek, remained in the Shenandoah Valley. In January its war-long leader, Stephen Thomas, went home. Because of a bureaucratic snarl, Colonel Thomas had been unable to reenlist and keep his rank of colonel when his three-year enlistment ended. He was subsequently informed he had been commissioned brigadier general, but it was too late to return to his unit. In April, after Lincoln's assassination, the Eighth hurried in from the Shenandoah to join other troops ringing the city of Washington, hoping to block the escape of John Wilkes Booth. (Booth was tracked down and shot on April 26 in a tobacco barn near Port Royal, Virginia.) Then the Eighth was nearly sent to Savannah, Georgia, its orders canceled at the last minute after Governor Smith intervened. After Appomattox the 10th regiment camped near Richmond until it was ordered to join the Vermont Brigade.

The Vermont cavalry was sent toward North Carolina with Custer's command, but just short of the state border, word was received of Johnston's surrender, and the regiment turned back. The Vermont cavalrymen passed through Richmond with Custer's division, riding with sabres drawn. Libby Custer rode with her husband near the head of the column. On May 23, in Washington, the Vermont cavalrymen joined in a grand review of all the Union armies. For two days the men of Meade's Army of the Potomac, and the veterans of Sherman's western forces marched past a reviewing stand where Ulysses Grant and the new president, Andrew Johnson, took their salutes. The only other Green Mountain unit present was the 17th Vermont Regiment, since the Sixth Corps was still on duty well to the south.

On June 7 Gov. John Gregory Smith held a grand review of his own for the Vermont troops, on the old parade ground at Bailey's Cross Roads. There on the field where the men once helped inspire "The Battle Hymn of the Republic," Smith and a group of Vermont dignitaries watched the home state troops pass in review. Peter Washburn, the state adjutant general who had fought in the war's first battle, Big Bethel, wrote:

> The occasion was one of deep interest—not merely as a fine military display of admirably drilled troops, executing every movement with the utmost precision, but as a review, with the Governor of the State, of the scarred, sunburned and war-torn veterans whom the state had sent into the field, intrusted with the maintenance of her honor, who had met the enemy in many a fierce and sanguinary conflict, and some of them in every battle in which the Army of the Potomac had participated, from the first Bull Run to the final surrender of Lee on the banks of the Appomattox. There were officers and men there present, whose names have been household words in Vermont for the last four years, and will stand upon the roll of honor of the state, as long as the state shall have a history. Numbering scarce 6,000 men, they were all that remained in active service of nearly 20,000, who had been sent from the state in the regiments reviewed.

On June 8 President Johnson, in a well-intentioned expression of honor for those who had missed the earlier parade, held a special review for the Sixth Corps. It should have been canceled, for the day was one of the hottest in Washington's history; hundreds of men fainted from exhaustion and sunstroke. But the Vermonters, as usual, bore up better than most as they passed the reviewing stand with sprigs of green in their caps. "The Vermont Brigade made the best display, and received the highest compliments," the *Boston Journal* reported.

On June 24 Gen. Lewis Grant issued a farewell address to his Vermont Brigade that concluded:

> Your record is a proud one. History records no braver deeds. Yet it is a record of blood and many a well fought field is stained with the life blood of brave comrades. We mourn their loss, and while we cherish their memories, let us emulate their virtues. Having successfully fought for the preservation of our common country, let us become good citizens, perpetuate its free and liberal institutions, and strive in all the arts of peace to make it, under the blessing of God, truly the wonder and admiration of the world.

The first contingent from the Vermont Brigade arrived at Burlington on June 23. Mayor Albert L. Catlin and a large crowd welcomed them at City Hall. A speaker, the Hon. Daniel Roberts, declared them to be "THE fighting brigade, of THE fighting corps, so pronounced by those who have studied best the history of the war."

The First Vermont Cavalry had reached Burlington by train 10 days earlier. The men marched to City Hall, where an artillery salute was fired by the Third Vermont Battery, home just three days. The Eighth Vermont arrived on June 29 to parade through the Queen City's streets to the cheers of the crowd.

The 10th Vermont came in on June 27, marching in rain and darkness from the train station to City Hall, where a warm supper prepared by the ladies of the community awaited.

Not until July 18 did the 17th Vermont arrive, to receive breakfast at City Hall. The Second Vermont Battery chugged in two days later.

On July 22 about two-thirds of the 11th Vermont detrained at Burlington; the regimental band played "Home Again" on the march up to a City Hall supper. Left behind for another month in Washington were 278 men, assigned again as artillerymen in the city's defenses.

The Seventh Vermont's was a much sadder story. The regiment that somehow never seemed to get a fair shake was sent to the Florida coast after its service in Louisiana and Mississippi, where it served around Pensacola, much of the time manning Fort Barrancas, a disease-ridden place infested with mosquitoes and snakes. In the late winter of 1865 the Seventh had finally got back into action, in the siege of Mobile. It experienced nearly three weeks of trench warfare, besieging Old Spanish Fort, one of the city's key defenses. The fort fell the day before Lee surrendered, and the city was found to be evacuated on April 12. But the Seventh was still a long way from home. After the fall of Mobile the regiment participated in one of the last actions of the Civil War, a skirmish on April 13 near Mobile. Then the Seventh was ordered farther from home than it had ever been, all the way to the banks of the Rio Grande in Texas. There it served until March 14, 1866. It was not until April 5, 1866, four days short of a full year since Appomattox, that the Seventh Vermont arrived in Brattleboro.

The Seventh had, of course, been disgraced by Maj. Gen. Benjamin Butler early in the war after the Battle of Baton Rouge. "Beast" Butler had forbidden the regiment to add the battle's name to its regimental flag, charging that the Seventh had disobeyed orders under fire. On July 10, 1866 the following order was issued from Headquarters Military Division of the Gulf:

In compliance with requirements of General Order, No. 19, 1862, from the War Department, and in accordance with the reports of boards convened to examine into the services rendered by the troops concerned, and by authority of the lieutenant general commanding the armies of the United States, it is hereby ordered that there shall be inscribed upon the colors of the following regiments the names of battles in which they have borne a meritorious part, as hereinafter specified.

Seventh Vermont Veteran Volunteer Infantry: Siege of Vicksburg, BATON ROUGE, Gonzales Station, Spanish Fort, Whistler.

The Fourth Vermont in Brattleboro, en route home.

The order was issued by a man who had seen, on many bloodstained fields, the true fighting qualities of Vermont soldiers. It was signed: Maj. Gen. P. H. Sheridan.

Just a few days after the Vermont troops reached the home state, they were mustered out of service. Then they were free to return home. So Ma and Pa, or brother and sister, came down to Burlington, or Brattleboro, in the buckboard to pick up their soldier and carry him home. Others got on the train to the nearest station, where they were met by loved ones. Some just walked on home.

Henry Houghton described his homecoming:

We arrived at Burlington in the afternoon of the 14th and was met at the depot by an escort of citizens and escorted to City Hall where we were welcomed by showers of bouquets by the ladies and speeches by several leading citizens, after which we had dinner, the best dinner I had tasted for nearly three years, then we marched out to the Marine Hospital where the regiment remained three days when we were paid off and started for home.

I arrived in the village of Woodstock about 1 o'clock in the night, shouldered my house and clothing, took "old trusty" and started for my father's home about three miles out; after some loitering on the way, I reached there about 3 o'clock.

Wilbur Fisk went back to Tunbridge, where he wrote on July 26:

Home at last. The Second Vermont Regiment was not paid off till yesterday. Now the most of the boys are at home, and have become citizens instead of soldiers of the United States. Our old regiment no longer exists as an organization among the powers that be, but must henceforth be reckoned as amongst the powers that were. There have been great changes in our ranks since their organization four long years ago, and so, too, we find among these hills and valleys great changes have occurred among the inhabitants with whom we used to delight to mingle. Some have removed to other places, but many have gone, alas! to return no more. How well I remember my parents' anxiety when we parted four years ago, but since then they have followed two of their dear children to the grave, while their soldier son still lives.

Here are the same hills and the same fields that we saw then, but they have passed into other hands, and somehow there seems a loneliness in contemplating them, which forces the impression that this world cannot be man's abiding place. We have seen home so often like a fairy vision in our imaginings and dreams, and so often have wondered whether, in the good Providence of God, we should be permitted to return and find it as we left it, that now the ideal is realized it almost seems as if we were dreaming still. To look back upon the campaigns of the Peninsula, of Maryland, of the Wilderness, Shenandoah Valley and others, it seems almost impossible that all the events which our recollection can recall, should come within the range of four years. A lifetime of experience has been crowded into this fierce term of war. If I was asked "how it seemed" to be a free citizen once more, I should say it seemed as if I had been through a long dark tunnel, and had just got into daylight once more.

TAPS FOR GILBERT LUCIER

In the aftermath of the Civil War it was calculated that Vermont had furnished 34,238 men to the war effort. Of those, 5,224 died. A familiar New England site helps measure the magnitude of Vermont's contribution and sacrifice. A crowd of 34,238 will fill Boston's Fenway Park to the rafters. Fenway's bleachers are nearly filled by 5,224 people.

Vermont's population when the war began was 315,098. The number of men killed per capita makes Vermont's sacrifice among the Union states second only to that of Michigan. It has been said, though not confirmed, that Vermont ranked first in the number of men per capita killed in combat. There is no record of numbers of maimed and crippled.

Long after the war the town historian in Ludlow wrote: "Of those spared to return home, nearly all came back wounded, and many maimed for life. Now and then a man is found who served his country faithfully for three years, and passed through the terrible baptism of fire unscathed, but such cases were rare."

Vermonters served not only in the Vermont Brigade and the other units noted in the preceding pages but also in the navy and marines, on the western plains, and in various staff positions. The names and numbers of folks who did not go to war, particularly Vermont women, but who made important contributions to the war effort will never be fully known.

The last guns had hardly been silenced on the Southern battlefields when many Vermont communities undertook to express their loss in public ways. The first Civil War monument was dedicated on October 31, 1866, in the Canadian border town of Derby. It stands, recently refurbished, with the astounding total of 239 names on its bronze plaques—the number of men who went off to fight from that small town. Other early monuments were placed in Williamstown and Rochester, two other communities hard hit by the terrible swift sword. St. Johnsbury citizens secured the services of the noted sculptor and former combat artist Larkin Mead. He produced a heroic female figure called *America* that stands by the courthouse on Main Street. Monument building continued well into the next century. Many took the form of soldiers carved in stone, some facing south toward the storied places where the men they honor once fought. Woodstock erected two memorials.

The boys settled back into civilian life quickly, and they had to, for in most Vermont homes much had been left undone during their long absences.

Wilbur Fisk wrote on his return from soldiering, "Old Vermont looks about as it used to, only they have closed the hills up nearer together and made them perhaps a little more steep and abrupt. We miss the large plains of Virginia."

Fisk moved west not long after the war, and in the years after 1865 a considerable exodus from Vermont occurred. A resident of Windham wrote many years later that one-half of all the boys who went to war from that community, though they came home for a while, eventually settled out of state. War-induced wanderlust was contagious.

Veterans' memories could at times be a nuisance, according to William Newton, who in 1928 published a history of Barnard: "This writer still holds vividly in mind some of the yarns these returned men were accustomed to spin while at work on the farm, or more properly while not working, for the war cost my father many a dollar which went not out in taxes or high prices for necessities, but which paid for work not done while the returned soldier talked of fields he fought and battles he won."

Veterans' organizations formed soon after the war: most former soldiers joined the Grand Army of the Republic, and GAR halls were built in many communities. Several remain, including the stone edifice in Hardwick where the Vermont Hemlocks, Civil War reenactors, now hold meetings.

The GAR gained wide political influence in Vermont. Many veterans rose, much on their war records, to political prominence. Among the veterans elected governor were Peter Washburn and Roswell Farnham, both of whom fought in the first battle; Samuel Pingree, badly wounded at Lee's Mills; and Redfield Proctor, commander of the 15th Vermont, who became Secretary of War in the Harrison administration and who also served as US senator. Urban Woodbury, the first Vermonter to lose a limb in the war, ran for office on a Republican ticket with another veteran who had lost an arm. "Two good arms between us," was their campaign slogan and both were elected. Woodbury's State House portrait shows him with an empty sleeve.

Wheelock Veazey, who stood with his 16th Vermont before Pickett's charge, became a Vermont Supreme Court justice and served on the Interstate Commerce Commission. George Stannard was for a time a customs commissioner in Vermont. Then he served for many years as a doorkeeper in the US House of Representatives.

William Wells became a prominent Burlington lawyer.

Oliver Otis Howard, who had prayed with the Second Vermont before Bull Run, fought all through the war, marching with Sherman from Atlanta to the sea. After the war he went west to fight Indians and single-handedly walked into the camp of Cochise to arrange terms for the Apache leader's surrender. He was for a time superintendent of the US Military Academy at West Point. Howard later became deeply involved in improving the lot of freed slaves and was named head of the federal Freedmen's Bureau. He went on to found Howard University and was instrumental in establishing Lincoln Memorial University. Howard spent the last 15 years of his life in Burlington, near his soldier son, who superintended construction of nearby Fort Ethan Allen. When he died, in 1909, an impressive military funeral procession wound its way down the hill from his Summit Street home to the Unitarian church, whose congregation had once fired the minister for presiding at the funeral of the abolitionist John Brown. Howard is buried in Lakeview Cemetery, close by the graves of George Stannard and William Wells.

"Baldy" Smith lived until 1903 and devoted much of his time to justifying his performance at Petersburg. He died in Philadelphia after a long engineering career.

After his two-term governorship expired in the spring of 1864, Frederick Holbrook perfected the plow he had invented, and he was fond of demonstrating it at agricultural fairs, often taking the reins of a team. He was not bashful about making the point that he had been Vermont's Civil War governor, and the plow sold well. Holbrook was president of the Brattleboro Savings Bank for 39 years and led the choir of Brattleboro's Center Congregational Church for 50 years. He died in 1906 at age 96.

John Gregory Smith left the governorship after two terms in 1866, returning to railroading, and was for a time president of the newly chartered Northern Pacific Railroad. He died in 1891.

Not long after the war people of the old Confederacy resumed northward treks. In 1878 Thetford elected a veteran of the Confederate navy, Thomas Chubb, to the legislature. Sydney Beauclerk, a British aristocrat who had fought with the Confederates and received both sabre and bullet wounds, came north to settle in Irasburg. He raised a large family on Mill Hill in a big Victorian house, and as a local historian recalled, "his wit, charm and generosity became more important to his neighbors than his early career as a rebel." When he died, both the American flag and the Confederate Stars and Bars adorned his casket.

After Robert Lincoln and his wife built Hildene in Manchester, a frequent guest was the wife of a Confederate general, Mrs. Benjamin Hardin Helm. She was the half-sister of Mary Todd Lincoln.

As warm weather came to Vermont in 1899, a portly Southern lady arrived at the Montpelier depot to be greeted by her host, Professor John Burgess. Varina Howell Davis, the widow of Jefferson Davis, spent the summer in a cottage adjacent to the Burgess home "Redstone" on a hilltop overlooking the Vermont State House.

"She charmed everybody in that old abolitionist state," according to Burgess. Varina, like Mary Lincoln three and one-half decades before, was fond of rides through the Vermont countryside. Burgess worried whether his buggy would bear the weight of his guest; one day, near East Montpelier, he heard a loud crack. Burgess pulled into a farmyard and inquired of a man raking leaves in his orchard whether he could make repairs. The man took a look at the damage, and at the former first lady, and replied, "Mebby." The wagon was soon fixed.

One Confederate never totally forgiven in Vermont was Melvin Dwinell. Dwinell was the Vermonter who had enlisted in a Georgia regiment and fought at Bull Run, writing home that he would not hesitate to shoot a man from his home state. Later, as a Southern newspaperman, he trumpeted the Confederate cause, once declaring, "It would be as easy for Abe Lincoln to reduce the White Mountains to the level of the ocean as to conquer these states."

After Dwinell's death in Rome in 1887 his body was brought home for burial in the East Calais cemetery. On Memorial Days, when schoolchildren placed flags on soldiers' graves, they placed one on Dwinell's though there was "strictly no comment about it."

In 1878 the Vermont Legislature passed an act appointing a state historian for the purpose of compiling "a History of the part taken by the Vermont soldiers and sailors in the War of the Rebellion." George Grenville Benedict was named and wrote the monumental *Vermont in the Civil War*, a two-volume history published in 1886. Benedict also became editor of the *Burlington Free Press*.

In 1876 the legislature authorized creation of a Civil War memorial, and a sum of $10,000 was provided for payment to the artist Julian Scott. Scott was, of course, the drummer boy who had carried wounded men across the bullet-riled Warwick River at Lee's Mills, becoming the first Vermonter to win a Medal of Honor. Scott visited the Cedar Creek field, brought Vermont veterans of the battle to his New York studio, and painted their portraits into the monumental work that graces the capitol in Montpelier. Philip Sheridan saw the painting in progress and declared it to fairly depict the boys as they looked "going in."

Sheridan visited the Vermont State House in 1867 and said: "When I saw these old flags, I thought I ought to say as much as this:—I never commanded troops in whom I had more confidence than I had in the Vermont troops, and I do not know but I can say that I never commanded troops in whom I had as much confidence as those of this gallant state."

George Meade, the victor at Gettysburg who later led the Army of the Potomac to Appomattox, came to St. Albans in 1870 with a detachment of US troops to keep order after the Fenians, an Irish and Irish-American secret society, organized raids into British Canada.

Ulysses Grant brought his presidential campaign to Vermont, speaking in Cambridgeport and Island Pond. Though his campaign from the Rapidan to Appomattox cost many a Vermont life and limb, he was enthusiastically received. Grant lived out his last days in a cottage on a hillside near Saratoga Springs, New York, hoping the mountain air would afford relief from the throat cancer that was killing him. It did not, but before Grant died he completed his memoirs and rescued his family from bankruptcy. Days before the end, as he drove toward completion of the book, Grant asked to be taken to an overlook near his cottage. Its view reached the long ridge of Vermont's Green Mountains, and one wonders whether Grant recalled that from among those distant ridges had come some of the finest fighting men he ever commanded.

Stephen Thomas, who had so bravely led the Eighth Vermont Regiment, switched from the Democratic party to the Republican party after the war, and in 1867 was elected lieutenant governor. He died in 1909 at the age of 94. Squire Howard, who fought with him, said, "He was the bravest man I ever saw."

George Foster, the seemingly indestructable giant who led the Vermont Brigade at Fisher's Hill, after the war became Vermont's US marshal and waded into a crowd of agitated Fenians to arrest their leader. But he soon became sick with diabetes. Not long before he died he told a friend: "I haven't over two years to live at longest. My disease is incurable, and will fetch me sooner or later; but I don't propose to be dying for years in the eyes of my family. I propose to be cheerful to the last. A man who has faced death in the past as I have, need not fear it now."

He died in Burlington on a winter night in 1879. Hundreds of veterans turned out for his funeral. A team of white horses pulled his hearse from the church to the cemetery through a driving snowstorm, as thousands lined the streets.

Charles Gould, the once-sickly youth who grew up to become the first soldier to enter into the Confederate works at Petersburg, fought off tuberculosis not long after the war. Then he settled into a career with the US Patent Office in Washington, retiring in 1916, the year before he died.

William Herrick, the diarist who had served in the Third Vermont's band, continued to work in the Fairbanks factories in St. Johnsbury. He led the St. Johnsbury Band and the North Church's choir for many years and delighted in trips to Boston to see opera performances. He died in 1894, and at a memorial service in the GAR hall a quartet that included the wife of cavalryman Horace Ide sang "Now the Day Is Over."

Edward Hastings Ripley lived a properous life and owned a prominent New York City hotel. He was a familiar sight in Rutland on days of parades, the old general coming down from his Mendon home in a fine carriage pulled by a pair of magnificent horses. As they clipped along, Ripley's long white hair flowed back from under his officer's hat. He died in 1916 and was buried by the imposing family monument in Evergreen cemetery alongside his brother William.

Not long after the war ended, the sculptor and former combat illustrator Larkin Mead, though living in Italy, was commissioned to carve statuary for the Lincoln tomb at Springfield, Illinois. Mead lived until 1908, and on learning of his death in Italy, the Vermont Legislature passed a resolution of condolence and messaged it to his widow. Back across the Atlantic came an offer of a bust of Lincoln "worked upon in a spirit of love and reverence," a study for the Springfield tomb. It stands today in the State House.

As the 20th century arrived the ranks of the veterans thinned ever faster. Most Vermont regiments held regular reunions, which became ever-sadder occasions. The Seventh Vermont met at Rutland's Bardwell Hotel (where John

Brown's widow had spent the night as she brought her husband's body back home) on August 10, 1910, and toward evening's end, former private Fenimore Shepard of Fair Haven offered the following toast: "Gathered again, as we are tonight near the first camping ground of our regiment, brings back to the memory of all those who camped here, vivid recollections of the past. We again seem to hear the voices of those we knew and again gaze into faces of those who long since left our side and faded from our vision."

Four years later, at the 12th reunion, the speaker again was Private Shepard, who summed up what the Seventh Vermont's service had meant:

> Nearly 50 years have passed since as a regiment we were mustered out of the United States service, and separated returning again to our usual avocations of life. What have the years brought to us? What to the country for whose preservation the Seventh Regiment gave nearly five years of its service? Its 200 dead slumber in the national cemetery at Chalmette, La.; for 50 years the waters of the Mississippi have flowed past their resting place. Under the shadows of Fort Barrancas and Pickens nearly a hundred more are sleeping. Though we should enter those sacred enclosures today, though the reveille should be sounded therein, it would not awaken them to glory again. But if life could be restored again to them as it was to that mighty force that lay in the plain of Esdraelon, as seen by the Prophet Ezekiel, we could say truthfully to them, 'Comrades, thy life was not spent in vain.'...
>
> Through the offerings of countless lives our flag, "Old Glory" waves over a united country and in deed and truth our country is a land of the free....The progress of this country in the past 50 years is almost beyond conception. In inventions, in engineering projects, in art, sciences and literature, in the progress of medical science, and in the growth of our industries, our country's progress has been wonderful. We are living in the Golden Age of the world. We have taken part, and to have lived in that age should be a subject of rejoicing to us all. The memories of past service as soldiers and as citizens will remain with us the few more years we have to stay.

He spoke in August 1914. An ocean away, the "war to end all wars" was beginning.

Vermonters held their Civil War veterans in high regard. Elba Jillson, a private in the Ninth Vermont who fought in one battle, died quietly in his sleep on a winter night in 1923 on his son's Pomfret hill farm. His grandaughter, my mother, Arlene Jillson Coffin, found him lying too still. It snowed hard that night, and the next morning, the men of the town came to clear the three miles of road from the farmhouse to South Pomfret so the old soldier's body could lie in the Grange hall.

The war memories lived as long as the veterans drew breath. One old soldier, Albert Kendall, roomed at the home of a Barnard family as a hired hand. Kendall had fought with the First Vermont Cavalry and been captured and imprisoned at Belle Isle and Andersonville. A descendant of the family with which he lived recalled: "The family were awakened in the dead of night by the Yankee yell,

Veterans of three wars: (left to right) Domic Calo, World War I; Adelbert Green, Civil War; Joseph M. Hodet, Spanish American War.

St. Albans Historical Society

such as he and others were accustomed to give as they rode the charge, to hear him bound out of bed, yelling as he had in many a battle, only to be awakened by coming into contact with the furniture or the side of the house and then, soldierlike, turn in again almost as though nothing had happened and go off to sleep."

Edwin Pierce, a private in the 14th Vermont, who faced Pickett's charge and found his best buddy dead beside him when the smoke cleared, lived to be 77. In 1913, at age 71, he and another Gettysburg veteran, John Quinlan, went from their homes in North Shrewsbury to the 50th anniversary of the Battle of Gettysburg. Pierce got a good way down the road before he realized he'd forgotten his false teeth, so he had to go back home for a moment. But the two friends who once fought for George Stannard made it to Gettysburg and joined veterans, blue and gray. Pierce died at his home in 1919.

The last veteran of the Civil War in Vermont was Gilbert Lucier. He had enlisted at age 16 in the 11th Vermont Regiment. Lucier was shot in the left leg at Cold Harbor, hospitalized at Alexandria where he nearly lost his leg, then nearly died. The leg hurt him at times for the rest of his life. Lucier came home to the Canadian border town of Jay, where he married Lucy Ann King in 1868. They had four children. Lucier later became road commissioner of Jay and twice represented the town in the Vermont House of Representatives.

In 1938 his nephew, Graham Lucier, drove him to Gettysburg for the 75th reunion. The old soldiers were quartered in tents on the battlefield, Confederates on one side of a road and Yankees on the other. Lucier's grandniece, Pauline

White-mustached Gilbert Lucier and wife Lucy.

(Peg) Barry of Brattleboro, told me that as the reunion went on, Graham got bored with sitting in the tent one night and went out for a walk. Upon returning some time later, his uncle wanted to know where he'd been. The nephew replied that he'd been across the road talking with Confederate veterans. Gilbert Lucier rose from his bed and told his nephew to start packing. They were going home. For Gilbert Lucier, almost three-quarters of a century after the guns of the rebellion fell silent, the war still had not ended. Lucier lived another six years in Jay, becoming bedridden toward the end, but still fond of recalling that once during the war he had seen President Lincoln. Peg Barry visited him not long before his death and remembered his old blue uniform hung by his bed. Lucier died on September 22, 1944 at age 97, in the Orleans County Memorial Hospital in Newport.

In 1987, in her 104th year, Daisy Turner of Grafton, the daughter of a former slave who fought in the Union army, talked of the Civil War: "The green fields of the southland is fertile with the blood of those Negro slaves and the true white men that went from Vermont to save us. Every one of those turning battles, where the victory was won, it was the Vermont boys."

Speaking years after the war at a reunion of Vermont veterans, former sergeant Lucius Bigelow of Burlington, who had survived the slaughter of Savage's Station, talked of the Vermont soldiers:

> The heroism of our boys had little of pride or pomp, of crashing music and royal banner and "vive l'Empereur!" boisterousness about it. It was, like themselves, homely and self-contained. They stood up firmly, fought stubbornly; when they

dropped they had grim humor and queer wit quite as often on their lips as groans, or cries or prayers. There was gold and there was dross in them. The soldiers who did their devoir most nobly in the awful solemnities of a great battle were not those who brawled and boasted either before or after the conflict; but those who with a human hate of bloodshed, turned it may be pale faces but stout hearts to the enemy, and fixed their unyielding feet firmly in the earth as the badger's claws, and made a badger's bitter fight, simply because it was the hard but single road to their full duty.

Indeed, as Erastus Fairbanks had promised Abraham Lincoln in the troubled spring of 1861, Vermont had done its full duty.

Sources and References

Abbott, Lemuel A. *Personal Recollections and Civil War Diary 1864*. Burlington, Vt.: Free Press Printing Co., 1908.

Abbott, Peter M. Civil War letter. Vermont Historical Society, Montpelier, Vermont.

Angle, Paul M., ed. *Lincoln Reader*. New Brunswick, N.J.: Rutgers University Press, 1947.

Antietam battle collection. Special Collections, Dartmouth College, Baker Library, Hanover, New Hampshire.

Basler, Roy P., ed. *Collected Works of Abraham Lincoln*. New Brunswick, N.J.: Rutgers University Press, 1955.

Bassett, T. D. Seymour. *Urban Penetration of Rural Vermont: 1840–1880*. Ph. D. diss., Harvard University, 1952.

———. "For Freedom and Unity, Vermont's Civil War." *Vermont Life*, Spring 1961: 36-39.

———. *The Growing Edge: Vermont Villages 1840–1880*. Vermont Historical Society, Montpelier, Vermont, 1992.

Battison, Edwin A. *Muskets to Mass Production: The Men and the Times that Shaped America*. American Precision Museum, Windsor, Vermont, 1976.

Bayler, John E. *Buck's Book: A View of the 3rd Vermont Infantry Regiment*. Burlington, Ill.: Balzer & Associates, 1993.

Beck, Jane C. (director). *On My Town: The Tradition of Daisy Turner*. Film produced by the University of Vermont and the Vermont Folklife Center, Middlebury, Vt.

Benedict, G. G. *Vermont in the Civil War*. Burlington,Vt.: Free Press Association, 1886.

———. *The Battle of Gettysburg and the Part Taken by Vermont Troops*. Burlington, Vt.: Free Press Print, 1867.

———. *Army Life in Virginia*. Burlington, Vt.: Free Press Association, 1895.

Bigelow, Edwin L. and Nancy H. Otis, *A Pleasant Land Among the Mountains*. Manchester, Vt.: Town of Manchester, 1961.

Bixby, George. Civil War letters. Special Collections, University of Vermont, Bailey/Howe Library, Burlington, Vermont.

Blaisdell, Jonathan. Civil War letters. Special Collections, Bailey/Howe Library, University of Vermont, Burlington, Vermont.

Booker, Warren E. *Historical Notes Jamaica, Windham County, Vermont*. Brattleboro, Vt.: E. L. Hildreth & Co., 1940.

Burdick, Winfield N. *My Gettysburg Corner*. Privately printed by the author, 1972.

Burlington Free Press, 1861–1866. Bailey/Howe Library, University of Vermont, Burlington, Vermont.

Burlington Relief Association clothing list, April–June, 1861. Special Collections, Bailey/Howe Library, University of Vermont, Burlington, Vermont.

Burns, Ken. *The Civil War*. Walpole, N.H.: Florentine Films, 1989.

Cabot, Mary R. *Annals of Brattleboro 1681–1895*. Brattleboro, Vt.: E. L. Hildreth & Co., 1922.

Carpenter, George N. *History of the Eighth Regiment, Vermont Volunteers 1861–1865*. Boston: Deland & Barta, 1886.

Catton, Bruce. *Glory Road*. Garden City, N.Y.: Doubleday & Co., 1952.

———. *A Stillness at Appomattox*. Garden City, N.Y.: Doubleday & Co., 1954.

———. *This Hallowed Ground*. Garden City, N.Y.: Doubleday & Company, 1956.

———. *Grant Takes Command*. Boston: Little, Brown & Co., 1968.

Chamberlin, George E. *Letters of George Chamberlin*. Springfield, Ill.: H. W. Rokker, 1883.

Chase, Peter S. *History of Company I, Second Regiment Vermont Volunteers*. Brattleboro, Vt.: Phoenix Printing Office, 1891.

Chittenden, Lucius. *An Unknown Heroine*. New York: Richmond, Grossup & Co., 1893.

———. *Personal Reminiscences*. New York: Richmond, Grossup & Co., 1893.

Closson, Harlan P. Diaries 1863–1864. Special Collections, Baker Library, Dartmouth College, Hanover, New Hampshire.

Collamer, Jacob. Family papers. Special Collections, Bailey/Howe Library, University of Vermont, Burlington, Vermont.

Costello, Bartley III. "Vermont in the Civil War." *Vermont History News,* April 1965: 220–26.

Crawford, Richard. *Civil War Songbook*. New York: Dover Publications, 1977.

Crockett, Walter Hill. *Vermont: The Green Mountain State*. New York: Century History Co., 1921.

Crosby, George R. Civil War diary. Vermont Historical Society, Montpelier, Vermont.

Crosier, Bernard. "Pardoned by Lincoln and Killed by the Confederacy." *Rutland Daily Herald*.

Cummings, Charles. Civil War letters. Vermont Historical Society, Montpelier, Vermont.

Dedication of the Statue to Brevet Major General William Wells. Privately printed, 1914. Special Collections, Bailey/

Howe Library, University of Vermont, Burlington, Vermont.

Dictionary of American Biography. New York: Charles Scribner's Sons, 1928.

Dodge, Grenville M. *Norwich University: Her History, Her Graduates, Her Roll of Honor.* Montpelier, Vt.: Capital City Press, 1911.

Doubleday, William O. Civil War letters. Collection of Hazen Kenneth Doubleday, Jr.

Dowden, Albert Ricker. "John Gregory Smith." *Vermont History,* April 1964: 79-97.

Doyle, William T. *The Vermont Political Tradition.* Published by the author, 1984.

DuClos, Katherine F. *The History of the Town of Braintree, Vt.* Vermont History Book Committee of Braintree, 1976.

Dwinell, Harold A. "Vermonter in Gray." *Vermont History,* Autumn 1968: 220–37.

Eastman, Seth N. Civil War journal. Vermont Historical Society, Montpelier, Vermont.

Emery, Edson. Civil War diary. Special Collections, Bailey/Howe Library, University of Vermont, Burlington, Vermont.

Fairbanks, Edward T. *The Town of St. Johnsbury, Vt.* St. Johnsbury, Vt.: Cowles Press, 1914.

Fairbanks, Erastus. Papers. Vermont State Archives, Montpelier, Vermont.

Faust, Patricia L., ed. *Historical Times Illustrated Encyclopedia of the Civil War.* New York: Harper & Row, 1986.

Foote, Shelby. *Fort Sumter to Perryville.* New York: Random House, 1958.

———. *Fredericksburg to Meridian.* New York: Random House, 1963.

———. *Red River to Appomattox.* New York: Random House, 1974.

Franham, Roswell. Papers. Special Collections, Bailey/Howe Library, University of Vermont, Burlington, Vermont.

Gale, Frederick. Civil War letters. Special Collections, Bailey/Howe Library, University of Vermont, Burlington, Vermont.

Garrison, Wendell Phillips, and Francis Jackson Garrison. *William Lloyd Garrison 1805–1879: The Story of His Life Told by His Children.* New York: Century Co., 1885.

Gay, Leon S., ed. *Brandon, Vermont: A History of the Town 1761–1961.* Brandon, Vt.: Town of Brandon, 1961.

George Houghton and Larkin Mead files. Brooks Memorial Library, Brattleboro, Vermont.

Gillett, Abel M. Civil War letters. Special Collections, Baker Library, Dartmouth College, Hanover, New Hampshire.

Glover, Waldo F. *Abraham Lincoln and the Sleeping Sentinel of Vermont.* Montpelier, Vt.: Vermont Historical Society, 1936.

———. *Mister Glover's Groton.* Published for the Groton Historical Society by Phoenix Publishers, Canaan, N.H., 1978.

Goff, John S. *Robert Todd Lincoln.* Norman, Ok.: University of Oklahoma Press, 1969.

Gould, Charles. Civil War letters. Special Collections, Bailey/Howe Library, University of Vermont, Burlington, Vermont.

Grant, Ulysses S. *Personal Memoirs.* Cleveland, Ohio: World Publishing Co., 1952.

Hance, Dawn D. *Shrewsbury, Vermont: Our Town as it Was.* Rutland, Vt.: Academy Books, 1980.

Harris, Joseph N. *History of Ludlow, Vt.* Charlestown, N.H.: Mrs. Ina Harris Harding and Mr. Archie Frank Harding, 1949.

Harris, Luther. "A Prisoner's Story." Special Collections, Bailey/Howe Library, University of Vermont, Burlington, Vermont.

Hatch, Benjamin. Civil War letters. Special Collections, Bailey/Howe Library, University of Vermont, Burlington, Vermont.

Haynes, Edwin M. *History of the Tenth Vermont Regt.* Lewiston, Me.: Journal Steam Press, 1870.

Haynes, Lyman Simpson. *History of the Town of Rockingham, Vermont 1753–1907.* Bellows Falls, Vt.: Town of Bellows Falls, 1907.

Hemenway, Abbie M. *Vermont Historical Gazetteer.* Rutland, Vt.: Tuttle Co., 1923.

Herrick, Henry W. Diary. Fairbanks Museum, St. Johnsbury, Vermont.

Hewitt, Lawrence H. *Port Hudson Confederate Bastion on the Mississippi.* Baton Rouge and London: Louisiana State University Press, 1987.

Holbrook, Frederick. Letter to Edwin Stanton. Newbury Library, Chicago, Illinois.

Holbrook, William C. *A Narrative of the Services of the Officers and Enlisted Men of the 7th Regiment of Vermont Volunteers.* New York: American Bank Note Co., 1882.

Houghton, Henry. "The Ordeal of the Civil War: A Recollection." *Vermont History,* Winter, 1973: 31-49.

Howard, Oliver O. *Autobiography.* New York: Baker & Taylor Co., 1907.

Janes, Henry. Medical record book. Special Collections, Bailey/Howe Library, University of Vermont, Burlington, Vermont.

Jeffrey, Nellie T. "The Story Of William Scott the Sleeping Sentinel." Pamphlet published by the Groton Public Library, 1959.

Johannsen, Robert W. *Stephen A. Douglas.* New York: Oxford University Press, 1973.

John Brown file. Bixby Library, Vergennes, Vermont.

Journal of the Times, The. William Lloyd Garrison, publisher. Collection of the Bennington Museum, Bennington, Vermont.

Kelly, John T. Civil War diary. Special Collections, Bailey/Howe Library, University of Vermont, Burlington, Vermont.

Kennedy, Frances H., ed. *Civil War Battlefield Guide*. Boston: Houghton Mifflin Co., 1990.

Kinsley, Rufus. Civil War diary. Vermont Historical Society, Montpelier, Vermont.

Lewis, Julius. Civil War letters. Courtesy of Richard Lewis and family.

Lewis, Thomas A. *The Guns of Cedar Creek*. New York: Harper & Row, 1988.

Lindsey, George R. "George Harper Houghton: The Civil War Photographer From Brattleboro, Vermont." *Vermont History News*, September, 1986: 106–08.

Lowell, Robert. *For the Union Dead*. New York: Farrar, Straus & Giroux, 1956.

Ludum, Richard M. *Social Ferment in Vermont*. New York: Columbia University Press, 1939.

Manchester Journal, 1861–1865. Skinner Memorial Library, Manchester, Vermont.

Marshall, Jeffrey D. "Voices of the Soldiers." *Liber*, Autumn, 1992: 3-6.

Matter, William D. *If It Takes All Summer*. Chapel Hill and London: University of North Carolina Press, 1988.

McFarland, Moses. *The Eighth Vermont in the Battle of Cedar Creek*. Hyde Park, Vt.: Lamoille Publishing Co., 1897.

McPherson, James. *Battle Cry of Freedom*. New York: Oxford University Press, 1988.

Mead, John A. Gubernatorial papers. Vermont State Archives, Montpelier, Vermont.

Meade, Larkin. Papers. Amherst College, Amherst, Massachusetts.

Melville, Herman. *Battle Pieces and Aspects of the War*. New York: Harper & Brothers, 1866.

"Memorial Sketch of Stephen Thomas." *Vermonter, a State Magazine*. February 1904.

Moore, Frank. *The Civil War in Story and Song*. New York: P. F. Collier, 1889.

Moore, Kenneth A. "Frederick Holbrook." *Vermont History*, April 1964: 65-77.

Morse, John. Civil War letter. Collection of Howard Coffin.

Morton, Louis. "Vermonters at Cedar Creek." *Vermont History News*, April 1965: 327–341.

Mosby, John S. "My Guerilla Operations." *Sunday Magazine*, August 1908.

Myers, John. "The Beginning of Antislavery Agencies in Vermont, 1832–1836." *Vermont History*, Summer 1968: 126-141.

———. "Captured by Rebels: A Vermonter at Petersburg, 1864." *Vermont History*, Autumn 1968: 230–235.

Nash, Hope. *Royalton, Vermont*. Royalton,Vt.: South Royalton Women's Club, Royalton Historical Society, 1975.

Nevins, Allan. *The Emergence of Lincoln: Douglas, Buchanan, and Party Chaos, 1857–1859*. New York: Charles Scribner's Sons, 1950.

Newell, Graham S. "Erastus Fairbanks." *Vermont History*, April 1964: 59-64.

Newton, William M. *History of Barnard Vermont*. Montpelier, Vt.: Vermont Historical Society, 1928.

Orcutt, Marjorie A., and Edward S. Alexander. *A History of Irasburg, Vt*. Rutland, Vt.: Academy Books, 1989.

Parcher, Tabor. Civil War letter. Collection of Howard Coffin.

Peck, Simon L. History of Ira, Vt. Rutland, Vt.: Charles E. Tuttle Co., 1970.

Pepe, Faith L. "The Shaping of an Artist: Larkin Meade and the Civil War." *Vermont History News*, September 1986.

Peterson, C. Stewart. *Last Civil War Veteran in Each State*. Baltimore, Md.: Published by the author, 1951.

Pettingill, Helen M. *History of Grafton, Vt. 1754–1975*. Grafton Historical Society, 1975.

Phelps, Edward W., ed. *Civil War Letters of Timothy B. Messer, Tenth Vermont Volunteers*. Bernardston, Ma.: Edward W. Hall & Co., 1986.

Pollard, Annie M. *History of the Town of Baltimore*. Vermont Historical Society, 1954.

Pratt, Fletcher. *A Short History of the Civil War* (original title, *Ordeal by Fire*). New York: Pocket Books, 1952.

Proceedings of Seventh Vermont Veteran Volunteers Association, Eighth Reunion, August 10, 1910. Troy, N.Y.: Henry Stowell & Son, 1910.

Randall, George. Civil War letters. Special Collections, Bailey/Howe Library, University of Vermont, Burlington, Vermont.

Revised Roster of Vermont Volunteers During the War of the Rebellion. Montpelier, Vt.: Watchman Publishing Co., 1892.

Ripley, Edward Hastings. *Vermont General: The Unusual War Experiences of Edwin Hastings Ripley 1862–1865*. New York: Devin-Adair Co., 1960.

Ripley, Thomas E. *A Vermont Boyhood*. New York: D. Appleton-Century Co., 1937.

Ripley, William Y. *Vermont Riflemen in the War for the Union*. Rutland, Vt.: Tuttle & Co., 1883.

Robbins, Daniel. *The Vermont State House: A History and Guide*. Barre, Vt.: Vermont Council on the Arts and Vermont State House Preservation Committee, 1980.

Robertson, James I., Jr. *Civil War Sites in Virginia*. Charlottesville, Va.: University of Virginia Press, 1982.

Robinson family papers. Rokeby Museum, Ferrisburg, Vt., and Special Collections, Bailey/Howe Library, University of Vermont, Burlington, Vermont.

Rochester, Vermont: Its History, 1780-1975. Rochester, Vt.: Town of Rochester, 1975.

Rosenblatt, Emil and Ruth Rosenblatt, eds. *Hard Marching Every Day: The Civil War Letters of Private Wilbur Fisk*. Lawrence, Ks.: University Press of Kansas, 1992.

Ross, Ishbel. *First Lady of the South: The Life of Mrs. Jefferson Davis*. New York: Harper & Brothers.

Rutherford, Joseph Case. Civil War letters. Special Collection, Bailey/Howe Library, University of Vermont, Burlington, Vermont.

Rutland Courier, 1861–1865. Bailey/Howe Library, University of Vermont, Burlington, Vermont.

Rutland Daily Herald, 1861–1865. Vermont State Library, Montpelier, Vermont.

Saint Albans Raid, October 19, 1864. St. Albans: North Country Press, 1953.

Sandburg, Carl. *Abraham Lincoln: The Prairie Years and the War Years.* New York: Harcourt, Brace & Co., 1954.

Scott, Erastus. Civil War letters. Special Collections, Bailey/Howe Library, University of Vermont, Burlington, Vermont.

Sheridan, Philip H. *Personal Memoirs.* New York: Charles L. Webster & Co.,1891.

Shores, Venila Lovina. *Lyndon Gem in the Green.* Lyndonville, Vt.: Town of Lyndon, 1986.

Siciliano, Stephen N. *Major General William Farrar Smith, Critic of Defeat and Engineer of Victory.* Ph. D. diss., History Department, William and Mary College, 1984.

Siebert, William H. *Vermont's Antislavery and Underground Railroad Record.* Columbus, Ohio: Spahr & Glenn Co., 1937.

Sisakis, Stewart. *Who Was Who in the Civil War.* New York: Facts on File, 1988.

Smith, John David. "The Health of Vermont's Civil War Recruits." *Vermont History,* Summer 1975: 185-92.

Smith, John Gregory. Papers. Vermont Historical Society, Montpelier, Vermont.

Smith, William Farrar. *From Chattanooga to Petersburg with Generals Grant and Butler.* Boston and New York: Houghton, Mifflin & Co., 1893.

———. *Autobiography of Major General William F. Smith.* Edited by Herbert M. Schiller. Dayton, Ohio: Morningside House, 1990.

———. Civil War letters. Special Collections, Bailey/Howe Library, University of Vermont, Burlington, Vermont.

———. Papers. Vermont Historical Society, Montpelier, Vermont.

Snyder, Charles M. "They Lay Where They Fell: The Everests, Father and Son." *Vermont History,* July 1964: 154-62.

Soule, Allen. "Vermont in 1861." *Vermont History,* April 1962: 149-161.

Stackpole, Edward. *Chancellorsville: Lee's Greatest Battle.* Harrisburg, Pa.: Stackpole Co., 1958.

———. *They Met at Gettysburg.* Harrisburg, Pa.: Stackpole Co., 1963.

Stevens, Charles A. *Berdan's United States Sharpshooters in the Army of the Potomac.* St. Paul, Minn.: Price-McGill Co., 1892.

Sturtevant, Ralph Orson. *Pictorial History: The Thirteenth Vermont Volunteers, 1861–1865.* Compiled by Eli N. Peck, secretary of the Thirteenth Vermont Regiment Association. Burlington, Vt., 1911.

Sumner, Samuel. Civil War letters. Special Collections, Bailey/Howe Library, University of Vermont, Burlington, Vermont.

"Twelfth Reunion of the Seventh Regt." *Vt. Veteran.* Aug. 5, 1914. Troy, N.Y.: Henry Stowell & Son, 1914.

Trimbie, Tony L. "Paper Collars: Stannard's Brigade at Gettysburg." *The Gettysburg Magazine.* January 1990.

Truesdale, Captain John. *The Blue Coats and How They Lived, Fought and Died for the Union.* Philadelphia: Jones Brothers & Co., 1867.

Van de Water, Frederic F. *The Reluctant Republic: Vermont, 1724–1791.* New York: The John Day Co., 1941.

Veasay, Wheelock. Papers. Vermont Historical Society, Montpelier, Vermont.

Waite, Otis F. R. *Vermont in the Great Rebellion.* Claremont, N.H.: Tracy, Chase & Co., 1869.

Walker, Aldace F. *The Vermont Brigade in the Shenandoah Valley 1864.* Burlington, Vt.: Free Press Association, 1869.

Walker, Mabel Gregory. *The Fennian Movement.* Colorado Springs,Co.: Ralph A. Myles Publishers, 1969.

Wallace, Lew. *Official Report on the Monocacy Battle.* Special Collections, Bailey/Howe Library, University of Vermont, Burlington, Vermont.

War of the Rebellion, Offical Records. Washington, D.C.: Government Printing Office, 1901.

Ward, Geoffrey C. *The Civil War, an Illustrated History.* New York: Alfred A. Knopf, 1990.

Watts, Isaac N. Civil War Letters. Special Collections, Bailey/Howe Library, University of Vermont, Burlington, Vermont.

Wells, William. Papers. Special Collections, Bailey/Howe Library, University of Vermont, Burlington, Vermont.

Wert, Jeffrey D. *From Winchester to Cedar Creek.* Carlisle, Pa.: South Mountain Press, 1987.

Wilkins, M.N. *History of Stowe to 1869.* Stowe, Vt.: Stowe Historical Society, 1987.

William Scott files. Groton Library, Groton, Vermont.

Williams, J.C. *Life in Camp.* Claremont, N.H.: Claremont Manufacturers Co., 1864.

Williams, John A. "A Lost Lincoln Telegram." *Vermont History.* Winter 1973.

Woodbury, Eri D. Civil War Letters. Special Collections, Baker Library, Dartmouth College, Hanover, New Hampshire.

Woodward, Jon. "The St. Albans Raid, Rebels in Vermont!...Oct. 19, 1864." *Blue and Gray Magazine.* December 1990.

Index

threatens Meade's supply lines 221; misses chance at Mine Run 224; in the field at Wilderness 239; wins race to Spotsylvania 244; orders Early on to Washington 289; peace offering rejected by Grant 334; surrenders 343

Lee's Mills, Battle of: 92-98, illus. 92, 93; battlefield 97

Lewinsville, skirmish at: 74

Lewis, John R.: 156, 174, 237

Libby Prison: cavalry officers sent to 162; Gen. Stoughton sent to 167; William Wells sent to 162; Edwin Dillingham in 231; attempt to liberate 230; prisoners freed 341

Lincoln, Abraham: portrait 48; debates with Douglas 45-46; remarks on John Brown 32; elected president 47; inauguration 49; sends telegram to Gov. Fairbanks 21; desires bloodless solution 25; visits Vt. troops 74; reviews troops in Virginia 78; orders Scott's sentence commuted 87-88; meets with Thomas Scott 89-90; reviews troops on Peninsula 112; at sharpshooter's training 123; visits Antietam hospitals 135; issues Emancipation Proclamation 136; replaces Burnside with Hooker 143; reviews troops on Rappahannock 157; comments on value of brigadiers and horses 168; reacts to defeat at Chancellorsville 175; on Mississippi Valley victories 209; Gettysburg Address 217; effect of "Forty Days" on 261-62; wants to see Vermont Brigade 292; watches battle from Fort Stevens 293; Vt. soldiers help re-elect 317; visits hospital at City Point 345; dismisses rumors of assassination plot 346-47; assassinated 347-48; funeral obsequies 348, broadside 347

Lincoln, Mary: 348

Lincoln, Robert T.: 345, 347, 348-349, 358

Looting: 128, 341

Lord, Nathan Jr.: 72, 95

Louisiana Native Guards: 149, 204

Lucier, Gilbert: 362-63

Malvern Hill, Battle of: 111; illus. 124

Manchester, Vt.: 105, 110

Manufacturers: 285-86

Marksmen (see Sharpshooters, First and Second United States Sharpshooters)

Marsh, George Perkins: 22

Marye's Heights (see Fredericksburg, First and Second Battles of)

Mattis, Dinah: 28, 37

McClellan, George B.: assumes command of army 74; reviews troops 78-79; approves formation of 1st Vt. Brigade 81; pardons Scott 88; in Peninsula Campaign 106-13; resumes command 130; at Antietam 132-35; relieved of command 135; loyalty of Vt. troops to 139

McDowell, Irvin: takes command of army 58; plans attack at Bull Run 60; orders Howard's brigade to halt 61; reviews 2nd Vt. 73

Mead, Charles: telegram informing family of his death (illus.) 270

Mead, John B.: 309, 310

Mead, Larkin: travels with 1st Vt. Brigade 114; sketch of Lee's Mills (illus.) 92; carves figure for St. Johnsbury 356-57; after the war 360

Meade, George G.: at Fredericksburg 140-41; at Gettysburg 186-89; fails to stop Lee's retreat from Gettysburg 214; victory at Rappahannock Station 222; advances, then withdraws from Mine Run 223-24; commands troops during Fenian Raid 359

Medal of Honor (see Congressional Medal of Honor)

Miles, Dixon S.: 126, 127, 128

Militia (see also Home Guards, Vermont soldiers): lack of preparedness 50; reviewed 50-51; new militia urged by Gov. Smith 319

Mine Run, Battle of: 223-25

Monocacy, Battle of: 289-91; battlefield 295

Monuments and historic markers (see also Battlefields): 356-57; Brattleboro 68, 120; John Brown and sons 33, 36; Camp Griffin 80; Stephen A. Douglas 43, 48; Fort Marcy 74; William Lloyd Garrison 28; Henry Janes 217-18; Manchester, Vt. 112-13; William Scott 15, 85; Woodstock, Vt. 55

Morale (see also Homesickness, Patriotism, War spirit): 73-74, 112, 115

Morgan horses: 99, 100

Mosby, John S.: forms guerrilla unit 161; saves Woodward's life 162; captures Wells 162; evades capture 163; captures Stoughton 164-67; wounded by Vermonter 167; exonerates Stoughton 168

Mosby's Confederacy 161; battlefields 168

Mud March: 142-43, 154, illus. 155

Musicians (see Bands, Drummer boys, Songs)

Mustering centers: 68

New Jersey soldiers (see Twenty-Sixth New Jersey Infantry)

New Orleans: 146

Newspapers: 29, 58; reaction to William Scott sentence 87; accounts from war zone 115, 284; support for war effort 283-84

Ninth Vermont Infantry: formation 125; builds fort 126; captured at Harper's Ferry 127; paroled to Camp Douglas 128; exchanged and sent to Virginia 158; returns to action 331; joins 18th Corps 332; in assault on Fort Gilmer 332; enters Richmond 339-40, illus. 341

Norwich University: 52, 127, 245-46

Noyes, William: 249

Old Constitution House (Windsor, Vt.): 27, illus. 26

Old Vermont Brigade (see First Vermont Brigade)

Opequon, Battle of: 298-303; battlefield 305

Parmlee, Moses: m. 87, 88, 89

Patriotism (see also War spirit): 22, 25, 105, 280, 281

Peninsula Campaign: 91-98, 106-13, 123-24

Petersburg, Siege of: 265, 327-39; battlefield 343-44

Petersburg Crater, Battle of: 329-30

Phelps, Edward E.: 77, 119

Phelps, John W.: 5, 72; appointed Col. of 1st Vt. Regiment 52; mistaken for Ethan Allen 53; leads reconnaisance into Virginia 54; captures Ship Island 144; abolitionist sentiments 146-47; proposal for black regiments rejected 147; resigns 147

Phillips, Wendell: 30, 31, 34, 35, 36

Photographers: 114-15

Physicians (see Surgeons)